Cosmic Defiance

Updike's Kierkegaard and the Maples Stories

David Crowe

Mercer University Press | Macon, Georgia
35 Years of Publishing Excellence

MUP/ H891

© 2014 Published by Mercer University Press, Macon, Georgia 31207

9 8 7 6 5 4 3 2 1

Books published by Mercer University Press are printed on acid-free
paper that meets the requirements of the American National Standard
for Information Sciences—Permanence of Paper for Printed Library
Materials.

Library of Congress Cataloging-in-Publication Data

Crowe, David, 1959- author.
  Cosmic Defiance : Updike's Kierkegaard and the Maples Stories / David Crowe.
    pages cm
  Includes bibliographical references and index.
   ISBN 978-0-88146-502-0 (hardback : acid-free paper) -- ISBN 0-88146-502-X
  (hardback : acid-free paper)
  1. Updike, John--Criticism and interpretation. 2. Kierkegaard, Søren, 1813-1855--
  Influence. 3. Literature--Philosophy. I. Title.
   PS3571.P4Z626 2014
   813'.54--dc23
                              2014035261

Cosmic Defiance

Contents

Acknowledgments

This book was born where Richard and Joan Maple were wed, in Cambridge, Massachusetts, where I took a very quiet part in the 2005 cohort of the Academy of Lutheran Scholars. I wish I could tell the late Ronald Thiemann of the Harvard Divinity School, who organized that seminar, that those weeks were a helpful kick in the pants. I thank the Luther College English Department and other college mentors of 1978 to 1982 for their gracious time and attention. Living and learning at Luther made a huge difference to me, in every part of my life. Soli Deo Gloria. I thank Augustana College for supporting research and writing time in the summers, and for rewarding the kind of teaching that led to this interdisciplinary book about the purposeful life. Mostly I thank my best friend, colleague, and wife Katie Hanson and our wonderful kids, Michael, Tyler, and Emily. Since my main role as husband and father is to be contentedly proud of you four and grateful to be around you, I find myself with no excuse to avoid reading and writing. I also thank Amanda Makula of the Augustana College Tredway Library for her diligent research assistance, and Marc Jolley, Director of the Mercer University Press, Marsha Luttrell, Publishing Assistant, Mary Beth Kosowski, Marketing Director, and the other editors, designers, and marketers at MUP for their excellent work.

Since God is the Judge, every righteousness of men is thrust into obscurity, every criticism which men exercise upon the ungodly and every busy attempt to convert them become of trivial importance. Beyond human good and evil the arm of God is extended in power; and men are advised to beware of too great daring.

Karl Barth, *The Epistle to the Romans*

There may be a rationalist who has never wavered in his conviction of the mortality of the soul, and there may be a vitalist who has never wavered in his faith in immortality; but at the most this would only prove that just as there are natural monstrosities, so there are those who are stupid as regards heart and feeling, however great their intelligence, and those who are stupid intellectually, however great their virtue.

Miguel de Unamuno, *Tragic Sense of Life*

Faith is the highest passion in a human being. Many in every generation may not come that far, but none comes further.

Søren Kierkegaard, *Fear and Trembling*

Introduction

> For me there has been no other contestant in the existential arena
> than the Christian creed, no other answer to the dread that one's
> mortal existence brings with it.
> —John Updike, "The Future of Faith"[1]

John Updike had a lifelong passion for Søren Kierkegaard's ideas. For readers who want to honor that passion, the most important passages to examine in Updike's novels and stories are those involving acts of non-erotic love, or situations that cry out for such acts of love. The logic that leads us to this unusual critical task unfolds this way.

Since both Updike and Kierkegaard endorse Martin Luther's understanding of the Christian faith, they understand—and make vividly known in their writings—that faith affords the believer no special power or efficacy, either in dealing with the world's many problems or in achieving personal goodness. Yet they also know that this sobering reality is no ground for despair or nihilism. Even if Christian faith does not lead to moral excellence, it does lead to hope. And so believers join together in acts of renewal and refreshment of which the Eucharistic meal is an emblem, and confession of sins a preliminary rite. The meal and the rite are celebrated by believers who will surely continue to sin, who may indeed immediately sin again, so that these believers require renewed hope again and again. Kierkegaard dwells on these continual processes of renewal and becoming whole, in doing so lending fresh meaning in his day and perhaps ours to the word *repetition*. He considers a range of meanings for repetition, reflecting characteristic ways of living. For the hedonist, he argues, repetition becomes monotony and leads to boredom; to the ethically motivated, repetition is ritual refreshment required for renewed work. To the person of faith, repetition is the promise of a second chance to live, and live differently.

In *Repetition, Either/Or, Works of Love* and elsewhere, Kierkegaard connects this spiritual process of renewal with marriage. He recognizes that marital love often begins as erotic love (*Elskov*), and that the marital relation involves particularities that other loving relationships between

---

[1] John Updike, *Due Considerations: Essays and Criticism* (New York: Knopf, 2007) 36.

people usually do not. But the wife must be "first and foremost the neighbor."[2] He means for us to hear the word "neighbor" in the sense of the mandate Jesus spoke at the Last Supper, that believers love one another as He has loved them, that the believer's first and really only task is to love the neighbor.[3] But Kierkegaard tries to make sense of this mandate too, which he begins to do by making a linguistic connection. In Danish, the word for "neighbor," *Næste*, is closely related to the word for "nearest," *Nærmeste*. Because believers are commanded to love the neighbor as one loves oneself, the nearest neighbor is, paradoxically, oneself. In Kierkegaard's somewhat sexist illustration, the husband learns to love himself, and then finds it possible to love the next nearest neighbor, the wife, and one supposes, the children and then a wider circle of neighbors. (Later he implies a more modern equality between husbands and wives because wives have an identical obligation to love the *Næste* and *Nærmeste*.) The husband must not make an "exception" in this duty toward the nearest and therefore usually most beloved neighbors. Especially concerning the wife, he must not confuse the feeling of love, or of being in love, with the experience of being a neighbor—which is to feel responsible for another neighbor's welfare.[4] Loving the nearest neighbors in an authentic way, unselfishly, non-preferentially and continually, the believer has the opportunity to learn something about the nature of God's love. And so we must search the behavior of Updike's characters—erratic, self-indulgent, libidinous, cruel, craven as they often are—for such acts of love.

It is clear to almost all of Updike's critics that he gains his subject and his fictional world's sociological realism from the quotidian manners of the American middle and upper-middle class of his day. Yet it is important to realize that Updike cares as much or more about the non-

---

[2] Søren Kierkegaard, *Works of Love: Some Christian Deliberations in the Form of Discourses*, trans. and eds. Howard V. Hong and Edna H. Hong. (Princeton NJ: Princeton University Press, 1995) 141. To avoid adopting Kierkegaard's implied sexism, I will substitute "spouse" for "wife" when discussing marriage in general, and will also use the word "partner" to indicate that I have no hostility toward any other genuinely loving, committed partnership.

[3] See John 15: 12. Terry Eagleton argues that the neighbor-love mandate "harks back to the Book of Leviticus and was assimilated into Judaism from Hellenism." The Gospel of John is thus incorrect in calling the mandate "new." See Terry Eagleton, *The Gospels: Jesus Christ* (New York/London: Verso/New Left Books, 2007) xxviii.

[4] Søren Kierkegaard, *Works of Love*, 17ff.

quotidian, existential questions his favorite theologians pose, especially this one: How are identity and action bound up with faith in God? The scholars who are most able and willing to elucidate Updike's existentialist theology, such as James Yerkes, Darrell Jodock, and George Hunt, have not carried theological conclusions very far into the fiction. I admire these three and some others for their willingness to understand Updike as a writer with a sophisticated theology. Unfortunately, most other critics make scant mention of Updike's faith and then neglect its impact on his writing, thus rendering him merely a painstakingly mimetic writer in a morally baffling world.

Updike tells us that many of his works are "illustrations of Kierkegaard," and yet for most critics that has simply meant that characters feel existential anxiety and, as they blunder their way into and out of mostly erotic relationships, seem hung up on God.[5] This narrative trajectory is correct, as far as it goes, but something important is missing here. Updike's favorite theologians and thinkers, including Kierkegaard, Karl Barth, Miguel de Unamuno and others, are so-called crisis theologians. They are dedicated to a rigorously thoughtful Christian neo-orthodoxy. Updike's interest in these thinkers surely means that his own theology was both complex and, in a way that accounts for modern understandings of human psychology and ideology, orthodox: declaring as true the existence of God, the divinity of Jesus Christ, the genuine activity of grace, and the reality of the afterlife. More importantly for these theologians, faith reforms conscience, and conscience leads to loving acts. This means that we still require a more rigorous sense of the facets of Updike's Kierkegaard, and a close reading of the novels and stories in that light. The Maples stories are a good place to begin because, along with the Rabbit novels, they epitomize Updike's theological interests, which are inspired in large part by Kierkegaard's central preoccupations.

The Kierkegaard I read has much to say about how people live their daily lives, the barriers and challenges in the way of authentic personhood and faith and right action. His indirect pseudonymous works are filled with tales and parables which parallel elements in Updike's narratives, and the more direct non-pseudonymous works offer equally relevant principles, precepts, lines of reasoning, teasing aphorisms, and startling interpretations of Biblical scripture. But

---

[5] John Updike, *Odd Jobs: Essays and Criticism* (New York: Alfred A. Knopf, 1991) 844.

Updike's critics have yet to apply Kierkegaard's theology in the simplest way: by diagnosing his major characters as living in one of the three stages of existence, the aesthetic, ethical, or religious. This move alone opens up many opportunities to make meaning out of the quotidian behavior of the characters. Reaching further into Kierkegaard, we realize that he has much to say about situations we find in Updike's works, including seduction, manipulation, sexual and material indulgence, heresy and other forms of theological error, violence and aggression, uncontrolled speech, egotism and narcissism, excessive pietism, spiritual denial, altruism, boredom, fear, and of course, love. Marriage is a major preoccupation of Kierkegaard's, along with holistic, non-neurotic personhood. Both are central to Updike's work, yet rarely connected in the criticism with Kierkegaard's ideas.

Like the Rabbit novels, Updike's Maples stories are diachronic, intricate, moving, and relevant to contemporary ethical and existential problems. Updike writes with pride about having invented what he calls the "fugal form" for the short story, collations of distinct, non-continuous scenes that bear on each other indirectly.[6] The Maples story "Plumbing" is one such story, and it is one of Updike's best. But a more important artistic achievement is the diachronic novel and story cycle, epitomized by both the Rabbit novels and Maples stories. Of course Harry Angstrom and Richard and Joan Maple appear long after Hemingway's Nick Adams, the characters of Dos Passos' *U.S.A.* trilogy, or those of Faulkner's Yoknapatawpha County. But Updike accomplishes two moves with the diachronic character that these forebears did not themselves accomplish: he allows Harry, Richard and their companions to appear across longer spans of time, and with each new installment focuses sharply on the character's evolved identity in a new facticity.[7] Even a novel with an extended historical sweep—*David Copperfield*, for instance, or Updike's own *In the Beauty of the Lilies*—tends

---

[6] John Updike, *More Matter: Essays and Criticism* (New York: Fawcett Books, 1999) 768.

[7] It is no coincidence that David Lodge's Philip Swallow and Morris Zapp are similarly diachronic and appear in novels with carefully rendered facticity. Lodge is another illustrator of Kierkegaard, so he is interested in time and context and identity transformation. See *Changing Places*. New York: Penguin,1975; *Small World*. New York: Penguin,1984; and *Nice Work*, New York: Penguin, 1988. Louise Erdrich is another important contemporary author employing recurring characters, but she seems more interested in historical facticity than in identity transformation through faith.

to make identity transformation seem plotted and inevitable, and rarely conveys social changes as vividly or particularly as diachronic installments do. Through this special diachronic form, Updike is able to explore and chart identity transformation (or more often characters' failures to transform because of personal incorrigibility) amid a realistically thick history—specifically a thick history of the Cold War, the sexual revolution, and the rise of the consumer society. In essence, Updike's diachronic works tell the story of the superego in decline. They question whether this psychosocial context is making the life of faith even more difficult and rare.

Significantly, both the Rabbit and Maples series are also about marriage. Some would say they are about adultery, but this is a misunderstanding. Luther, Kierkegaard, and Updike understand faithlessness in all its forms, sexual and otherwise, to be endemic, essentially unavoidable, a sort of background noise in the spiritual realm. The signal believers are supposed to pick up clearly through the noise is the call of grace and the mandate to love the neighbor. When marital partners are also believers, behavior within marriage becomes a matter of conscience rather than custom or law. If this is a genuine clarification, then it is not the only relevant one that can come from an understanding of Updike's theological commitments. Some of these clarifications will arise out of a theology familiar to Protestant believers of the liturgical churches. Others are more challenging, which is to say, less familiar: in this book I will attempt to describe an extraordinary notion of Christian faithfulness, in and beyond marriage, that has everything to do with freedom, and little to do with laws, commandments, codes, and traditions.

In other words, I will try to avoid enrolling Updike in a Sunday School—an acid phrase he once applied to a theologically Christian and, he thought, over-simple reading of his early Maples stories. [8] We avoid excessive simplicity by paying attention to Updike's reading of Kierkegaard, distinguishing that reading from sharply countervailing

---

[8] "[T]hey tend to enlist me in their own Sunday School a little too quickly and efficiently, so that in some cases where I meant to raise a question they take it that I provided an answer." James Plath, *Conversations with John Updike* (Jackson MS: The University Press of Mississippi, 1994) 92-93. Updike made this remark about Alice and Kenneth Hamilton's 1970 readings of the first nine Maples stories, readings he admired, except apparently for their oversimplifying of his theology. For these readings, see Alice and Kenneth Hamilton, *The Elements of John Updike* (Grand Rapids MI: Eerdmans, 1970).

ones offered by Theodor Adorno, Jacques Derrida, Martin Buber, Edward Said, and others. We gain further complexity by considering readings of Kierkegaard that Updike found ingenious and powerful, such as those of Miguel de Unamuno, Iris Murdoch, and Denis de Rougemont. Finally, we will consider readings of Kierkegaard's best and most enlightening contemporary scholars engaged in the task of unpacking the first existentialist's notoriously indirect and elusive writings. If these efforts do not make this study altogether distinctive, then perhaps the effort to restore a missing logic in Updike's understanding of Kierkegaard does. That is his insistence that the gift of God's grace—the energy behind the leap itself—is not truly accepted or owned until the believer works for the neighbor's benefit, enacting what Kierkegaard calls works of love. Updike, we will see, takes these works of love very seriously, and makes marriage an even more important site for them than Kierkegaard does.

&

In this book I tell the story of Updike's first encounter with Kierkegaard and then propose a way of understanding the specific existential effect that reading had upon the young American author. I make a comprehensive survey of Updike's writings about Kierkegaard and his interpreters, attempting to crack the implicit theological logic that informs Updike's fiction. Tracing that logic, I explore two specific preoccupations of both Updike and Kierkegaard, both central leitmotifs of the Maples stories, the consuming duty to love the neighbor, and the particular love that animates the new Christian or Protestant marriage— a model of marital practices that emerged in the sixteenth century and continues to challenge both married Christians and other committed partners today. I assemble a compact and continuous narrative of Richard and Joan Maples' relationship so that we can see more clearly their parallel though non-identical trajectories through Kierkegaard's stages and toward authentic personhood, a transformation that is all the more difficult because it occurs in a permissive consumerist and therapeutic society. And I read the eighteen Maples stories as illustrations of Kierkegaard's schema and as interesting treatments of the existential problems and blessings of faith generally. Unlike many contemporary critics, I have sought to find the fun as well as the complexity in the stories. Updike clearly meant them to be fun, as well as exasperating.

The Maples stories correspond closely to the biographical and historical circumstances of John and Mary Pennington Updike's 22 ½ - year marriage (1953-1976) and a moment in their lives a decade after their divorce. All 18 stories evidently correspond to the mutual and personal meaning-making attempts of the Updikes as partners and parents. I assume so in this study—or assume rather that the Maples struggle with existential issues that obviously concerned Updike during his first marriage and early career, and applied to a facticity much like his own, largely shaped by the sexual revolution, the Cold War turned hot in Vietnam, and new dominance of consumerism. The Maples appear in 1956 with "Snowing in Greenwich Village." Four years later, Updike wrote a second Maples story, "Wife-Wooing," and in doing so began to build a story cycle. Every one to three years for about two decades, he published individual Maples stories in *The New Yorker*, *Playboy*, *The Atlantic Monthly*, *Harpers*, and a couple of less well-known magazines. In 1979 he collected the first seventeen stories in a paperback volume titled *Too Far to Go*, including two that use only pronouns for central characters but seem to involve the Maples because of what Updike calls "internal evidence."[9] That same year, 1979, NBC broadcast a two-hour film titled *Too Far to Go*, starring Michael Moriarty and Blythe Danner as Richard and Joan Maple. Updike added to the cycle only once more after the book and film, a *New Yorker* story titled "Grandparenting" (1994). In the final weeks of his life, Updike welcomed the first hardcover and complete collection of the stories, the Everyman Pocket Classic *Maples Stories* (2008).

What are the autobiographical Maples stories about? What problems do Richard and Joan seek to solve? Finding a reason to remain married, finding the love and energy to raise their children with imagination and care, finding ways both to honor and control their natural impulses, finding help with managing their psychological health, finding ways to relate meaningfully with others, and ultimately, finding a loving God with whom each might relate—these are the most important tasks the Maples take up. This final task of finding God seems always frustrated among Updike's characters, including the Maples, though we know it was not totally frustrated in Updike's life.

---

[9] John Updike, Foreword to *Too Far to Go: The Maples Stories* (New York: Fawcett Crest, 1979) 10.

In his memoir *Self-Consciousness* (1989), in many famous personal essays such as "The Dogwood Tree: A Boyhood" (1965), in reviews of books that had particularly moved him across his writing life, in interviews, in two long self-parodic and confessional poems, *Midpoint* (1969) and *Endpoint* (2009), Updike generously shares his own struggles to solve personal existential problems. These problems become the particular focuses of the Maples stories—complications of purpose, marriage, and love of neighbor, basically, which are certainly central Kierkegaardian themes. All of the stories illustrate particular conditions of anxiety and despair. They point to the factors in modern life that make the leap into faith a scandal, a potential embarrassment, an ethical offense to nominal Christians and non-Christians alike. If one of the Maples were to make the leap of faith, we would expect to see in that person sudden and serious unselfing, relinquishment of narcissistic traits, and the performance of loving acts determined by a newly activated, creative conscience rather than by received ethical standards alone. But we would also see that person continue to live with existential problems. For even the most devout believer, the task of loving the neighbor is deeply complicated and, as we will see Adorno and Derrida pointing out, almost impossible to carry out. Kierkegaard tells us that it takes alertness and imagination to love the neighbor. There simply are no ethical codes—not the Ten Commandments, not the Beatitudes, not the developed theology of any given Christian denomination—adequate to the project of properly loving the neighbor, including the typical nearest neighbor, whom I have noted Kierkegaard calls "wife." Those who know the Maples stories know that Richard and Joan find it a challenge to love each other. They tend to love their neighbors promiscuously rather than faithfully. Their half-acknowledged difficulties with love are symptomatic of the Kierkegaardian category of anxiety, its synonym, dread, and its condition of crisis, despair.

Updike and Kierkegaard both realize that to live is to seek meaning, usually unconsciously and always desperately. Seekers travel through stages of meaning-making in an attempt to solve the existential problems of boredom, anxiety about perfect freedom, and despair over finding a proper ground for right action. (As we will see, each of these states of consciousness has a specific meaning for Kierkegaard.) Kierkegaard's own stages are well-known, if sometimes mystifying to those of us who seek, with our differing levels of interest and commitment, to understand his extraordinarily dialectical and dialogical works. He sees lives in Christendom—clearly we should now add post-Christian societies—as repeating the strategies of one of three stages or spheres of existence, the aesthetic, the ethical, and the religious.

People in the least self-aware stage, the aesthetic, first depend upon pleasure-seeking and interpersonal gaming to give their lives meaning. They do so because the experience of physical and psychological pleasures keeps at bay the great existential questions about eternity. This aesthetic stage gives way, for some, to an ethical stage, in which seekers recognize the God-granted, universal nature of human values. They attempt to live rightly, aligned with these values. Because genuine ethical conduct will not allow for the particular exploitations of the other upon which the aesthetic life depends, the aesthetic motive collapses in the ethical, even while aesthetic pleasure remains possible. This ethical life can be the ground for satisfying mutuality in marriage and other widely sanctioned relationships.

But there is a reason that the ethical life is a penultimate rather than ultimate stage in Kierkegaard's vision. Mere ethics do not solve the problem of death. The ethicist can only do good and then die. For Kierkegaard and Updike, all anxiety is rooted in anxiety about one's own death, not just because annihilation is frightening, but because death closes off the possibility of defining choice on one's own behalf. It is this anxiety that leads some out of the ethical, and into a shift in consciousness that Kierkegaard and other Christians call "faith." Believing that the teachings and promises of Christ solve the problems of death and purposelessness, these believers have made a leap into faith, a leap into an utterly absurd system of meaning-making which is qualitatively distinct from the busy-ness of living by ethics, even religious ethics. Personal busy-ness is supplanted by authentic work for others in need, work related to one's own ecstatic gifts and to a freedom that can arise only out of gratitude and hope.

What saved Updike's own life and career, he tells us in these writings, was reading Kierkegaard and accepting as true the *teleological suspension of the ethical*. Updike acknowledges that his faith is an ethical and rational scandal, an offense to many. But he also insists that any life lived in the aesthetic or ethical stages—which are of course prior to the leap into faith—any life absent the leverage provided by the Archimedean point, the existential fixed point of faithful conscience and its endless task of loving the neighbor, must be despairing. Such a life can only be loosely, abstractly ethical. Updike accepted Kierkegaard's argument that neighbor-love after the leap is more rigorous, demanding, and encompassing than any altruistic ethics derived, as ethics must be, from more arguable public standards for right behavior. For Kierkegaard and thus for Updike, the leap of faith is incomplete, hollow, even vain if it does not lead, through a changed consciousness and charged conscience, to work on behalf of those in need, no matter who they are or what they believe. Updike's faith thus gave him genuine and meaningful work to do, without creating the illusion that he was working his way into God's favor.

George Hunt and Marshall Boswell emphasize the dialectical character of Updike's Kierkegaard. The strength of this approach is that the two of them find common ground between Kierkegaard and Karl Barth, both dialectical thinkers and both very important to Updike. In *John Updike and the Three Great Secret Things: Sex, Religion, and Art* (1980), Hunt aptly describes the fundaments of Kierkegaard's thought: the three stages or spheres of existence, their character, the nature of the leap from stage to stage culminating in the leap of faith, the passionate character of choosing, the scandalous nature of Christianity, and the miracle of the God-man, Christ. I will review Updike's understanding of these fundaments, much updated in his nonfictional writings since the publication of Hunt's study, and offer my own understanding of them. Hunt views Updike's fiction as posing "a moral debate about goodness and its opposite."[10] This dialectic is present in Updike's work, to be sure, but to focus wholly on it is to collapse Kierkegaard's religious stage back into the ethical. No one makes the leap because of discerned and attained "goodness." As Kierkegaard writes in *The Sickness Unto Death*, "the opposite of sin is not virtue but faith."[11] Boswell's view unfortunately erases even more of the matters Kierkegaard did not leave in unresolved tension: the necessity of faith and consequent works of love. In *John Updike's Rabbit Tetralogy: Mastered Irony in Motion* (2001), Boswell argues that Updike learned from Kierkegaard the use of the dialectical tool of "mastered irony"—as though Kierkegaard's or Updike's uses of irony

---

[10] George Hunt, *John Updike and the Three Great Secret Things: Sex, Religion, and Art* (Grand Rapids MI: William B. Eerdmans, 1980) 48.

[11] Søren Kierkegaard, *Fear and Trembling* and *The Sickness Unto Death*, trans. Walter Lowrie (Garden City NY: Doubleday Anchor Books, 1954) 213.

were somehow distinctive, constituted a vocation, or solved existential problems.[12]

So Updike's double-minded diffidence can be unduly emphasized. Though it is true that Updike has spoken eloquently about the "Yes, but—" character of his fiction ("Yes, in *Rabbit, Run*, to our inner urgent whispers, but—the social fabric collapses murderously"), and that it is fundamental to Updike to see people as both sinful and lovable in the sight of God, Updike insists on the centrality of existential choosing.[13] Too great an emphasis on unresolved dialectics, which I think Hunt and Darrell Jodock avoid but some others before and after them have not, yields an Updike who is complex but has little to argue for, an essentially mimetic writer in a morally baffling world.[14] This Updike interests himself only in the quotidian matters of people's ethical and psychological struggles. This is not the Updike I read. Updike understands that to be convinced by Kierkegaard means to be open to grace, willing to adopt a sudden and serious change of consciousness and behavior—to accept through repentance or *metanoia* a radical existential freedom. As Jodock aptly puts it, the experience of faith, so conceived, confers "freedom *from* coercion, freedom *for* service, and freedom *to* tell the truth."[15]

As Jodock notes, in *Self-Consciousness*, Updike writes that as of 1989 he does not read Kierkegaard or Barth any more, that his life is "mostly lived." Jodock understandably takes Updike at his word. When it comes to Updike's theological heroes, he writes, "their assistance is over. [Updike] remains neither a disciple nor a student of their theologies."[16] On the contrary, no matter what he felt was true while writing *Self-Consciousness*, Updike read and wrote about Kierkegaard, and about Barth, Unamuno, and others in a Kierkegaardian light, throughout his entire career. This writing is affirmative, emphatic, and healthily critical. Updike's last extended essay on Kierkegaard appeared in 2005, only four

---

[12] Marshall Boswell, *John Updike's Rabbit Tetralogy: Mastered Irony in Motion* (Columbia MO: University of Missouri Press, 2001) 1.

[13] Charles Thomas Samuels, "John Updike: The Art of Fiction No. 43." *The Paris Review* 45 (Winter 1968). http:// www.theparisreview.org/interviews/ 4219/the-art-of-fiction-no-43-john-updike

[14] Darrell Jodock, "What is Goodness? The Influence of Updike's Lutheran Roots." In *John Updike and Religion: The Sense of the Sacred and the Motions of Grace*, ed. James Yerkes. (Grand Rapids MI: Eerdmans, 1999).

[15] Ibid., 132.

[16] Ibid., 131.

years before his death, and the final lines of the *Endpoint* poem, dated thirty-five days before Updike's death, express the Kierkegaardian formula of Christian subjectivity:

> The tongue reposes in papyrus pleas,
> saying, *Surely*—magnificent, that "surely"—
> *goodness and mercy shall follow me all*
> *the days of my life,* my life, forever.[17]

"My life" is, of course, the defiantly Kierkegaardian expression, the insistence that when it comes to faith one goes it alone, but going it alone one can accept God's offer of eternity. Updike spoke with this cosmic defiance often throughout his career. He spoke of neighbors and neighbor-love less often, but no less emphatically, as we will see. One problem with emphasizing dialectics in Updike's work, then, is that in doing so we tend to neglect the *telos* of Kierkegaard's scheme, the idea that God's motion of grace is completed by the motions of believers, cleansed if only briefly of grandiosity and thus able to love others more genuinely.

Updike tells us clearly and repeatedly that his fiction tends to reveal God's loving presence in even the most depraved behavior. Wretched and depraved acts in the fiction are meant to aggravate the despair that doubters and seekers already feel incipiently, so that they may feel more sharply the passion for the leap. As Kierkegaard argues in the non-pseudonymous *The Sickness Unto Death*, when "despair is more intense, salvation is in a certain sense nearer."[18] This is not to say that Updike simply adopts the role of Kierkegaard's disciple. Indeed, we will see that Updike's calling brought him into serious theological engagement and debate with Kierkegaard. Specifically, Updike simply could not accept Kierkegaard's late-career ananthropic and misogynistic conclusions (which I will review), arguing instead for an understanding of God's mercy that, he hints, might extend even so far as to a doctrine of universal salvation.

Certainly Updike's fiction offers few orthodox Christian consolations. For Kierkegaard and therefore for Updike, it is a Hegelian

---

[17] John Updike, *Endpoint*. In *Endpoint and Other Poems* (New York: Knopf, 2009) 29.

[18] Søren Kierkegaard, *The Sickness Unto Death*. In *Fear and Trembling and Sickness Unto Death*, trans. Walter Lowrie. (New York: Anchor, 1954) 196.

mistake to offer readers any model of Christian faithfulness that might appeal to them, or show them some kind of practical advantage for being a Christian. Such believers would be invited to choose faith for self-serving reasons. In Kierkegaard's world, no Christian feels faith, or leaps into it genuinely, without experiencing, both before and after the leap, doubt, embarrassment, anxiety, sense of failure, alienation from loved ones, and other causes of suffering. This suffering is right and true because free will leads to pain, and pain confers benefits. The central benefit is that the grandiose self is corrected. Kierkegaard is willing to state plainly what in my experience many who teach at Christian colleges find it difficult to talk about with their students: God does not promise happiness as promised by triumphalist American civil religion, or the flattering consumer society, or its sometime agent, the admissions office. One's calling may be to live a life of great difficulty and even pain, so long as one's work squares with prayerful conscience. If we are offended at the idea that we are not wholly lovable in the eyes of God, and that faith will not inevitably lead to our material benefit, this would not surprise Kierkegaard. He writes in *Works of Love* that offended grandiosity is the typical state of the incipient believer.[19]

Far from promoting the Christian life, Updike's fiction often seems to taunt the more pious and conventionally Christian reader. Shocking offenses of ethics and taste in the fiction seem calculated to rile readers into an irritated state, and perhaps then into a desire for a better way to live and act. Yet, even when we are irritated, we should realize that Updike is neither a manipulative nor malicious writer. He merely describes moments in life so fraught, so tortured, and so private that few other writers or artists will make a similar attempt. Feeling existential irritation prepares the seeker for a new consciousness, and perhaps for a leap. In this sense, Updike's many distressing scenes, especially the coital ones, are perhaps meant to be a gift to spiritual seekers. We will see that he speaks directly about writers who seem to intend to irritate, an intention he admires especially in his favorite Catholic writers.

Through his interest in Kierkegaard and students of Kierkegaard such as Barth, Unamuno, de Rougemont, and even a secular writer such as Iris Murdoch, Updike became a crisis theologian, a student and amateur professor of Christian neo-orthodoxy. The term "neo-orthodoxy" (or its rough synonyms, "crisis theology," "dialectical theology," and the pejorative "fideism") is contested, but I depend upon

---

[19] Søren Kierkegaard, *Works of Love*, 59.

Updike's own articulation of the neo-orthodox task, which I develop more fully in succeeding chapters. Updike implies this definition of neo-orthodoxy in the negative: Any Christian theology which poses God as near and simply loving, which seeks proofs outside the human heart, which believes that rationality, teaching, or suasion play a role in bringing people to faith, which views Christian impulses played out in society as anything other than penultimate, which denies the ultimate matter of the believer's or seeker's existential desperation—such a Christianity fails to be orthodox, which is to say, true for believers like Updike. As Updike says of Barth's gift to clear-thinking orthodox believers, "The Christian believer, awaking from the medieval dream wherein Church and State, faith and science, thoughts and things seem to merge, has been restored with a vengeance to his primitive desperation [by Barth's and others' neo-orthodox writings]."[20] Barth and other crisis theologians owe a debt to Kierkegaard, whose project was to distinguish habits and traditions of Christendom from the absurd experience of faith in the human heart.

♬

The first four chapters of this study deal with three fundamental features of the Maples stories, which illustrate and epitomize Kierkegaard's existential theology. "Chapter One: Updike's Kierkegaard" seeks to identify those core ideas of Kierkegaard's which Updike tells us he tried to illustrate in his early fiction. Because it is not at all clear that Updike's Kierkegaardian theology changed significantly over the course of his adult life (though it must have deepened), I consider every significant utterance Updike recorded about Kierkegaard from the early 1960s to the mid-2000s. "Chapter Two: The Neighbor-Love Problem for the Relatively Antinomian Believer" examines the Kierkegaardian result of the leap of faith, freely chosen obedience to Jesus' mandate that believers love one another. Since Kierkegaard's neighbor-love principles are the most contested in all his work, this chapter presents an implicit debate between Kierkegaard and such critics as W.H. Auden, Theodor Adorno, and Jacques Derrida. Updike sides with Kierkegaard in these debates, refusing to rate neighbor-love as either ananthropic or absurdly ineffective. "Chapter Three: Kierkegaard's Marital Ideality and Updike's

---

[20] John Updike, "Faith in Search of Understanding." In *Assorted Prose* (New York: Knopf, 1965) 281.

Reality" examines three marital idealities—Martin Luther's, Kierke-gaard's, and Updike's own. These we need to understand so that we are better able to parse Richard's and Joan's existential successes and failures as husband and wife. Updike posits a culture of narcissism in which existential and marital success means restraining the hungry ego. "Chapter Four: The Maples Marriage and Identity Transformation" examines in Kierkegaardian terms the psychological and historical facticity which informs the stories and places new demands upon the spouse and believer. This is the story of a waning cultural superego, a record of the diminution of its characteristic repressions. Richard, living in the aesthetic stage, welcomes freedom from childhood repressions, while Joan, living in the ethical, must square greater sexual freedom, which she embraces, with her good works. The Maples' therapeutic culture teaches them that discarding or disregarding repressions will lead to peace and satisfaction, but Richard and Joan do not experience these benefits. Their despair deepens as they find ways to avoid genuine existential choosing. Only after divorcing do they display signs of corrective, beneficial, or blessed identity transformation.

In "Chapter Five: 'Oh But They Were Close'," I argue that "Snowing in Greenwich Village" (1956) and "Wife-Wooing," (1960) are intentional meditations upon secular and orthodox ideas of the neighbor.[21] Rebecca Cune is quite literally a neighbor of the young and newly-married Maples, who have just moved into a Greenwich Village apartment down the street from hers. Rebecca's "closeness" becomes a crucial question. Do the Maples treat her as their neighbor in the Christian sense? Certainly not. Though Richard comes close to kissing Rebecca as he drops her off at her apartment, and is tempted to move her toward the large bed so noticeable in her room, love does not guide him. Clearly, in this opening story of the cycle, Updike wishes to examine the mechanics of sexual desire in encountering the neighbor. Richard's decision to resist temptation and return chaste from Rebecca's apartment to the unwell Joan is a brief victory for the retreating forces of sexual repression, but

---

[21] The titles for chapters five through ten, those dedicated to an interpretation of the individual Maples stories, though also charting shifts in their historical context and theological import in groupings, are drawn from striking and tellingly relevant lines within the stories—but not necessarily the stories involved in that chapter. For example, the title "Etiquette of Adultery" is drawn from "Gesturing," while in that chapter I deal with adulterous manners in "The Taste of Metal," "Your Lover Just Called," "Waiting Up," and "Eros Rampant."

leaves us with doubts about Richard's conscience. In "Wife-Wooing," Updike confronts a related mystery, how the wife who is supposed to be one flesh with the husband is in fact still an object of courtship, still a neighbor at some emotional distance from her partner. To put this in Kierkegaard's terms, Richard finds himself performing a loving repetition, courting his own wife, returning to a heightened awareness not just of her body but of her whole person. In this case he is eventually guided by love, and his success in wooing feels to him like a moment of grace. In later years he will fail to perform this loving repetition, and this failure will become a measure of his despair, of his resistance to the motions of grace.

In "Chapter Six: Fathoms Deep in the Wrong," I note that the narcissistic and ruthless Richard who appears in stories of 1963 and 1964, "Giving Blood," "Twin Beds in Rome," and "Marching Through Boston," has begun to seize essentially hedonic satisfactions. More clearly than in the first two stories, he epitomizes Kierkegaard's aesthetic stage. At the same time, Joan, like the society the Maples live in, has become more alert to questions of social justice and the welfare of fellow citizens. She epitomizes the ethical stage. These mismatched commitments to the aesthetic and ethical of course lead to conflict between the Maples, just as self- and other-oriented ethics cause conflict within American government and society. But the conflict is not Updike's central focus. He is more interested in the specific character of Richard's narcissism and personal grandiosity, which is expressed in the stories as psychological illness—psychosomatic symptoms and psychotic breaks. This sickness has the character of contagion. For the first time in the Maples stories, we see the children frightened by their father's raving narcissistic speech, and as a result, they become incubators of their own anxiety. Meanwhile, Joan's ethical commitment makes her feel contempt rather than love for her husband.

Kierkegaard calls personal grandiosity and cruelty "sickness unto death," drawing the phrase from the New Testament story of Lazarus, whom Jesus raises from the dead.[22] Sickness unto death is sin, but not sin understood as misdeed. It is original and endemic separation from God. Born like all other people to this wretched sickness, Richard is different only in degree from anyone else, literally anyone, since according to Kierkegaard all live in separation punctuated intermittently, for the willing, by moments of grace. Joan contrasts with Richard in these

---

[22] See John 11.

stories, having found not only a calling of her own in serving others (her aunt in "Giving Blood," Richard himself in "Twin Beds in Rome," and disenfranchised African-Americans in "Marching through Boston") but apparently the author's sympathy. Yet, Joan too is prone to self-delusion and grandiosity and unworkable theories about love. She is also on the edge of emotional crisis, one that will lead her to thoughts of suicide in later years. These stories confront the existential problem of why people tend to minimize love, even their own love for others in interpersonal and civic forms, when such love lends much needed meaning to individual lives. In "Marching through Boston," we see that Dr. Martin Luther King transformed this love into a broad-based and effective civic movement—but Richard especially finds cause to ignore King's example.

The aesthetic and ethical tables begin to turn in "Chapter Seven: An Etiquette of Adultery." In these chilling stories of 1967 and 1968, "The Taste of Metal," "Your Lover Just Called," "Waiting Up," and "Eros Rampant," the entire Maples family suffers the effects of the culture of narcissism, of an ethics perversely based in a society's shift to the aesthetic. This discarding of repressions, which we sometimes associate with the counterculture, but which Updike observed in the prosperous Boston suburbs, eventually led to a new established and understood ethic, or etiquette, of adultery. Updike has said that frank adultery and sexual play could be found anywhere in the East throughout the 1960s. He carefully chronicles the absurd rules by which this play was governed. He notes that this sexual play was in his experience both destructive and liberating, but in these stories Richard seems more compulsive than free. As in earlier stories, love does not guide him. Updike's diagnosis of this newly permissive world is complex and consistent with his crisis theology. In these stories he contrasts the ethics of adultery with a set of Christian allusions and anagogical images which point to another way, one in which sexual play might be understood or forgiven or even accepted, but in which marital healing and parental dedication become a more serious and rightful project of awakened conscience. In other words, even while depicting in frank detail the ways he and his neighbors conduct their affairs, Updike is able to point slyly but insistently toward Kierkegaard's works of love.

I argue in "Chapter Eight: Frightened People Discussing," that in the final years of their marriage, the Maples enter into a debilitating existential crisis. In these stories of 1971 to 1974, "Plumbing," "The Red Herring Theory," "Sublimating," and "Nakedness," Richard and Joan escort each other into this crisis. These stories plumb, very directly, the most crucial of human questions: Why do we die? What do our brief lives mean? How do we lend them meaning? How do we defeat those impulses in us that further degrade meaning and purpose? In these four stories, the Maples have come to live in evident dread, the sort that Kierkegaard describes in *Sickness Unto Death*. In that book Kierkegaard describes adults who, failing to "choose themselves"—that is, confront mortality, feel intense dread, and solve that dread by leaping into eternity—live their lives in perverse, determined egotistical childishness.[23] So it is with Richard and Joan in these stories. Their dread is expressed in perverse gaming over sexual dalliances, in heavy drinking, in mutual taunting about sexual and other forms of fidelity, and occasionally in physical violence. As the Maples fail to recognize their own existential fear in themselves and each other, they cause more ordinary daily fear in their children. As usual, of course, Updike offers alternatives to fearful dread through a complex subtext dealing with such issues as time, art, psychoanalysis, and an Augustinian theology of incarnation. The story "Nakedness," through its play with images of Eden, Adam and Eve, the Fall, and the persistence of love between partners in a postlapsarian world, even offers the possibility of regained innocence

"Chapter Nine: Sanctified Unhappiness" involves two of Updike's best stories: "Separating" (1975), and "Gesturing" (1979). "Separating" crystallizes Updike's literary methods and interests, his ability to turn the particularity of a modern family's struggles into the universality (for him and Kierkegaard) of human dread and its alternatives. Specifically, in this story Updike retells the story of the Last Supper in distinctly modern and half-profane terms, showing the Kierkegaardian formulation that the most important separation in an incipient Christian's life is separation from Christ, a loss the diners at the Last Supper anticipated and later of course experienced. Updike goes so far as to claim in his memoirs that this is America's great problem, that it is a "country severed from Christ by the breadth of the sea."[24] "Separating" illustrates the particular personal and social problems that stem from this great one. The Last Supper also traditionally gave believers the mandate to love the neighbor, so we must evaluate Richard's love for his mistress living nearby, comparing that love to the love he shows intermittently

---

[23] See, for example, Kierkegaard, *The Sickness Unto Death*, 191ff.

[24] John Updike, *Self-Consciousness: Memoirs* (New York: Knopf, 1989) 103.

for his children and for Joan. "Gesturing," a story not published until 1979 but dealing with action of the final year of the Maples' marriage, specifically the summer of 1975, is the only story Updike placed in his own *Best American Short Stories of the Century*.[25] So it too has at least a claim to being his best. This story also dwells on human incapacity—our ability to gesture only—in the face of eternal death and a Wholly Other God. Updike questions whether marriage and faithful life in general are in fact at best forms of "sanctified unhappiness."[26] Joan threatens to kill herself in "Divorcing: A Fragment" (unpublished until the appearance of *Too Far to Go* in 1979), so in these three stories the stakes of failing to choose oneself and, as a result, continuing to live in enervating anxiety are shown vividly, palpably, chillingly.

The final two Maples stories, "Here Come the Maples" (1976) and "Grandparenting," (1994), round out the story sequence in a strikingly peaceful and hopeful mood. In "Chapter Ten: Reality is Sacred," I argue that at the moment of their separation and for years afterward, Richard and Joan finally undergo a beneficent kind of identity transformation. They relinquish their need to manipulate and control each other, and enter into a more loving partnership than we had seen before. Indeed, these stories question whether a loving marriage really ever ends, even after a divorce decree. For Updike, if not for Kierkegaard, a true marriage, one in which love is present, transcends legal or social agreements. If a loving partnership continues, in a sense the marriage continues. Certainly love of the near-neighbor does. These stories continue the existential suggestion Richard makes in "Gesturing," in which Joan tells Richard that he is the only person she can talk with freely and easily—a compliment that, ironically, obliges him to listen to her tell about her sex life with second-husband-to-be Andy. Joan seems unable to resist sharing her most intense experiences with Richard, as she has done while they shared a home for some twenty years. Richard realizes what Joan is really saying, that the two of them, joined together, are "sacred as reality is sacred."[27] Through Richard's memories of the marriage in "Here Come the Maples," and his reunion with Joan at the birth of their first grandchild, he comes to realize, perhaps dimly, that if

---

[25] John Updike and Katrina Kenison, eds. *Best American Short Stories of the Century* (New York: Houghton Mifflin, 2000) 565ff.

[26] John Updike, *Too Far to Go: The Maples Stories* (New York: Fawcett Crest, 1979) 234.

[27] Updike, *Too Far to Go*, 231.

the marriage contract between himself and Joan was not essential, permanent, or ultimately real, their love for each other was and is.

The Maples may have gestured their way into and then out of their marriage, and that matters to Updike. But it matters only penultimately. What Updike cares more about is whether Richard and Joan accept the grace of a God of pure possibility. In both of these final two Maples stories, Richard and Joan achieve a notable calm and sanguinity. Richard's patience and calm in "Grandparenting," his ability to think about his daughter's pain in childbirth rather than his own waning years—even after a nearly sleepless night in a cold coffin of a hotel room—raises the most interesting existential question: has his retreat from aesthetic gaming resulted merely from his aging, with its inevitably shrinking sexual interest and opportunity? Or has he truly moved along the stages on life's way to an ethical or even religious consciousness? No pattern of Richard's behavior will answer this question for us. Kierkegaard notes in *Fear and Trembling* that the genuine believer, the Knight of Faith, is indistinguishable from ethical others.[28] The leap of faith is wholly inward, and acts of loving conscience look like merely ethical acts. Nevertheless, Updike may have felt that depicting a Richard and Joan who had each made the leap of faith was not too far to go.

---

[28] See Kierkegaard's imagined Knight of Faith, who might look like an ordinary citizen, a tax collector. Søren Kierkegaard, *Fear and Trembling*. In *Fear and Trembling* and *Repetition*, eds. and trans. Howard V. Hong and Edna H. Hong. (Princeton NJ: Princeton University Press, 1983) 38ff.

1

Updike's Kierkegaard

> After *Fear and Trembling*, I had a secret twist inside, a precarious
> tender core of cosmic defiance; for a time, I thought of all my
> fiction as illustrations of Kierkegaard.
>
> —John Updike, *Odd Jobs*[1]

This is the clinching line of John Updike's tale about his first encounter
with Søren Kierkegaard's writings, an epiphanic moment if ever there
was one in a doubting Christian's life, and the origin of Updike's calling
as a particular kind of existentialist writer. Recalling this moment about
a decade after, Updike writes that as a 23-year old he enjoyed the
"paradisiacal" days of his first summer in Manhattan, reading Proust
and, also for the first time, Kierkegaard. He was newly married, newly a
father, living in a city where he had always wanted to live, employed by
The New Yorker, the magazine he had loved since he was a little boy
reading the cartoons in his mother's copy. But his Manhattan happiness
seemed fragile. Updike felt he had existential problems to solve,
especially the problem of achieving a sanguine sense of identity and
purpose. "I was not only a would-be writer," he writes, "but a would-be
Christian." Reading Proust was helping, teaching Updike that the deceit
and absurdity he encountered in daily life need not distract him from the
world's mysterious loveliness. Kierkegaard was helping even more,
providing a particular intellectual, emotional, and spiritual support that
Updike believed his courses at Harvard had neglected. Between Proust
and Kierkegaard, Updike found himself able to "walk safely down the
street, the street of my life."[2]

In his memoir *Self-Consciousness* (1989), Updike refers to Kierkegaard as one in a list of existentialist Protestant and modernist Catholic
writers whom he admires: Unamuno, Kierkegaard, Barth, Chesterton,

---

[1] John Updike, *Odd Jobs: Essays and Criticism* (New York: Knopf, 1991) 844.
[2] John Updike, *Picked-Up Pieces: Essays and Criticism* (New York: Knopf,
1976) 167.

Eliot. These were the "very few" writers who helped Updike find a credible Christian theology in a vapid American Christendom in which "almost no one believed, believed it really"—"it" being the faith of his childhood, expressed best by the Apostle's Creed.[3] Two years later, in a requested essay on a book that changed him, Updike wrote more specifically and lovingly of his encounter with Kierkegaard's *Fear and Trembling*. The book, he writes, was a pumpkin-colored Anchor paperback with an Edward Gorey cover, *Fear and Trembling* bound together with *The Sickness Unto Death* in this 1954 edition. Updike read the book in 1955 or early 1956, again while living in New York City with his wife and first child. His new duties as father, husband and breadwinner had left him feeling "fearful and desolate." He saw that he would die, and that "the substance of the earth was, therefore, death." Elsewhere, Updike speaks of those terrible days in terms of an enervating despair: "I've touched a kind of bottom [. . .] when I've felt that existence itself was an affront to be forgiven. I've felt in myself and in those around me a failure of nerve—a sense of doubt as to the worth of any action."[4] Reading Kierkegaard gave Updike the nerve he felt missing in himself and others, along with the confidence and will to act.

In the first few pages of *Fear and Trembling*, Updike encountered the story of Abraham's hastening to Mount Moriah to sacrifice his son Isaac. Kierkegaard tells this story in a series of brief versions, a "mesmerically repeated evocation" as Updike puts it, of Abraham's state of mind as he pondered the terrible act he would have to perform. The sacrifice God had called Abraham to perform was really to be an appalling murder of a beloved child. It was therefore "an incomprehensible act," Updike writes, "that marked the beginning of Judaic faith and God's stated covenant." Here he repeats the logic of Kierkegaard's "teleological suspension of the ethical"—the idea that Abraham's intention, obedient to God's command, is an unthinkable ethical offense even while it is an essential acknowledgement of God's presence and guiding influence in his life. Faith itself is such an offense, Kierkegaard argues, an absolute violation of the community's expectation, of the demands of compassionate good sense. Yet Updike took comfort from *Fear and Trembling*. The Abraham and Isaac story in Kierkegaard's captivating, repeating evocation of it "corresponded," Updike writes, "to my inner state of alarm" and "rather sketchy Lutheran upbringing." Finding the

---

[3] Updike, *Self-Consciousness*, 230.
[4] Plath, *Conversations*, 14.

sketchy theology of his youth confirmed in the writings of the first existentialist, Updike had discovered a reason, a kind of intellectual if not rational permission, to believe in the living and loving God he had heard about through childhood. "I took from Kierkegaard," he writes, "the idea that subjectivity too has its rightful claims, amid all the desolating objective evidence of our insignificance and futility and final nonexistence; faith is not a deduction but an act of will, a heroism."[5]

Updike knew that the believer's acceptance of God's gift of faith is anything but heroic. The God of the neo-orthodoxy Updike adopted from Kierkegaard is so qualitatively different from the incipient believer that, as one of Kierkegaard's characters argues, in the face of this God a person is always already in the wrong.[6] Mired in sin, which Kierkegaard defines as separation from God leading to misdeeds, rather than misdeeds themselves, the incipient believer cannot choose God. The leap of faith is at best an acceptance of God's grace, which somehow pierces the carapace of illusion and denial in which the unbelieving yet instinctively seeking person lives. Using the word "heroism" here, Updike must mean that he felt the leap of faith to be heroic in the social realm, a willingness to seem scandalously irrational and credulous in signing on for an ancient myth under sustained and coherent philosophical attack. As we will see, scholars of Kierkegaard such as Jamie Ferreira and Sylvia Walsh develop this idea of the "offense" of Christian faith, the outraged reaction of those who cannot or will not understand such an absurd personal choice, and the offense believers feel before the leap, their grandiose selves struggling with the idea that they are not completely lovable and capable and righteous, that they desperately need God's help.

So Updike tells us that in the face of "desolating objective evidence" of a Godless universe and certain objections from others, he leapt into a consciousness shaped by eternity rather than by the brevity of ordinary

---

[5] Updike, *Odd Jobs*, 844.

[6] Søren Kierkegaard, *Either/Or*, eds. and trans. Howard V. Hong and Edna H. Hong. 2 vols. (Princeton NJ: Princeton University Press, 1987) 2:346-354. In the closing pages of *Either/Or*, the ethically-minded Judge William makes a sermon that begins with a correct theological insight emerging from the existence of the Wholly Other God. The title of this sermon is "The Upbuilding That Lies in the Thought That in Relation to God We Are Always in the Wrong." William begins correctly but then is not quite able to play out the full consequences of this truth—which is that incipient believers require God's grace, that they cannot be ethically sound on their own.

life-span. As a result, he tells us, he leapt into consciousness and conscience shaped by immediate relation with God. When confronted by despair, "one has nothing"—as he once put it—"but the ancient assertions of Christianity to give one the will to act, even if the act is only the bringing in of the milk bottles off the front porch."[7] He implies here that conscious despair is utterly disabling, that it renders absurd the simplest action. If the assertions of Christianity help, he also suggests, these assertions are not the Christianity of recorded commandments, of pious adherence to rules and codes and habits. Updike writes of himself as "somewhat antinomian" in his faith, but in fact he seizes a particular Christian logic which is at once both orthodox—declaring original sin, the divinity of Jesus Christ, the resurrection, and the assurance of an afterlife all to be real and true—and perfectly free and open with regard to enacting ethical responsibility. "I decided I nevertheless would believe," Updike writes, in spite of the "priests and executors" who, "to keep order and to force the world into a convenient mould, will always want to make Him the God of the dead, the God who chastises life and forbids and says No. What I felt, in that basement Sunday school of Grace Lutheran Church in Shillington, was a clumsy attempt to extend a Yes, a blessing, and I accepted that blessing, offering in return only a nickel a week and my art, my poor little art."[8]

The No and Yes here are Karl Barth's, though Kierkegaard's dialectics employ the same logic. The No Updike felt is the human dilemma in the face of the chastening, punishing, Wholly Other God, a life-constricting and life-denying ethic which has everything to do with fear of death and the God who allows it, and nothing to do with relation with God and the love that overcomes death. The Yes is the effect of the Easter miracle, of Christ's sacrificial death and then defeat of death. According to Barth's and Kierkegaard's theology, Christ's death justifies the errant believer to the Wholly Other God, making relation to this distant and chastening God possible.[9] This Yes is life-granting because the moral-ethical life becomes a project of individual and communal imagination rather than constraining obedience to codes expressed in the

---

[7] Plath, *Conversations*, 14.

[8] Updike, *Self-Consciousness*, 230-31.

[9] See Updike, "Faith in Search of Understanding, in *Assorted Prose*, 273. Here, for the first time in his writings, Updike introduces his readers to Barth's No and Yes, and names the first work of Barth's that he read, *The Word of God and the Word of Man*, trans. Douglas Horton. (New York: Pilgrim, 1958).

negative—Thou Shalt Not. Believers, acknowledging their ethical weakness and the inevitability of their sinning, feel the freedom to "sin boldly," as Luther put it, which means to live boldly in spite of one's known flaws.[10] And so, in story after story, Updike's characters explore and test the complex relation between imagination, the moral life, and existential freedom.

To paraphrase the final act of Kierkegaard's drama, when believers stand before God and experience God's love, they release an inevitably compulsive egotism. They are suddenly able to love themselves genuinely, and find themselves able therefore to love the neighbor. The believer's conscience is suddenly "before God," as Kierkegaard often asserts, meaning that awareness of God as both present and loving awakens the believer, however dimly, to tasks that must be performed as a neighbor on behalf of the neighbor. In *Works of Love* Kierkegaard suggests that worldly love is person-to-person love, while Christian love adds God as the middle term, and loses its worldliness.[11] It is simply impossible, Kierkegaard argues, to choose oneself before God, live in gratitude for the meaning provided by God's love and promise of eternal possibility, and then neglect the neighbor. As Anthony Rudd elegantly summarizes the post-leap ethical life, "Ethics then ceases to be a striving to realize a *telos*, but becomes simply an outlook of trust and gratitude."[12]

This remark captures the mood of received belief, according to Kierkegaard, but perhaps not his emphatic assertion in *Works of Love* and elsewhere that the performance of works of love is an absolute duty, a necessary consequence of thankfulness and reformed conscience. In *Either/Or* he argues that this God-informed conscience may not tell the believer the right loving acts to perform, which requires personal judgment and creativity which any given individual may or may not own, but certainly will alert the believer to wretched or destructive acts that they have mistakenly contemplated or performed.[13] Even though

---

[10] Luther's advice to believers that they "sin boldly" is actually a paraphrase of a passage in a letter to Melancthon in which Luther argues that Christians should "be a sinner, and let [their] sins be strong." See Letter From Luther to Melanchthon, Letter no. 99, 1 August 1521, trans. Erika Bullmann Flores. In *Dr. Martin Luther's Saemmtliche Schriften*, ed. Johannes Georg Walch. (St. Louis MO: Concordia, n.d.) 15:2585-2590.

[11] Kierkegaard, *Works of Love*, 106-7.

[12] Anthony Rudd, *Kierkegaard and the Limits of the Ethical*. (New York: Oxford University Press, 1993) 153.

[13] Kierkegaard, *Either/Or*, 2:167.

genuine believers will often ignore this conscience, it provides just enough help to eliminate utter, absurd relativity in one's actions. This is exactly the consequence of the leap that Updike describes in his own experience.

Whether Updike's leap into faith strikes us as an offense, as baffling silliness, as an understandable but meaningless gesture, or as an affirmation of our own Christian commitments, we have the same task: understanding how this epiphanic reading of Kierkegaard, both the first event and events to follow, changed Updike's sense of cosmic meaning and thus his fiction. Updike's faith is not merely an irrationalist, completely private category that critics had best avoid. Paying attention to Updike's nonfiction and fiction, we will see that he leapt not only into faith, but also into a meaning-making philosophical system in which loving regard for the other and right action on the other's behalf become possible. The Maples stories test the practical realities of Kierkegaard's entire scheme, but especially the reasonableness of the love mandate.

Because Updike spoke and wrote so emphatically of what self-consciousness feels like, we tend to neglect what he felt self-consciousness is for. According to Kierkegaard, and thus to Updike, it is the part of oneself that feels existential anxiety and then despair, that yearns for God, that seeks and finds its own transformation in relation with that God of pure possibility. Titling his 1989 memoirs *Self-Consciousness*, Updike points to his adoption of this key insight of Kierkegaard's. He declares in that book that he has taken up the same work of love taken up by his theological hero. This is not the work of teaching, suasion, or mediation, as Kierkegaard's writings make clear. It was the hated Hegel's mistake to think that Christian faith was finally rational and subject therefore to logical dialectics, indeed, that to the truly dialectical thinker the very mind of God might be known. Kierkegaard and Updike both understand God as Wholly Other and faith to be absurd, so that teaching and mediation about faith become useless. (This is not to say that teaching and mediation about how to live with faith are also useless, or that understanding other seekers in their struggles is anything other than a duty.) Updike's fiction must therefore have some purpose other than demonstrating the virtues or benefits of faith. The only fictive task consistent with the theology is to tell the truth about human relations, making readers more self-conscious, even sometimes terrifically irritated, in order to prepare them for the unmediated leap.

Shortly after reading Kierkegaard for the first time, Updike would compose such God-haunted works as *The Poorhouse Fair* (1959), *Rabbit, Run* (1960), *The Centaur* (1962)—and dozens of autobiographical short stories about sacred and profane ecstasies, including the early Maples stories. Updike does not tell us precisely which of Kierkegaard's works he read during the time of this earliest fascination, other than *Fear and Trembling*, and probably *The Sickness Unto Death*. But since he reports that he immediately saw his stories and novels as illustrations of Kierkegaard, he had begun to enact a logic of vocation. He learned this logic in church as a child; we know this because of a brief speech Updike offers in *Rabbit, Run*. Rabbit's mistress Ruth recalls learning in Sunday school the essential Lutheran idea that "everybody God made was good at something," and ought to use that talent in a needy world.[14] There is no reason to believe that Updike demurred from this logic of divine calling to purposeful and fitting vocation—especially since it is at the heart of Kierkegaard's theology also.

Updike was good at writing mimetic fiction about postwar America, presenting situations with theological import even when there is no explicit theological content. Even though Updike felt that his work illustrated Kierkegaard *for a time*, we know that his existential Christian calling was life-long. "I have felt free to describe life as accurately as I could, with especial attention to human erosions and betrayals," Updike writes in *Self-Consciousness*. "What small faith I have has given me what artistic courage I have. My theory was that God already knows everything and cannot be shocked. And only truth is useful."[15] In a 1997 speech accepting the Campion Medal, Updike tells an abridged version of his discovery of Kierkegaard and Barth, and of the vocation of truth-telling that resulted. He goes on to declare that this truth-telling is courageous Christian work, a "noble and useful profession." What truth needs to be told? That "the reality around us is created and worth celebrating; that men and women are radically imperfect and radically valuable." This Augustinian dialectical tension animates all of Updike's writings.

The Campion speech is important because in it Updike takes pains to explain the character of his fiction, and of Christian fiction generally. "Is not Christian fiction, insofar as it exists," he writes,

---

[14] John Updike, *Rabbit, Run.* (New York: Knopf, 1960) 74.
[15] Updike, *Self-Consciousness*, 231.

a description of the bewilderment and panic, the sense of hollowness and futility, which afflicts those whose search for God is not successful? And are we not all, within the churches and temples or not, more searcher than finder in this regard? I ask, while gratefully accepting this award, to be absolved from any duty to provide orthodox morals and consolations in my fiction.[16]

Updike requests absolution, but does not retreat from his vocation. Indeed, Updike's mission and choice of genre is remarkably consistent with Kierkegaard's. In early career Kierkegaard wrote dialectical, maieutic, Socratic dialogues in which he interests himself deeply in the claims of his pseudonymous authors and characters while taking no responsibility for any particular claim.[17] Later, in part worried that his pseudonymous works were evasive and excessively elaborate, he wrote edifying or "upbuilding" discourses under his own signature. In these writings his central purposes are hermeneutics and dogmatics, the systematic interpretation of holy scripture and its implications for believers. So: Kierkegaard trained in and was willing to perform both the roles of Socratic philosopher and Christian apologist. After his Harvard years, Updike trained himself as a theologian too, and in a sense accepted the same two roles. He wrote dialogical fiction exploring the behavior of libidinous, God-haunted seekers, and nonfiction about his experience of faith and dependence upon Christian scripture and theology.

In this chapter I attend to the nonfiction, what it reveals about Updike's understanding of Kierkegaard's thought. It will become clear that Updike illustrates a particular version of Kierkegaard's schema or vision, an existential version of a distinctly Lutheran narrative in which the despairing person, at first avoiding relation with God, either through hedonic or ethical distractions, gains a more genuine self-consciousness and then, perhaps, with God's grace, makes a leap of faith. This leap provides the new believer with an "Archimedean point," Kierkegaard's geometrical emblem for the fixed point of God-informed conscience, also adopted by Updike. Another benefit of the leap is a corrected self-love, which replaces a socially-shaped form of narcissism, inauthentic self-love. This aspect of the leap I develop in the second and third chapters of

---

[16] John Updike, *More Matter: Essays and Criticism*. (New York: Fawcett, 1999) 851.

[17] "Maieutic" refers to the role of midwife, who assists a birth but has nothing to do with its existence or essence.

this study. A corrected self-love allows the believer to love more truly, which is to say selflessly and non-preferentially. Meanwhile, the conscience leads the believer to work on behalf of human need. Updike makes this matter of self-love even more crucial than Kierkegaard does, because grandiosity, exaggerated self-regard, and insincerity become an even greater problem in the mid-twentieth century Boston suburbs—for Updike, a microcosm for America as a whole—than in mid-nineteenth century Copenhagen.

Through his fiction, Updike illustrates this narrative, but also illustrates a matter of sharp difference with Kierkegaard: the issue of God's love and mercy. As Updike notes, late in his brief career, Kierkegaard began to denigrate erotic love and the possibility of healthy human relation generally. He argued so strenuously for the solitary, hermitic Christian calling that he literally called for the setting-aside of Biblical scripture involving God's mercy. He writes that it would be better for Christians to know nothing about certain stories—Jesus calling for children to come unto him, or Barabbas being forgiven his sins and crimes and freed from his cross—because weak Christians exploit such stories, living in self-serving pleasure, belatedly accepting God's mercy in a spasm of deathbed desperation.[18] Some self-serving Christians read these stories wrongly, and neglect to give themselves life-long to the work of being Christ to the neighbor, a work that Kierkegaard believed required solitude and great suffering. "Solitude" really meant bachelorhood to Kierkegaard, meaning that his solitude involved a rejection of the nearest neighbor and the daily acts of marriage. In his own life Kierkegaard famously renounced his relationship with fiancé Regine Olsen for this central reason. He used his solitude to produce an impressive *oeuvre*, but twelve years to the day after he was first engaged to marry Regine Olsen, and eleven years after he had chosen solitude as his neighbor, he was calculating whether he would meet Regine on his daily walk and be able to nod silently her way, as he often did.[19]

Updike found this argument about solitary suffering objectionable, indeed, neurotic. In "vomiting up" these ananthropic doctrines— "vomiting up" is Updike's—Kierkegaard seems to have forgotten his own logic of complete human freedom and activated conscience. His argument is paternalistic and controlling rather than freedom-seeking, a

---

[18] Updike, *Picked-Up Pieces*, 120.

[19] Joakim Garff, *Søren Kierkegaard: A Biography*, trans. Bruce H. Kimmsee. (Princeton NJ: University of Princeton Press, 2007) 684-88.

problem Updike notices. There is clear scriptural warrant, he argues, for God's mercy. It is one of the Bible's most persistent and emphatic themes. For this reason Updike finds himself unable to accept these over determined implications of Kierkegaard's schema, suggesting (as we will see) that it is Kierkegaard's tortured family history rather than the logic of his existential dialectics that gave shape to these chilling attitudes.[20] We will see that such familial psycho-histories recur in Updike's fiction as well, and pose a particularly vexing theological problem. Where Kierkegaard feels that people resist God with frantic, determined, and intricate denial, Updike takes account of Freud and his interpreters, building a picture of human incorrigibility and anxiety that resides even deeper in identity, even less available to consciousness and volition— and even more destructive to self and other. Updike also rejects Kierkegaard's absolutist distinction between erotic and Christian love, *Elskov* and *Kjerlighed*, while still finding them useful. Again he presents scriptural warrant for an incarnational view of erotic love in which God is present in human sexuality—even, apparently, in some extra-marital sexuality, where God's presence does not necessarily imply God's endorsement of the act—and in which erotic love is a crude that might be refined into something more beautiful and powerful.

Following the logic of Updike's argument for a merciful God, we see that indeed his is a fiction of tolerance in which the erotic and agapic forms of love coexist, in fact, nearly meld. As far as Updike is concerned, it is up to the perfectly free Christian to relate with God and neighbor, guided by a creative, intelligent, and prayerful conscience. Laws, codified practices, etiquettes and other forms of paternalism cannot save struggling believers; nor can essentially secular dialectics. Only God can. As Updike sees it—and here he is in perfect accord with Kierkegaard—

---

[20] Gillian Rose offers a corrective to Updike's view of Kierkegaard's elective solitude. She notes that Martin Buber, who celebrates Kierkegaard's passion for immediate relation with God, somehow got him wrong on this score: "Thus, according to Buber, it is 'the Single One' who renounces Regine and the feminine as such, marriage and all ethical relationships, because only God is essential and everyone else, all otherness, is inessential" (161). Rose warns against Buber's mistake, made also by many others: confusing Kierkegaard with his personae. She argues, "The knight of faith inherits the world in all its mediation and law; it is the knight of resignation who renounces the world and the ethical for the sake of a lost love." See Gillian Rose. "Reply from the 'Single One': Soren [sic] Kierkegaard to Martin Buber." In *Martin Buber: A Contemporary Perspective,* ed. Paul Mendes-Flohr. (Syracuse NY: Syracuse University Press, 2002) 163.

Christians must learn not only to do the right things, but they must avoid spiritual treason and do them for the right reason. And that is love of the neighbor. Creative loving needs to trump obedience to received doctrines. Neurotic solitude of the kind Kierkegaard chose for himself, and promoted for some others, looks to Updike like a withdrawal from the task of being a neighbor, and runs counter to scriptural descriptions of a merciful and loving God. For these reasons, Updike rejects prickly solitude as a sound Christian calling.

While we take Updike at his word, and attempt to read his stories as illustrations of Kierkegaard, we should also of course feel free to honor other issues and impulses in the fiction as they appear. I certainly do in the critical portions of this study. Yet given Updike's confessional writings, it seems hard to deny that his fiction is finally primarily existential-theological. The Maples stories teach us what it feels like to spend decades yearning for faith, yet to fear that faith so much—or the freedom it confers, or the God who offers it, or the offended reactions of others—that it seems better to live a life of determined distraction, to submit instead to personal compulsions, habits, and convoluted projects. The stories also teach us what it feels like to love, both selfishly and selflessly. In their intricate, diachronic way, the Maples stories hold out hope for the leap of faith, for blessed identity transformation, and for the freedom to perform genuine works of love.

&

Updike took Kierkegaard's work both seriously and personally throughout his entire career, as the record we are about to review shows clearly. Fortunately for him, as we will see, the first works he read, *Fear and Trembling* and *The Sickness Unto Death,* then apparently *Repetition, Either/Or, The Concept of Dread,* and at least parts of other works, provide an essentially complete and coherent version of the three stages, the motive energy that moves people through them, the leap, and the nature of faith. *The Sickness Unto Death* is particularly important because in that edifying work Kierkegaard establishes unambiguously that personal authenticity, and the moment of choice that leads to it, may only be secured through the help of the God of pure possibility. We know that during the early 1960s, Updike also read Walter Lowrie's biographical scholarship, which of course clarifies key concepts in Kierkegaard's writings, the three stages particularly. Lowrie also summarizes each major work in Kierkegaard's career, so Updike would have known about aspects of the schema he had not read first-hand in Kierkegaard's works at that time.

In the late 1960s, Updike began to write and speak overtly about his conversion a decade before to Kierkegaard's reading of Christian mysteries. By this time he had also read *Concluding Unscientific Postscript*, a number of *Edifying Discourses*, and *Stages on Life's Way*. Around that same time, he reviews the *Late Journals*, and shows special interest in Kierkegaard's attack on the Danish Lutheran church. Updike knows Kierkegaard's life story well enough to formulate a 1966 argument about psychological causes for Kierkegaard's late-career severities. By 1971 Updike reviewed at least another ten secondary works on Kierkegaard's life and works, which he lists in a brief biography of Kierkegaard published in a biographical encyclopedia entitled *Atlantic Brief Lives*.[21] During the next three decades he also seizes opportunities to review books on Kierkegaard, offering some of his longer, more involved examinations of the existential schema. In the 1990s through the mid-2000s he shows that he knows *Works of Love* in detail, and in reviewing one of the longest and best of the biographies of Kierkegaard, Joakim Garff's *Søren Kierkegaard: A Biography* (2000) he shows even greater command of the late-career writings and Kierkegaard's final years. Just more than a month before his death Updike wrote a poem (which I quote in the Introduction) expressing the nature of his faith in Kierkegaardian language, terms of subjectivity and orthodox Christian hopefulness: "*Surely*—magnificent, that 'surely'—*goodness and mercy shall follow me all the days of my life,* my life, forever."[22] The story of Updike's learning from Kierkegaard is both a picaresque tale—a man, living by his wits, makes discoveries—and, in the literary sense, a comedy.

---

[21] See John Updike, "Søren Kierkegaard." In *Atlantic Brief Lives: A Biographical Companion to the Arts*, ed. Louis Kronenberger. (Boston MA: Little, Brown, 1971). There is no way to know how carefully Updike read these works by James D. Collins, Thomas H. Croxall, Louis Dupré, Vernard Eller, Jerry H. Gill, Kenneth Hamilton, Johannes Hohlenberg, Regis Jolivet, and Peter P. Rohde. By 1971 he has read Lowrie, whom he also lists among these others. In the essay he specifically criticizes Josiah Thompson's *The Lonely Labyrinth* for neglecting Kierkegaard's heroic Christian orthodoxy while describing his "self-administered, and eventually futile, therapy" (429). So he has read scholarship on Kierkegaard, and read it critically and knowingly.

[22] Updike, *Endpoint*, 29.

Updike's first printed references to Kierkegaard's work appear in *The New Yorker* in October of 1963. In a review and comment on a new 1962 translation of Karl Barth's *Anselm: Fides Quaerens Intellectum*, Updike lays out a particular understanding of God and grace. In the first paragraphs of this essay, Updike links Barth's theology with Kierkegaard's. Both theologians, he writes, predicate their claims upon "[t]he real God, the God men do not invent, [who] is *totaliter aliter*— Wholly Other." Updike then offers his Lutheran formulation of faith, which he finds confirmed by these two: "We cannot reach Him; only He can reach us. This He has done as the Christ of Biblical revelation...."[23] Both Barth and Kierkegaard accept this uni-directional nature of grace and the salvific reality of Christ on the cross, the actor and act justifying believers to the Wholly Other God. Tracing out the logic of this absurdity, both deny the possibility of human mediation in preparing another for the leap of faith. As Barth confirms, "The aim of theology cannot be to lead men to faith, to confirm them in the faith, nor even to deliver their faith from doubt. Neither does the man who asks theological questions ask them for the sake of the existence of his faith; his theological answers, however complete they may be, can have no bearing on the existence of his faith."[24]

Kierkegaard is emphatic on this same point, as Updike knows, for Hegel with his false dialectics believes in the ultimate efficacy of reasoning processes and mediation. Hegel goes so far as to identify God with nature's physical laws, and to argue that dialectical processes and thus human effort might lead to a complete understanding of both God and nature. Kierkegaard is appalled at such a deflation of the Wholly Other God, and so he replaces Hegel's orderly processes of growth and change (faith felt—demands of reason felt—faith converted to philosophy or "Absolute Mind") with a scheme both less rational and more realistically psychological (anxious denial—miraculous immediacy—personal concretion). Updike concludes this essay by noting how this schema has changed the situation for modern believers, in contrast to the situation of the Middle Ages. "The Christian believer, awaking from the medieval dream wherein Church and State, faith and science, thoughts and things seemed to merge, has been restored with a

---

[23] Updike, *Assorted Prose*, 273-74.
[24] Ibid., 277.

vengeance to his primitive desperation." It is out of this desperation, the terror of nothingness, that the believer raises "the cry for God."[25]

In *The New Yorker* a month later, in a brief essay on a visit to St. Peter's Basilica, Updike turns these impersonal-intellective comments to the comically personal-existential. "Mea Culpa: A Travel Note" also honors Barth's chastening sense of a "fierce God above the kind God," to use Updike's own phrase from this note. He also implies Kierkegaard's existential understanding of faith as a fundamental change in consciousness in contrast to the humanistic or "merely ethical" religious understandings epitomized by modern Catholicism and liberal German Protestantism. Updike's report on his visit to St. Peter's adopts the tone of a 1960s "Talk of the Town" piece. He recounts his reaction to the vast building, which his Hachette guide warns sometimes disappoints. "DISAPPOINTS?" Updike writes. "Better, 'appalls.'" Not only is the sheer size of the building out of human scale, implying a false notion of human relation to God and Church, he complains, but the statues of saints have a movie-set falsity, and the tacky gift shop on the building's roof, complete with Coca Cola sign, implies a distinctly commercial intention within the Vatican walls. "Reverence was not in the air," Updike writes.[26]

In a story set in the same year the Updikes traveled to Rome, "Twin Beds in Rome," Richard Maple has a similarly appalled response to the city of Rome itself—comically modeled, as I argue in chapter five of this study, on Martin Luther's unhappy 1510 visit to the Holy City. This travel essay also focuses on Updike's distaste for Catholic architecture and other ideas the city embodies, such as Catholic confidence in the role of the priesthood in helping others to faith. Both building and theology, he suggests, fail to account for the individual's existential anxiety and need. Updike offers an image to communicate this idea, the graffiti of names scrawled all over the inner dome ceiling in the Basilica, acts of vandalism made famous around that time by a scene in the 1960 film *La Dolce Vita*. He adds his own name in an act that suggests his own laying claim to faith. As he signs, the gigantic scale of Michelangelo's dome collapses to the intimate, personal scale of the signature. Updike worries that he might be caught defacing this great building, but his worrying is distinctly theological: "Caught in the middle of the leap of faith, is one

---

[25] Ibid., 281-82.
[26] Ibid., 217.

eternally embarrassed?"[27] In this explicitly Kierkegaardian remark, Updike suggests, as he will throughout his memoirs and other theologically-oriented essays, that one's faith is absurd, a scandal to the ethically-minded, a kind of brash misdeed by the community's standards (even the Christian community), but a life-saving leap for the believer. We recall Kierkegaard's point in *Fear and Trembling* that Abraham's willingness to sacrifice his son Isaac is wretchedly, shamefully wrong by community standards, yet obedient to God and ultimately life-affirming.

Three years pass before Updike again brings us extended comments on Kierkegaard. Then, in February of 1966, he offers his first meditations on Kierkegaard's life in "The Fork," a *New Yorker* review of *The Last Years: Journals 1853-1855*. In this essay, Updike seizes the opportunity to introduce his readers at length to the life and work of his mentor theologian. Indeed, Updike offers his first fragmentary version of his Kierkegaardian conversion experience, attached to the essay as an unfinished threnody about Kierkegaard's greatest biographer and translator of that day, Walter Lowrie. The incomplete poem is a series of fourteeners in three-line stanzas including this stanza:

> I never read his forty books, I never sought him whole;
> I had to pass right through him when, returning from a stroll,
> I flung myself on Kierkegaard to save my flagging soul.[28]

It is not much, but for three more years this would be the only clear statement Updike would make about his debt to Kierkegaard, a debt implied in the essay through appreciation.

Actually, in "The Fork" this appreciation is qualified for the first time, though not the last. While Updike clearly identifies with the younger Kierkegaard, noting that "many weak boys with sharp tongues are born into the world," he is not wholly charmed by the grown man with "a somewhat elderly mind" all his short life long.[29] The two of them may share a Lutheran upbringing, and an existential logic predicated on the inhumanity of God, but Updike clearly regrets Kierkegaard's narrow circle of concerns ("five people and a few key concepts"), the strangeness of his relationship with both father and rejected fiancé Regine Olsen,

---

[27] Ibid., 221.

[28] Updike, *Picked-Up Pieces*, 107.

[29] Ibid., 110, 112.

even the tiresomeness of his continual evocation of "the individual." It is the existential principle that moves Updike:

> But, by giving metaphysical dignity to "the subjective," by showing faith to be not an intellectual development but a movement of the will, by holding out for existential duality against the tide of all the monisms, materialist or mystical or political, that would absorb the individual consciousness, Kierkegaard has given Christianity new life, and handhold, the "Archimedean point."[30]

This image of the Archimedean point is a touchstone for Updike. In *Self-Consciousness* (1989), he writes that faith itself is the "Archimedean point outside the world from which to move the world," which is an almost perfect echo of a line he used in his 1971 *Atlantic Brief Lives* biography of Kierkegaard.[31] It is an image he borrows from Kierkegaard.

Kierkegaard first develops his own notion of the Archimedean point in the "Rotation of Crops" essay of *Either/Or*, in which Johannes the seducer of "The Seducer's Diary" argues for forgetting as a useful technique of the hedonic life. In making this argument, Johannes mentions that "the artistically achieved identity is the Archimedean point with which one lifts the whole world."[32] (295). But we are not meant to trust seducers. Johannes's valorization of this aesthetic life is not only quickly and directly countered by Judge William later in *Either/Or*, as we will see, but ironized by the entire Kierkegaardian scheme with its countervailing valorization of faithful, loving, authentic living. In the later and non-pseudonymous *Works of Love*, Kierkegaard develops the Archimedean point more sincerely. He notes that even a charwoman, the most menial worker, ceases to work for wages once she becomes an authentic Christian. As a believer, she works "for the sake of conscience." This inward change, this sense of calling, is the Archimedean point by which the believer can move the world. If you "make Christianity your own," Kierkegaard writes, "...it will show you a point outside the world, and by means of this you will move heaven and earth; yes, you will do something even more wonderful, you will move heaven and earth so quietly, so lightly, that no one notices it."[33] This is not the Seducer Johannes's version of the Archimedean point, and Updike makes clear that he has adopted the image and its meaning.

---

[30] Ibid., 121.
[31] Updike, *Self-Consciousness*, 232; "Søren Kierkegaard," 430.
[32] Kierkegaard, *Either/Or*, 1:295.
[33] Kierkegaard, *Works of Love*, 136.

In the biographical portion of this essay we learn some of the possible reasons why Kierkegaard was such a tortured adult, at least in Updike's view, and how his torments gave shape to his theology. Kierkegaard was the seventh and final child of Michael and Ane Kierkegaard. Michael, a widower, wed his second wife when she was a house servant, far pregnant with his child. Years later Søren was born, a weak but precocious child who grew up to become an odd man, one who eventually wrote out of the energy of a renounced love for the attractive Regine Olsen to become, Updike declares, "the most remarkable writer in Denmark."[34] Kierkegaard grew to consider organized Christianity, the habits and rituals of Christendom, as corrupt and unspiritual, as interference to an existential, immediate and personal relation with God. As Kierkegaard pursued the logic of this insight, he conducted continual attacks on the Danish national church establishment, which he felt cloaked the vital, passionate choosing of faith in a fabric of moribund traditions and locutions. Eventually, church worship itself seemed to him a sin. Indeed, the dying Kierkegaard refused a deathbed Eucharist because only clergy were available and willing to serve it, which according to his extreme reading of Luther's 'priesthood of all believers' would not do. This same logic led the younger Kierkegaard to renounce his engagement to Regine, in favor of hermitic solitude, study, prayer—and elective suffering.

Indeed, Updike sees that for the late-life Kierkegaard "Christianity is torture, and God a torturer."[35] Though Updike accepts the understanding of God as Wholly Other, he finds it difficult to accept the idea of God as torturer, especially a torturer of those who have been reconciled to God through Christ's death and resurrection. Updike considers a relevant passage from the journal, part of which reads,

> To be a Christian is the most terrible of all torments, it is—and it must be—to have one's hell here on earth.... One shudders to read what an animal must suffer which is used in vivisection; yet this is only a fugitive image of the suffering involved in being a Christian—in being kept alive in the state of death.[36]

---

[34] Updike, *Picked-Up Pieces*, 110. Hans Christian Anderson, who attended Kierkegaard's funeral, thus ranks no higher than second place in Updike's panoply of Danish writers.

[35] Ibid., 112.

[36] Ibid., 113.

Updike proposes a psychoanalytical-theological way of under-standing this strange and terrifying vision. The father of Isaac and father of faith, Abraham, Updike argues, apparently melded in Kierkegaard's mind with the "searing experience of his [own] father."[37] As Updike notes, Kierkegaard is not entirely wrong to pursue this kind of identification. The orthodox Christian simply must grapple with the duality of God's nature. After all, Jesus' loving Father would hear "Christ's outcry on the cross" without interceding on His son's behalf.[38]

Yet that Father was also God, working in human time to produce grace, and Jesus was willing to make the ultimate sacrifice. So Updike sees little reason to accept Kierkegaard's notion of God as torturing father. Indeed, using psychoanalytic reasoning, Updike finds cause in this essay to dismiss or minimize some of Kierkegaard's most severe, seemingly misanthropic and clearly misogynistic ideas about the nature of faith. Updike connects Kierkegaard's late-career absolutism with childhood psychological trials, a connection he makes in his own life and the lives of his characters. (Richard Maple is one of these characters.) He notes that Kierkegaard wrote enigmatically of a shame, an "earthquake" in his youth that had a defining effect on later thoughts and works. Updike speculates that Kierkegaard found the concupiscence of his elderly parents disgusting, or that his father's tale of cursing God while working as an eleven-year old shepherd was too uncanny for Søren to put out of his mind. Whatever the specific cause, Updike suggests that, "Kierkegaard's attack upon Christendom is a repetition of his father's curse—an attack, ostensibly directed against the Danish Protestant Church, upon God himself, on behalf of the father who had suffered, and yet also against the same father, who had made his son suffer and bound him to Christian belief."[39] Updike notes that Kierkegaard attacks another forefather, Luther, who transformed Christianity into "a matter of calming anxious consciences" for the utterly personal reason that he suffered neurotically anxious feelings himself. Kierkegaard wants no such calming. He wants a religion that brings people to a crisis of faith through intolerable anxiety and irritation. It is in this context that Kierkegaard dismisses scriptural evidence of a genuine compassion in Christian doctrine—Jesus' love of children, criminals, the beaten.

Updike does not wish away these stories of Christian compassion.

---

[37] Ibid., 117.
[38] Ibid., 116.
[39] Ibid., 119.

He differs quite sharply with Kierkegaard on this point: "Surely here he is attacking something essential to Biblical teaching—the forgiveness that balances majesty. He seems impatient with divine mercy, much as a true revolutionary despises the philanthropies whereby misery is abated and revolution delayed."[40] Updike is certain that there is a "softer side" to the gospels—communicated by the wedding at Cana, Jesus calling the children to his side, or promising the thief on the cross eternal life. Bringing his own counterargument to conclusion along with the essay, Updike takes evident pleasure in relating the story of Kierkegaard's deathbed renewal of faith in God's love, when the dying young man's comments seemed to move him suddenly to the theological extremity of universal salvation—perhaps the happy *reductio ad absurdum* of the distant God who offers a present Son, and possibly Updike's own stance.[41]

Apart from the single stanza of iambic heptameter lines attached to "The Fork" in 1966, Updike's special interest in Kierkegaard was only implicit until 1969. In that year everything changed when he published his confessional poem, *Midpoint*. The poem's fifth section, "Part V: Conclusion," is the most relevant to our concerns because it opens with a hymn of praise to Kierkegaard, Barth, Henry Green, Walt Disney, and Jan Vermeer.

> An easy Humanism plagues the land;
> I choose to take an otherworldly stand,
> The Archimedean point, however small,
> Will serve to lift th'entire terrestrial Ball.
> * * *
> Praise Kierkegaard, who splintered Hegel's creed
> Upon the rock of Existential need;
> Praise Barth, who told how saving faith can flow
> From Terror's oscillating Yes and No.... [42]

---

[40] Ibid., 119-20.

[41] Updike raises the possibility of universal salvation directly in "The Fork," and notes that Kierkegaard mentions the possibility in his *Late Journals*. Notably, one of the theological heroes Updike mentions only once—but places alongside Kierkegaard, Barth and Unamuno—is avatar of Christian universalism, Nikolai Berdyaev. Updike makes this remark in a 1982 review of *The New Oxford Book of Christian Verse*. See John Updike, *Hugging the Shore*. (New York: Vintage, 1984) 644.

[42] Updike, *Picked-Up Pieces*, 38.

Updike goes on to praise English novelist Henry Green for inaugurating a fiction of "gestures" and "silly drift," Walt Disney for transforming cartoons into films, and Jan Vermeer for painting light realistically. He also praises Pointillism and the Calculus for showing that "The Infinite is littleness heaped high." Within a few years, critics such as Edith and Kenneth Hamilton and George Hunt would cite the lines about Kierkegaard and Barth, beginning the task of understanding Updike's investment in Christian neo-orthodoxy. In *Midpoint* Updike offers a personal but much less existential account of Kierkegaard's ideas. He decries "easy Humanism" and only implies Kierkegaard's arguments against Hegelian dialectics. Readers are on their own in the task of discovering why Kierkegaard, in his love-hate relationship with Hegel, rejected the role of intellection, mediation, and process in religious matters.

Updike clarifies this issue in a two-page biography he contributes to Louis Kronenberger's 1971 *Atlantic Brief Lives*. In the essay Updike describes Kierkegaard's hostility to "German idealistic philosophy," specifically Hegel's systematics. Updike notes that Kierkegaard contrasts sharply and favorably with Hegel in believing that "to be human is inherently to be a problem." Kierkegaard had his own neurotic problems, Updike suggests, but to focus on them unduly "is to excuse ourselves from his truth and his heroism." Kierkegaard wanted his readers to believe the Christian story, which provides the "'Archimedean point' outside the world, from which the world can be lifted, admitting, like a crack of light in a sealed cave, the possibility of faith, that is to say, of escape from death." For the first time in Updike's writings, the Archimedean point has become not just a matter of leverage required to do non-absurd work in the world, but also relief from mortal dread. Updike here implies Kierkegaard's deep personal importance for him, and also a hint of his former despair, his intimations of death. On the other hand, there is no hint yet that early in his first marriage the simplest act had become absurd to Updike.[43]

In 1973, that story would be out, in comments Updike offers to Frank Gado in an installment in his *First Person: Conversations on Writers and Writing*. Apparently questioned about the importance of Kierkegaard's writings for his work, Updike answers, "somehow the whole idea I got from [Kierkegaard] of existence preceding essence was very liberating for me; it seemed to give me some kind of handle on my

---

[43] Updike, "Søren Kierkegaard," 429-30.

own life." He continues with remarks that make clearer both the Archimedean point metaphor and philosophy of the balked act:

> As a young person, I felt that thinking of myself as being suspended quite pointlessly in an immense void of indifferent stars and mathematically operating atoms made it difficult to justify action. To act because, if you don't, you'll get hungry—to act simply because of animal reaction to stimuli—was not to act in a way that gave shape to my life.[44]

Here the Archimedean point becomes a matter of physics: the universe is immense, empty, and without purpose. To live is to be set adrift in this universe. But faith in God, which is not possible without that God's grace, provides the fixed point in the void against which a lever can be placed, and the entire earth moved. It is an absurdly hopeful vision.

Mystifyingly, Updike in this interview claims to have "quite forgotten Kierkegaard's books or even his sentences."[45] This is an odd remark given that he had published "The Fork" only three years before. In that essay Updike makes clear that he has consulted at least *The Attack Upon 'Christendom'* again, along with W.H. Auden's introduction to an edition of the book, and also *The Point of View for My Work as an Author* and earlier journals.[46] He clearly reread *Fear and Trembling* while preparing to write the essay, or at least reviewed early passages carefully enough to capture the cadences and fugal arrangement of differing versions of Abraham's setting out for Mount Moriah.[47] He recalls the combination of aesthetic and neo-orthodox content, speaking of his suspicion that most readers swallow "the aesthetic coating and leave the religious pill."[48] During the same year he published "The Fork," 1966, Updike demonstrates detailed knowledge of *Repetition*, which he cites in a review of a novel by Sylvia Townsend Warner.[49]

Clearly, even if he has forgotten particular sentences of Kierkegaard's by 1970, as he claims, Updike has command of Kierkegaardian ideas, whether early or late, merciful or severe. During the decade of the 1970s he would seriously deepen his knowledge of Kierkegaard's work. Hunt reports in 1980 that Updike wrote him a letter listing his reading of Kierkegaard's works up to that moment. These

---

[44] George Hunt, *John Updike and the Three Great Secret Things*, 14.
[45] Ibid., 14.
[46] Updike, *Picked-Up Pieces*, 111, 119.
[47] Ibid., 116.
[48] Ibid., 121.
[49] Ibid., 231.

include *Philosophical Fragments, The Sickness Unto Death, The Concept of Dread*, parts of *Concluding Unscientific Postscript*, and "a good number" of the *Edifying Discourses*.[50] Updike forgets the *Late Journals*, which he reviews in 1966, and the other texts he read in the 1960s and which I have listed in the previous paragraph. Since *Fear and Trembling* is so memorably important to Updike, this is unusual forgetfulness, or perhaps a tacit admission that knowing the particular works of Kierkegaard is not terribly important for his application of the first existentialist's work. We can be sure, however, that by the early 1970s Updike had read—and read carefully enough to mark or recall key passages—at least ten or parts of ten of Kierkegaard's books. By the 1990s, Updike had demonstrated command of *Either/Or* and *Stages on Life's Way* in addition, though it is not clear whether he knew *Stages* while writing the Maples stories or other early fiction.[51]

In any case, by the mid-1970s Updike had either developed, or felt inclined to confess an earlier development, of a reader-response theory about Kierkegaard's literature and his own. The telling remark is a brief one, in a 1974 review of E. M. Cioran's *The New Gods*. Writing about the works of Nietzsche and Kierkegaard, and noting their methods as existentialist authors, Updike suggests that he detects a particular phenomenological aim or intention regarding their readers' responses: these existentialist writers want to "inflame readers to the point of crisis and cure."[52] It is not clear exactly what cure Updike felt Nietzsche might have sought to provide, but his notion of Kierkegaard's cure is clear. He wants to heighten despair in readers, or awareness of despair, so that those readers might realize their own inner willingness to make the leap of faith. That leap must be authentically their own in concert with God, but Updike hints that conditions matter and can be shaped by an artistic experience of the kind that Nietzsche and Kierkegaard clearly provide.

What is remarkable about this brief observation is that it is reflexive. Updike has noted over the years that his fiction somehow fails to please readers completely. Even as he makes this rueful observation, he knows why it is so. He has given us the broad hint: he also means to inflame through his writing, albeit while entertaining and fascinating readers as well. As he admits in *Self-Consciousness*, a book we will consider further below, there may even be something downright cruel in his writing, a

---

[50] Hunt, *John Updike*, 216 n. 19.
[51] Updike, *More Matter*, 140.
[52] Updike, *Hugging the Shore*, 602.

"vengeful element of 'showing' people, of 'rubbing their noses' in our sad human facts," as he puts it. In the next sentence, he acknowledges that this is a lesson he learned from Kierkegaard and Barth.

> I had learned from Kierkegaard and Barth to say the worst about our earthly condition, which was hopeless without a scandalously super-natural redemption; but I harbored a hurt hostility, also, an anti-Christian or at least anti-ecclesiastical bias, toward the church itself—a rubbing of the nose in the antique absurdity of what it professed.[53]

Kierkegaard also hated his church, and argues that "sad human facts" and the despair they cause are precisely the irritants prodding people on toward cosmic meaning, the desire for which he believes is innate in us. Again we see that Kierkegaard has provided Updike not only with a theology to illustrate, but with specific literary methods consistent with that theology. Judging by certain frank and ironic (and to many, distasteful) coital scenes in *Rabbit, Run*, by 1960 Updike had adopted the artistic mission of "irritate to crisis."[54] The Maples stories first appeared in magazines, and therefore cannot be quite so sexually frank or similarly irritating, but they certainly do offer sources of irritation, the most important of which, we will see, is Richard's and Joan's perverse dishonoring of a love for each other that they obviously feel.

For some reason, for more than fifteen years after the 1973 Gado interview, Updike seized no occasion to explain other deep facets of his interest in Kierkegaard. Then, beginning in 1989—perhaps in that year because he had been composing his first book-length memoir, *Self-Consciousness*, and thus revisiting his own history—Updike commenced a period we might call his Kierkegaard renaissance. During the next sixteen years, he wrote four of his most important meditations on Kierkegaard's work. First, there is the concluding chapter to his prose memoir *Self-Consciousness*,[55] a thoroughly Kierkegaardian confession titled "On Being a Self Forever." In this essay Updike lays out the personal calculations of his own Christian faith, naming Kierkegaard specifically among his theological heroes, and employing the Kierkegaardian code words "self" and "Archimedean point" in his

---

[53] Updike, *Self-Consciousness*, 149-50.

[54] I explore such arguably distasteful but also communicatively ironic coital scenes in *Rabbit, Run* in "Young Man Angstrom: Identity Crisis and Works of Love in *Rabbit, Run*." In *Religion and Literature*. 43/1 (Spring 2011).

[55] The poetic memoir *Endpoint* was yet to appear, which it did in 2009.

argument. In 1991 he writes the brief but clarion "IN RESPONSE *to a request from* The Independent on Sunday, *of London for a contribution to their weekly feature "A Book That Changed Me,"* which supplies my epigraph for this chapter, and tells us the story of his first reading of *Fear and Trembling*. In 1997 he writes an introduction to the Princeton University Press's *Seducer's Diary*, and in 2005 a review of Garff's *Søren Kierkegaard: A Biography*. In these latter two essays, as with others, Updike recoils from Kierkegaard's less merciful late-career words and acts. Yet the total presentation is intensely admiring. In all of these essays Updike plumbs the vocation of writer, examining differences and similarities between Kierkegaard's and his own choices of genre and method.

In the 1989 "On Being a Self Forever" chapter of *Self-Consciousness* Updike describes his faith as he experienced it both before reading Kierkegaard and after. To be more accurate, Updike recollects his early Christian beliefs in Kierkegaardian terms, as well as the nature of his faith after reading *Fear and Trembling*. He opens the chapter with a meditation upon the self, which he defines as a bundle of tics, habits, and physical flaws. He wonders whether he really wants this self, radically imperfect in an Augustinian sense, to "outlast the atomic universe."[56] He does. He experiences his self as a window on the world, which he "can't bear to think of shutting." He begins to quote Kierkegaard's Basque disciple Miguel de Unamuno, who speaks most persuasively to Updike's own desire for an afterlife. Unamuno helps Updike to understand that the "yearning for the afterlife is the opposite of selfish: it is love and praise for the world that we are privileged, in this complex interval of light, to witness and experience." Unamuno's *The Tragic Sense of Life* (1954), he writes, teaches us that what we want of the afterlife is not some other world but this world, going on forever.[57] Unlike Kierkegaard, who views enervating doubt as a condition to be discarded through faith, Unamuno argues that the yearning to live, which leads one to faith in eternal life, exists in unresolved, lifelong tension with our rational capacity, which leads to profound doubt in such an absurdity as an eternal afterlife. The believer must return to desperate trust in God over and over again—a slightly different take on repetition than we will see

---

[56] Updike, *Self-Consciousness*, 214.
[57] Ibid., 217.

from Kierkegaard. It is not entirely clear whose scheme is more compelling to Updike.[58]

Updike acknowledges in this chapter that his self emerges from Oedipal developmental processes and in this sense from others: mother, father, community. He names the communities in which he has lived, recalling flawed aspects of his childhood Shillington self, the self that moved and later commuted to Manhattan to work for *New Yorker* editor William Shawn, his young adult Ipswich self, taking pleasure in new wealth and sexual opportunities, the contemporary self that ponders the religions of others. Every few paragraphs in this meditation on versions of himself, Updike turns to another aphorism from Unamuno: "Consciousness is a disease"; "Work is the practical consolation for having been born"; "I do not want to die—no; I neither want to die nor do I want to want to die; I want to live forever and ever and ever."[59] Thankfully, writes Updike, there is a God of "bottomless encouragement" to help us with these desires and terrors. This is a God Updike had deduced in early adolescence, through the following syllogism:

1. If God does not exist, the world is a horror-show.
2. The world is not a horror-show.
3. Therefore, God exists.[60]

If the Christians around the boy Updike were any indication, few shared this belief. Updike recalls his disappointment that no one really believed the core Christian story of utter transformation through faith, and utter confidence in an afterlife. Neither ministers of the church, nor his own father, nor his father's father—none of them really believed. Updike wanted to believe, wanted it really, and so he began to read the theologians who, as I explain more thoroughly in the beginning of this chapter, gave him spiritual aid and the writing vocation.

At this point in his spiritual confession, Updike admits that he has grown uncomfortable with this "worthy attempt" to describe his faith, which he does at the behest of others—ambitious editors and interested

---

[58] See Miguel de Unamuno, *The Tragic Sense of Life*, trans. J.E. Crawford Flitch. (New York: Dover, 1954) 113-119. These pages contain Unamuno's best articulation of this stance, drawn from his "In the Depths of the Abyss" chapter, which I quote as one epigraph for this book.

[59] Updike, *Self-Consciousness*, 226-29.

[60] Ibid., 230

readers, apparently. This pious sort of confession is a miscarriage. His vocation does not involve working "an altruistic good." He feels that his own faith should be, as it always is in his fiction, *"behind:* behind the façade, the human courtesies, my performance, my 'act.'"[61] We understand this calculation better once we remember Kierkegaard's hostility to spiritual education or mediation, to dialectics leading in an orderly way to faith, to the Hegelian project, to rote pieties of Christendom. Updike here follows the Kierkegaardian logic, acknowledging that the Christian existentialist author writes behind a veil, working a good not through courteous rational argument, but through irony, double-dealing.

Still, Updike feels he can allow himself one last sincere credo: "one believes not merely to dismiss from one's life a degrading and immobilizing fear of death but to possess that Archimedean point outside the world"—outside because the Creator also lives Beyond— "from which to move the world." The language clearly comes from Kierkegaard, specifically *Either/Or* as we have seen, as does this potent statement a few lines along: "The self is the focus of anxiety; attention to others, self-forgetfulness, and living like the lilies are urged, to relieve the anxiety."[62]

Updike continues with a Kierkegaardian parable based in his recent experience, the kind of parable of existential terror and then relief that is repeated in different forms in Richard Maple's life. In this tale, Updike returns to his elderly mother's farmhouse in Pennsylvania. She has been ill. He moves in a world of memories and feels intense anxieties about his mother's illness and pending death, which are sad in their own right but also of course prophesy his own. After a long day of doctor visits, already exhausted from a long drive in sleet coming home from an irritating reading at a Midwestern university, he experiences insomnia, which he has said is symptomatic of an anxious sense of self. During this anxious, mostly sleepless night he cannot stop thinking about his mother, his boyhood house, a stirring mouse, clammy sheets, the inevitability of death. Finally, the blessing of selflessness overtakes him. He sleeps. In the morning, chilly, clammy objects of the night before seem warm and luminous. His mother stirs with relative health and contentment in her kitchen, and his self has been restored to him,

---

[61] Ibid., 232, emphasis Updike's.
[62] Ibid., 232.

acceptable. He has experienced what Kierkegaard calls a repetition—whether aesthetic or religious in nature we cannot quite tell.

For the dweller in the religious stage, a repetition is simply grace—an undeserved gift of God's loving acceptance. But Updike will not conclude this essay on such a grace-filled moment. This potent chapter ends in the style of the first pages of *Fear and Trembling,* with mesmeric evocations of dread and its sources. The essay is also like *Fear and Trembling* in offering an answer to this dread. Updike catalogs the causes of his dread: movies about outer space; memories of dear friends and associates now dead; thoughts of his own advancing age and its doddering symptoms; materialist theories emerging from Freud, Darwin, and armies of physicists. Past homes. Happiness. Christmas. Innocent as these things are, each causes the aging middle-aged Updike some discomfort stemming from his awareness of the nearness of death—and of death-in-life, which Kierkegaard suggests is really a dreadful sense of uselessness. Yet Updike finds, eventually, a kind of comfort, though a kind that is far less orthodox than the kind we encountered earlier in the chapter. His parents, he tells us in closing out this chapter, both seemed to him, finally, and a bit disappointingly, materialists. They had been children of science and nature. This disturbs him, since he is no materialist. But he takes comfort from an instinct his mother had shared with him, one that he somehow respected and absorbed: "that our instincts and appetites are better guides, for a healthy life, than the advice of other human beings."[63] This remark may disturb those who find Updike impious, since the "instincts and appetites" he refers to seemed likely to be concupiscent ones, as they often are in his fiction. But in fact, given the context of his remarks and the nature of his just concluded parable, he is speaking of the instincts Kierkegaard and Unamuno argue for, specifically that instinct that seeks pure possibility and wants to live forever. Updike senses this instinct in his mother, whom he knows he will soon lose, and experiences the relief of recognizing that she, like him, is a seeker of eternal and pure possibility. He experiences a repetition of hope.

In 1994, in the midst of this Kierkegaard renaissance, Updike writes his final Maples story, "Grandparenting." If we need clear evidence that he remained interested in Kierkegaard around this time, and thus throughout the entire Maples cycle (which by the way encloses the entire Rabbit cycle, apart from the 2000 coda-novella, *Rabbit Remembered*), we

---

[63] Ibid., 257.

have the important 1997 Campion speech I cited earlier, as well as Updike's 1997 Introduction to *The Seducer's Diary*. The latter is a relatively brief and essentially pedagogical essay. In it, Updike presents an introduction to Kierkegaard's indirect or maieutic methods; the nature of *Either/Or* and its fictional editorship by Victor Eremita and, in the first volume, authorship by A; the specific nature of "The Seducer's Diary" section as a found manuscript which A simply passes along to others. None of these remarks helps us particularly to understand Updike's fiction, but the conclusion of the essay does.

Updike notes that one purpose of the "Diary" is to convince Regine Olsen that she is the fictional Cordelia Wahl, the lovely and innocent girl to be seduced, and that Kierkegaard is the seducer. As he composed the "Diary," Kierkegaard had just ended his engagement to Regine, and she had been taking the rejection hard. Posing himself as the seducer Johannes, and thus putting himself in a despicable light, Kierkegaard hoped to help Regine get on with her life. This he tells us directly. He seems to have felt that this double-dealing was an act of love. Though Updike is himself a maieutic and indirect writer—we have just seen that he prefers his authentic beliefs to be "behind" the performance—this purpose of Kierkegaard's strikes him as deceptive, or at best as "convoluted gallantry."[64] Clearly, Updike finds "The Seducer's Diary" and the rest of *Either/Or*, with its particularly deceptive double-dealing, less compelling than *Fear and Trembling*, with its portrait of a heroically offensive faith. This distinction may be important for understanding Updike's own fiction, which also illustrates a preference for heroic offenses in seeking faith over-against convoluted gallantry in doing good.

Even more important is the evident implication of a passage he offers in "Incommensurability," a 2005 review of Garff's biography of Kierkegaard. Describing Kierkegaard's stories, Updike effectively describes his own relation to his key characters. The portrait is distinctly theological: "What he wrote about," Updike writes about Kierkegaard, "was himself, a singular being tricked up in many alter egos and attacked from many angles, not only examined but cross-examined, an intricately guilty defendant on trial."[65] This seems a perfect description

---

[64] John Updike, Introduction to "The Seducer's Diary," a chapter of *Either/Or*. In *More Matter: Essays and Criticism* (New York: Fawcett, 1999) 139-44.

[65] John Updike, "Incommensurability." In *Due Considerations: Essays and Criticism*. (New York: Knopf, 2007) 512.

of the Updike only-child-man, the autobiographical character that appears repeatedly in Updike's fiction. Richard Maple is one such self. Of course we know from his acceptance speech for the Campion Medal that Updike views these incredibly guilty persons as incredibly valuable in God's eyes also. For this reason they will not become objects of his overt satire. Still, within this dialectic many critics lean, perhaps, the wrong way. They often believe that Updike celebrates and defends characters the author himself tells us he views as guilty defendants on trial.

Certainly Updike accepted and celebrated Kierkegaard's portrait of the embattled believer. Though in his 1966 "The Fork" Updike argues against Kierkegaard's late misogynistic and misanthropic attacks on a merciful Christianity, in 2005 he returns to these ideas and lends them great emphasis through quotation. "Human unhappiness [is] intrinsic to traffic with God"; to be a Christian "one must be educated in the school of abuses"; it is "the greatest tragedy for a family if one of its members becomes a Christian"; Kierkegaard's God is so severe that this faith is "hard to distinguish from atheism." Worst of all, "Christianity is the invention of Satan, calculated to make human beings unhappy."[66] Reacting to these aphorisms, Updike this time offers no countervailing scriptural stand for God's mercies. He does, however, repeat his psychoanalytic diagnosis that the attack upon Christendom is a "vomiting up of the gloomy religiosity that the father had worked upon the son." A few lines later Updike admits to finding "sophistry in Kierkegaard's attack"—but notes with seeming approval that the attack also conveys "the powerful nay-saying passion of Paul and Augustine: life and the world are the enemy."[67] Given Updike's 1989 approval through Unamuno of life in the physical world, perhaps it is best to conclude that this is one of those matters where for Updike the Yes and No of God's and the world's character are in unresolved dialectic. He seems to be rethinking, but not conclusively, the torturous feelings Kierkegaard confessed in his final years.

What is especially notable about both "The Fork" and "Incommensurability," and what we have not yet properly considered, is the intense focus on the Regine Olsen jilting and Updike's sense that in writing about it Kierkegaard acted in bad faith. The Regine Olsen story is the second of four scandals in Kierkegaard's life, by Updike's count in

---

[66] Ibid., 521-22.
[67] Ibid., 522.

this essay. The first is Kierkegaard's father's cursing of God while a youth, then as a widower much later in life, impregnating and marrying his serving maid "well within the conventional year of mourning for his first wife." The third involves the vicious attacks of the Copenhagen journal *Corsair* upon Kierkegaard, an act of journalistic bullying exacerbated by many Copenhagen neighbors who joined in the ridiculing. The fourth is Kierkegaard's own counterattack on the people with his attack on Copenhagen's Christendom. The second and seemingly most important to Updike is the story of Regine's release from her engagement with Kierkegaard, and his duplicitous writing and speech during the immediate months after. The story seems to grow in importance for Updike, as though he feels contempt he can hardly contain for his existentialist mentor. Certainly Kierkegaard's behavior raises intriguing questions about neighbor-love. Kierkegaard believed himself to be doing right by Regine after their separation, but there is a demonic self-centeredness to his approach in the "Seducer's Diary" of *Either/Or* and "Quidam's Diary" of *Works of Love,* both thinly fictionalized retellings of the jilting of Regine and its aftermath, in which the man who does the jilting then poses as roué in order to give the girl supposed relief.[68] This matter, then, helps us get to the heart of Updike's judgments about neighbor-love, as opposed to Kierkegaard's—a subject I take up more fully in the next chapter.

Surely, Updike implies, it would have been better for Kierkegaard to have told Regine some fuller version of the truth of his qualms about marrying, even if he were observing sexual manners of 1840s Copenhagen. Surely this would have been more loving than the linguistic manipulations, the deviousness, the duplicity of Kierkegaard's indirection. Kierkegaard must have caused Regine real and to some degree unnecessary pain. Updike, whose fiction is filled with depicted acts of needless pain and its causes, invites readers to imagine more compassionate alternatives. Once again he argues on behalf of Christian mercy. In "The Fork" and in "Incommensurability," he hints broadly at the necessity for honesty and kindness between loving partners. Thus it becomes clearer that part of his calling as writer is to help people become alert to others' pain, and more responsible in finding ways to cause less of it.

It is right and true that Updike's concluding statement on the importance of Kierkegaard's work for his own should be this

---

[68] Ibid., 515-518.

compassionate response to Regine Olsen and condemnation of Kierkegaard's demonic manipulations. We will see that the Maples stories call readers not only into feelings of irritation and despair on the Maples' behalf, but also into deep feelings of sympathy and compassion for both of them. Joan especially—late in the Maples' marriage, at the moments of the couple's separation and divorce, Joan Maple becomes Richard's Regine Olsen, an innocent but self-aware object of a demonic man's manipulations. Joan nearly dies over her own abandonment, and over the falsehoods Richard offers and which she must stomach.

Even if the actual Regine Olsen story irritated Updike, Kierkegaard nevertheless offered him a core existential schema to live by. Updike's fiction illustrates Kierkegaard, but so does his life and vocation. As Updike showed through these personal and intellectual meditations across forty years, and through his fiction during that same span, Kierkegaard's theology removes faith from the realm of the despicably ethical—where argument, cant, demonstrated piety, religious philistinism, rock-hard ideology, and the negation of freedom prevail. Kierkegaard argues that Christianity occurs in the individual's heart rather than in a congregation of believers, in a believer's conscience rather than in the recorded doctrines of its sect. In their hearts, Updike seems to have hoped, incipient believers may find room for a faith enacted in conscience and compassion, rather than one that promotes either the sentimental vapidity or ruthless certainty of the greater part of American Christendom.

2

The Neighbor-Love Problem for the
Rather Antinomian Believer

As soon as I enter into a relation with the other, with the gaze, look, request, love, command, or call of the other, I know that I can respond only by sacrificing ethics, that is, by sacrificing whatever obliges me to also respond, in the same way, in the same instant, to all the others. I offer a gift of death, I betray, I don't need to raise my knife over my son on Mount Moriah for that.

—Jacques Derrida, *The Gift of Death*[1]

John Updike called himself a "Protestant, Lutheran, rather antinomian" Christian.[2] This declaration that laws and codes have limited hold upon him may be heretical, but likely is not. In the 1520s Martin Luther coined the term "antinomianism," as part of his argument that grace confers freedom but will not allow for total lawlessness. The antinomian heresy is the error of concluding that grace confers perfect freedom from all communal or religious law.[3] Given the arguments about Kierkegaard which we have just reviewed, Updike's remark almost certainly implies something less radical and non-heretical: that he is guided by God-informed conscience, and perhaps feels freer to follow his conscience creatively than do the many legalistic Christians so common in American popular culture of his day. Certainly the antinomianism of many of Updike's characters—who often are frankly heretical—has given rise to criticisms of his fiction and indeed his theology on moral grounds.

---

[1] Jacques Derrida, *The Gift of Death*, trans. David Wills. (Chicago: University of Chicago, 1996) 68.

[2] Updike, *Self-Consciousness*, 234.

[3] Julius H. Bodensieck, ed. *Encyclopedia of the Lutheran Church*, vol. 1. (Minneapolis MN: Augsburg, 1965) 89. This encyclopedia is the most thorough of those I find available, but renames "Antinomianism" as "Enthusiasm (*Schwärmerei*)," and then reviews the Reformation and later antinomian controversies under that name (783-788).

The most direct of these objections is Ralph C. Wood's. Wood accuses Updike of "an ethical quietism" which derives from "an overly transcendent sense of God's otherness." Wood argues that it is important to view God as "incarnate in [both] Christ [and] the church." He implies that the believer, informed by that understanding of God's commensurability with human insights and efforts, and tutored by Christ's example and the church's teachings, recognizes a clear moral structure to obey. Somehow this Christian worker also finds the discipline to honor that moral structure. Wood is especially concerned with defending faithful marriages and condemning adultery. He faults Updike especially and specifically for failing, in *Couples* and elsewhere in his fiction, to "point an accusing pen at our adulterous generation."[4]

The Maples stories offer clear evidence that Updike did not fail on this score. Considering stories that do in fact seem to imply sharp criticism of casual adultery, I confront this objection in later chapters of this study. The typical error among Updike's critics is much like Wood's error, even when these critics have little interest in theological matters: to believe that Updike's central characters epitomize his commitments, spiritual, ethical, political, and other. We have seen, on the contrary, that Updike learned from Kierkegaard to keep "his act" behind a screen, to employ a double-dealing fiction with some care, to employ personae at some apostate distance from his own commitments, to bring readers through irritation to the verge of a leap into God's presence.[5] He views key characters as thoroughly guilty defendants on trial. True, Updike asks us to see these characters' flaws and faults as understandable, and their drives as natural, endemic, and often nearly impossible to control—impossible at least without God's assistance through grace. Yet Wood's question remains crucial and must be answered: Does Updike believe that post-leap, rather antinomian Christians have any hope of restraining their urges, honoring vows, changing the world for the better, or making any altruistic effort at all?

Updike tells us that he does hope for these things, and with good theological cause. As I will show in this chapter, he believes that God-inspired individual conscience trumps civil and church law. Yet altruism neither diminishes nor disappears in this Kierkegaardian world. The

---

[4] Ralph C. Wood, *The Comedy of Redemption: Christian Faith and Comic Vision in Four American Novelists* (Notre Dame IN: University of Notre Dame Press, 1988) 190.

[5] Updike, *Self-Consciousness*, 232.

conscientious believer, even when "rather antinomian," joins in common cause with other conscientious believers in selecting and addressing human needs. Casual adultery and other hurtful acts almost certainly do diminish or disappear among such ideal conscientious adults, who now find fewer delusional excuses for betrayal—or so Updike strongly implies in the Maples stories and nonfiction writings. These transformed people also employ their imaginations to address pain, hunger, poverty, and other injustices. As Denis de Rougemont suggests in an argument Updike calls our attention to in 1963, a proper Christian love will address threats to "marriage, social stability," and even "international peace."[6]

Updike notes in this essay that de Rougemont's doctrines emerge from earlier doctrines of Kierkegaard's. Yet Kierkegaard has been roundly criticized for his neighbor-love doctrines. Christians within other theological traditions (like Wood), thinkers of varying other faiths, and especially Marxists and other secular materialists have all found fault with Kierkegaard's framing of the ethical as penultimate and framing of neighbor-love as all-consuming. The neighbor-love problem is among the most vexing for those who would understand Kierkegaard's work, Updike included. The complaint Derrida makes in my epigraph for this chapter is perhaps only an especially striking expression of these objections, though it is important enough for us to address in some detail before this chapter closes.

As we will see in more detail below, Derrida joins Wood—strange bedfellows indeed—in viewing neighbor love as deeply problematic when it emerges from recognition of a Wholly Other God. Wood finds God's will to be comprehensible to congregations of believers, and indeed incarnate in their loving acts. But for Derrida, any altruistic act is a plunge of the knife into Isaac's heart. Derrida argues that whenever an ethically-minded person meets one other person's need, the needs of countless others go unmet. This paradox he names a "gift of death." As he asserts in my epigraph, the logic of the gift of death is so self-evident to Derrida that it strikes him as wholly unnecessary for Kierkegaard to retell Abraham's intended sacrifice of Isaac in *Fear and Trembling*. As he sees it, we all kill the innocent, all the time. Like Wood, Derrida believes that Kierkegaard's crisis theology lacks earnest intent and a proper consciousness of the incredible magnitude of real human need. The question both Wood and Derrida lead us to is whether Updike cares

---

[6] Updike, *Assorted Prose*, 285.

about human need and moral responsiveness to it among Christians, or whether Kierkegaard somehow gives Updike permission not to care—or to care, but not to work on the gigantic project of human need. Put another way, the question is whether the rather antinomian believer like Updike is freed from altruistic responsibility and thus able to engage mostly in erotic play.

If this were Updike's conclusion, it would be based in an appalling misreading of Kierkegaard's work. Updike's acceptance of the leap, which he confesses repeatedly, implies that the rest of the Kierkegaardian scheme also moves him. And indeed we will see in this chapter that certain key terms upon which Updike depends—he names "the absurd," "the leap," and "dread"—imply the necessity of the three stages of existence. The third and ultimate religious stage, which one leaps into, implies the necessity of a calling or vocation for believers, a calling based in love. If neighbor-love does not exist, the whole schema collapses. We will see in this chapter how necessary it is that Updike's fiction evokes these and other key terms of Kierkegaard's. And we will see that he has his own coherent answer to challenges—including Wood's criticism of his own work, and Auden's, Adorno's, and Derrida's criticisms of Kierkegaard's—an answer based in the bafflingly paradoxical nature of Christ's, and thus Kierkegaard's, neighbor-love mandate.

⊗

We begin with a return to Updike's 1966 portrait of Kierkegaard, "The Fork," in which he notes that certain key terms Kierkegaard often employs in his works, specifically the absurd, the leap, and dread, do not appear in the journals of *The Last Years*. Five people do—Jesus, Socrates, Hegel, Kierkegaard's one-time fiancé Regine Olsen, and his father Michael Kierkegaard. Updike also mentions an additional "few concepts," but he does not name them.[7] It seems to be part of Updike's "act" to remain quiet about certain Kierkegaardian concepts he employs. We will have to speculate upon these concepts, or rather, find them implied, because they will be essential to our further understanding of Updike's Kierkegaardian theology, with its neighbor-love *telos*.

There are many more than "a few" concepts in Kierkegaard's schema, but there is a core list that we can confirm do matter deeply to

---

[7] Updike, *Picked-Up Pieces*, 112.

Updike. They are: sin as sickness unto death; the aesthetic stage and its related concept of rotations; the ethical and its related concept of repetition; the essentially indescribable religious stage which redefines and magnifies the idea of loving repetition; and of course, as Updike himself names them, dread; the absurd; and the leap of faith. These we must review, and not necessarily in this order, for there is a particular logic and narrative coherence binding these terms inextricably. In later chapters we will consider other, less central terms as well.

The most important, most dialectical, most counter-intuitive, and therefore most difficult of these concepts is *dread*, which Updike calls "all encompassing" in Kierkegaard's work. Since the "angst" in Harry Rabbit Angstrom's name is the German word for dread or anxiety, the concept is also clearly central to Updike's work. In *The Concept of Dread* (translated *The Concept of Anxiety* in the Princeton edition), Kierkegaard defines dread as the "dizziness of freedom," a psychological condition felt by those who sense the full freedom of their choices.[8] As Mark C. Taylor aptly paraphrases this principle, "Confrontation with one's own protean possibilities evokes the dread that is inseparable from authentic selfhood."[9] If dread leads to dizziness, it is because pure possibility might lead either to personal authenticity or, if one chooses badly or fails to choose at all, to personal negation, death in life. Dread is present because this choice is defining. Nothing matters more. As Paul Ricoeur notes in his study of *The Concept of Dread*, one of the choices any of us might make is for "the narrowness of a mediocre life, the loss of a horizon," the inevitable results of a "lack of infinity."[10] As his argument makes clear, the very practical matter of living well thus becomes a matter of relenting to God's offer of grace, standing before God, and then acting by transformed, clarified conscience. Only through this transformation of one's identity, beginning in unsuccessful strain and ending in the utter relief resulting from God's gracious gift, is liberation from dread or anxiety possible.

Sin is a traditional religious word for the condition that causes

---

[8] Søren Kierkegaard, *The Concept of Anxiety: A Simple Psychologically Oriented Deliberation on the Dogmatic Issue of Hereditary Sin*, ed. and trans. Reidar Thomte and Albert B. Anderson. (Princeton NJ: Princeton University Press, 1980) 61.

[9] Mark C. Taylor, *Journeys to Selfhood: Hegel & Kierkegaard* (Berkeley CA: University of California Press, 1980) 175.

[10] Paul Ricour, "Kierkegaard and Evil." In *Søren Kierkegaard*, ed. Harold Bloom. (New York: Chelsea House, 1989) 56.

dread: separation from God. Since this separation leads to death, Kierkegaard labels it the *sickness unto death*. Sins are not (as we usually think) countable, execrable deeds, but rather the entire fabric of human acts made within a condition of alienation from God, of failing to stand before God.[11] Ricoeur helps us to understand this connection of sin with dread and with its condition of crisis, *despair*. His distinctions are elusive, as they are in Kierkegaard's writings, but he suggests that sin understood as misdeed is incomplete, a function of the penultimate ethical life. A fully authentic religious consciousness understands sin as failure to stand face to face with God. For Kierkegaard, to attempt to lend meaning to one's life through ethical work, or more primitively, through physical and psychological pleasure, is to live in dread. Such modes of living are avoidance strategies, ways to elude ultimate choosing of God, of an eternal version of oneself, of the demands of enlivened conscience. Despair is a mode of living in unconscious but determined avoidance of a living God. In *The Sickness Unto Death*, Kierkegaard pictures despair as a pathological illness, just around the corner from death. Indeed, Lazarus, who was fully dead before Jesus brought him back to life, is Kierkegaard's avatar of the sickness unto death, and because he was brought back to life and into joyful celebration of Jesus' presence, also an avatar of its cure.[12]

Certainly, dread is a concept that for Kierkegaard draws other issues into its orbit. In defining dread in his journals, Kierkegaard explains (perhaps to himself) why he feels it was necessary to break off his engagement with Regine Olsen. In this journal entry Kierkegaard lists his own great sins, which he views as too wretched to share with Regine through marriage. These include his melancholy, his lusts, his "terrible" relationship with his father, his "aberrations from the truth." All these, he says, were "in God's sight. . . not so atrocious, for indeed it was dread which caused me to go astray."[13] Clearly, then, even when we live in a condition of received faith, dread is an existential category of experience, one that is defining but out of our essential control. Dread is a psychological condition that in some way mitigates responsibility for faulty acts even while it makes life's choices difficult. It is also a

---

[11] Even linguistic distance is fatal: to speak of God in the third person rather than the second—I relate with you, God—is to accept separation and thus to sin.

[12] See John 11.

[13] Walter, Lowrie, *A Short Life of Kierkegaard* (Princeton NJ: Princeton University Press, 1970) 102.

condition that the most intent and devout believer, as we must consider Kierkegaard to have been, finds difficult to transcend or escape.

The most primitive or natural way to accept separation/sin and live with dread is called the *aesthetic stage*, which involves the consoling forgetfulness of hedonism. Updike's favorite fictive situations demonstrate that the aesthetic involves much more than sybaritic fun as a stay against genuine God-consciousness. The person living in the aesthetic stage also enjoys engaging in social gaming, even the appearance of ethical commitment, so long as that person can enjoy manipulating people and circumstances in an effort to avoid spiritual awareness. Updike often depicts his aesthetes, Rabbit Angstrom and Richard Maple among them, as Freudian narcissists.

More ordinarily, the aesthete is desperate to avoid boredom. In *Either/Or* Kierkegaard describes a method for avoiding boredom in the aesthetic stage, a method modeled after the agricultural practice of rotating crops to restore nutrient levels in the soil. Just as a single crop planted season after season in the same field will deplete the soil's crucial nutrients, a life lived in habit and tradition will deplete the energy that opposes both boredom and fuller self-awareness. Boredom is one of those irritants which Updike suggests might bring us into identity crisis, and thus to the leap of faith. But of course the person fearing freedom must evade this result or even thoughts of its possibility. According to the aesthete/narrator of "Rotation of the Crops," the best way to put off these thoughts is to engage in interpersonal gaming. He retells the stories of Creation and The Fall as a story of boredom and compulsive gaming. The "gods" created the world because they were bored, Adam and Eve and Cain and Abel were bored *"en famille,"* nations grew bored *"en masse,"* and finally people built a tower—presumably the Tower of Babel—in order to decrease their boredom. But these people grew as bored as the tower was tall. Thus, "humankind stood tall and fell far."[14] Boredom, we see, is one cause of misdeeds.

The Maples stories develop the anti-boredom strategy of *rotations*, which we will see not only in Richard's wish to till soil other than Joan's, but also in the enjoyment he takes in manipulating her own desires and attitudes toward neighbors such as Mack Dennis and Andy Vanderhaven. Nowhere does Kierkegaard call such efforts at interpersonal gaming "rotations." Rather, he develops an earthy farming metaphor: "The method I propose does not consist in changing the soil,"

---

[14] Kierkegaard, *Either/Or*, 1:286.

writes Kierkegaard in the persona of a seducer of women's attentions, "but, like proper crop rotation, consists in changing the method of cultivation and the kinds of crops."[15] We will use the term "rotations," however, because Walker Percy does. In *The Moviegoer* (1960), Binx Bolling somewhat over-elaborately defines a rotation as "the experiencing of the new beyond the expectation of experiencing the new."[16] Of course the Binx who offers this definition is still striving to forget truer existential possibility, so we might define the word more simply: titillating diversions providing existential forgetfulness.

Fortunately for incipient believers, rotations and other aesthetic strategies eventually lose their power to distract. When these people realize that to live for fun is finally disappointingly thin gruel, they may enter the *ethical stage* or sphere. They realize that they need to seek deeper satisfactions through justice-centered efforts on behalf of others. If Kierkegaard's ethical avatar Judge William is any indication, ethicists can go about their business with a profound sense of altruistic commitment, with gratitude for the beauty of loving relationships, and even with passion for a God that loves justice. Still, the central failing of such ethicists is that they do not recognize Kierkegaard's warning that "[p]leasure disappoints; possibility does not."[17] They have realized this truth only about bodily pleasure, still fearing eternal possibility and keeping it at arm's length through the consuming activity of good works. In this sense, the ethical life is a kind of ur-rotation, socially useful avoidance of the existential. Kierkegaard believes the behavior distinct and characteristic enough to be a stage of its own because of a key difference: unlike contemporary situational ethics, Kierkegaard's ethicists believe that their ethical duties are God-granted. This is the reason why the ethical stage is qualitatively distinct from the aesthetic, because its adherents at least recognize a God who provides law and encourages ethical goodness. Additionally, while the aesthete is involved in ecstatic being, the ethicist has begun a process of moral becoming, strenuously seeking after goodness and self-awareness rather than self-indulgence. She has begun to realize that she is a synthesis of the physical and the spiritual.

Through the lengthy address of a serious man named Judge William (or simply B), Kierkegaard connects the ethical life with the

---

[15] Ibid. 292.

[16] Walker Percy, *The Moviegoer* (New York: Vintage, 1998) 144.

[17] Kierkegaard, *Either/Or*, 1:41.

repetitions of marriage.[18] These remarks are the source for a crisp understanding of ethical *repetition* in another fine Kierkegaardian novel, David Lodge's *Therapy* (1995). The novel's central character Tubby Passmore realizes that "a beloved wife (or beloved husband) is repetition. To appreciate the real value of marriage you have to discard the superficial idea of repetition as something boring and negative, and see it as, on the contrary, something liberating and positive—the secret of happiness, no less."[19] Like his forebear Binx describing rotations, Tubby is also partly mistaken here. In his valorization of the ethical, Tubby recognizes how continued or repeated efforts to do good in the world are like the repetitions of marital love. There is a wish to fulfill ideals, to keep promises, to love the near one. Yet Tubby exaggerates the benefits of the ethical life and the capacity of people to be so loving and faithful. For even though the ethically noble person attempts to obey God dutifully, she has not entered into relation with God lovingly, and for this reason she will continue to live in unrelieved dread. Because she honors abstract duty to love instead of feeling passionate love for God and neighbor, her happiness will be elusive and finally illusory.

Though dread is unpleasant to live with, and deadly in the end, it is existentially propitious. Nothing other than dreadful desperation—or despair—will bring the believer to the point of *the leap*. The seeker comes to know God by making the leap into faith, entering at that moment into the so-called *religious stage*.[20] This stage Kierkegaard believes to be ineffable, incommensurable with human reasoning. Aesthetes and ethicists who hear about this experience are offended by its absurd nature, and by its implied premise that they are perilously incomplete beings. To the extent that they ponder their existences, aesthetes and ethicists are offended to hear that they require God to secure their authenticity as persons.

There is a great body of scholarship on the leap, much of it contesting the nature of the choosing or accepting, the activity or passivity of the leaper. These are important arguments because a simple

---

[18] In Chapter 3 I consider Judge William's arguments in some detail.

[19] David Lodge, *Therapy* (New York: Penguin, 1995) 127.

[20] I do not italicize the phrase "leap into faith" or use the more popular "leap of faith" here because this is a good place to note that Kierkegaard never uses that formulation. It is an invention of Kierkegaard's explainers. Kierkegaard uses the verb "to leap" often, and in many forms. Updike uses the phrase "leap of faith," however, and so will I, when I am not describing Kierkegaard's schema with care, as I am here.

volitionist notion of the leap would defy the Lutheran theology which grounds Kierkegaard's thoughts on grace: Luther observed that we cannot work our way into presence with the Wholly Other God. Yet human choice and action are clearly involved. The theory which best accords with Updike's talk of a changed consciousness and the granting of an Archimedean point is Jamie Ferreira's. She suggests that the leap of faith may be likened to a gestalt shift in psychology, or a phase shift in physics. Just as the viewer of the famous "duck-rabbit" can see only a duck in one moment, and only a rabbit in the next, or as a container of water climbs toward the boiling point, reaches it, and only then converts to steam, in the leap into faith there is a "critical threshold" change, a dramatic change of substance while the original substance remains. In Ferreira's application of the gestalt shift metaphor for the leap, a strange mingling of activity and passivity combine with change of consciousness. One does not really *will* to see rabbit or duck, but rather *accepts* rabbit or duck as the represented image—or rather, accepts the shift from one to the other. In just this way, with the leap the believer's entire vision of the world is simply shifted, utterly and all at once.[21] It is an elegant metaphor.

A homelier and more direct illustration involves the sense of calling that avid artists and scholars feel. There are those for whom piano practice or hours of reading and writing would be a torturous duty, while for others who feel a calling to these activities, they are endlessly fascinating, a function of what Parker Palmer calls the "can't not" of vocation.[22] Kierkegaard proposes that the post-leap believer attains this loving passion for the neighbor, and "can't not" respond lovingly to another's need. The essential difference is the new conscience, which Kierkegaard and Updike associate with the emblem of the Archimedean Point, a fixed point against which the person can place an altruistic lever and do good work. Kierkegaard argues, as we will see, that loving conscience is like Jesus' fictional good Samaritan: it cannot walk past evident need.[23]

---

[21] Jamie Ferreira, "Faith and the Kierkegaardian Leap." In *The Cambridge Companion to Kierkegaard*, eds. Alastair Hannay and Gordon D. Marino. (New York: Cambridge University Press, 1998) 217-18.

[22] Parker Palmer, *Let Your Life Speak: Listening for the Voice of Vocation* (San Francisco CA: Jossey-Bass, 1999) 26ff.

[23] See Luke 10: 25-37.

Both with his own confessions and with remarks such as one he makes in a long 1999 essay on "Religion and Literature," Updike seeks to illustrate the paradoxical experience of faith. Because faith is *absurd*, he can really only describe its cause, the swelling of despair which finally erupts into indescribable personal change. Updike tells us directly that fine literature can accelerate this swelling. Christian novelists, he writes, such as Graham Greene, Muriel Spark, Evelyn Waugh, Flannery O'Connor, Francois Mauriac, and Georges Bernanos—and presumably himself—may grant "little orthodox comfort" to readers. They do not write of the world of "arrived faith and its consolations." Rather they display a "bleak world, often comic in its desolation and inconsequence." Yet this bleakness of their real and fictive worlds may have "led these authors to make the leap of faith."[24] Updike here clearly describes his models in the world of Christian literature. Readers know that his own fictive world is also intentionally bleak, lacking comfort, and offers few consolations to Christians. For Updike, each person's leap will have to emerge from existential desperation, personally and uniquely felt, and the best a writer can do is to depict accurately the character of this desperation, perhaps in order to swell the same feeling in readers.

Updike recognizes that the religious life solves certain existential problems, namely the problem of enervating dread and balked agapic love.[25] However, no believer other than Jesus has been able to remain in continual, total relation with God—and perhaps not him, if we read the story of his suffering in the Garden of Gethsemane in a certain light. Therefore the ordinary believer, even one who has made the leap into faith, will certainly return again and again to a condition of dreadful doubt, and will require the miracle of *repetition.*

As I note in my Introduction, each of the three stages involves a different form of repetition, ranging from the comic to the miraculous. The aesthete pursues the repetition of rotations, which are amusing but difficult to keep fresh and novel. The threat of boredom always hovers over daily repetitions, as we see in Richard's fear of a monogamous and monotonous lifetime with Joan—a fear that results in his frantic pursuit of sexual and other excitements. Ethical repetition is more satisfying to the identity because the ethicist works on projects that seem more

---

[24] Updike, *More Matter*, 61.

[25] One never releases penultimate forms of dread, as Richard Maples' and John Updike's night terrors show. See Chapters 7 and 10.

meaningful. For Kierkegaard this ethical meaning derives from the knowledge that God endorses altruistic work, but for Updike it seems that ethical commitments may also arise from a more general and even secular commitment to human welfare. Yet Updike accepts Kierkegaard's deconstruction of the ethical life. The ethicist comes to understand her own weakness, the contradictory character of her personal drives, the final impossibility of changing the world very much, and the difficulty of discerning the good.

If ethical repetition involves experiencing refreshment that makes possible further meaningful work on behalf of others, then religious repetition is the thankful acceptance of grace, again and again. These repetitions are necessary because, as Miguel de Unamuno argues, any person can believe in eternity only intermittently. The rational person, always finding convincing reasons to doubt that eternal life is real, is as energetic as the inner person that wants to live forever. So periods of doubt are profound and enervating. Repetitions are a Kierkegaardian category, but Unamuno provides a clearer reason to believe in them. Again and again, the believer must return from rational doubt to absurd faith in eternity. As important as these repetitions are, we see few of Updike's characters engage in them. When it comes to the Maples stories, these characters pray sporadically, repent rarely, and worship not at all. Richard and Joan Maple do experience spiritual epiphanies in their daily lives, but do nothing in their daily practices to seek or return to these experiences. Updike, on the other hand, does describe his regular worship and prayer habits, particularly in *Self-Consciousness*. He closes his memoir with a recent experience of post-worship (and post-coital) happiness.[26] Ever the truthful realist, he also describes in both memoir and stories the other side of the existential coin, night fears and insomnia that occasionally accompany his most severe doubts.

These key Kierkegaardian concepts constitute a coherent, interlocking, and necessary scheme. We see that Kierkegaard is interested in identity transformation, in which the primitive or incomplete self, avoiding relation with God, moves through either hedonic or ethical distractions, or both, and finally comes to a condition of psychological crisis. This crisis is propitious in the sense that it leads to a despair that only God can relieve. As Kierkegaard tells us in *The Sickness Unto Death*, this incomplete person is usually not even aware of

---

[26] Updike, *Self-Consciousness*, 254-57.

her despair.[27] But despair determines her every gesture. It bubbles up in alienated behavior, in cruel or selfish acts that are only possible because of separation from God. These acts are the core existential material in the Maples stories, as well as in the rest of Updike's fictional works.

If we review Kierkegaard's terms with reference to the Maples stories we see even more clearly how carefully Updike illustrates Kierkegaard, including the neighbor-love doctrines. Richard lives in the aesthetic stage, gaming his wife and his neighbors' wives for purposes of consoling forgetfulness, or rotations. He lives in fear of the boredom that will ensue if and when these rotations cease working. He lives in dread of the real choice he might make: himself, standing before God in eternity, newly alive to his real neighbors rather than merely their sexual selves. Joan too avoids this moment of existential choice. She avoids this moment mainly through commitment to the ethical stage. She is somewhat better adjusted than Richard is to their community and family, but she still lives in unknowing dread because her ethical commitments, though noble, distract her from the immediacy of loving God and neighbor. Both of the Maples, and evidently many of their neighbors, eventually feel dread so sharply that they can be said to be in despair. This despair leads them repeatedly into experiences that shame them intensely. They believe that their neo-Freudian commitment to shedding repressions will lead to a richer life, but they find that they pay for sexual liberty with wrenching regrets about their lies, pretenses, and shaming admissions of their affairs. They come to feel self-contempt and contempt for each other. Far from releasing anxiety and achieving comity, the Maples come to blows while their children watch. Richard feels terrific guilt about the fear he causes in his children, and neither he nor Joan can feel anything but horror at Joan's suicidal feelings in the year before their divorce is decreed. Amid all this pain, Joan and Richard repeatedly return to and sustain a loving companionability which they cannot properly honor.

To speak psychoanalytically of a problem with a Christian theological telos, the Maples often display aggressions and other narcissistic traits. Their self-love is not authentic, and so their love of neighbor is also inauthentic and often destructive of identity, their own and that of others. They rend the local social fabric. They speak of childhood theological training, sometimes wistfully, sometimes dismissively. They find themselves unable to pass those principles,

---

[27] Kierkegaard, *The Sickness Unto Death*, 178.

which cannot deliver faith but can set the stage for it, along to their children. They consider their secular aesthetic and ethical ways, which display as right and becoming manners, to be more sophisticated than religion in the Kierkegaardian sense. They are embarrassed, Updike shows, by the very writings and practices that might save their lives, as his own was saved. But to be saved requires acceptance of the absurd, of a life lived before God. This life would give both Richard and Joan freedom from many of their compulsions, Kierkegaard argues—and even freedom from the imposed laws of religious and legal others. It would also give them some genuine work to do, in applying their imaginations and intellects to the despair of their neighbors, who include each other, their children, their friends and acquaintances. They might also address the physical and psychological hungers of the disenfranchised African Americans of "Marching through Boston" and the embattled Vietnamese of "Your Lover Just Called."

If it were not for the passages of memoir in which Updike describes the nature of his own vocation, we might conclude that his Kierkegaardian drama ends with the leap of faith and the perfect freedoms it confers. After all, he declares himself to be a rather antinomian man, and his characters seem nearly lawless, in their sexual pursuits especially. Certainly many have misread Updike's characters as utterly free—free to fornicate, to betray, to pretend, to run away from loved ones, that is. However, if we listen to Updike we hear him say that he presents us with an intentionally and meaningfully bleak world requiring escape through the leap. He only seems to offer the orgasm as an existential solution, or to celebrate the erotic bazaar in which physical and falsely spiritual satisfactions are to be gained. Like his hero Kierkegaard, Updike honors the charwoman who no longer works for wages, who has come to live with her God-informed conscience and the never-ending task of loving the neighbor. It is just that he honors her mostly in his nonfiction writings, with his repeated use of the phrase "Archimedean Point." As my previous chapter shows, in those writings he states directly what in his fiction he only implies: faith allows for right action and a sense of purpose. The only non-absurd actions for the believer, in Updike's Lutheran tradition especially, are praising God and serving the neighbor as Christ might have. This is a principle Updike understands and endorses.

Indeed, given Kierkegaard's arguments about the nature of purpose, Updike had little choice but to accept the neighbor-love principle if he wants to "illustrate Kierkegaard." Especially but not only in *Works of Love,* Kierkegaard explicates the opportunities, difficulties, and paradoxes of the mandate to love the neighbor. Scholars pay a great deal of attention to these ideas, in particular Ferreira in her monograph *Love's Grateful Striving* (2001), which explicates *Works of Love* chapter by chapter. Ferreira argues that in assessing the realism of Kierkegaard's call to the "duty to love," we must recognize that God not only commands but also supports love of the neighbor. Whether Kierkegaard's charwoman can change her own attitudes or the socio-economic circumstance in which she lives will be largely up to her imagination, which is fired by that God. Of course her associations with other like-minded altruists (whether religious or not) will also matter. Taylor emphasizes this religious life as a matter of "deeper involvement in concrete existence," while John Elrod argues that loving the neighbor as one loves oneself means that the neighbor simply ceases to be "the means of one's own self-seeking."[28] This change in consciousness and involvement in the lives of others is thus as ordinary as it is potentially powerful—if adopted and enacted together by networks of people in community. Kierkegaard implies that what stands in the way of pervasive justice is not Christian weakness or indolence or iniquity, but widespread denial of eternity.

There are of course those who disagree with such claims about the reasonableness of Kierkegaard's call to love the neighbor, and Updike writes with an awareness of their logic if not their work. J.L. Mackie calls the mandate "the ethics of fantasy." George Steiner uses the same root word, arguing that "these fantastic moral requirements mock and undermine mundane values. They set anarchic love against reason, an end of time against history."[29] W.H. Auden worries that the Christian who knows he cannot fulfill the neighbor-love mandate falls back on "Grace" (his capitalization). Auden complains, "The trouble about such a type of Christianity is that to the outside observer it might appear to make no practical difference."[30] In 1939, Adorno laid the groundwork for

---

[28] Taylor, *Journeys to Selfhood,* 271; John Elrod, *Kierkegaard and Christendom* (Princeton, NJ: Princeton University Press, 1981) 129.

[29] Anthony Rudd, *Kierkegaard and the Limits of the Ethical* (New York: Oxford University Press, 1993) 164. Rudd cites Mackie's *Ethics* and Steiner's *Bluebeard's Castle,* somewhat eccentrically, so I do not reproduce those citations here. My bibliography supplies complete citations of obtainable editions.

[30] Ibid., 170.

these arguments with one from his Marxist point of view. He argues that Kierkegaard's notion of love is so alienated from living people such as the "fishermen and peasants, herdsmen and publicans" with whom Jesus consorted that such love lacks real meaning. "It is unnecessary to point out how close this love comes to callousness," Adorno writes. He is not above a little confusing hyperbole: "Perhaps one may most accurately summarize Kierkegaard's doctrine of love by saying that he demands that love behave towards all men as if they were dead."[31]

More recently (as we have seen and will review further), Derrida has challenged Kierkegaard's doctrines with a typical deconstructive turning of the tables in an untypical tone of pointed accusation. He argues that a good work on behalf of any one person is a betrayal of all others.[32] The loving act is thus not only impossible to accomplish, but multiplies into manifold betrayal. Derrida even deconstructs the orthodox notion of the gift of Christ's death, asserting that in offering up one's life for another one can at best modestly lengthen another's life by shortening one's own—a materialist rewriting of the Christian passion story.[33]

Scholars more sympathetic with Kierkegaard's thought and more interested in a generous or fair-minded interpretation of it, such as Elrod, Ferreira, and many others, have pointed out that Kierkegaard has an answer to these kinds of objections. Specifically (and very briefly), Kierkegaard's supposed demonic and ananthropic or unfeeling qualities fade when we realize that his schema presumes a fundamental adjustment in the believer, post-leap. This believer is so relieved to experience God's genuine love that her conscience and other mental faculties are largely corrected. She cannot ignore, walk away from, or minimize need—not without betraying and losing immediate relation with God. This believer will choose acts or projects of love based on possibility and the neighbor's need, a kind of loving ethical triage. She will begin with her nearest neighbors, such as spouse and children when they are present. The person who experiences faith also feels a calling to a particular, personal form of loving work, tied to aptitudes and dispositions and sense of the neighbor's need. This is why Updike became a writer. Ideally, this work is a way to enact love most

---

[31] Theodor Adorno, "On Kierkegaard's Doctrine of Love." In *Søren Kierkegaard*, ed. Harold Bloom. (New York: Chelsea House, 1989) 23.

[32] Derrida, *Gift of Death*, 68-71.

[33] Ibid., 43.

thoroughly, avidly, and creatively—as Updike thought about his own work when he chose to write about his favorite human situations in order to bring others to the propitious despair he once felt and fortunately overcame.

This triage method will seem less absurd to the believer than to the nonbeliever because the believer is confident that God ordains and participates in the work, and forgives failures, large and small. Kierkegaard acknowledges that it may seem offensive to doubting others to think of God's participation in human ethical work. But it is a leitmotif of the entire body of Kierkegaard's thought that genuine Christian faith is an offense. Indeed, as Sylvia Walsh points out, Kierkegaard argues that people must "either believe, or be offended."[34] But with the leap, offended resistance gives way to complex opportunities for freedom and responsibility. Ferreira points out that Kierkegaard's apparent callousness is in fact a function of his argument that all authentic believers are capable of and called to acts and feelings of mercy. Even the poor are called to this work because they must be merciful toward the rich and all others if they wish to be genuinely faithful. Non-preferential love does not first think about which neighbor is disadvantaged and which is advantaged, or which class is destined by history to gain or lose economic power. But will such doctrines inevitably quash revolutionary change or ameliorating welfare policies? Certainly not, because we recall that individual Christians are still charged with being imaginative, effective, and just in their application of mercy and meeting of need, and the rich are as obligated to love the neighbor as the poor are.[35]

We have direct evidence that Updike adopted a remarkably similar logic. In a long footnote in the "On Not Being a Dove" chapter of *Self-Consciousness*, he cites with tacit approval an argument of Paul Tillich's, that the "power of the state" is a work of love. "The power of the state, which makes it possible for us even to be here or for works of charity to be done at all, is a work of God's love," Tillich writes. "The state has to suppress the aggression of the evil man, of those who are against love; the strange work of love is to destroy what is against love."[36] The force of Updike's chapter, which is about his stance on America's war in Vietnam, is similar. Updike asserts an explicitly Christian-Augustinian

---

[34] Sylvia Walsh, *Kierkegaard: Thinking Christianly in an Existential Mode* (New York: Oxford University Press, 2009) 157.

[35] Ferreira, *Love's Grateful Striving*, 198.

[36] Updike, *Self-Consciousness*, 130n.

rationale for supporting the Johnson administration and American combatants during that conflict. He argues that intervention on behalf of dominated Vietnamese people and a wish to improve their lives is consistent with American liberalism, and that liberalism, like any other movement, must fight fiercely for its way. Having bloody hands comes with having hands at all, Updike writes, implying that even though people are faulty they had better use their hands to improve others' lives.[37] Ferreira points out that for Kierkegaard meeting another's need is a kind of nourishment to the troubled person, as necessary as food.[38] Updike's nonfiction writings and the nature of his career both demonstrate his acceptance of this kind of view, and, as I will show in the latter six chapters of this study, the fiction can be read convincingly in support of it too. Whether through state power or local, individual acts of charity and kindness, or the publishing of novels that address existential despair, the work of love is fundamental to Kierkegaard and his followers, the anodyne to despair and enervation, and ideally the route to a just and clement society.

What Updike gathered from his reading of Kierkegaard is that a rigorous logic of renewed interpersonal compassion emerges from the leap of faith. The leap may be absurd itself, but the believer's response to God's presence in their lives is predictable, assured, and necessary. Yet, paradoxically, because these believers have chosen freely, they live in freedom. Kierkegaard makes clear that dread and despair as conditions of unbelief are incredibly corrosive of the human identity and sense of efficacy. Even the ethically-minded persons, latter day Judge Williams such as the dedicated and ultra-sincere Joan Maple, confront their own limitations and the conditions which make ethical striving so difficult and frustrating. Even committed ethicists rarely know how to help others, and their efforts are often half-hearted, mistaken, or ineffectual. Accumulated frustration leads to enervation, to despair, and perhaps to hopelessness and submerged self-contempt. This is Joan Maple's story in a nutshell. On the other hand, as Elrod so aptly explains, the leap of faith is an overwhelming experience of God's love. Unlike erotic human love, God's love is humbling rather than aggrandizing, and since it is involved in eternity, this love rests in hope rather than quotidian frustrations. The important ethical tasks may remain the same for believer, seeker, and doubter, all three, but for the believer there is newfound energy to

---

[37] Ibid., 136.
[38] Ferreira, *Love's Grateful Striving*, 260-61.

engage in the tasks, a reformed conception of the value of others, and hope in God's consummation of one's limited efforts. In this way, God's love makes possible authentic, healthy self-love, which re-orients one to the neighbor.

As Elrod argues, the leap of faith properly understood replaces the false faith of Christendom, which as Kierkegaard puts it, "grafts 'grace,' if you will, directly onto the secular mind."[39] In other words, this false believer lives just as he pleases while depending indolently on God's grace to secure his future. As the great theologian and anti-Nazi martyr Dietrich Bonhoeffer writes, such easy grace is completely hollow, lacking love, only nominally transforming.[40] Easy grace nourishes narcissism. Genuine grace is so precious that it simply must not be employed primarily for projects of self-aggrandizement or passive self-satisfaction. "One may legitimately refer to God's grace," Elrod writes, "only as that which makes possible the fulfillment of ethical obligation."[41] The word "obligation" has a special sense here and in *Works of Love*, where Kierkegaard declares that "only duty is liberating."[42] As the book unfolds it becomes clearer that Christian duty liberates one from interestedness, the sense that one needs to investigate or judge the merit of the neighbor before selecting her as an object of attention.

In *Works of Love*, Kierkegaard repeatedly refers to the story of the good Samaritan, a story Jesus gives in reply to a lawyer's question, "Who is my neighbor?" The good Samaritan is neighbor to the beaten man by the roadside, not walking past but caring for the man. Then when other responsibilities call the Samaritan away he pays for the beaten man's continued care. Kierkegaard writes, "Christ does not speak about knowing the neighbor but about becoming a neighbor oneself, about showing oneself to be a neighbor just as the Samaritan showed it by his mercy. By this he did not show that the assaulted man was his neighbor but that he was a neighbor of the one assaulted."[43] Self-consciousness here turns the tables: rather than leading to self-obsession, genuine religious self-consciousness leads to one's absolute duty to be a neighbor, to see oneself in, and act out, caritative connection with others. As I have

---

[39] John W. Elrod, *Kierkegaard and Christendom*, 79.

[40] Dietrich Bonhoeffer, *The Cost of Discipleship* (New York: The Macmillan Company, 1959) 35.

[41] Elrod, *Kierkegaard and Christendom*, 79-80.

[42] Kierkegaard, *Works of Love*, 38.

[43] Ibid., 22.

noted, Updike read *Works of Love* as he read all of Kierkegaard's other works—with appreciation.[44]

However, merely to point to Updike's appreciation for Kierkegaard's work is not necessarily to explain or defend either man's religious ideas. Some of those who argue against Kierkegaard's ideas also make compelling arguments which may not finally devolve into differing doctrinal premises. There may also be real, substantive debates from shared premises. Derrida's argument in *The Gift of Death* is one of these compelling cases.

Updike apparently saw Derrida as a worthy challenger on the matter of neighbor-love and the Christian marriage, as the epigraph and central themes of *Memories of the Ford Administration* make clear. In that 1992 novel, Updike first points to Derrida by citing him as the source of an epigraph by Heidegger (which is not important here). He then devises a plotline in which a deconstructionist English professor backs water on his Derridean commitments in an effort to save what post-structuralism (in his version) says that he cannot defend intellectually: his bourgeois marriage. As John Duvall has pointed out, though in the novel the "flaming deconstructionist turns out to be a closet traditionalist," Updike's interest in Derrida is complex, and not entirely negative.[45] Certainly Updike shares with Derrida a distaste for overly simple and stable binary oppositions. For example, *faithful/faithless* is a binary Updike often casts into dialectic tension, by expanding the meanings of these words beyond the sexual. However, if he is to be true to Kierkegaard's thought, Updike must preserve and honor one binary distinction toward which Derrida displays vivid hostility: *presence/absence*. For Kierkegaard and Updike, divine presence does exist. The material universe serves a transcendental surplus both in and beyond it, and the existence of this transcending presence—God— underwrites meaning in life. In his 1995 book, *The Gift of Death*, Derrida makes a direct and pointed assault on Kierkegaard's faith in God's living presence, and the loving acts that this faith underwrites.

---

[44] Updike's appreciation for *Works of Love* is apparent in his use of the Archimedean Point metaphor for reformed conscience in *Self-Consciousness* and essays throughout the 1990s. See my discussion of this metaphor in Chapter 1 of this study.

[45] John Duvall, "Conclusion: U(pdike) and P(postmodernism)." In *The Cambridge Companion to John Updike*, ed. Stacey Olster. (New York: Cambridge University Press, 2006) 169.

In this book, Derrida offers surprisingly lucid passages of a kind rarely found in his earlier writings. He engages Kierkegaard's ideas in a straightforward debate for long stretches, considering their implications for marital ideals and other aspects of neighbor love.[46] Derrida opens his argument by complaining about Kierkegaard's exclusively Christian preoccupation, since Judaism and Islam are also religions of The Book. However, far from defending the distinctive claims of Judaism and Islam, Derrida apparently wishes to dissolve differences between and among religions. Throwing down his philosophical gauntlet, he declares that "Religion is responsibility or it is nothing at all."[47] With this claim about the strange monolith, "religion," he overturns Kierkegaard's ethical/religious dichotomy, which of course privileges the immediate experience of the Judeo-Christian God's presence. Religion may be responsibility for Derrida, but even responsibility he deems impossible. Derrida points out the hopelessness of ethical right action with regard to "Others," human and animal, since to give ethical attention to any one being is to deny that attention to many, many others. Derrida is contemptuous of the transcendentalism underwriting the religious stage, or perhaps of Kierkegaard's confidence in proposing it, or perhaps of his Victorian way of posing it as exclusively Christian. And so Derrida proceeds to deconstruct the privileged term: responsibility, or its synonyms, duty, help, obligation.

After creating deconstructive poems out of the French quasi-homonyms for "secret," "sacred" and "sacrifice," the usual demonstration of unstable signification, Derrida offers an acute summary of Kierkegaard's central argument in *Fear and Trembling* about the nature of faith:

> The knight of faith can neither communicate to nor be understood by anyone, she can't help the other at all…. The absolute duty that obligates her with respect to God cannot have the form of generality that is called duty. If I obey in my duty towards God (which is my absolute duty) *only in terms of duty*, I am not fulfilling my relation to God.[48]

Derrida correctly notes that Kierkegaard thus denies a Kantian sense of duty to all, pointing beyond human responsibility to a "gift of

---

[46] I will not attempt to do justice to Derrida's semantic, etymological play. I concede the deconstructive principle that language is complex and underdetermined.

[47] Derrida, *Gift of Death*, 2.

[48] Ibid., 63, emphasis Derrida's.

death," an incommensurable subjectivity raised to consciousness by choices that must be made before death. Through this choosing, Derrida accurately notes, the believer relates to God and neighbor through the emotion of love, which is felt secretly and even demonically, in defiance of social expectation.

Derrida's challenge sharpens as he notes Kierkegaard's interest in Luke 14:26. In that gospel passage, Jesus tells his potential disciples that in order to follow him faithfully they must come to hate their families and their own lives. This "duty of hate" strikes Derrida as a compelling competitor to a Christian duty to love, and indeed as a crucial element in the Abraham/Isaac story as related in *Fear and Trembling*. Once God insists upon the sacrifice of Isaac, Abraham must come to hate his son in order to love God.

Here Derrida believes he has found not only a scandal and an offensive paradox but a deconstruction. Every act of love, he argues with surprising sincerity and passion, is also an act of hate. Every time one honors an urge to love or help the neighbor, one denies one's love and help to countless others who might benefit from some time and effort. "But I am sacrificing and betraying at every moment all my other obligations: my obligations to the other others whom I know or don't know, the billions of my fellows (without mentioning the animals that are even more other others than my fellows), my fellows who are dying of starvation or sickness."[49] Not only does Christianity fail in its project of loving every neighbor, then, but much of the worldwide church creates terribly destructive myths around the love mandate. For example, Derrida notes that the place where Abraham gave us our gift of death is not only the site of the House of the Lord of Jerusalem but also the grand Mosque of Jerusalem. All religions, then, he poses as ferociously competing appropriations of a compelling myth, and an occasion for "bloody, holocaustic sacrifice."[50] Even in the domestic realm, altruistic acts have the character of betrayal. The owners of a pet cat, he argues, cannot justify the "fact" that they sacrifice all other needy cats in the world.[51]

This logic would not have seemed strange to the John Updike of 1955, who also realized that choices and actions were absurd, so absurd that the substance of the earth was death. But in contrast to Derrida's

---

[49] Ibid., 69.
[50] Ibid., 70.
[51] Ibid., 71.

conclusions, Updike felt that Kierkegaard's leap of faith afforded him an exit to this logic of death, freed him to accept his vocation as a writer, and helped him to feel the work was noble rather than a betrayal. But why? After all, calling any vocational commitment or generous act a "work of love" does not seem to lend added sense to it, or make an act on one other's behalf less of a betrayal to all the other others. Furthermore, as Derrida notes with some asperity, it avails nothing simply to "deny...the aporia and antimony, tirelessly," to "treat...as nihilistic, relativist, even poststructuralist, and worse still deconstructionist, all those who remain concerned in the face of such a display of good conscience" as that of Kierkegaard and his students.[52]

Yet Derrida seems not to recognize that Kierkegaard also found antimonies compelling, and found displays of good conscience equally hollow. This is why he posits God's grace rather than a sense of "responsibility" as necessary for right action. Derrida certainly lends new language to the logic of annihilation and paralysis that plagued the young Updike before he read *Fear and Trembling*. Derrida raises the question whether Updike or any other follower of Kierkegaard can either reason or leap out of this conundrum. Yet clearly, within Updike's theologic, Derrida has failed to cancel out the either/or at the heart of Kierkegaard's writings—*either* fail to choose and live in frantic purposelessness *or* find the energy to choose, accept God's blessing, and find one's conscience reoriented. Indeed, Derrida provides a demonstration why Kierkegaard proposes such an exit as the leap in the first place: the paralyzing absurdity of what Lutherans call "works righteousness," the fantasy of pleasing God through good works, which Kierkegaard also accepts as absurd. Derrida has sketched, powerfully and economically, the unavailing character of merely human effort, devoted to non-dialectical or monist principles ("religion is responsibility or it is nothing at all"), and in doing so, has exposed the unavailing character of the ethical stage only, not the telos of Kierkegaard's scheme, the religious stage.

In spite of Derrida's efforts to ground his deconstruction in unstable signification, *The Gift of Death* offers an essentially rationalist and materialist ethical objection to Kierkegaard's schema, which as we have seen depends upon an a-rational suspension of the ethical. In a sense, then, by understanding and labeling the leap into faith an offense, Kierkegaard inoculates himself against objections like Derrida's. All such

---

[52] Ibid., 85.

arguments attacking faith (faith in God's presence and help) finally demonstrate that the offense Kierkegaard speaks of is real indeed. In other words, Kierkegaard has already deconstructed his own schema, acknowledging that no human intellective power can seek or find adequate grounding either for the leap or for its consequent works of love. These works will always be, as Derrida notes, incomplete, inefficacious, ambivalent, even mistaken. But according to Kierkegaard, the believer knows that God works in her conscience and thus she engages in a discernment of works that she feels she can and, through free conscience, must perform. Nowhere does Kierkegaard promise that Christian love of the neighbor will perfect the world, bring about sweeping justice in the social realm, or even adequately meet need on one's own block. Christian love will likely not save all the cats, not in this world at least. Kierkegaard implies strongly that, unless God comes to treat human freedoms differently, most people will continue to suffer lives in the aesthetic and ethical stages, wasting energies that might be directed to the neighbor's benefit. Notably, Derrida is oddly satisfied with his deconstructive observations and offers no description of more reasonable help to the "others," animal and human, with whom he is so concerned.

By illustrating Kierkegaard in his fiction, Updike also provides a kind of answer to Derrida's conundrum. For instance, Richard epitomizes Derrida's position in "Giving Blood," when he complains about giving part of his day off to donate a pint of his blood for Joan's cousin's surgery. "Well hell," he grumbles, "every goddam body in New England is some sort of cousin of yours; must I spend the rest of my life trying to save them all?" Also a bit of a deconstructionist, Richard here employs a *reductio ad absurdum* argument in order to show that "giving" is nonsensical. His implied argument is that one person can only scratch the surface of human need, so one need not bother to "give" at all. In "Marching through Boston," Richard implies that working for African-American civil rights is similarly absurd, but for another reason: imperfections among leaders and other marchers. Since the Reverend Abernathy and other speakers that day depend on a poetry of common feeling, an appeal to conscience rather than a display of hard logic concerning trans-racial justice, Richard is unmoved. He ends his day making vicious fun of the Reverend Abernathy's speech: "'Onteel de East German goes back t'East Germany, onteel de Luxembourgian hies hisself back to Luxembourg—'"[53] In sharp contrast, Updike himself called Martin Luther King's civil rights work one of the few genuinely heartening religious movements of the last century.[54] There is no logic available to move Richard toward his author's compassion and sense of justice. The change will have to be inward, a matter of trusting conscience, as Kierkegaard understands.

God-informed conscience will also have to shape Richard's marital commitments. He is chronically tempted away from his love for Joan by his many other sexual and relational options and opportunities. Why remain attentive and fair to Joan when he lives in a newly opened sexual bazaar, one that happens to accord with his manifold desires—and especially when his time and energy are freed up from serving every goddam neighbor? Though sociologists tell us that people do reason their way back into fidelity—the "needs of the children" argument is especially common and sometimes persuasive—such reasoning does not move Richard.[55]

Counterarguments to such reasoning are too easy to find when conscience is absent, such as Richard's own therapeutic argument that his health depends upon shedding sexual repressions. It becomes obvious that his "health" depends on no such thing, since greater sexual freedom and the coital encounters this freedom leads him into almost always increase rather than reduce his guilt and anxiety. For Updike, only the leap of faith will help Richard. He will have to gain a new self, a newly charged conscience, and then see what he can and cannot take on as rightful tasks.

Still, as Derrida so eloquently demonstrates, to live is to betray. Updike happens to agree, arguing (as he does in his infamous but coherent stand on America's involvement in Vietnam) that "shameful things [are] intrinsic to life," that bloody hands come with having hands at all. People make room for their desires, erotic and otherwise, through violence and other forms of self-assertion. They also neglect others' needs through denial. They always have.[56] This is precisely why he once felt he needed to overcome the logic of imminent annihilation and present paralysis, as he tells us, and why the ironies of the Maples stories

---

[53] Updike, *Too Far to Go*, 89.
[54] Updike, *Due Considerations*, 30.
[55] See Karla B. Hackstaff, *Marriage in a Culture of Divorce* (Philadelphia, PA: Temple University Press, 1999) 212.
[56] Updike, *Self-Consciousness*, 134-36.

finally defend the goodness of marriage, even though it is a penultimate goodness. Everyone who wishes to be good, within marriage and in meeting all other responsibilities, realizes that the wish cannot be wholly fulfilled. The late Harvard Chaplain Peter Gomes suggests that "It can be argued that the whole energy of the Bible is an attempt on the part of people who would be good to cope with the reality of the fact that they are not good."[57] This seems to be the whole energy of Updike's work as well, but it does not keep him from illustrating the world's great need for love, such as the needs of the frightened Maples children. Properly understood, the illustrating is itself an effective work of love on Updike's part.

---

[57] Peter J. Gomes, *The Scandalous Gospel of Jesus: What's So Good About the Good News?* (New York: HarperCollins, 2007) 132.

3

Kierkegaard's Marital Ideality and Updike's Reality

> "[W]ho has described marriage and all these aspects of human existence more beautifully, more charmingly, than I?"
> —Søren Kierkegaard, *Papirer* X[1]

Though his fictional marriages are often sadly realistic, Updike learned theologies of marriage from two persuasive idealists: Martin Luther and Søren Kierkegaard. For this reason, he presents his fictional marriages as "social fabric," which he knows is often torn apart by adultery and other dubious expressions of freedom, and also as incarnate love, which he suggests can transcend and even redeem the sadness of reality. The social fabric involves important legal and other agreements and promises, while the incarnate aspect of marriage involves images, drawn from scripture, of partners as "one flesh" joined in unselfish or spiritual love.[2] Images of the latter appear often in the Maples stories, in persistent references to flesh and blood. While giving blood with Joan in a Boston hospital, for instance, Richard dreams of their blood spilling onto the floor beneath their adjacent beds. As their individual essences mingle into one conjoined flesh, they grow coincidentally less irritable, mutually more patient and loving. Years later, as their legal-social marital agreement nears its end, Richard thinks about how every cell of his body is composed of Joan's cooking.[3] If these images seem rather flippantly rather than theologically carnal, we have Richard's own words in "Gesturing" about his marriage with Joan: "We are reality. We have made children. We gave each other our young bodies. We promised to

---

[1] Gregor Malantschuk, *The Controversial Kierkegaard*, trans. Howard V. Hong and Edna H. Hong. (Waterloo, Ontario: Wilfred Laurier University Press, 1976) 45n.

[2] This imagery is consistent with Luther's Two Kingdoms theology, which is too complex to describe here, except to say that Luther views the social/natural world and the spiritual world both to be real and worthy of respectful attention.

[3] Updike, *Too Far to Go*, 48 and 215.

grow old together."[4] This remark is less important for Richard's marriage than for his existential state. It communicates his inkling that marriage is a piece of the social fabric before the leap, but a laboratory for agapic, unending love after.

The notion of marital partnership as "reality" need not be explicitly Christian, of course. Though Updike is obviously interested in the incarnational aspect of marriage—the presence of God in, with, and under (as the Lutheran theologians say) the bodily partnership—he may also be suggesting here that marriage is in a secular sense somehow natural, nearly inevitable, a given, and involved in bodily conjunction. Or Richard may simply be noting his participation in cultural training about marriage, the peculiar ideology of the 1950s "profamily period" Stephanie Coontz describes in *The Way We Never Were*: "[M]arriage was almost universally praised; the family was everywhere hailed as the most basic institution in society."[5]

Updike tells us that he has considered many serious challenges to ideal models of marriage, those of Nietzsche, Marx, and Freud particularly. Nietzsche and Marx he lists as losers in the game of cultural influence. He does not even bother to describe how they redefined marriage, not in any complete or coherent way. Freud is Updike's great cultural winner, as we will see.[6] The larger point is that Updike is a historian, sociologist, and theologian of marriage, and we must be too if we hope to avoid merely personal-ethical judgments of Richard and Joan Maples' behavior in their marriage. In both his nonfiction and fiction, Updike identifies and illustrates important shifts in Christian and secular marital ideality since the Protestant Reformation, from new models of marriage that have liberated men and women from restrictive roles to destructive models which emerge from what Updike and others recognize as a deeply narcissistic culture.

---

[4] Ibid., 231.

[5] Stephanie Coontz, *The Way We Never Were: Families and the Nostalgia Trap* (New York: Basic Books, 1992) 24.

[6] "Freud more than Marx would bias our lives; the suburban home would replace the city street as the theatre of hopes; private fulfillment and not public justice would set the pace of the pursuit of happiness." John Updike, *Hugging the Shore: Essays and Criticism* (New York: Vintage, 1984) 201. Updike cites a slightly different grouping in this provocative remark in the mid-1990s: "Darwin, Freud, and Derrida left not a stick standing of the old faith, though millions of churchgoing Americans haven't quite got the news." Updike, *More Matter*, 472.

As Updike clearly knows, a new model of Christian marriage emerged amid Reformation efforts of the sixteenth century, Martin Luther's especially, a model whose ideals of mutual respect and common purpose many in the West still look to today. He knows too that Kierkegaard rewrote Luther's idealistic, earnest, pleasantly domestic marital theology into a much more challenging ideality. Updike recognizes key differences between the two visions, and since he respects both, they compel him to make a choice. Kierkegaard allows persuasive talkers, especially his ethical avatar Judge William, to define marriage as a realm of deeply satisfying but difficult fidelity. Where Luther emphasizes cheerful moral purpose, discipline in the reading and enacting of scripture, and erotic and caritative love in the marital partnership, Kierkegaard through William emphasizes the partners' anxious wish to feel more authentic through idealistic loving partnership. Kierkegaard thus seems to shift emphasis from the theological to the psychological for married partners, from mutuality through shared Christian principle to mutuality through passion for God, for goodness, and for each other.

But Kierkegaard then performs a kind of deconstruction of his own implied scheme. As we will see in more detail below, William has only just concluded his encomium to marriage when Kierkegaard challenges those same ideals, using William's own words and Luther's logic of faith to present even more demanding exceptions to marital mutuality. These are exceptions that Luther seems not to have worked out in his own theology. The Christian, Kierkegaard suggests, may be called to a life of solitude, to the "duty of hate" we saw Derrida confronting in my previous chapter. Indeed, Kierkegaard notes that a blessed, happy marriage might very well be a distraction from the real event, the leap into genuine relation with God. As we have seen, this demanding life was Kierkegaard's own choice, as he eschewed marriage with Regine Olsen in favor of a severe and lonely vocation as Christian prophet. Faced with Luther's and Kierkegaard's theologies, Updike must choose between marriage as a sacred practice, fully worthy of one's time and attention, or as an interference to the existential demands of personhood, yet another unwanted erosion of personal liberty and cause of deferred authenticity. It may or may not help him that Kierkegaard appears to have made the latter choice.

Living in the erotic bazaar of the American consumer society, Updike considers, confronts, and updates both of these idealistic models, along with the social and theological problems they raise. He tests a marital theology of his own, a constellation of practices and traditions and Christian ideals mediating the never-ending tensions of selfhood and mutuality. Perhaps surprisingly, in a very real world of compromises, betrayals, failures, neuroses and delusions, Updike affirms—or at least hopes for—something like Luther's ideality. We have seen that Updike rejects Kierkegaard's late-career ananthropic severities in favor of a more orthodox view of God's loving mercy. As they struggle to remain married, the Maples and their friends test whether the love and mercy Updike finds at the heart of the gospels really has a chance to keep marriages intact, to set aside a broadly cultural narcissism, and to reduce betrayals among married partners. In the years leading up to their divorce, the Maples mostly fail in this task. But Updike is careful along the way to provide scenes that contrast with the narcissism and the betrayals. He shows just how important it is that married partners love each other unselfishly, and that they both love and teach their children with care.

&

Marriage, for Luther, is not a sacrament as his medieval Catholic training would have it, but a worldly institution with a spiritual character deserving theological attention. As one Reformation historian puts it, Luther views marriage as theologically significant "because it is an institution of God's purposing" and because of "the manifold hardships and temptations it entails, especially when there are children." Wedding promises are so difficult to fulfill that marriage "almost 'compels' faith." Genuine mutuality virtually requires God's assistance.[7] Of course life itself is so difficult that it almost compels faith and requires God's assistance, so this is to say little about marriage specifically.

Facing up to such difficulties, Luther and his followers redefined marriage in the early sixteenth century, and in doing so redefined more than the Christian self and Christian family. They reshaped Western culture for all. For sociologists and historians, marriage and the so-called "simple" or nuclear families emerged as regimes of control on excesses of medieval Catholic consciousness. According to religious historian

---

[7] Bernd Wannenwetsch, "Luther's Moral Theology," in *The Cambridge Companion to Martin Luther*, ed. Donald McKim(Cambridge UK: Cambridge University Press, 2003) 131-32.

Susan C. Karant-Nunn, late Medieval Christendom was characterized by a "surfeit of allegiances, occasions, and gratifications," a variety of social institutions and practices operating under a loose metaphor of family. So, for example, guild membership and apprenticeships might be characterized as brotherhoods, and monastic commitments might be referred to as a marital commitment. Corruptions of quasi-familial commitments abounded, such as the apparently widespread role of priests' housekeepers serving secretly as sexual and emotional partners as well.[8] As Stephanie Coontz notes, marriages among the laity also bore the weight of these multiple alliances and commitments, so that a good marriage served primarily as a "link in a larger system of economic and political alliances."[9] The Protestant spirit of reform motivated a rethinking of this surfeit of allegiances, a simplification and purification of relationships between believer and God and between husband, wife, and child.

At first, the Reformation pastor, newly married to a fervently Christian wife, modeled for a larger congregation of believers a loving relationship and pastoral calling both more chaste and more frankly affirmative of human sexual connection than its Catholic precedents. Honoring Luther's emphasis on living the Christian life rather than proselytizing for it, these pastoral couples were to model a loving, faithful, and cooperative life, one that was sanctified but not sanctimonious. They were to embody a purer and more intense love of God and neighbor, to engage in the cultivation of children as newly volitional selves participating in a life of faithfulness, and to practice familial relationships based in mutual esteem and respect.

Most important of these transformations in esteem involved the question of marital obedience and role-sharing. Where Catholic culture heaped scorn upon any man who let himself be dominated by his wife, the emerging Protestant culture of the early and middle sixteenth century urged husbands to exercise Christ-like love and restraint—even while retaining legal dominion in the relationship. Wives were to remain domestic workers, and were in no way invited into full partnership in civic and ecclesiastical roles—not for centuries, and not yet today in many Protestant denominations—but in the home and sanctuary, and

---

[8] Susan Karant-Nunn, "Reformation society, women and the family," in *The Reformation World*, ed. Andrew Pettegree (New York: Routledge, 2000) 436.

[9] Stephanie Coontz, *Marriage, a History: From Obedience to Intimacy or How Love Conquered Marriage* (New York: Viking, 2005) 146.

with their husbands' blessings, these Reformation-era wives took up tasks that they shared with the Protestant state. Namely, these wives were to sacralize the functions of daily life, imposing discipline upon Christians' behavior, and in doing so creating a "community of faith," albeit one officially presided over exclusively by men, the husband, father, and male pastor. Marriage had become much more than a civil matter. It was now a holy calling, and the site of the core spiritual exercises (sociologists say "social disciplines") of Protestant culture.[10] These exercises included doing the work one is called to—from charwoman to pastor to prince, Luther tells us—with prayerful integrity and all the excellence one can muster; relating to family and neighbor with love and respect; restraining selfishness, petulance, anger, and violence; attending worship and teaching each other (especially the children and new believers) both biblical and catechetical principles. This scheme has had unanticipated theological and social consequences. The emphasis on ideal love and justice has led to less rigid role-taking, so that now the pastor in the parsonage is often the wife, while the more domestic partner with more of the child-rearing duties is often the husband. Both embrace the task of sacralizing quotidian acts, ideally at least.

Kierkegaard's theology of marriage matches and then trumps the idealism of Luther's theology. Kierkegaard too accepts and celebrates the unselfing practices of ideal Christian marriage—necessarily, because the leap of faith is itself an act of unseating egotism and learning to love oneself and one's neighbor properly, including the near neighbors of spouse and children. But Luther's ideal marriage and society would appear to Kierkegaard another version of the moribund ethical society he saw in his Copenhagen. Too great an emphasis is placed on daily habits. The pastoral marriage is deeply invested in teaching, training, and practicing theological principle, the systematic spiritual mediation that Kierkegaard believes plays no essential role in the drama of achieving existential authenticity. Kierkegaard insists on another ideality in which married persons are transformed as individuals first, and only then, as a result of that transformation, able to participate properly in a loving, agapic marriage.

As a character named Judge William argues strenuously and lengthily in *Either/Or* and *Stages on Life's Way*, it is the husband especially who needs to develop humility over time, for "an ideal husband is not

---

[10] Karant-Nunn, "Reformation Society," 436-449.

one who is ideal once in his life but one who is that every day."[11] The word "ideal" here means kind, attentive, patient, honest. Whether the focus on the husband's moral life is sexist or realist we may decide for ourselves. But Kierkegaard believes himself to be telling a truth about becoming, how all fallen persons come to have integrity through life-long struggle and finally through God's help with moral orientation. Apparently, marriage may have a place in the process. Its difficulties swell dread into despair, while the presence of love (when it is present) hints at the nature of the God who urges seekers to leap into authenticity. However, Kierkegaard is also willing to set aside marriage as a spiritual blessing. Pursuing the logic of his own teleological suspension of the ethical, he argues for a strange logical ground where God might require spiritual solitude and rejection of others' love. He believes men are more likely than women to feel this stern sense of calling.

Some of Kierkegaard's critics regard this severe religious requirement as misogynist, its presentation shrill and ananthropic. This is hard to deny, yet Kierkegaard never wholly discards a concern for communities like his Copenhagen, in which marriage and churchgoing and practices of citizenship still matter. Both the pseudonymous first literature and non-pseudonymous second present marriage as an ethical blessing, and hold out the possibility that even the knight of faith may be called to faithfulness in marriage—and "faithfulness" here means much more than avoiding extramarital sexual dalliances. Faithfulness is primarily about one's duties to love unselfishly and justly. Misogynist conclusions may have struck the 19th century Danish bachelor-philosopher as reasonable, but the logic of his post-leap schema hardly requires such conclusions. Humble service of the neighbor may take many forms, some far from extreme. In *Fear and Trembling*, for instance, the wife of the knight of faith sometimes shows her love merely by serving her husband his favorite meal of roasted lamb's head.[12]

We will see that Updike accepts and endorses both the unselfish ethical and transcending religious possibilities for marriage. Updike has

---

[11] Kierkegaard, *Either/Or*, 2:135.

[12] Kierkegaard, *Fear and Trembling*, eds. and trans. Victor V. Hong and Edna H. Hong. (Princeton NJ: Princeton University Press, 1983) 39. I refer in this study to another edition of *Fear and Trembling*, the Lowrie edition Updike read in the mid-1950s, but unless I stipulate otherwise, all citations of *Fear and Trembling* refer to this Princeton edition.

concerns, on the other hand, with one significant aspect of Kierkegaard's schema, his notion of the religious "exception," his choice of a celibate life and his supposedly selfless and spiritual manipulating of Regine Olsen. As we have seen, Updike does not find Kierkegaard especially unselfish or spiritual in his relation to Regine. In the Maples stories, this tale of manipulation becomes a target of Updike's satire—or at least deliberate testing. He shows how destructive manipulative lovers can be, and how necessary honesty is to a healthy marriage.

The fictional Victor Eremita ("victorious hermit") moderates Kierkegaard's extended discussions of marriage. He is the editor of *Either*, in which an aesthete we know as A tells us why he needs to manipulate his fiancé into a separation, and *Or*, in which Judge William promotes the ethical validity of marriage. William is the spokesman for Kierkegaardian marital ideality. He contrasts the giddy experience of being in love, which he calls "first love," with the unselfish, sustained, harmonious quality of a good marriage. Time is the enemy of first (or romantic) love, while marital love endures over time.[13] The aesthete's preference for "first love" is just one way in which he falls short of the ethicist. The Judge realizes that the aesthete favors the giddy fascinations of first love, while the married couple understands that their mutuality cannot be based in such a fleeting emotion. Their focus will have to be loving companionability, and therefore ethical goodness, especially with regard to each other. He also grants that passionate loving and long-term faithfulness are possible within marriage, even normal within a good one. He makes a personal confession that "there is one thing for which I thank God with my whole soul, and that is that [my wife] is the only one I have ever loved, the first, and there is one thing for which I pray to God with my whole heart, that he will give me the strength never to want to love any other."[14]

William realizes that this passionate love is not enough, that husbands like him must apply themselves to particular Biblical priorities. Marital love, he argues in an obvious paraphrase of I Corinthians 13, is "faithful, constant, humble, patient, long-suffering, tolerant, honest, content with little, alert, persevering, willing, happy."[15] Kierkegaard certainly approves of these qualities in marriage, though conditionally—

---

[13] Kierkegaard, *Either/Or*, 2:135ff.

[14] Ibid., 2:9.

[15] Ibid., 2:139.

because, as it happens, in *Either/Or*, Judge William's theology of marriage is lovely and compelling but eventually exposed as inadequate.

Kierkegaard stages a similar outcome in *Stages on Life's Way*. Two years after the 1843 publication of *Either/Or* Kierkegaard published a Victor Eremita redux when Victor appears as a speaker at a banquet of aesthetes early in that book. The Judge listens to the others at table belittling women's spirituality. His friend, Constantin Constantius, supposed author of *Repetition*, argues, shockingly, that women cause ideality by doing men the favor of dying. Johannes the Seducer of the "Seducer's Diary" also chimes in, arguing that only the element of deception in a seduction partakes of the eternal, only erotic possibility. Ethical, faithful marriages annul the erotic. The irony is heavy here, as Kierkegaard satirizes self-serving, objectifying, and misogynist views of women by male aesthetes. As in *Either/Or*, Judge William's response to these ideas is to argue earnestly that these aesthetic, somewhat cynical understandings of marriage are inadequate, that marriage involves genuine mutuality between married partners.[16]

At first it seems that Judge William has twice won the day, both in *Either/Or* and *Stages on Life's Way*. In *Stages*, he rejects his fellow diners' cruelty and cynicism. He also shows convincingly that the aesthetic life is driven by habits and impulses that involve only penultimate rather than existential choice. He describes marriage as a spiritual category rather than, as we might expect, a matter of duty, personal integrity, or community expectation. He even suggests that husbands should "have faith" in marriage.[17] *Either/Or* presents an even more emphatic defense of marriage. In a series of compelling epigrammatic statements, interlarded in a lengthy exposition in which the Judge's somewhat tedious qualities come forward, William describes marriage as a divine state open to all who have the energy of choice, choice which when genuine is personally transforming and God-ordained:

> Romantic love can be portrayed very well in the moment; marital love cannot, for an ideal husband is not one who is ideal once in his life but one who is that every day.[18]

---

[16] Søren Kierkegaard, *Stages on Life's Way,* eds. and trans. Howard V. Hong and Edna H. Hong. (Princeton NJ: Princeton University Press, 1988) 89-184.

[17] Ibid., 91.

[18] Kierkegaard, *Either/Or*, 2:135.

[The romantic lover] has not fought with lions and trolls but with the most dangerous enemy, which is time.[19]

[W]hat is important in choosing is not so much to choose the right thing as the energy, the earnestness, and the pathos with which one chooses...Therefore, even though a person chose the wrong thing, he nevertheless, by virtue of the energy with which he chose, will discover that he chose the wrong thing.[20]

Your condition of despair is propitious...because the one who despairs finds the eternal human being, and in that we are all equal.[21]

When a person has truly chosen despair, he has truly chosen what despair chooses; himself in his eternal validity.[22]

He repents himself back into himself, back into his family, back into the race, until he finds himself in God.[23]

As soon as I love freely and love God, then I repent.[24]

As the Judge asserts, the aesthetic is a matter of being, while the ethical is a matter of becoming, of growth in personhood and movement toward God, of an arrived humility through chosen repentance.[25] William's arguments seem to have Kierkegaard's endorsement, as repentance involves living "before God," the essence of the religious stage. The Judge seems to have found a way to grow into a genuine religious experience through participation in marriage, through the personal refinements that come from loving mutuality and permanent commitment. This is not marriage merely as a laboratory of love, where lovers find out what love can do ethically. This is marriage as a refinery of human personality and producer of faith.

However, the Judge then offers a sermon that he has found in a letter, but which he feels crystalizes his own commitments, "The Upbuilding That Lies in the Thought That in Relation to God We Are

---

[19] Ibid., 2:138.
[20] Ibid., 2:167.
[21] Ibid., 2:209.
[22] Ibid., 2:214.
[23] Ibid., 2:216.
[24] Ibid., 2:216.
[25] Ibid., 2:225.

Always in the Wrong." As the sermon commences, the logic of the Judge's own argument gets the better of him. To alert readers, his former positions are exposed, specifically the notions of personal will and autonomy that underwrite the "choosing" he speaks of. The Judge's sermon-writer works through a logic of being "in the wrong," of consciousness of sin before God. His language hints that he is trying to find his argument and come to some personal conclusions. We know that he is an ethicist, confident in a person's ability to see valid ethical tasks and then perform them. The sermon juxtaposes that confidence with an exposition of Lutheran theology, the originally Lutheran kind that emerges from Luther's fear of a chastening, judging God. The sermon-writer argues that the healthiest human move, essential for personal authenticity, is to realize that God is always right, so transcendently right that human beings are always in the wrong. A faith that begins with this principle of "original wrongness" is devoid of doubt, and doubt is what disables human action.[26]

Judge William does not seem to realize it, but in offering this argument he claims to have found, in which the *totaliter aliter* God is incommensurable with human hopes and desires, he has dissolved his own idea of a human personhood with the will and the energy and the perspicacity to choose ideal marriage—or despair, or himself, or anything else with existential import. Living in the ethical, the Judge is groping toward a cause for the leap, the need to be justified through Christ to this Wholly Other God. But he remains far too confident that his ethical scheme is perfectly sound, that he has cleansed his commitments of all doubt.

In a study of the continuation of Judge William's ethical ideality in *Stages on Life's Way*, Mark C. Taylor sees clearly—and expresses brilliantly—why Judge William's idea of marriage as an existential good will not do:

> But what if this form of life is the domestication, not the realization, of spirit; what if the end of life is not secure, meaningful occupation and a *hyggelig* [cozy, comforting, life-affirming] family life; what if self is not fully actualized in community; if individuality is not best expressed in universality; what if eternity is not within time; if infinitude is not in finitude; what if desire and duty conflict; what if God does create dreadful collisions; if God demands renunciation, not consummation, of love; if God requires lover to forsake beloved; if God orders the sacrifice

---

[26] Ibid., 2:337-354.

of a son, perhaps his own son, perhaps the son of another; what if...; what if...; what if...?[27]

Of course in his second literature Kierkegaard confirms each of these "what ifs" as true rather than conditional. It turns out that the Judge has been making essentially Hegelian arguments about marriage. He has viewed marriage as a rational process which, entered into with care and discipline, will lead husbands and wives into full and finalized communion with God. But even if people have the moral strength to choose faithfulness within marriage, they do not have the power to choose God, nor to discover a life devoid of doubt and anxiety.

Late in the Judge's remarks on marital love and mutuality (a set of papers Victor steals from the Judge on the street, just after the banquet), Judge William acknowledges that marriage is not "the highest life." The highest life is the religious, in which one lives in direct communion with a God to whom one is justified by Christ's sacrifice and God's love. From the true believer, the knight of faith, God can require an "exception" from universal ethical requirements. Kierkegaard describes, through Judge William, how a believing man might need to eschew marriage in order to follow in the steps of Christ and accept some of His suffering.[28] Here we encounter the severe requirements of faith that some find misogynist and strident. The Judge here seems to realize that marriage and religious faithfulness do not solve all human problems or result in a wholly blessed life. Faith may help the believer to live with suffering rather than avoid it. Indeed, for some, suffering is a genuine Christian calling. It is not clear how many might be called to this life rather than life in the triadic love of marriage: husband, wife, and God bound faithfully through promises. But some are.

If this were all that Kierkegaard's fictions implied about marriage, we might conclude that in the land of Denmark two-hundred years after Luther, marriage remains a blessing for the genuine believer, an honorable estate and aid to religious identity. The only real modification to the early modern pastoral marriage is Kierkegaard's idea of exceptions for the believer who feels that special calling. We have only to decide what these exceptions mean for faithful love and marriage, decide to whom this exceptional life applies, and live accordingly. However, both *Either/Or* and *Stages on Life's Way* offer the Judge's encomia and

---

[27] Taylor, *Journeys to Selfhood*, 250. The emphasis is Taylor's, the translation of *hyggelig* mine.

[28] Kierkegaard, *Stages on Life's Way*, 169ff.

eventually their exposure alongside proxy versions of the strange tale of Kierkegaard's abortive engagement with Regine Olsen. This story also interrogates the meaning of marriage and the faithful life. Because the two fictionalized versions of the tale are so palpably personal for Kierkegaard, complex and heartrending, they present a yet more authentic marital ideality. They lead us to the center of this unresolved problem of the Christian exception, where we find another deconstructive moment.

Kierkegaard and Regine met in 1837 at a mutual friend's house outside Copenhagen. Kierkegaard immediately fell in love with the fourteen year-old girl, and she seems to have liked him as well. The two contrived to meet briefly and casually in shops and friends' homes, though there was no true courtship. In September of 1840, just after taking the examinations for his divinity degree, the twenty-seven-year-old Kierkegaard found a private moment with Regine and announced his longings for her. She replied with a confession of similar feelings, and accepted his proposal of marriage. Her father did not oppose the engagement. As the existing correspondence between the lovers shows, almost immediately Kierkegaard began to write notes and letters that communicated his doubts about the marriage. Privately, he wondered whether his own calling wasn't an "exception" to the ordinary relational life—both because his theology was so strange and demanding, as he knew, and because he had inherited from his father a deep melancholy, perhaps even a somatic disorder such as epilepsy or a sexually transmitted disease. In August of 1841, Kierkegaard broke the engagement. Regine tried for a time to persuade Kierkegaard to reconsider, but eventually she gave him up. In 1847, she married her former private tutor, a man named Schlegel. Throughout the years before that marriage began, Kierkegaard tried to help Regine with her disappointment. Kierkegaard tried to convince himself that he needed to pose as a cruelly cynical roué, like his proxies in *Either/Or* and *Stages*, the Seducer Johannes and Quidam, so that Regine would have no "dialectical" feelings about the broken engagement. That is, he felt he needed to be cruel to be kind, to convince Regine that he was beneath her attention after all, and to convince her that she bore no responsibility for their breakup.

Scholars agree for the most part that in *Either/Or* and *Stages* Kierkegaard was exploring the nature of Christian calling, but the theology is inextricably bound up with his personal working-through of torturous feelings he clearly still harbored for Regine. The two diaries in particular were a first treatment, taken up more fully in the later second literature, of the severities that Christ calls into being when he says that his followers must "hate" family members in order to give Him their full attention and devotion. Of course, many informed and alert readers also detect in the diaries feelings of doubt and guilt and self-indictment in Kierkegaard's arguments. Later he renounced at least some part of this effort. In his later years, Kierkegaard began to consider his own pseudonymous indirection to be overelaborate, turning to the straightforward apologetics of the second literature. He began to treat Regine differently too. According to biographer Joakim Garff, Kierkegaard went to his grave craving Regine's time and attention. About a decade after their broken engagement, the two tacitly contrived for a time to meet for an exchange of greetings in churches and on walking paths.[29] Kierkegaard willed his worldly goods to Regine as well, noting to his brother that he considered an engagement to be "as binding as a marriage."[30]

So perhaps Kierkegaard did not eschew marriage with Regine so much as he created a new form of loving fidelity. By the same token, perhaps the question implied by the Seducer's and Quidam's diaries is not whether marriage might or might not aid in authentic living, nor whether people should consider living as a Christian exception. Those scholars who believe that Kierkegaard wrote the diaries simply to worry these questions after he parted ways with Regine Olsen may be missing the point. The diaries only seem to establish two ranks of Christians: ordinary ones who like Judge William and his wife may find daily satisfactions and blessings through marriage, and exceptional ones who like Quidam/Kierkegaard can share Christ's sufferings with Father, Son, and Holy Ghost, but not with a spouse. Read another way, with less emphasis on the autobiographical, Kierkegaard may be demonstrating that there is only one way to be married or engaged or in love, or simply alone, and that is creatively. A marriage based in law, even the benevolent laws of patient unselfing that the apostle Paul urged the people of Corinth to accept, is a rather rote thing, qualitatively different from God's creative love. The diaries in fact point to a problem and a question every married or lovingly committed person must answer: How to love this person rightly? This is a question of conscience, and we

---

[29] Garff, *Søren Kierkegaard*, 598.
[30] Ibid., 801.

know that for Kierkegaard the conscience is lawless, perfectly free, a creative faculty rather than an ethically obedient one.

Updike jokes in his Introduction to *The Seducer's Diary* that it was odder of Kierkegaard to decide to marry Regine than to decide to break off from her. As we have seen, Updike considers Kierkegaard neurotic in his treatment of Regine. He views his theological mentor as suffering something like an identity crisis proposing that God lacks mercy and in dishonoring Regine's love for him. These kinds of theological and personal neuroses become a central focus of the Maples stories. One of Richard Maple's hallmarks is his manipulative gaming of Joan, his sly and sometimes crude attempts to get her to end their marriage so that he does not have to. He often excuses his gaming through antinomian theological arguments, the needs of self to his mind always trumping marital ethics. Thus he mirrors the duplicity of Kierkegaard's seducers, if not their aims. This trait of Richard's, this trend in his behavior, is in part a satire on a demonic or narcissistic vein in Kierkegaard's personality—a self-centeredness that causes pain in a loving woman. Thus Updike points to his commitment to honest loving between spouses or lovers, to an updated version of Luther's rather than Kierkegaard's model of the Christian marriage.

To put this slightly more precisely, what Updike affirms and embraces is Judge William's marital ideality up to the point where the Judge implies that spouses have the power, the will, the discipline to be faithful to each other in all things. What do we mean by "faithful?" Kierkegaard supplies an answer in a footnote to *Concluding Unscientific Postscript*. Working through differences between objective and subjective thinking, he offers a parable. Imagine a maiden who "yearns for her wedding day because this would give her assured certainty" about the nature of her future. It would make her "comfortable in legal security as a spouse." This is unfaithfulness, Kierkegaard argues. He at first jokes that this maiden prefers "marital yawning to maidenly yearning," but then more seriously declares that "this, after all, is the essential unfaithfulness in an erotic relationship; the incidental unfaithfulness is to love someone else."[31] Marital fidelity, in other words, is *primarily* about subjective focus, earnest and passionate investment in the person of the beloved, rather than about external circumstances such as material

---

[31] Søren Kierkegaard, *Concluding Unscientific Postscript to Philosophical Fragments*, eds. and trans. Howard V. Hong and Edna H. Hong. (Princeton NJ: Princeton University Press, 1992) 1:74n.

security or the presence or absence of a rival lover. In the same way, marital love is *primarily* about the beloved, rather than about the feeling of being "in love." And in the same way, faith is *primarily* about trust in God, rather than about enacted pieties. As Howard and Edna Hong note, Judge William offers an "ennobling" message when he describes proper marriage as "faithful, constant, humble, patient, long-suffering, tolerant, honest, content with little, alert, persevering, willing, happy." The Hongs are also right to note that "[i]n a time of decay of the family, his portrayal of the meaning of marriage is refreshing and invigorating."[32] Updike endorses the same model of meaningful marriage, while remaining realistic about the partners' ability to achieve and sustain it. Indeed, this realism will be the hallmark of his own marital ideality.

In his fiction Updike confronts the vestiges of Luther's and Kierkegaard's marital idealities. Along with these vestiges, Updike confronts and illustrates a third ideality more relevant to the particular challenges of his own two marriages. This is a specifically psychoanalytic version of ideal marriage that shaped the unique facticity of his day, in his own community of Northeastern intellectuals. This facticity involved new freedoms, especially sexual freedom for men and professional freedom for women. In Updike's version the new self-consciousness for men and women both tended toward self-indulgence or narcissism. For most of those neighbors of Updike's, narcissism is an effect of a permissive culture, or of interrupted developmental processes. For Updike, narcissism is dread, self-aggrandizement, sin as separation from God, the sickness unto death. He poses failing marriages, especially that of the Maples, as symptoms of this specifically existential sin.

Updike's college days and early marriage coincided with a period of psychoanalytic ascendancy. Psychoanalysts and their students busily rethought and updated the fundaments of their practice, turning from a focus on guilt to one on tragedy, from the "maturity ethic" of intrapsychic autonomy to the "esteem ethic" of intersubjective analysis. This shift would have a profound impact on American marital practice, even beyond the circle of those reading psychoanalytic literature or undertaking psychoanalysis. The maturity ethic saw the healthy *telos* of psychoanalysis in marriage, the parenting of children, and the adoption

---

[32] Howard V.Hong and Edna Hong, Introduction to *The Essential Kierkegaard*, eds. and trans. Howard V. Hong and Edna H. Hong. (Princeton NJ: Princeton University Press, 2000) x.

of a meaningful calling.[33] This ethic thus aided and abetted the male breadwinner family of the 1950s. By contrast, the esteem ethic, like the emerging counterculture of the 1960s, sought a wider range of relationships and activities as meaningful, even if they had no evident social purpose. Psychoanalytic questions of self-esteem, authenticity, and freedom would filter into the popular culture and underwrite the so-called sexual revolution, which in psychoanalytical terms was a rethinking of repression and individual restraint. While Freud presents repression of instinctual desires as necessary to the fabric of personal restraints that make up a clement civilization, intersubjective psychoanalysts saw repressions as overly abundant in Cold War culture, a hindrance to happiness and fulfillment. They argued that fulfilling unreflective desire led to deeper satisfaction and meaning. At least some of these psychoanalysts believed a more peaceable society would result from increased libidinal freedom and resulting satisfactions in self-esteem and authenticity.

This is the time, roughly the period when John and Mary Updike and Richard and Joan Maple were legally married, when American divorce rates tripled. These rates stabilized in the early 1980s with half of all first marriages and 60 percent of second marriages ending in divorce within forty years.[34] Given the chance, Luther and Kierkegaard might regard many of these divorces as acts of moral failure or even sin, but the Maples illustrate a more dialectical view. They honor a marital ideality of their day by marrying young, focusing deliberately upon questions of personhood and identity during their marriages, seeking freer exercise for their libidos than their parents probably had, and concluding that divorce has become the best route to personal satisfactions. Divorce may have been for the Maples the only way to negotiate their individual commitments to personal self-esteem, autonomy, and happiness. Like Kierkegaard and Regine, the Maples contrive after their breakup to meet and share private moments. The divorce was less a moral failure than a perceived psychoanalytic anodyne. This is Richard's sense at least; Joan's attitude is less clear.

Each of the Maples subscribes to a favored psychoanalytic theory. As we will see in my next chapter, Richard Maple seems to pattern his conduct after a psychological scheme offered by Herbert Marcuse and

---

[33] Eli Zaretsky, *Secrets of the Soul: A Social and Cultural History of Psychoanalysis* (New York: Vintage, 2004) 314-15.

[34] Coontz, *The Way We Never Were*, 3.

his followers, who believed that infant narcissism, necessary as a shield to the helpless infant's fear, was not to be defeated but allowed to flourish in adult erotic and artistic play. Joan, on the other hand, seems to honor the humanist psychotherapy most often associated with Carl Rogers and Abraham Maslow. They preached a basic trust in the goodness of nature, the possibility of human comity, and the emergence of an identity in accord with this hopeful vision. These choices of Richard's and Joan's accord with his hedonism and demands for sexual freedom, and her ethical commitments in her childrearing and work for social justice. Notably, the theories of Marcuse, Rogers and Maslow were quite prominent in the 1960s and 1970s, but have since declined in importance even more sharply than psychoanalysis as a whole.

As psychoanalytic historian Eli Zaretsky notes, psychoanalysis emerged as a dominant explanatory system among post-World-War-Two intellectuals, partly because more than two hundred refugee psychoanalysts had arrived from Axis-controlled countries during the war, and because the U.S. Army required all its physicians during the war to take psychoanalytic training. Most of the physicians who survived filtered back into their communities after the war.[35] The only other intellectual framework to compete effectively for attention in the early Cold War was existentialism and, as Zaretsky puts it, "existential theology."[36] Students at good colleges and universities in the 1950s encountered both the psychoanalytical and existentialist systems in their studies, if not existentialist theology, and some of these students, like Updike at Harvard, seem to have found their world-views permanently shaped along these lines. Updike's investment in existential and psychoanalytical meanings was profound. Throughout his fiction, Updike casts Protestant Christian and neo-Freudian models of identity into dialectical tension, in doing so posing a tension of spiritual and psychoanalytical explanations for his characters' behavior, identifying neither as a clear winner.

As early as the second Maples story, "Wife-Wooing" (*New Yorker*, 1960), Richard and Joan Maple frame their experiences in psychoanalytic terms. Richard thinks that people say "dreadful things" about God now, such as the suggestion that "rose windows in churches are vaginal symbols." Later in the story he views his baby son as an "egotist."[37]

---

[35] Zaretsky, *Secrets of the Soul*, 276 and 280.
[36] Ibid., 276.
[37] Updike, *Too Far to Go*, 32-33.

These kinds of references are common in the stories, if not pervasive. By the twelfth Maples story, "Sublimating" (*Harpers*, 1971), Updike implies an even deeper investment in psychoanalysis among the older three Maples—Richard, Joan, and daughter Judith. Richard and Joan decide with dubious logic that because "sex was their only sore point in their marriage" (Richard wants more than Joan does) they should experiment with a period of sexual abstinence. As the title word "sublimating" implies, the two of them expect surplus libidinal energy to be available for other tasks. Sure enough, Joan turns to increased household chores and kid-taxiing, while Richard turns to his professional work, golf game, and comedic teasing of his children with mock-Oedipal props, garden shears and a cabbage. Seventeen year-old Judith goes to sleepovers with a druggy crowd and thus may or may not be abstaining from sex herself. But she has plenty of surplus energy, which spills over in the form of aggressively knowing speeches about her family's states of mind. At one point she says, giggling, "Daddy's a narcissist." Richard is so shocked at her bluntness and perceptiveness that he overreacts in response: "Judith!" This is as sharply, we are told, as he has ever spoken to her.[38]

Her diagnosis is correct within its paradigm, and this moment, along with many other fictive situations focusing on Richard's self-indulgence and family history, is clear evidence that Updike wished to engage the "culture of narcissism" arguments of his day. These were arguments by which intellectuals in the 1970s, using their favored psychoanalytic terms, sought to explain the wrenching shift in public mores they witnessed between the 1950s and 1970s. These shifting mores had a profound impact on marital ideality and reality, an argument made by such public intellectuals as Philip Rieff, Erich Fromm, Otto Kernberg, Melanie Klein—and John Updike's former Harvard roommate for three years, historian Christopher Lasch, who does us the favor of summarizing a clinical debate about narcissism as pathology.[39]

I am not proposing that Lasch and Updike debated or compared visions with each other as adult professionals. Though Sam Tanenhaus of the *New York Times* reports that the two followed each other's work after college, they make no references to each other in their published

---

[38] Ibid., 174.

[39] Christopher Lasch, *The Culture of Narcissism: American Life in an Age of Diminishing Expectations* (New York: Norton, 1979) 31-51.

writings.[40] Rather, I am proposing that the two shared a mid-century Harvard worldview, and that therefore Lasch is an excellent source for Updike's concerns. Both examine carefully the mechanics of primary and secondary narcissism, and the impact of character disorders on the psychological states of American individuals and society. Both also view eroding marriages as key symptoms of cultural narcissism. As Lasch and others suggest, the common psychological disorders in a society always shape the society as a whole, and so the personal category of narcissism becomes a cultural category. Lasch's account also has the virtue of being rigorously grounded in the classical and reformed Freudian theory Updike often cites, and of drawing on a useful array of psychoanalysts, cultural critics, and historians of the 1960s and 1970s. For our purposes, Lasch provides a diagnosis of marriage and society during the time of the Maples' intact household, a diagnosis that will help us to understand Updike's ironies.

In *The Culture of Narcissism* (1979), Lasch asserts that narcissism in America is a cause for problems of identity, work, sport, schooling, sex, senescence, and of course marriage. Because Americans have, he argues, a despairing view of the future arising from both social evidence (the bomb) and psychic disposition, they have lost traditions of enlightened individualism and local action. Both traditions involve deferring gratification and investing selflessly in children and communities—functions of a hopeful view of the future. But when nuclear extinction or social anarchy seem imminent, people do not invest time and effort in children and communities. The fearful individual finds it best to keep intense feelings at bay along with the commitments that tend to produce such feelings. And so parenting and partnering both become cool, distant, noncommittal, and pro forma. Promiscuous sexual attachments become common, as well as emotional abandonment of children. These children, who have already experienced a deep sense of loss in separating from the mother in pre-Oedipal processes—this sense of loss is a reason psychoanalytic models of the world are often described as tragic—now find themselves disappointed during the Oedipal stage as well by their parents' self-congratulatory but inadequate care. This disappointment produces aggressive impulses outward, and an inner sense of having little hope. These basically unhappy people realize, if

---

[40] Sam Tanenhaus, "The Roommates: Updike and Christopher Lasch," *The New York Times,* June 20, 2010, http://www.nytimes.com/2010/06/21/books/21roommates.html?_r=0.

only dimly, that they are unprincipled and corruptible. As the children of narcissists, they also defend themselves against deep and threatening feelings, and thus tend to recapitulate a narcissistic family and society. "The ideology of personal growth, superficially optimistic, radiates a profound despair and resignation," Lasch writes. "It is the faith of those without faith."[41] Work becomes an enterprise in vanity, sport a distracting spectacle, schooling a mere commodity, sex a form of exercise without deep feeling, aging the end of personal attractiveness and thus of opportunities for sexual fun. Death is simply unthinkable. Marriages lack both genuine feeling and genuine mutuality, divorce merely confirming both partners'—but especially the father's—emotional absence.

These are the symptoms, but the disorder has a precise etiology which Lasch, as historian and advocate of classical maturity-ethic psychoanalysis, develops carefully. To summarize: sharply higher incidents of narcissism as character disorder emerged after the Second World War caused largely by a national shift in economic priorities from production to consumption. Both economic tendencies are to blame. The production economy of the 19th and early 20th centuries removed the breadwinning father from the home, where he formerly farmed or conducted a craft in cooperation with his wife. A father's absence places unreasonable demands upon the mother, unreasonable not just because parenting is hard work but because no one parent should be the sole object of the children's psychological energies. According to this theory, the mother represents to the children primarily an oceanic unity with nature, while the father represents primal authority. The psychic problem with the production economy, then, is the loss of an authority figure in the household during the father's long working hours. Developing children feel this lack especially. This is not a problem primarily because the absent father is unavailable for instruction of the children in healthy responses to the world, or for the modeling of healthy impulses. Rather the father's absence is important to Lasch because, within his psychoanalytic scheme, paternal authority is an important ally of the superego.[42]

Within normal Freudian developmental processes, the infant in a state of primary narcissism acts out feelings of personal grandiosity, fantasies of omnipotence which protect it from full knowledge of its

---

[41] Lasch, *The Culture of Narcissism*, 50-51.
[42] Ibid., 170-75.

absolute vulnerability. During this pre-oedipal stage, if the child is lucky, the mother (as feeding breast rather than complex companion) meets the child's needs. But as the child develops it has wrenching feelings of loss in store. Ordinary development involves growing awareness of the mother's sexual difference if the child is male, and generational difference in any case. The child also encounters evidence of the mother's limitations as a caregiver. The primal sense of omnipotence is shaken. This child has to establish a more realistic view of life's risks. Primary narcissism has been a defense, only temporarily effective, which has helped the child to cope with vulnerability until the superego develops further. This development provides the child with a more realistic view of its place in a civilization of voluntary and involuntary restraints.

Secondary narcissism is another matter. While primary narcissism has a role in natural development toward self-regulating identity, secondary narcissism is a character disorder entailing serious deleterious consequences for the family and society. Lasch's version begins with the centrality of patriarchal authority in the forms of father, teacher, and pastor, and a consequently weakened or underdeveloped social superego when those authority figures disappear or lose authority. Lacking these social helps in its development, the superego turns to primitive fantasies about its parents. These fantasies involve "boundless rage," a spilling-over of the inborn pool of aggression normally devoted to survival and defenses.[43] The enraged superego becomes harsh and punitive. The narcissistic personality emerges not from this rage but from fear of it. This fear is why the narcissist tends to engage only in cool, detached relations with others, in conduct that avoids strong feelings. The narcissist requires decadent and self-centered consolations for the disappointment of no longer having a perfect provider. The flatteries of the consumer society tend to exacerbate this character disorder, as do careless or casual or mistaken therapists who urge upon adherents a personal authenticity or "awareness" that is really solipsism, self-absorption.[44]

Richard Maple epitomizes this adult selfhood; his condition emerges from causes Lasch has identified. As we will see in more detail in the next chapter, Richard recalls a doting mother whose self-centered moods and demands seem to him to have been suffocating. His father

---

[43] Ibid., 176-79.
[44] Ibid., 218.

has been too weak a figure of authority to instill in Richard a sense of independence and functional guilt, both of which Freud says are required for useful work, leisure, and relation in civilization. Richard's ego is apparently unable to resist pre-Oedipal urges for oceanic reunion with the mother-provider, the breast. As a result, he is relentlessly oral, hungry for pleasure and attention, self-serving, and compulsively promiscuous. He justifies his behavior in therapeutic language, implying for instance in the eleventh year of the marriage that he and Joan have "come very far and have only a little way to go" to escape the tyrannical repressions of their mutual marital promises. As Lasch sees it, such

> "Radical" therapeutic wisdom urges men and women to express their needs and wishes without reserve—since all needs and wishes have equal legitimacy—but warns them not to expect a single mate to satisfy them. This program seeks to allay emotional tensions, in effect, by reducing the demands men and women make on each other, instead of making men and women better able to meet them.[45]

And so, because of his existential hunger, Richard feeds his inherited narcissism, accepting early in his marriage the pop-therapeutic message that in order to be emotionally healthy he needs more than one sexual partner.

Updike clearly does not accept or wish to illustrate all of this rather over-determined narrative. Indeed, thanks to his Kierkegaardian commitments, Updike departs sharply from Lasch on one central matter, and is able to close out a logic that Lasch only begins. Updike recognizes that character disorders, like sin, are endemic and out of personal control. Lasch sometimes writes as though secondary narcissism were the personal fault of those afflicted with the disorder. At the very least, he sometimes fails to distinguish those acts and policies for which people are ethically responsible and those emerging from their psycho-cultural narcissism. Thus, part of his opening remarks on "The Sexual 'Revolution:'"

> The "repeal of reticence" has dispelled the aura of mystery surrounding sex and removed most of the obstacles to its public display. Institution-alized sexual segregation has given way to arrangements that promote the intermingling of the sexes at every stage of life. Efficient contraceptives, legalized abortion, and a "realistic" and "healthy" acceptance of the body have weakened the links that once tied sex to love, marriage,

---

[45] Ibid., 200.

and procreation. Men and women now pursue sexual pleasure as an end in itself, unmediated even by the conventional trappings of romance.[46]

Had sexual conduct become cheapened by 1979 because college administrators lacked the moral strength to honor a principle of premarital sexual restraint which might be honored by segregating men and women in different dorms, or because the mothers and fathers of these administrators had failed to provide psychic stays on their infant narcissism? Lasch implies the former, but Updike is more interested in the latter, the complexity of sexual disposition as an endemic condition. When that condition is destructive, Updike is interested in both the misdeed and alienation from God leading to misdeed.

To what extent are the Maples' choices determined by their psychological states? Or, on the other hand, to what extent are the Maples free to create their own relationship and marriage, to honor, if they see fit, the marital standards of Paul's first letter to the Corinthians? For now we can say this: clearly Updike not only presents Richard as a narcissist, but also the Northeastern suburbs as a microcosm of a narcissistic nation, a consumerist feeding system for psycho-existential hungers like Richard's. Joan, on the other hand, seems much better adjusted than the Laschian narcissistic mother, who sees the child as an extension of herself and "lavishes attentions on the child that are 'awkwardly out of touch' with his needs, providing him with an excess of seemingly solicitous care but with little real warmth."[47] On the contrary, Joan is a loving and attentive parent, if somewhat permissive (to my loosely ethical and thus irrelevant sense). Still, Updike does not withhold his ironies regarding Joan, who in "Eros Rampant" (*Harpers*, 1968) self-servingly says of her therapist, "It's not his job to scold me [for my affairs], it's his job to get me to stop scolding myself."[48] Yet in spite of Joan's Maslowian line, hostile to repressions and overconfident in human goodness, Updike seems determined to portray her as a faulty but relatively mature and well-adjusted woman, rather than a victim of narcissistic character disorder. Warmth Joan has, not only for her children but for friends and neighbors too. Updike tends to portray Richard as the more thoroughgoing narcissist and thus as the central problem in the Maples marriage and family. Since Richard's narcissism is partly pathological and partly chosen by him, one of the most difficult

---

[46] Ibid., 191.
[47] Ibid., 171.
[48] Updike, *Too Far to Go*, 137.

critical tasks is to determine when he is authentically responsible for his regular betrayals and acts of cruelty.

In his treatment of Joan, Updike seems to anticipate some of the corrective arguments directed at Lasch's psychoanalytic diagnosis. Most but not all of these arguments come from feminist psychoanalysts, such as Stephanie Engel and Jessica Benjamin, who find in *The Culture of Narcissism* a "nostalgia for paternal authority and the old gender hierarchical family."[49] The Maples stories communicate no such longing. In Updike's work in general there seems to be a greater openness to social changes that Benjamin celebrates. Most of these run counter to Lasch's nostalgia for a pre-industrial, populist society. Benjamin lists the most welcome of these changes: "fewer children per family, shorter working hours for parents, less labor in the home, a culture of family leisure, increased paternal involvement in the early phases of childrearing, and the trend toward understanding rather than merely disciplining children."[50] It is not that Updike writes as a feminist *per se*, but that he thinks dialectically and with an eye toward justice. He likes to balance human error and efficacy in all his characters, and weigh the gain and loss in all social changes in his real and fictive worlds. Marriage is his favorite site for this dialectical weighing. We need to consider how Updike felt that the maturity and esteem ethics contended over marriage, and which ethic he found most persuasive.

Updike questions intersubjective psychoanalytic schemes not primarily because, as Lasch argues, they neglect guilt, thus thwarting maturity and damaging society, but because these schemes solve only penultimate problems, not the existential ones. Also, to the extent that psychoanalytic arguments become clichéd, they contribute to the vapidity of American Christendom. For both Lasch and the therapeutic culture he attacks, religion is merely a form of social order and regime of authority that might be either useful or damaging to the psyche. Lasch sees religion as "*the* organizing framework of American culture," but names only Puritanism and Weberian Protestantism as theologies of humble prospering, orders of repression on "personal aggrandizement"

---

[49] Jessica Benjamin, *The bonds of love: psychoanalysis, feminism, and the problem of domination* (New York: Random House, 1988) 156. See also Stephanie Engel, *The Initial Impact of Psychoanalysis on Feminism in America* (Cambridge MA: Harvard University Press, 1976).

[50] Benjamin, *The Bonds of Love*, 139.

and corrosive vices such as drinking.[51] A modern-day Montesquieu, Lasch thinks of religions as regimes of social control only.[52] He seems unaware of doctrinal, theological or even traditional differences among churches; he just desires an authoritarian ally for the superego. In other words, he desires the regimented Christendom from which Kierkegaard recoils.

Updike and Kierkegaard want solutions to the kind of alienation Lasch describes. Both classical and intersubjective psychoanalytic schemes hold out little hope of breaking cycles of sin and error. If it is true that narcissism recapitulates itself in families and cultures, and that the psychoanalytic community, whose influence is waning anyway, has lost interest in a maturity ethic that might counter the seductions of the consumer culture, then it is unlikely that a powerful alternative to narcissism will emerge any time soon. Even if it does, this alternative ideology may not have the methods required to pierce the psychic defenses of narcissists like Richard. Though we like to believe that our futures are open, and that we routinely rethink our personal dispositions, in narcissism's generational recapitulation freedom and an attractive future seem to evaporate. We know that Updike, generally hopeful, finds that logic hard to accept, even while he accepts that sin is not something we can overcome by merely human effort.

The Updike I read, even the Updike of the early 1970s, would also find it hard to accept both the symbolic sexism of classical Freudianism—the mother as irrational unity and father as enlightening authority—and the kind of direct sexism we encounter in Lasch's vision of the teacher and pastor as attractively "patriarchal" forms of authority.[53] Strong women may sometimes be witches in Updike's work, including the Maples stories, but the imagery is playful and his appreciation for these women's powers is real, when they are non-aggressive and non-narcissistic powers.[54] We join Updike in admiring Joan for her courage in her African-American civil rights work, for her

---

[51] Lasch, *The Culture of Narcissism*, 13, emphasis mine; 71.

[52] Judith N. Shklar, *Ordinary Vices* (Cambridge MA: Belknap Harvard University Press, 1984) 12. Shklar singles out Montesquieu as the epitome of this radical shift in focus, from religion's spiritual benefits to its merely social disciplines.

[53] Lasch, *The Culture of Narcissism*, 11.

[54] In chapter 6 I note more than one bewitching in "Marching Through Boston," and in chapter 10 identify a witch in the Cambridge City Hall in "Here Come the Maples."

knowledge of modern art, for her sharp logic in practical matters such as Richard's logical consistency and the children's safety. The masculinism of psychoanalysis—now undergoing critique—is out of sync with Updike's theology of original sin and redemption, which if it is affected by gender at all does not differ on the question of who sins and who may gain faith. (Answer: men and women both.) Because sin has been with us always, furthermore, accounts of a better day in the past, such as the day of healthful patriarchal authority which Lasch believes he recalls, really do seem to be largely, to use Coontz's great phrase, a way we never were.

However, there is strong evidence that as early as 1963, Updike understood the threat of narcissism to lasting marriages, and wished to take a specific stance on the question of narcissistic personhood as it affects loving, enduring relationships generally. Narcissism is also, after all, the very problem Kierkegaard addresses most often. Excessive or warped self-regard is the central form of resistance to a repentant disposition. Updike accepts and extends Kierkegaard's critique of excessive self-regard. In a long review of Denis de Rougemont's *Love Declared* (1963) and consideration of *Love in the Western World* (1939, rev.1956), Updike considers de Rougemont's sophisticated theological treatment of passion, marriage, the incarnation, and the battle between Eros and Thanatos. The Swiss theologian's project, which Updike endorses, is to establish enduring marriage as existentially superior to ephemeral passion. De Rougemont centers his theory on the myth of Tristan and Iseult, whose problem is that they are not in love with each other, as they believe, but in love with being in love. They crave the feeling of being appreciated, overestimated by the other. Thus erotic love is, in de Rougemont's words, a "twin narcissism."[55]

This is to speak, as Updike sees, in psychoanalytical terms. But de Rougemont is also dealing with a Christian heresy, the neo-Manichaean heresy of Catharism, which denies the incarnation of Christ by rendering the Blessed Virgin an emblem of the church rather than a real woman. Lovers of Catharism, or even lovers of the experience of being in love, hold Creation in contempt. Just as these unknowing heretics find it better to love a disembodied and emblematic Christ, some lovers prefer to prolong the ecstasy of being in love rather than fashioning a quotidian life in mutuality with the real, attainable partner. Notably, Updike employs Kierkegaard's vocabulary and reasoning in this analysis, calling

---

[55] Updike, *Assorted Prose*, 284.

the attainable woman "in legal terms, our 'wife'; in Christian terms, our 'neighbor,'" and naming Christ the "God-man," a locution Kierkegaard uses in *Practice in Christianity* (1850) to refer to Jesus as incarnate deity. De Rougemont's theology is complex, but the importance of the Tristan myth, of the ecstasy we now call Tristanism, is simple. Updike summarizes de Rougemont's central insight this way: "A man in love ceases to fear death."[56] Such ecstatic forgetfulness seems to be psychologically beneficial, but it also keeps people from honoring non-heretical, unselfish, agapic love-in-action. And it leads to painful betrayals such as those caused so often by adultery.

A man in love ceases to fear death: this could be the motto for Updike's fiction, at least the fiction that illustrates Kierkegaard. Yet this is not to say that Updike approves wholeheartedly of the man in love. In this essay, Updike next moves to a consideration of narcissism and its key methodology—Tristanism—as a dialectical tension. We must find ways to restrain our narcissism, he argues, but should not disown it. The narcissist seeks a lover's "overestimation" in which he himself becomes lovely. But there can be a non-narcissistic result to these processes: "The selfish and altruistic threads in these emotions," writes Updike, "are surely inseparable."[57] The love that animates Tristanism also has the potential to animate caritas. The incarnation applies to love in all its forms as well as to the God-man, so that eros and agape are blood kin. If this is so, it is perhaps better to understand rather than condemn the man or woman who falls giddily in love, while remembering that when that love leads to betrayal or pain in others that is an act of cruelty participating in sin. Another "Yes, but—" of dialectical understanding, but one in which eros is an early stage in spiritual evolution and agape the much more desirable evolved stage.

De Rougemont exposes a basic philosophical problem—that God or nature made people sexually avid and giddy while orderly civilization demands that they prefer monogamy and exercise restraint. Yet in Updike's judgment, de Rougemont denigrates Tristanism as heresy rather too quickly, with too little consideration. De Rougemont should have read Kierkegaard more closely, Updike implies, because "[o]ur fundamental anxiety is that we do not exist—or will cease to exist."[58] We are narcissists and so we seek an "other" to overestimate us. This will

---

[56] Ibid., 286.
[57] Ibid., 289.
[58] Ibid., 299.

feel consoling if the other is lover, but much more than consoling if the other is Wholly Other, as Updike implies: "This exalted arena [where we love], then, is above all others the one where men and women will insist upon their freedom to choose—to choose that other being in whose existence their own existence is confirmed and amplified."[59] To choose a beloved is also to choose love. Since God is love, choosing love is choosing God. Thus even erotic love partakes of sacred ideality.

Marriage, Updike implies a few lines later, is unfortunately not certainly a result of proper choosing. The duties of marriage restrict freedom, which is existential and essential to the leap of faith. The purpose and goodness of marriage are underdetermined. Thus erotic love partakes of tragic reality. Updike's marital ideality, which is nowhere better expressed than in this de Rougemont review, preserves the importance of love and unselfing practices as we find them in Luther's and Kierkegaard's idealities, while granting spouses greater freedom to follow their consciences, and even their psyches, in a new historical moment. With this emphasis on God-granted conscience, Updike honors Kierkegaard's core logic—faith by grace leading to love of neighbor—more diligently than Kierkegaard seems to with his talk of rigid, uncreative "exceptions." Updike endorses Luther's loving mutuality in marriage while accounting for both existential and more ordinarily psychological difficulties. And he places responsibility on individual lovers for loving justly and creatively, though they are broken people. But since the God-man is their hero and their model, just and creative these lovers must be.

In his fiction especially, Updike wishes to deconstruct our conception of the great American *bête noir*, the sexual sin, and to direct our attention to the real good news, the imperatives of neighbor-love and community. Unlike many Christians (including, in my experience, many Lutherans), Updike follows Luther in refusing to rate the sexual sin as somehow more wretched than any other sin—and to call into question whether some behavior rated as sin by certain legalistic Christians is really sin at all. As the late Peter Gomes recently and elegantly argued, American Christendom is currently mired in an "extrabiblical prejudice" regarding sexual behavior, especially but not exclusively behaviors associated with homosexuality. Gomes calls instead for an "inclusive gospel," involved in a thoughtful reading of the Bible as a historical document, understood as well as we can manage through the mind of

---

[59] Ibid.

Christ. He argues that Christians should honor "biblical principles that extend beyond the limits of social location and are always and everywhere true: the love of God and neighbor, the example of Jesus Christ, the call to discipleship and service, God's mercy and justice, and, as Roman Catholic theology puts it, the preferential option for the poor."[60]

Updike endorses every word of this description of Christian principles. Not only has he teased out and celebrated love and mercy in Kierkegaard's work, but is on the record, for instance, celebrating "an improved, relatively tolerant" world for American homosexuals, as opposed to the years of gay-bashing he witnessed in his youth.[61] Updike of course focuses more sharply on heterosexual relationships, but in that realm too he wishes to deconstruct the sexual sin, rejecting legalistic judging. Instead, he attempts to understand the potential and power of creative love. For Updike, adultery certainly may be a sin against the sixth commandment of the Old Testament or the commandment to love one's neighbor of the New; it may be a sin against the marriage promise made before God. It may, on the other hand, be a momentary mistake or compulsive habit committed by fallible or even ill men and women who mostly mean well. Is the mistake more execrable than, say, cruel neglect of or emotional terrorizing of a child? Updike seems to like this kind of question, and indeed takes it on directly in the Maples stories, as it becomes clear that Richard's and Joan's betrayals of each other are far less execrable than their betrayals of their children. Updike has little interest in simple, absolutist definitions of marital fidelity, definitions which turn upon sexual thought and action alone. Though Updike's vision leaves him open to charges of ethical quietism, as we have seen, his theological reading helps him to recognize that faithfulness is a complicated matter of both thought and deed emerging from endemic brokenness.

And finally, Updike knows that the real show is not institutional and ethical, as marriage must always be. The real show is existential. Marriage is indeed a new institution in the late 20th and early 21st centuries, complicated and defined by variables that have grown very significant since Updike began this story cycle in 1956. New Christian

---

[60] Gomes, *The Scandalous Gospel of Jesus*, 199-200.

[61] Updike, *Due Considerations*, 464. In this same essay Updike implies support for gay marriage, yet notes that even after the sexual revolution, people tend to "create nuclear families."

marriages have been and continue to be negotiated by contemporary partners in marriage, and when those partners are believers in or seekers of God, they must become theologians, consciously or not. They must interpret the public commandments and private urgings of their God, address the inconclusive either/or of duty and desire, consult their consciences, and navigate their ways into, through, and sometimes out of marriages. In all this, Updike and Kierkegaard argue, they should seek to be just and Christ-like. But their central responsibility is to accept grace and choose themselves as eternally valid.

4

The Maples Marriage and Identity Transformation

> [Jesus] is presented as homeless, propertyless, peripatetic, socially marginal, disdainful of kinfolk, without a trade or occupation, a friend of outcasts and pariahs, averse to material possessions, without fear for his own safety, a thorn in the side of the Establishment and a scourge of the rich and powerful. The problem of much modern Christianity has been how to practice this lifestyle with two children, a car and a mortgage.
> —Terry Eagleton, Introduction, *The Gospels: Jesus Christ*[1]

There is a trajectory to the Maples story, one we will never see if we read the stories as individual performances only. Obviously, the marriage ends in the disappointment of divorce, though a companionable one that allows for Richard and Joan to perform friendly and mutual if intermittent parenting. The existential trajectory of the Maples' individual lives is a different matter. Even though both are degraded and deeply hurt by the conflict in their marriage—perhaps because they are degraded and hurt—Richard and Joan make hopeful progress on the stages on life's way. The degradation and suffering the Maples experience tends to deflate the grandiose selfhood with which each suffers, in differing degrees. Richard particularly requires this deflation, the unseating of his narcissistic self, so that he can begin to see and respond to suffering others, especially Joan.

Though both Richard and Joan experience acute anxiety during the middle and later years of their marriage, suicidal anxiety on Joan's part, they both meet their divorce date with calm acceptance. Years after the divorce decree, both seem psychologically whole, well-adjusted, free from the frantic compulsions of their married years. Has the patient, self-critical, sanguine new grandfather we meet in "Grandparenting" made the leap of faith, or has he simply gained emotional relief resulting from a waning libido and narrowing sexual opportunity? I close this book

---

[1] Terry Eagleton, introduction to *The Gospels: Jesus Christ* (New York: Verso, 2007) xxii.

with an educated guess. This chapter charts the existential progress the Maples make, especially during the married years, within a thick historical facticity.

In a comment he makes in his incisive *Kierkegaard and Christendom* (1981), John W. Elrod provides a likely reason why Updike decided to illustrate Kierkegaard with a series of stories about Richard and Joan Maple: "Kierkegaard noted in *Either/Or* that the self is constituted by social, historical, economic, and cultural factors, as well as by biological and psychological ones, but he did not develop this insight in early writings."[2] Kierkegaard did develop these ideas to some extent in the edifying, non-pseudonymous "second literature" (Elrod's useful phrase), but not with reference to the paradoxes and dialectical tensions of the early pseudonymous literature, including masterworks such as *Fear and Trembling, The Sickness Unto Death,* and *Either/Or.* Elrod realizes that this is a weakness in Kierkegaard's larger argument, as an atomized and abstract self emerges in the first literature. This is a problem, since the passionate, choosing self who leaps into eternity is anything but atomized and abstract. Realizing that this is so, and that the emerging liberal Danish state of the early nineteenth century is significantly different from the American late-capitalist superpower of the mid-twentieth, Updike offers the Maples stories not only as illustrations of Kierkegaard's ideas, but as illustrations in a newly relevant context and richly particular existential situations.

In the Maples stories Updike creates what Mikhail Bakhtin calls a literary chronotope, a depicted social and historical context with a particular authorial inflection and horizon of fictive possibilities.[3] We witness Richard and Joan Maples' actions within a new American Christendom undergoing revolutionary change, as the religious and political regimentation of the early Cold War gives way to a marketplace model of religious and sexual satisfactions, a model that the political structure does not resist but in fact aids and abets. In the prosperous American Northeast especially, as we have seen, a psychotherapeutic community gives further aid, redefining basic existential states and

---

[2] John W. Elrod, *Kierkegaard and Christendom* (Princeton NJ: Princeton University Press, 1981) 87.

[3] Caryl Emerson and Michael Holquist, *Mikhail Bakhtin: Creation of a Prosaics* (Stanford CA: Stanford University Press, 1990) 366ff. As with most of Bakhtin's terms and concepts, these two explain the "chronotope" most clearly and helpfully.

redefining the individual's relationship to a community of neighbors. The Maples cooperate with, and endure, this social context. In this chapter we will consider the Maples story, not stories, in a continuous, diachronic fashion, consulting thinkers who fascinated Updike and clearly gave shape to his treatments of psychological health, authentic love, and genuine faith in Cold War America. These thinkers include especially Sigmund Freud, Erik Erikson, Denis de Rougemont, and Iris Murdoch. The kinship binding these four, and binding them to Kierkegaard's thought and that of Updike's other theological heroes, is their interest in controls on the pathologically grandiose self, as well as help for the anxious, fearful one.

Alice and Kenneth Hamilton claim that the Maples stories amount to a "marriage-history," which has become a truism in the Maples scholarship.[4] The history of a marriage is there, to be sure, but not the typical marital landmarks: ceremonies, holidays, anniversaries, the births of children and celebrations of their accomplishments. Instead, Updike creates fraught moments in which the Maples marriage has come into sharp focus for Richard and Joan. When the story is about conflict rather than mutuality, as most are, Richard especially fails to haul himself back from some emotional precipice and personal indignity. The focus is on choosing. Until Richard, mired in the aesthetic, decides to commit fully to the marriage and to the unselfish love for his wife and his children on which it should ideally be founded, he will have to come up with reasons to remain married and decide again and again to go further with Joan. The occasions for the individual Maples stories are times when any choice, marital or existential, seems most pressing to Richard.

The Maples live in a home dominated by lively talk. In his introduction to *Too Far to Go*, Updike provides us with a broad hint about the importance of language to the Maples stories, telling us that Richard and Joan talk

> more easily than any other characters the author has acted as agent for. A tribe segregated in a valley develops an accent, then a dialect, and then a language all its own; so does a couple. Let this collection preserve one particular dead tongue, no easier to parse than Latin.[5]

---

[4] Alice and Kenneth Hamilton, *The Elements of John Updike* (Grand Rapids, MI: Eerdmans, 1970) 52.

[5] Updike, Introduction to *Too Far to Go*, 10.

Updike's anthropology here is playful, but it does suggest that his concern is with human language use generally, not just the cadences of these characters or of his own first marriage. Updike is concerned with language as an index to moral conditions. In the "Getting the Words Out" chapter of *Self-Consciousness* he dwells specifically on how his stutter affects his speech whenever he feels "in the wrong." The first examples he gives hardly seem indicting. He stutters when reading others' awkward writing aloud, or when speaking to contractors who seem bored and impatient. But further along he lists among those who excite his stutter "children I have harmed," the most important of these his own children after he "left them."[6]

Updike is not simply sharing autobiographical trivia here. In his seemingly associative meditations on speaking with difficulty and speaking with ease he eventually arrives at a psychological theory of sin or malfeasance. In this chapter Updike tells a kind of parable of his own cruelty and its psychological origins. Describing his own claustrophobia and its beginnings (he believes) in a vivid scene in a radio play in which an escaping prisoner is trapped in a prison heating duct, Updike recounts his reluctance to enter into any confined space. Yet, ironically, he causes a similar claustrophobic crisis. His own cruel teasing of his first pet, a dog named Copper, drives the animal into a narrow culvert in which it seems permanently stuck. The dog crawls out after a frightening time, but the thirteen-year old Updike recognizes his responsibility for the near-tragedy. The adult man remembers, and ponders, "What is our tremendous human cruelty, after all, but the attempt to discharge our pent-up private nightmares onto the open ground of actuality?"[7] As though to illustrate this theory, he goes on to describe other personal charges and discharges, his first affair and attempt to leave his marriage in 1962, his seemingly psychosomatic asthma during the Ipswich years of "falling in love with other men's wives," and the re-emergence of his childhood stutter when he finally leaves his wife and children. The final sentence of this chapter identifies the stutter as a "guilty blockage."[8] In each case he associates his guilt with his adultery and the related betrayals and abandonment.

Speech, for Updike, is a bellwether to the frightened, hungry, unconscious self and to its worthy foe, the conscience. Speech emerges

---

[6] Updike, *Self-Consciousness*, 95.

[7] Ibid., 90.

[8] Ibid., 111.

from the self, and reveals that self as essentially guilty, confused, despairing. Kierkegaard's doctrines suggest that the true believer, the knight of faith, has transcended this condition, has foresworn the life of anxiety in favor of the life of faithful calm.[9] But in both Kierkegaard's and Updike's works this claim has a wistful quality. Both authors recognize that this serene Christian life is more ideality than actuality. So is the Christian marriage as described in Paul's first letter to the Corinthians, Chapter 13: "Love is patient; love is kind; love is not envious or boastful or arrogant or rude. It does not insist on its own way; it is not irritable or resentful; it does not rejoice in wrongdoing, but rejoices in the truth."[10] Both authors describe their own faiths lifting them out of a debilitating existential ennui, but not out of the difficulty of living authentically as a Christian or as a whole human being, moment by moment. As Updike's essay about his stutter illustrates, believers are plagued by their own errors, their tendency to be cruel, and their bad faith emerging from biological urges.

In all this sociological concreteness, Richard and Joan are incomplete selves desiring completion. Like all other anxious seekers they desire to be, in Elrod's words, "concrete, identifiable, and worthy, " a deep desire he sees Kierkegaard implying is the "essential motivation of all human activity."[11] What Richard and Joan will have to discover and accept—and perhaps they never do—is a God-granted shift from a socially corrosive self-love (*Elskov*), in which the neighbor is an object to be manipulated and exploited, a means to other ends, to a spiritualized self-love (*Kjerlighed*), in which the neighbor's need provides rightful focus and work for the more fully-realized, worthy self.

&

Just as Updike grew up in a small village a few miles outside the small city of Reading, Pennsylvania, Richard grows up twelve miles outside of Morgantown, West Virginia. His parents drive him into the city for dancing lessons, and teach him the Lord's Prayer.[12] Yet his is not a family of prudes. His mother, interested in *avant garde* ideas and health fads,

---

[9] Kierkegaard, *Fear and Trembling*, eds. and trans. Howard V. Hong and Edna H. Hong, 39-40.
[10] 1 Cor. 13:4-7 (New Revised Standard Version).
[11] Elrod, *Kierkegaard and Christendom*, 188.
[12] Updike, *Too Far to Go*, 53, 149.

sunbathes nude with her young son.[13] He recalls his mother as attentive, one might say doting, waiting up for him even during his high school years of relative independence. But her "blood-deep...moods...and secrets" keep young Richard begging her to speak to him.[14] We never see siblings, but Richard does think (in the late Maples story "Gesturing") about developing his personal act among "parents and grandparents, siblings and pets."[15] Since the word "siblings" here is literally the one word in the Maples stories referring to Richard's unnamed brothers or sisters, he seems to be a psychic if not literal version of the gifted only-child-man we meet often in Updike's short fiction. True to autobiographical form, then, Richard is raised in a Christian home, and is apparently baptized and catechized. (Later, as a father of pre-teens, he even attempts to keep a promise he made in his children's presumptive baptism liturgies, teaching "his" version of the Lord's Prayer to his daughter.) He does well enough in school to be admitted to Harvard, where he earns a bachelor's degree. In Cambridge he meets a Radcliffe student named Joan, a Unitarian clergyman's daughter who now finds the concept of God somewhat oppressive. She had to sit through many sermons as a child.[16] Both study literature and art history most avidly. Even though their colleges do little to support their faiths, neither Richard nor Joan abandons the church. As married adults, they send their kids to Sunday School, apparently attending irregularly themselves. Joan becomes emotionally "agitated" and cries in church. She is more comfortable playing the piano in the children's Sunday school.[17]

---

[13] Ibid., 186.

[14] Ibid., 162. From Updike, *Self-Consciousness*, 84: "As I remember the Shillington house, I was usually down on the floor, drawing or reading, or even under the dining-room table, trying to stay out of harm's way—to dissociate myself from the patterns of conflict, emanating from my mother, that filled the air above my head. Darts of anger rayed from her head like that crown of spikes on the Statue of Liberty; a red 'V,' during those war years, would appear, with eerie appositeness, in the middle of her forehead."

[15] Ibid., 219.

[16] John Updike, "Grandparenting," *The Afterlife and Other Stories*. (New York: Knopf, 1994) 305, 312. Since I cite *Too Far to Go* for the first seventeen Maples stories, in order to retain details that Updike changes in the 2009 *Maples Stories*, I also cite the first non-periodical publication of the final Maple story throughout this book.

[17] Updike, *Too Far to Go*, 120.

In spite of their secular educations, the Maples' dialect is the language of modern American Christendom. Throughout his first marriage, Richard thinks in theological terms, with persistent reference to purity, innocence, the church, the Bible, sin, death, and more. Of course these are Updike's preoccupations, but they are consistent with Richard's character as well. He is a product of a casually Christian home, so he is also complacent yet God-haunted, homesick for a faith that eludes him, or rather, that he eludes. Throughout the course of his marriage he thinks of churches amid skyscrapers gaining proper attention, of God as a tall friend, of rose windows as vaginas, of his children as "blasphemous brats," of presenting his "statistics to eternity," of laying the marriage in its tomb, of loving Alabama state troopers as neighbors, of an afternoon in the rain as his crucifixion, of himself and Joan drunkenly hiding eggs as celebrating Easter, of suicidal self-pity as a sin. When drunk or distressed he imitates characters from Christian melodramas, Tiny Tim of *A Christmas Carol* and Tom from *Uncle Tom's Cabin*. He sees the crowd in a pornographic movie house as characters in *Inferno*. The Maples' cats are named Esther and Esau. More than once, Richard imagines his church funeral. Seeing people naked on a beach he thinks of Adam and Eve, Noah seen naked by Ham, Susannah seen naked by the elders. He believes he has a soul.[18] Just before his divorce is decreed, he thinks of how his vow, "With this ring / I thee wed," will outlast his and Joan's deaths.

None of these is a merely literary reference, or an allusion Updike makes without Richard being aware. They are emanations of Richard's consciousness. Meanwhile Joan says during one marital contretemps that she could believe in a little more bourbon.[19] It is not that she is blasphemous, but that she has greater irony about her own speech and dispositions. Richard and Joan are conspicuously self-conscious, notably literate in theology, and, after college at least, unusually privileged— traits that will give them existential trouble as well as opportunities.

---

[18] Ibid., 220. This citation confirms that Richard believes he has a soul: "Even unseen [the skyscraper] was there; so Richard himself, his soul, was always there." The other narrative details I have just listed in quick succession are cited in discussions of the individual stories in which they appear. I distinguish casual Christian references from specific theological traits or assumptions of the Maples.

[19] Ibid., 121.

They meet in 1952 or 1953, if we presume that their history mirrors that of John and Mary Pennington Updike. It does, in great detail, but with meaningful departures. When filing for divorce, Richard requests a 1954 copy of his marriage license rather than the 1953 marriage year of the Updikes.[20] The reason for this difference is apparently Updike's wish to erase his and Mary's year in Oxford, England while he studied at the Ruskin School of Drawing and Fine Art.[21] We can otherwise, however, have great confidence in the Updike/Maples historical synchronicity. The March 1965 death of Mrs. Liuzzo in Selma, Alabama is one historical detail that confirms our suspicion that both the historical and fictive action of each story occurs just a few months before each story is published.[22]

Richard recalls in "Here Come the Maples" that he first meets Joan in a Harvard English course, English 162b: "The English Epic Tradition, Spenser to Tennyson."[23] They first talk in the library while looking at Blake's illustrations for *Paradise Lost,* and agree to have a beer together after the upcoming exam. Joan never shows up either for the exam or the date because she is hospitalized with a spell of unusual vaginal bleeding resulting from a platelet deficiency. She reports to her interne and then to Richard, as he begins to court her in her hospital room, that she is a virgin. This fact seems to hold some interest for Richard, but Joan is no unsophisticated inferior, no rib of Adam. She is a talented teacher,

---

[20] Ibid., 239.

[21] Rather, there is no mention of the year in England until "Grandparenting" (1994), in which we learn for the first time that Judith was born there. (See Updike, *The Afterlife and Other Stories,* 299.) Updike's first child, daughter Elizabeth, was born in England in 1955. Since Updike seems to use his family life not only as a mine for rich material but as a control on continuity of detail in the Maples stories, he probably felt safe in offering this detail. However, there is a problem. The action of "Snowing in Greenwich Village" recounts autobiographical events that are supposed to occur after the trip to England, yet in that story there is no child. Since no sojourn in England is recorded or mentioned in any story before "Grandparenting," either before or after the Maples' Manhattan years, we seem to have a small continuity problem here.

[22] Ibid., 75.

[23] Ibid., 246. In the original *New Yorker* and *Afterlife and Other Stories* versions of "Grandparenting," Richard recalls the course as a seminar in the English Romantics, which for continuity's sake might be read as Richard's older and faultier memory at work rather than Updike's error. It probably was an error, since Updike corrects it to "a seminar on English-language epics" in the omnibus *Maples Stories.*

musician, art historian and citizen, so there are presumably many reasons Richard is attracted to her.

The Maples' marriage mirrors a sociological trend of the American 1950s: the partners marry young. Wed as college students, Richard and Joan cannot be more than twenty or twenty-one when they become the Maples. Partners in the male breadwinner marriages of the American 1950s married younger than at almost any other moment in Western history. Social historian Stephanie Coontz calls a period from 1947 to the early 1960s the "Golden Age" of American marriage, a brief period of rampant youthful marrying, decreased divorcing, and male breadwinning that many falsely call "traditional" marriage.[24] Traditional or not, the Maples marriage is highly representative of marriages of the depicted years, a time when high male breadwinner salaries and limited professional opportunity for women made the simple or nuclear family the temporary norm.

We learn little about the courtship—just an image of Richard following Joan upstairs in her Cambridge walk-up, he fearing that the landlord will put a halt to their intimate trysts. We know nothing, unfortunately, about the mutual decision to marry. We do learn of middle-aged Richard's sense that both entered the marriage with "the same regressive impulses."[25] Richard's regression is most apparent to us, if not to him, as his parents drive him from West Virginia to Cambridge for the wedding day itself. Not only does Richard ride like a child in his parents' car, but he shelters beneath his coat on the trip, consciously trying to get some sleep but unconsciously expressing some regressive anxiety. Richard may or may not be correct in assessing Joan's state of mind as also regressive. She is shown bathing for the wedding with either her sister or mother in the bathroom with her, perhaps an act of regression to childhood bathing, perhaps not. Richard and Joan are wed in an unnamed Cambridge church in the summer of 1954. Joan is working as a teacher and Richard is still a college student. Both have been living in the Harvard Square area of Cambridge, he in a Harvard Yard dormitory and she a few blocks away in an Avon Street apartment near Radcliffe. The two have been sexually intimate before the wedding, we learn just after they are married. "[T]he whole business, down to the last intimacy, had become formula," Richard thinks.[26] But since in "Wife-

---

[24] Coontz, *Marriage, A History*, 229ff.

[25] Updike, *Too Far to Go*, 251.

[26] Ibid., 25.

Wooing" Richard recalls their sex while on the honeymoon as involving "blood badly spilled" and "clumsiness of all sorts," the Maples have apparently saved full intercourse for marriage.[27] In the flashbacks of "Here Come the Maples" Updike is careful to imply a kind of sexual innocence prevailing between the couple during courtship, and also a casual and wholesome bodily intimacy. On the day of their marriage, Richard knows what Joan looks like in the bathtub. It seems likely, then, that like many couples of the buttoned-up 1950s, Richard and Joan married partly in order to have socially-sanctioned sex. This particular sanction would change quickly after the wedding, both in their lives and in America generally.

Richard and Joan honeymoon in an ocean-side cabin south of Boston, then travel to New Hampshire where they have contracted to work the rest of the summer at a camp on Lake Winnipesaukee.[28] This camp supplies imagery for memories Richard recalls in the days just before his divorce decree—mismatching single beds pushed together in a cabin in the woods, a boat ride across the lake disturbed by loud whistles at each of its stops—images and incidents that imply to Richard's mind the imperfect matching of identities and unexpected shocks that complicate a marriage. Richard's overreaction to the boat whistle illustrates his fundamental anxiety about the marriage: "He both blamed her and wished to beg her forgiveness for what neither of them could control."[29] This is an Augustinian remark about living with one's own and others' original sin, but also a remark about Richard's psychological pathology. Throughout the marriage, Richard's emerging and finally fully flowering identity crisis will involve this confusion amplified: Joan as mother who fails properly to dote, Joan as whore who fails tests of fidelity. Early in their marriage, Richard fails to establish a genuine partnership with Joan, largely because in early childhood he did not separate properly from his controlling, doting mother. He is not wrong to think of himself as regressive, not at any time before the divorce.

---

[27] Ibid., 32.

[28] In other early Updike stories such as "Walter Briggs" (1959) this is a YMCA camp, but its purpose or affiliation is not given in "Snowing in Greenwich Village" as first published in *The New Yorker* or *Too Far to Go*. Updike adds the identifier "YMCA" to the story in both *Early Stories: 1953-1975* (2004) and the Everyman complete *Maples Stories* (2009) for some reason, perhaps the quiet reference to the word "Christian."

[29] Ibid., 245.

We learn nothing of the young Maples' first months of marriage, other than that they spend the first three months at the lakeside camp. Unlike the young Updike family of three, the childless Richard and Joan move to Manhattan in their second year of marriage, where they begin to host the gatherings, usually boozy, that will fuel their marriage's eventual demise. Their very first, rather sober gathering involves only Joan's former college classmate Rebecca Cune and a few glasses of sherry. Richard's fascination with Rebecca, signaling his boredom after only a few months of his wife's lovemaking, suggests that he considers a sexual affair a real risk or possibility. Certainly, he nearly kisses Rebecca in her apartment. Still, there is no indication at this time that Richard is about to begin having regular affairs. Richard's rejection of Rebecca's bodily offer—if Richard does not imagine it—is rather a struggle of conscience, which we have seen is a Kierkegaardian category.[30]

In spite of such temptations, the Maples' marriage remains companionable into its seventh year. "Three children, five persons, seven years," Richard thinks in 1960, have brought "no distance" between himself and Joan.[31] Joan has begun her piano playing at the Sunday School—almost certainly for the children's sake or to answer community expectations, since we notice no religious avidity in her. Because of Richard's self-mockery in this story, it is difficult to tell whether he really embraces the roles of loving father, breadwinner, working professional, and churchman. It seems so: since Richard evokes imagery of girders, right angles, circuits, and grids when thinking about his work, his profession seems to be that of engineer or architect—but Updike clearly wishes the profession not to be definite. Joan seems to have embraced her role at home with the children, perhaps because of limited choices: Richard notes around this time that the Maples' babysitters, inevitably female, move on to "nursing school or marriage."[32] Money seems never to be a problem for the Maples, here or at any later moment in the marriage. The two of them enjoy discussing ideas. Joan reads about Richard Nixon because she hates him, while Richard quotes some unidentified Augustinian theologian—"We're all guilty. Conceived in concupiscence, we die unrepentant"—in a discussion of whether Alger Hiss deserved Nixon's hatred.[33] He and Joan make love regularly,

---

[30] Ibid., 13-28.
[31] Ibid., 30-31.
[32] Ibid., 55.
[33] Ibid., 34.

though not as often as Richard would like. They share in parenting duties, and talk amiably.

At nine years, around the year 1963, the Maples' marriage enters into its characteristic troubles. Clearly, the sexual revolution has become real for the Maples. These troubles seem to stem primarily from Richard's self-obsession and childishness, as when he chides Joan for asking him to give blood on his day off. He expresses his irritation and a general sense of dissatisfaction in attack, calling Joan sexless and smug, and taunting her about her interest in men in their social circle. In interior monologue, Richard admits that he has been employing a strategy of match-making, encouraging Joan to interest herself in male friends of theirs so that he can begin an affair with a friend named Marlene Brossman. But his verbal excesses put him in the wrong—as they often will throughout the rest of the marriage.[34] A pattern emerges in which Richard is sarcastic, self-involved and cruel, apparently tormented by successive failures of his projects for sexual titillation, while Joan responds with weary patience or aloof detachment, and goes about some personally meaningful work.

In Kierkegaardian terms, Richard typically acts out his commitment to the aesthetic, behaving as badly or charmingly as he wishes while he seeks out adventures of sexual and social gaming (rotations), while Joan typically acts out the ethical, keeping her good manners intact and engaging in parental or civic concerns. Richard in his way and Joan in hers are thus fending off full consciousness of their existential situations. Neither has faced up to mortality or made the leap into eternal relation with God. Occupying these two differing spheres does not necessarily indicate a deep incompatibility. On the contrary, the two can make each other a special project, in a social rather than existential sense—Richard helping Joan to broaden her freedoms and realm of pleasures, Joan helping Richard to behave more properly. They can, that is, until the community changes its sexual ethics in ways that happen to accord with Richard's attitudes. As this cultural shift to aesthetic pleasure occurs, Richard and Joan seem to become more confused about their core values. The society's emphasis on health through diminishing repressions conflicts with their own instinctive love for their children and each other, non-erotic love requiring restraints that have nothing to do with physical pleasures. The Maples begin to act out deeper anxieties, often chiding each other over perceived failures and limitations. Though they joke and

---

[34] Ibid., 37-58.

laugh and share ideas and interests during these days, they also quarrel bitterly and often.

Indeed, as events on a 1963 trip to Rome make apparent, Richard suffers unknowing inner despair. He develops pains in his stomach and feet, symptoms with no apparent physical origin. These symptoms are clearly psychosomatic, like the arthritis symptoms he suffers in the mid-70s as the marriage ends. Both sets of symptoms signal an identity crisis in full flower. Updike calls particular attention to behaviors that emerge in later stories and that make Richard seem poorly adjusted: his raving, sarcastic, self-involved speech; his unrestrained sexual desire; his regressive fear of pain and responsibility; his unreasonable belief that another life-partner will decrease his boredom over the long term. In Rome, the pains are linked somehow to visiting churches and ruins, and the indignity of paying exorbitant tips and entrance fees. Richard seems unconsciously disturbed that Rome's churches are mere tourist sites rather than spaces for worship and hopeful understanding of death.[35] This is a Kierkegaardian identity crisis, both psychological and existential-theological.

We have seen that these symptoms are consistent with the condition of secondary narcissism, a result of improper separation from the mother or feeding breast. A hungry, grandiose personality emerges from this Oedipal narcissism, the liberated personality of our time, Lasch calls it, one that reminds us of Richard,

> with his charm, his pseudo-awareness of his own condition, his promiscuous pansexuality, his fascination with oral sex, his fear of the castrating mother..., his hypochondria, his protective shallowness, his avoidance of dependence, his inability to mourn, his dread of old age and death.[36]

As we have seen, Lasch connects this personality with larger disorders in the culture. We need not adopt Lasch's longing for lost patriarchal authority in America to see that Richard epitomizes a fragile therapeutic-consumerist self, now replacing the regimented self of the wartime and immediate postwar period. Describing his own asthma attacks during the 1960s, Updike proposes a practical angle which might apply to Richard's identity crisis: "We didn't know what it was—pure

---

[35] Ibid., 59-72.
[36] Lasch, *The Culture of Narcissism*, 50.

inner demons, or an ingenious psychosomatic mechanism to make my wife feel guilty about being still married to me, or what."[37]

Why does Richard's narcissistic personality shift into full identity crisis at this stage in his married life, and does Joan undergo a crisis of her own? As Erik Erikson argues, the identity crisis typically occurs first in "young people in their late teens and early twenties" who naturally seek an ideology to serve as a center of their personal energy. In *Young Man Luther* (1958), however, Erikson shows vividly how a more mature adult in his late 20s, Martin Luther of course, could also enter into an identity crisis while trying to "learn to derive out of the modes of his psychobiological and psychosexual make-up the prime modality of his creative adaptation." More simply put, Erikson suggests, Luther had to "combine intellectual meaning with an inner sense of meaning it."[38] He had to find a cosmic truth that made sense for himself. Significantly for our purposes, this seeking after a personal ideology often has a religious or quasi-religious character, as the young person seeks a world-view with cosmic overtones—cosmic because for a secularist like Erikson as well as a theist like Kierkegaard, one's well-adjusted identity must account for fears of death. With such a cosmic ideology, a healthy sense of vocational purpose is possible, along with greater maturity and patience in the marital relation. When Updike first read Kierkegaard in the mid-1950s, this was his situation and the outcome of his changed mind—a shedding of some anxieties and the adoption of a vocation. In Richard's and Joan's cases, unlike Updike's, this seeking after an ideology remains thwarted or incomplete. So does their yearning for purpose, for meaningful rather than merely remunerative work, and for a realm in which acts of love make sense rather than frivolous nonsense. Neither enters into a phase of full adult responsibilities with a durable world-view. Whether the struggle to do so is within their ken is an interesting question. However, according to both psychoanalytic and existentialist schema, both Richard and Joan should be in crisis.

Indeed they are, both in Rome and the rest of the marriage after that 1963 journey. They live in deep uncertainty about their world-views, act continually in bad faith, and flout promises they have made. They accept counseling which emphasizes needs of the ego, gives license to the id, and dangerously denigrates the work of the superego. In Kierkegaardian

---

[37] Updike, *Self-Consciousness*, 99.

[38] Erik Erikson, *Young Man Luther: A Study in Psychoanalysis and History* (New York: Norton, 1993) 176.

terms, Richard is in crisis because as he dwells in a thoroughly aesthetic sphere, he cannot meet the ethical demands of his marriage and family. Joan, it seems, is brought into full crisis by her husband's selfishness. She is vulnerable to this crisis because of a naïve ethical commitment, unleavened by a functional ideology that acknowledges the incorrigibly iniquitous behavior of all, and the redemptive hope that Kierkegaard says emerges from faith. The two cannot quite convince themselves that their childhood Christian world-views are completely silly. Mainly they seek to live in a world that they consider more sophisticated than that of their childhoods, even while their sophistication causes them pain.

On the other hand, Joan seems to gain surprisingly genuine purpose when in the spring of 1965 she joins the freedom marchers in Alabama. Joan is putting her life at risk, so the depth and seriousness of her inner ethical commitment become clear. On her return flight home she learns of the assassination of the historically real Mrs. Liuzzo of Detroit. Like Joan a suburban wife and mother, Liuzzo had been shocked by televised images of marchers being beaten at the Edmund Pettis Bridge. She flew to Alabama to work with civil rights activists. Driving in a rural area after a march in Selma on March 25, 1965, she was shot in the head and killed. Here we come to understand another dimension of Joan's deeply ethical character. She is committed to social justice as well as to interpersonal kindness. This is consistent with Kierkegaard's notions of the ethical, which in his mind springs from a universal and God-granted human equality. Though the ethical is a stage that must be transcended for genuine communion with God and full realization of the other as worthy individual, Kierkegaard sees the stage as a gift springing from God's love. In his Victorian way, Kierkegaard argues that women live in the aesthetic stage, dwelling upon the physical immediacy of the domestic realm. He argues, in fact, that women who make the leap of faith often do so *"ex tempore"* directly from the aesthetic.[39] Updike observes a different pattern. Like Kierkegaardian novelists Walker Percy and David Lodge, Updike updates Kierkegaard's schema with a new view of women, granting them the capacity not only to live in the ethical but often to epitomize that stage.[40]

Joan's civil rights work is not only an illustration of Kierkegaardian categories though. John Updike's autobiography is involved. Mary

---

[39] Malantschuk, *The Controversial Kierkegaard*, 56.

[40] See, for example, Percy, *The Moviegoer*, in which Aunt Emily epitomizes the ethical stage, and Lodge, *Therapy*, in which Sally does.

Pennington Updike also took part in the freedom marches. She was raised to honor the ethical, to view ethical goodness as intrinsic to the religious experience. Her father, the Reverend Leslie Pennington, was a well-known Unitarian pastor who was, as one amateur historian writes, "especially prominent in advocating international peace and promoting neighborhood racial integration." Pennington himself leaves little doubt about his commitments when he writes in 1950 about "the essential condition of maturity in high ethical religious faith."[41] This equation of ethics and religion was not persuasive to Updike. He devotes an emphatic passage of *Self-Consciousness* to Pennington and his Unitarian church, noting that he loved his father-in-law but could not accept his idea of God, a God with no attributes. Updike connects Unitarianism with the ethics of his Emersonian friends, such as one who asserted that personal extinction is less of an existential problem than "global pollution."[42] Though Joan feels some ideological and psychological distance from her apparently Unitarian father's commitments, she lives out these Unitarian/Emersonian ethical views.

Richard, on the other hand, is no nearer Updike's stance when he expresses great skepticism about the motives of Dr. Martin Luther King and other civil rights leaders, questions the purity of his wife's passion for justice, and doubts the efficacy of marches like the one in which he reluctantly takes part in Boston. His objections are far from principled. Richard simply cannot stand attention being diverted from himself—even while he recognizes and honors human need around him. Perhaps because of this inner contradiction, he has a psychotic break on the trip home from the march. It is an alarming episode, Richard raving in racist imitation of the day's speakers, seemingly unable to stop. The episode frightens the Maples children badly.[43] Like the psychosomatic symptoms of a few years earlier, these behaviors indicate Richard's severe inner turmoil.

We do not see another such episode for years. Both Richard and Joan find other less civically engaged outlets for their overflowing energies. Seemingly because of dissatisfactions stemming from their

---

[41] Alan Seaburg, "Leslie Pennington." In *Dictionary of Unitarian and Universalist Biography*, an on-line resource of the Unitarian Universalist History & Heritage Society, 1999-2013. http://www25.uua.org/uuhs/duub/
articles/lesliepennington.html.

[42] Updike, *Self-Consciousness*, 132-33.

[43] Updike, *Too Far to Go*, 83-90.

fundamental political differences, in the thirteenth and fourteenth years of their marriage, 1967 and 1968, Richard and Joan commence a series of poorly concealed affairs. Simultaneously, Joan stops her work for social justice. She has her own reasons, we suppose, but there also seem to be some of which she is unaware. Updike explains in a 1975 essay: "Freud more than Marx would bias our lives; the suburban home would replace the city street as the theatre of hopes; private fulfillment and not public justice would set the pace of the pursuit of happiness."[44] This would remain true, he tells us, beyond the mid-sixties, when because of the Vietnam war the public and private realms would begin to chafe against each other. Yet the Maples' own interests demonstrate Freud's longer-term victory over Marx (read: sexual freedom over political consciousness), as marching through Boston was a brief experiment. For Joan as well as Richard, cocktail parties, intimate lunches and dinners, and sometimes sexual encounters in hotels and lovers' homes become primary diversions. As Philip Rieff argues throughout *Freud: The Mind of the Moralist*, by 1959, "psychological man" begins to define culture. Even when this man is a woman, the pursuit of health in therapeutic terms "takes precedence over social concern and encourages an attitude of ironic insight on the part of the self toward all that is not self," including, apparently, African-American kids needing better schools in the Maples' Boston.[45]

The brevity of Joan's civil rights work, and her adoption of many of the traits of the aesthetic stage afterward—social gaming, sexual self-indulgence, preoccupation with psychological and physical fitness—signal the beginnings of her own crisis. But the crisis has roots in the ethical, which for Joan was not fully-enough realized. Kierkegaard would agree with Freud that the natural person is essentially narcissistic, certainly so in the aesthetic stage and less obviously but just as certainly in the ethical. For the ethical person, the other exists as an object of duty, and deserves one's ameliorating efforts, but exists in the abstract only, as a means to the quasi-altruist's improved feelings rather than a radically valuable end in herself. The reason: the ethical subject still seeks personal consolations for a dreadful existence, even while working on behalf of the other. This is true even of Joan's otherwise admirable freedom marching, as Richard sees. Thinking apparently of the Biblical injunction

---

[44] Updike, *Hugging the Shore*, 201.

[45] Philip Rieff, *Freud: The Mind of the Moralist* (Chicago: University of Chicago Press, 1979) 329ff.

to love your enemies, Richard asks her whether she isn't "to love the troopers" who oppose freedom marchers. "Only abstractly," Joan answers, "Not on your own.... Once you're in a march, you have no identity. It's elegant. It's beautiful."[46] Apparently, in the rush of self-esteem that Joan feels in this important work, she begins to feel the false satisfactions of the aesthetic stage. Kierkegaard would say that she is being a good citizen, but not Christ to her very particular neighbor. Unfortunately, her self-diagnosis, that she "has no identity," is largely and unfortunately correct, according to Kierkegaard's notions of authentic identity.

Updike has written that the American civil rights movement was one of the most heartening religious movements of modern times. He notes that King's methods were based in a coherent Christian theology as well as other influences.[47] But here he ironizes Joan's sense of her ethical work and its aesthetic benefits. For Kierkegaard, one never loves anyone else "abstractly," and seeking identity is the mission of life. Identity and neighbor love are logically linked. Egotistic self-love is sin—egotism is separation from God—but loving oneself with God's aid (grace) is qualitatively different. Choosing oneself as a radically valuable end, one suddenly finds it possible to love others as radically valuable ends also. Elrod goes so far as to argue that unless the believer turns to the neighbor in loving action, she has not in fact made a genuine leap of faith. Valid identity simply requires the other.[48]

Ironically, the force that brings the Maples closer to their own leaps is despair over various dissatisfactions and dangers of adultery. As Jane Barnes notes, Richard seems to seek out the adventure of his affairs, while Joan's seem merely retaliatory.[49] In this way Joan's adultery is consistent with her ethical stance: Do unto him as he is doing unto you. The chilling inadequacy of such a world-view is exactly why the ethical deconstructs itself, according to Kierkegaard. In stories such as "A Taste of Metal," "Your Lover Just Called," "Waiting Up," "Eros Rampant," and "The Red-Herring Theory,"—that is, from the middle 1960s to the middle 1970s—both Richard and Joan speak very frankly with each other about the people they've slept with, and neither seems to feel much

---

[46] Updike, *Too Far to Go*, 74.

[47] Updike, *Due Considerations*, 30.

[48] Elrod, *Kierkegaard and Christendom*, 80.

[49] Jane Barnes, "John Updike: A Literary Spider." In *John Updike*, ed. Harold Bloom. (New York: Chelsea House, 1987) 119.

regret about their own infidelities. However, these mutual revelations always cause both Maples to feel shock and pain.

Richard and Joan have adopted the sexual ethic of their place and day. Sociologists Stephen Mintz and Susan Kellogg argue in *Domestic Revolutions* that during the very years of the Maples' marriage we see "the proliferation of loose, noncontractual sexual relationships [that] are symptoms of increasing selfishness and self-centeredness incompatible with strong family attachments."[50] They note that self-fulfillment and liberation theorists such as Norman O. Brown and Herbert Marcuse argued during these years for an emancipation of the libido, a new responsiveness to pleasure-seeking life instincts, or, as Marcuse put it, the "free gratification of man's instinctual needs." This emphasis on gratification is consistent with, or symptomatic of, a new societal emphasis on "autonomy, independence, growth, and creativity," which he saw as existing in opposition to the marital and courtship status quo.[51]

Even those American citizens not reading Brown or Marcuse seemed to be getting the message: Mintz and Kellogg report—and somehow equate—news stories from the 1950s citing suburban wife-swapping, drug and alcohol abuse, and battering of children, among other seeming consequences of emerging commitments to self-gratification.[52] Like Updike, though for different reasons, these sociologists have very serious concerns about "free gratification" as an alternative to marital fidelity and other social ethics under attack.

This dialectic between sexual gratification and moral authority becomes vivid to Richard in the winter of 1967, as he and Joan leave a cocktail party. The Maples offer a ride home to Eleanor, a woman Richard desires. Richard is very drunk and the roads snow-covered. He drives carelessly, loses control, and slams his new Corvair into a telephone pole. Joan walks for help, and though Eleanor now has a seriously injured leg, Richard kisses and gropes her, even as a police car arrives.[53] Richard's drinking is an increasing problem, but the larger problem here is his increasing contempt for social codes regarding marital respect, care for a hurt neighbor, safety of the community, and

---

[50] Stephen Mintz and Susan Kellogg, *Domestic Revolutions: A Social History of American Family Life*. (New York: Macmillan, 1988) 204.

[51] Ibid., 206.

[52] Ibid., 194.

[53] Updike, *Too Far to Go*, 91-100.

obedience to reasonable law. Beyond law, Kierkegaard notes, there are the obligations of conscience.

In the late 1960s, the Maples begin dealing with their society's, and thus their own, changing notions of valid authority. Updike is certainly attentive to the sexual revolution, but also attentive to a less sinister but no less transforming shift to a matriarchal domestic realm focusing on the children. As the dominant parent, Joan seems to epitomize the unconditional love and regard urged upon parents by Dr. Spock, and also the parental permissiveness of which Spock is often and perhaps unfairly accused. She speaks of respecting the children as individuals, an ironic remark given that her own ethical viewpoint is so thoroughly involved in the diminution of individuality. Richard is even more permissive, as his parental style is shaped by his daytime absence (he commutes thirty-some miles to Boston every workday) and leisure-time indifference to, or rather moral quiescence about, the children's lives. Thus he contributes to Joan's matriarchal dominance. The roles he takes with the children—"scoutmaster, playmate, confidant, financial bastion, factual wizard, watchman of the night"—feel to Richard like impersonations.[54] He directs less energy and imagination to his kids' benefit than to the financial, social and erotic contacts he finds at cocktail parties and workday luncheons. Like his friend Mack Dennis, Richard strikes us as one who might be surprised to discover when his divorce is finalized that he misses his kids.[55]

When Richard accuses Joan in 1967 of having a recent affair, she replies sarcastically, "My days are consumed by devotion to the needs of my husband and his many children."[56] In fact, Joan has been spending time on an affair of her own, as well as tennis, yoga, and volunteering in the community. Of course exercise and leisure are important to a balanced life, but Updike also hints here that neither Joan nor Richard seems very devoted to the children. Even when Richard tries to express his vestigial Christianity, joining his little daughter in a bedtime prayer, he surrenders to her embarrassment—"Daddy, no, don't!" He recognizes that he is too easily embarrassed in this situation, too prone to retreat from what he recognizes as his vocation as nominal Christian parent. He prefers to protect himself from unpleasant or even strong emotions.[57]

---

[54] Ibid., 127.
[55] Ibid., 105.
[56] Ibid., 103.
[57] Ibid., 149.

Joan also finds church too emotional, as we have seen. We recall that Lasch predicts exactly this behavior from contemporary narcissists. They are typically promiscuous; their relations with friends and family are cool and distant; they are emotionally unavailable to the children even while congratulating themselves for their skill and good sense in parenting.

These references to learning prayers and attending church hint at Updike's interest in the eroding social disciplines of Protestant culture under erosion, the failure of modern Protestant parents to meet or even approach the promises they make in the baptism liturgy to teach the fundaments of creedal Christianity to children.[58] Neither a matriarchal nor patriarchal dominance is required for this teaching, and when these practices are authentic, Kierkegaard argues, they do not partake of the moribund character of Christendom. (His entire second literature is devoted to the study and reasonable application of Biblical scripture.) Notably, the Maples children resist talk of religious matters, and come to repeat and even trump Joan's ethical and Richard's self-oriented aesthetic commitments. Judith emerges as the pious vegetarian, the ethical "sociologist" (according to her irritated brother), while Dickie and John struggle with boredom and other preoccupations of the self-involved inner life. These children also enact typical teenaged Oedipal dramas of misdirected libido (teenager Judith French-kisses her mother goodnight), incestuous energy (Dickie "finds his sister's body painful" and notes how she "flaunts her charms"), and, like their father, aggressive speech (Judith to her brother: "You and a very *spoiled* and *selfish* and *limited* person!").[59] While this behavior in teenagers seems developmentally normal enough, we wonder whether the Maples children will someday improve upon their father in his limited ability to develop properly past these psycho-dramas. We receive a minimal answer. Judith is the only Maple child we meet as a thirty-one-year-old

---

[58] I am speaking here of Updike's Protestantism, which is represented in the Maples stories by Richard's sketchy Lutheran upbringing. (He teaches his children a specifically Lutheran version of the Lord's Prayer, while his daughter is learning an Episcopalian version at church.) In a Lutheran baptism service, parents promise to bring children to church, to teach the Lord's Prayer and certain creeds. I recognize that Joan too learned a form of the baptism service from her Unitarian father, one in which the child is celebrated as new life, a gift from God, but in which parents make no promises to instruct children in creedal or catechetical matters.

[59] Updike, *Too Far to Go*, 124, 173.

adult, in the mid-1980s, and then only for a few moments the day after she delivers her first child. She seems well-enough-adjusted—but then we know nothing of her inner life, either its past or its future. Neither she nor her husband speaks of God or faith.

As I will argue much more fully in readings of the later Maples stories, Richard and Joan conduct their affairs according to a rather complex etiquette widely accepted among their friends. There seems to be a general agreement among the participants that repressions are unhealthy, so people should seek increased sexual freedom. Updike routinely connects this ethic with Freud's writings, but psychoanalytic historians make clear that Freud saw at least some repression as necessary for civilized, well-adjusted restraint. Actually, Updike and his characters assign to Freud the tenets of a certain mid-century interpretation of his theories, one in which sexual license means health. The Maples and their neighbors apparently pick up this message from the popular culture too. People have been reading Norman O. Brown and Herbert Marcuse, and listening to their therapists. The Maples are also close to friends who conduct quasi-open marriages, such as the Masons,[60] who model an etiquette of adultery that at first surprises Joan. She is no prude herself. She has been sleeping with Mack Dennis, but is shocked when Richard's affair with Mrs. Mason is exposed—not shocked at Richard's philandering but at the Masons' determined etiquette in a subsequent discussion. They tell Joan to be angry, implying that emotional honesty is imperative, but they will not in fact allow her an honest emotional reaction. They think that indignation is childish. They encourage her to adopt an attitude in which she willingly gives Richard away—for sexual trysts—as a gift to dear friends. They believe that all four of them should help each other to realize greater freedoms. Joan realizes that this is not so much an etiquette as a creed: "It was like church...." Joan feels she is going crazy, but only because she retains vestigial standards of marital fidelity and moral limits, standards that don't finally have much purchase on her.[61]

Her confused feelings on this night lead to no new existential commitments, but rather, to ethical commitments much like those of the Masons. In succeeding months and years, she and Richard both have affairs, unapologetically. The etiquette seems to be primarily aesthetic,

---

[60] I cannot refer to the Masons by first names; for his own reasons, Updike refers to them otherwise as "he" and "she" only.

[61] Updike, *Too Far to Go*, 118-20.

not a code based in human dignity, worth, and natural rights. According to this code, flirtation may be public and known to all, including marital partners, but affairs themselves are to be conducted discreetly. If and when an affair is exposed the participants and others affected are supposed to speak honestly and directly about both the history of the affair and feelings it conjures. The honesty is limited by community standards, though. Once the other spouse knows about an affair, it is "grotesque" for the lovers to continue sleeping with each other[62]—a hint that these neighbors are more invested in illusion and delusion than in honesty and frankness. Joan is less sure than her neighbors that indignation is so childish.

Between approximately 1967 and 1971, or the thirteenth through sixteenth years of the Maples' marriage, Joan and Richard both begin to undergo psychoanalysis. In fact, both can be said to adopt a therapeutic model of existence, a model Updike presents as problematic. Not only does this ethic lack the only real ground for healthy identity Updike and Kierkegaard regard as valid—God's assistance in forming unselfish conscience—but it actively thwarts such a grounding. Richard and Joan, with their vestigial Christian consciousnesses, must sense something like this, as they maintain a certain irony about their therapies. This irony arises, it seems, from their youthful Christian training with its moral fundamentals—ideal scriptural descriptions of love and marriage, for instance. Joan is perhaps the more trusting of the two in her therapist's counseling, telling Richard sometime in 1968, "It's not his business to scold me, it's his job to get me to stop scolding myself." Normally a Maslowian, here she has accepted a Marcusan ethic, the idea that one should throw off the yoke of the superego and of repressive institutions generally, that one should resist "normalization" on all fronts. Marcuse was particularly hostile toward what he called the heterosexual family. It is not clear that either of the Maples' therapists actively invites them to abandon each other and shed the family life. If so, Richard and Joan miss the larger point, both moving from divorce to another family situation immediately. Yet it becomes clear that, partly because of the messages they receive in therapy, Richard and Joan find themselves balked on questions of identity and purpose. Should they, like their therapists, be wholly hostile to normalization when the "normal" includes their home, careers, and kids? Joan doesn't think so. Around 1968, she feels that her

---

[62] Ibid., 136.

affairs have gotten out of control, and she looks to her analyst to help her curtail them.[63] She does not receive that help.

Both she and Richard begin to express their relationship problems primarily in therapeutic-developmental language. They have throughout their marriage, but never so consistently as in these years of marital crisis. Richard says, for instance, during their 1963 trip to Rome that they have "come very far" in pursuing their marriage toward its expected end.[64] Again, in the early 1970s, as the Maples plan the delayed separation they have already announced to the children, Joan says, "Things are stagnant...stuck; we're not going anywhere."[65] Both remarks imply the presumption that marriage is a process of development, that it must go somewhere—a presumption Iris Murdoch, a long-term favorite of Updike's, satirizes in her great anti-therapeutic novel *A Severed Head* (1961).[66]

Updike read and enjoyed this novel in the early-1960s, and some of its satire resonates in the Maples stories. The novel's central character, Martin Lynch-Gibbon, has been conducting an affair, but finds himself shocked, hurt, and indignant (or wishing to be) when he learns that his wife and psychoanalyst have been conducting an affair of their own. He struggles with this logical inconsistency. The analyst, Palmer Anderson, urges Martin to accept the current *ménage* because, he asserts, all of them can use the situation to help each other grow. Martin's wife Antonia agrees, saying that the marriage is going nowhere. Martin complains that a marriage is not a conveyance, which is only the beginning of his indignant resistance to Palmer's cant, to his own moral and ethical inconsistency, and to a culture devoted to delusional self-aggrandizement. After enduring a number of further shocks and indignities, Martin relinquishes his own affair and commitment to almost total sexual freedom. This outcome accords with Murdoch's philosophical writings, especially *The Sovereignty of Good* (1970), in which she finds secular substitutes (some, ironically, drawn from Freud's works) for Kierkegaard's key terms—original sin, repentance, reformed conscience, and identity.[67]

---

[63] Ibid., 137.
[64] Ibid., 61.
[65] Ibid., 213.
[66] Iris Murdoch, *A Severed Head* (New York: The Viking Press, 1961).
[67] Iris Murdoch, *The Sovereignty of Good* (New York: Ark Publishing, 1985.

Updike's appreciation for Murdoch's work, which we find in book reviews and other allusions throughout his career, is not surprising, given that she too works out a philosophy that calls for controls on the grandiose self, and illustrates that philosophy in realistic fiction. He tells us that *A Severed Head* reached Ipswich in the early 1960s as a "species of news," sexual news to his neighbors, that is.[68] Updike seems to have heard another kind of news in the novel: that a rhetoric of total moral freedom is logically inconsistent.

For the most part, Richard and Joan do not question their own affairs or freedoms, not after the first contretemps with the Masons in 1967 or 1968. Certainly they experience no epiphany of conscience like Martin Lynch-Gibbon's. They turn their freedoms into consoling games, engaging in a variety of psychological experiments and moratoria, such as diagnosing each other's stratagems for concealing affairs and refraining from sex in order to better understand the mental-emotional dimensions of their relationship. But all of this play has a severe cost. At one point during this period, Richard half-jokingly reports admiring Joan's "discreet death wish."[69] This wish will seem less funny to Richard as it grows less discreet. In 1975, as the Maples' marriage finally collapses, Joan threatens to kill herself. She feels "suicidal, depressive, beaten."[70] Updike is aware of the irony. Joan and Richard have viewed themselves as psychological subjects, and have carefully tended their psychological health. They have based this health on an ethic of sexual freedom, but the possibility of realizing that health-conferring benefit seems to have collapsed even before the marriage.

During 1971, Richard also displays vivid symptoms of his own maladjusted death wish. As the Maples move from one house to another, we find Richard obsessed with death, as he reviews events that occurred in the house he is leaving. Most depressingly, he remembers a quarrel with Joan that finally turned violent. She throws a book at him, nearly choosing a more dangerous ashtray. When he speaks back defiantly, she hits him, and he punches her side, realizing unkindly that she is merely "a sack of guts." The children watch it all. They "sneak quietly up and down the stairs, pale, guilty, blaming themselves, in the vaults of their innocent hearts, for this disruption."[71] Perhaps because he realizes the

---

[68] Updike, *Due Considerations*, 563.
[69] Updike, *Too Far to Go*, 219.
[70] Ibid., 232.
[71] Ibid., 149-50.

kind of pain he has begun to cause his wife and children, Richard's psyche turns toxic. Things remind him of death: his wrecked car, his dental work, his home's aging plumbing. He cannot respond to his daughter's question about her eventual death.[72] He prunes a bush with such aggression that his children are shocked, and he teases them about forced trimmings of their hair. More aggressively, he suggests to his sons that they try out a school-project guillotine on themselves. Not only is he un-funnily aggressive, but as he reports to Joan, he now dreams of death:

> "I keep having this little vision—it comes to me anywhere, in the middle of sunshine—of me dead."
> "Dead of what?" [Joan asks.]
> "I don't know that, all I know is that I'm dead and it doesn't much matter."[73]

Years before, it was the "exploded civic dream" of Rome that threw Richard into a night terror, and helped produce painful psychosomatic symptoms. Now, nearly ten years later, as he attends parties where people argue about Vietnam, the terrors recommence for new reasons. Richard and Joan seem desperately uncomfortable with their many recent affairs, with the civil war that has become their marriage. Richard dreams of Joan confessing affair after affair, of her describing to him newly learned coital position after coital position. She admits in this dream that she willingly has sex with any man who comes to the door, such as a septic tank salesman.[74] The imagery of human filth communicates some of the complexity of Richard's deeper feelings about such promiscuity. Richard knows that their death wishes and fears are involved. He muses about himself and Joan, who have become characters in his memories: "What are they saying, what are these violent, frightened people discussing? They are discussing change, natural process, the passage of time, death."[75]

Still, the Maples weather these dark days, eventually reaching individual conclusions about their future. Richard wants a divorce, and Joan does not. Sometime in 1971, Richard begins the final affair of his first marriage with a woman named Ruth. She will become his second

---

[72] Ibid., 153.
[73] Ibid., 171-78.
[74] Ibid., 142.
[75] Ibid., 150.

wife. Joan begins an affair with her eventual second husband, Andy, around this time as well, but makes clear that she is ready to drop the relationship if Richard will only ask her to.[76] But he will not. He is determined to move on to a freer future—though ironically this future also involves another marriage. Richard's somewhat contradictory persistence wins out, and in June of 1974 he and Joan announce to their children their intention to separate. They express this separation as a temporary trial, but all five of the Maples know or sense the truth. This is the break-up of the family household, if not the family. Three of the children object only briefly, but Richard's namesake elder son fills Richard with dread by asking, "Why?" Richard has forgotten why. Nothing comes to mind, not lover Ruth's desirability, not his own need to be happier, not his frustrations with Joan—none of the reasons he has spoken to Joan. The elder Richard's conscience seems to be at work. He makes no rational calculation about what he can or should say in reply to Dickie's "Why?" A force in him simply will not allow him to speak, to explain himself, wretched as he feels.[77]

During the next few summer months, Richard occupies a seaside shack only two miles from home, where he returns for meals and occasional sexual favors from Joan. His actions suggest that he is less committed to this separation than he says. During this period, Joan too seems to back water on the decision to separate, gladly accepting Richard's company. But in September of 1974 she finally invites Richard to move out of the family house. Her suggestion is a bluff, but it double-crosses her when Richard agrees. Thus neither of them really chooses this divorce genuinely—a perfect illustration of the non-choosing life Kierkegaard predicts prior to the leap of faith. Richard takes an apartment on Boston's Beacon Hill, where he has a view of the brand-new but window-shedding John Hancock Tower. He and his presumptive second wife Ruth meet at the apartment for naked floor-cleaning and sexual fun. Though Joan is also deeply involved with Andy, she too visits Richard for conversation and sexual benefits—a situation that offends Ruth ("In *our* bed?"), who apparently expects Richard to observe a sexual fidelity with her that she did not expect him to honor with Joan. Living in Boston, Richard sustains this separation for about two years. These are not completely contented years. After a year and a half Joan enters into her period of suicidal depression. Richard's

---

[76] Ibid., 214.
[77] Ibid., 192-211.

happy moratorium from his marriages, present and future, is over. Joan wants Richard to come back to her, to renounce the happiness and health he has found since the separation began. Richard refuses to return, telling Joan that her seemingly genuine contemplation of suicide is a sin.[78] It is ironic that for Kierkegaard, sin is separation from the source of love.

The Maples' marriage ends in 1976, just as the laws of the Commonwealth of Massachusetts allow for no-fault divorces. Thus, the Puritan pieties that for better or worse gave rise to the first state in Massachusetts give way to the pervasive moral relativity in the modern State of Massachusetts. Richard and Joan undergo the legal proceedings with great calm and mutuality, driving together to the courthouse and sharing private moments behind the backs of their lawyers. Liberally educated, they realize the scene is a Daumier. Apparently Joan has overcome her depressive, suicidal emotions. Richard and Joan seal their divorce decree with a friendly kiss.[79]

This mutuality is more than merely temporary peace, as we will see some ten years later. In 1986, Richard and Joan come together in parental partnership once again, as Judith goes to the hospital in labor with her first child. Both Richard and Joan seem to have functional second marriages, yet second spouses Ruth Maple and Andy Vanderhaven display evident and similar personal limitations—impatience, petulance, jealousy, insecurity, intellectual simplicity—while the former Maples share a witty sense of humor, a broadly philosophical outlook, knowledge of each other's habits,[80] a daughter they love, and now a grandchild. We shouldn't be surprised at the companionability. As the final three stories of *Too Far to Go* unfold, Updike gives special attention to Richard's and Joan's compatibility, their common love of wit and art and conversation. He also pays attention to the one issue they never discuss, the sanctity of the marriage bond that both of them seem to feel but only Richard expresses, and then only through his interior monologue: "...these lovers [who are about to become second spouses], however we love them, are not us, are not sacred as reality is sacred. We are reality. We have made children. We gave each other our young

---

[78] Ibid., 212-235.

[79] Ibid., 236-256.

[80] Joan brings Richard crackers with his soup, though Andy would refuse them, and Richard didn't request them.

bodies. We promised to grow old together."[81] But the Maples are now the Maples and the Vanderhavens, and after witnessing their first grandchild's birth, Richard and Joan go their separate ways without conscious regret.

જી

Of course there is a cost to this exercise of treating the Maples' marriage as a continuous story rather than eighteen discreet moments. Through the interpretive work of the next six chapters, I try to repay the greatest cost by attending, as I have only sparingly here, to the particular expressions, emblems, and ironies of the individual stories. What we gain from the unified story is some clarity on the nature of Richard's identity transformation across forty years, and to a lesser extent, the nature of Joan's. Rarely have scholars even mentioned any change from story to story in Richard's or Joan's emotional states—a reasonable omission since these scholars have expressed no particular wish to find Kierkegaardian content or otherwise chart emotional changes across the Maples stories. Though when we do chart the Maples' mental and emotional changes, and set them in relief against material and ideological changes in their lives, we discover that the stories present definite signs of Kierkegaard's causes of identity transformation. Richard and Joan both feel increasing dread in the fifteen or so years leading up to their divorce, partly because this is inevitable for those living in the aesthetic and ethical stages, and partly because the two of them, with the help of their suburban subculture, make particularly dreadful choices that lead them to become ever more personally grandiose. Kierkegaard would say that the two of them, during their married years at least, moved more deeply into sin, experienced pain, and unknowingly felt the sickness unto death.

Beyond this transformation to the Maples' identities, Updike offers contemporary fictional corollaries to a range of deeply human responsibilities with theological resonance for himself and other orthodox or neo-orthodox Christians. These include regarding husband and wife as one flesh (or blood), honoring parental and community promises of the baptism ritual by teaching and protecting children, contemplating historical theologies of royal responsibility as models for general human responsibilities, admitting the frightening "No" of a

---

[81] Updike, *Too Far to Go*, 231.

judging God while desiring the liberating forgiveness or the "Yes" of the loving God, and living with the knowledge of our basic fragility and mortality. The Maples are challenged in these tasks by their own grandiosity, Richard's self-indulgent form, the aesthetic, and Joan's self-righteous form, the ethical. As the moment of their divorce nears, the two of them achieve greater sanguinity, perhaps because they have both found new partners who seem (for the moment) suitable, or perhaps because one or both of them has, under the intense pressure of dread and despair, made the leap of faith.

As for the works of love that are supposed to follow the leap, Richard and Joan do love each other unselfishly—even after they begin telling each other that they do not love each other at all. For example, during that 1963 trip to Rome, a trip they take "out of marital habit," they also discuss their failed love, and reach agreement on a separation. At one point, Richard makes Joan cry with some particularly cruel words. Watching her cry, Richard feels a "force as powerful as lust" move his hand onto her arm in a gesture of comfort.[82] What specific habit is this, and what is this force? We can tell—the habit is companionship and the force is love, a love that is notably caritative rather than erotic, *Kjerlighed* rather than *Elskov*.

The same kind of love is evident, perhaps surprisingly, during the terrible fight Richard and Joan have sometime in the late 1960s, the one where their children watch them scream and throw punches at each other. Neither parent apologizes to the other; neither takes time to comfort the frightened children. But there is both regret and love in Richard's awareness of the children's feelings: "Children sneak quietly up and down the stairs, pale, guilty, blaming themselves, in the vaults of their innocent hearts..."[83] It is true that this regret would be better expressed to these children, for then it would be love-in-action, a genuine work of love. However, Richard's thought communicates real shame on his part, and a real wish that his children would not have to endure his deep moral flaws. This too is caritative love—in potential.

Notably, Richard and Joan begin to fall in love as college students, not in a potentially erotic meeting over a beer, as planned, but in a hospital where Joan has been admitted for unusual vaginal bleeding. Richard recalls that a "force of nature drove him to brave the long corridors and the wrong turns and the crowd of aunts and other suitors

---

[82] Ibid., 60-61.
[83] Ibid., 149-50.

at the foot of the bed." Thus his first love for Joan—this force that makes him endure potential unpleasantness—appears to be caritative. Once Joan's "interne" reveals that she is a virgin, a more erotic love kicks in for Richard, or so we assume.[84] The Maples' relationship will involve more than illustrations of the damages of *Elskov*, but a dialectic of *Elskov* and *Kjerlighed*, eros and agape.

Not only should we honor the Maples' capacity to love one another and their children, but we should probably emulate Updike himself in withholding harsh judgment of his characters and their flaws. After all, the Maples are simply trying to address existential problems—their own despair and psychological programming—in the best way they know how. Waiting up for Joan to return from her conference with the Masons, Richard has an unusually sharp insight. "[E]ven as a child he had seen there was nobody to be angry at, only tired people anxious to please, good hearts asleep and awake, wrapped in the limits of a universe that itself, from the beauty of its details and its contagious air of freedom, seemed to have been well-intentioned."[85] In the particular context, this remark is potentially self-serving, of course. Neither arguing for the rightness of his affair, nor confessing its wrongness, Richard hopes to be excused of all responsibility for his philandering on this evening. But he has had a Kierkegaardian insight. In a theological sense, there really is no one to be angry at because all people are broken and flawed, groping toward greater authenticity.

Kierkegaard would clearly censure neither Richard for his aesthetic self-indulgence nor Joan for her ethical pieties—but would rather see both involved in "stages on life's way." Richard's inability to meet the demands of love in his own life seems to have been largely determined by the quality of his mother's love and father's authority. It is not clear that we can blame Richard for his childhood or its incomplete Oedipal processes. Joan too is doing her best with her own existential anxieties. As the sociological literature of marriage tells us, she grew up bathed in an ethical ideology of marriage in which she is to marry young, give her support to a husband-breadwinner, and give shape to a matriarchal child-centered home in order to bring the children to responsible citizenship and personal health. Her ethics also seems to lend a deeper existential purpose to her life, as she allows her maternal stewardship of the children to brim over into a stewardship of the ill (such as the "sort

---

[84] Ibid., 247.
[85] Ibid., 117.

of cousin" of "Giving Blood") and oppressed (such as the civil rights marchers and speakers of "Marching through Boston"). Perhaps she is trying to supply herself with ethical alternatives to the aesthetic-based adulteries into which her husband has taunted and pressured her. In any case, few who see the rightness of Kierkegaard's version of Christianity would excoriate her, as Luther unfortunately and notoriously did the Jews of his day, for failing to recognize the benefits of faithfulness to Christ. Darrell Jodock makes an elegantly simple and apt remark: Updike "has not given up on" his characters.[86]

Updike was further along Kierkegaard's stages on life's way than Richard and Joan Maple are—or so he asks us to understand through his confessional writings. Yet the Maples feel and even act upon genuine love. They often confuse that love with lust and fantasy and ethical busyness, but the moments when they feel this love least selfishly—such as their spontaneous embrace while watching the mounted police in Greenwich Village, or together seeing a Masaccio or Daumier in a scene they view, or helping each other through the stressful day of their divorce decree—these are the passages where the critic ought to begin. Here a contrast is possible between the unselfish love of *Kjerlighed* and the often frivolous, childish, irresponsible, and profane *Elskov*. Knowing that difference, and committing to it, the reader, Updike hopes, can set aside laws and codes, and begin the creative, loving activity of conscience.

---

[86] Jodock, "What is Goodness?," 125.

5

Oh But They Were Close

"Snowing in Greenwich Village" and "Wife-wooing"

Applaud your Neighbor; admire his style
That grates upon you like a sawtooth file.
His trespasses resemble yours in kind;
He too is being crowded from behind.

—John Updike, *Midpoint* [1]

The first two Maples stories test the power of marital and neighborly love. For Kierkegaard, there is no difference between the enduring love of marriage and the non-preferential love the believer is supposed to enact on the neighbor's behalf. For Updike, as we have seen, erotic love, within marriages or without, can evolve into this enduring, caritative neighbor-love. In "Snowing in Greenwich Village" we see neighbor-love failing a test; in "Wife-Wooing" we see a momentary victory for caritative love in a carnal, erotic act. Both stories of erotic and caritative love are set in relief against half-comic references to the Cold War and the so-called Golden Age of Marriage.

As the two gerundive titles of "Snowing in Greenwich Village" (1956) and "Wife-Wooing" (1960) imply, these stories involve deceitful language. Snowing and wooing two women, Richard engages in uses of language we would not expect from a Christian breadwinner husband living in a nation trying, through social disciplines, to win a struggle for liberty, privacy and wealth. On the contrary, living out the key traits of the aesthetic stage, its pleasure-seeking diversions, manipulations, and self-delusions, Richard illustrates why social disciplines accomplish so little good, often devolving into regimes of coercion. The Maples marriage has always been such a regime, as Joan and Richard manipulate each other into situations that yield advantages for the

---

[1] Updike, *Midpoint*, 41.

manipulator. In these stories the Maples are so young and inexperienced that these manipulations strike us as relatively benign. Updike understands that coercion is natural and necessary in this world—a claim he makes in the "On Not Being a Dove" chapter of *Self-Consciousness*, where he defends the utility of law enforcement and war.[2] But he also understands that any coercive effort on the part of a government, class, union, tribe, clan, or family tends to destroy freedom, dignity, and even life, if that movement lacks a deep inner motive of love.

Updike likes to turn private matters into public meanings. In "Snowing in Greenwich Village," Richard and Rebecca Cune nearly snow each other into bed for a tumble—or so Richard believes. But if we focus on Richard's fun, as Richard himself does, we miss important details about Rebecca's needs as a lonely *neighbor*—a word I use in both theological and ordinary senses. Joan fails to recognize the real Rebecca too, in her less libidinal but also self-absorbed way. The seeds of the Maples' later pathological narcissism have already been sown before these incidents take place in the young couple's lives. Both of the Maples tend to negate Rebecca's personhood, her evident loneliness and need for attention. "Wife-Wooing" is only marginally more hopeful, a story in which, precisely because he gives up his continual erotic pressure, Richard receives a gift of erotic grace from his wife. Joan offers herself to Richard at their bedtime because, briefly at least, he has ceased wooing, pressuring her for sexual favors. Such moments of relatively selfless loving union on the Maples' part will be rare because his aesthetic needs clash with her ethical ones in another kind of Cold War.

The Cold War references are not only emblematic. In "Snowing," Rebecca Cune has very real communist friends (real but perhaps not authentic), and arranges her domestic life for a time along communal lines. In "Wooing," Richard and Joan talk frankly about the legitimacy of the anticommunist efforts of the House Unamerican Activities Committee in the early 1950s, during Congressman Richard Nixon's tenure. These connections express not only the sometimes tense division prevailing between the Maples, but also the fact that they, like the Western and Soviet blocs, are bound together by their deep responsibilities for human lives under imminent threat of death.

To many Cold Warriors, the family meant life and refuge. The so-called "Golden Age" of marriage, usually dated 1945-60, scripted a

---

[2] Updike, *Self-Consciousness*, 112ff., especially 130n.

matriarchal home supported by masculine work. Many viewed this model of marriage as the central stay against rival communist models of home. But because of a series of popular books that criticized suburban family life, these roles quickly became stereotypes rather than attractive callings to many thoughtful people—like Updike. *The Organizational Man, The Crack in the Picture Window, The Man in the Gray Flannel Suit, How the Bough Breaks, No Down Payment,* and *The Split-Level Trap*—all of these books, according to Scott Donaldson, blamed the American suburbs for fostering conformist, isolationist, and matriarchal attitudes.[3] Updike too explores all these themes alongside other contradictions of Golden Age marriages. Updike will not satirize the Maples marriage—he recognizes universal human failing too clearly to imply that he and others have risen above such marital failing—but he is not content with their Christian marriage either. For this reason, he slyly supplies contrasting models of home, such as Rebecca's temporary union with two freethinking friends. Updike notes that this union dissolves for the typical human reasons of exploitation, unfairness, and misdirected libido: Jacques and Georgene live on Rebecca's labor, and Jacques attempts to seduce his neighbor, the Swedish "bomber." Updike invites us to consider whether these novel, leftist domestic arrangements threaten the Maples' marriage.

Of course they do, but not in the way nostalgic or reactionary family theorists imagine. If Richard and Joan cannot defeat their grandiose selves, his pleasure-seeking one and her complacently ethical one, the two of them have no chance to become authentic and worthy selves. They will continue to negate others, as they do Rebecca Cune in "Snowing in Greenwich Village," and each other, as they do in "Wife-Wooing." Richard's double in "Wooing," Richard Nixon, destroys rivals viciously in a dubious effort to protect the American home, but the Maples, though they dislike Nixon, are little better. They exploit each other's real and perceived weaknesses in a search for consoling forgetfulness and as a result never construct a true home. Kierkegaard teaches that no coercive law, social plan, or revolutionary rearrangement of family will solve this problem. Only free conscience and God's assistance will. If Richard and Joan are to engage more meaningfully and justly with each other, and with their neighbors, Updike implies, it will not be because of Lenin's or Marx's models of communal or revolutionary living, but because of the gospel's message of love.

---

[3] Mintz and Kellogg, *Domestic Revolutions*, 184.

ॐ

"Snowing in Greenwich Village" opens and closes with a remark about "being close"—comments that pun upon each other, as we will see. The occasion for the story is Richard's and Joan's first night in an American apartment of their own, surrounded by their own things, as they feel a married couple ought to be.[4] They want to practice the roles of host and hostess. This plan is self-serving, very different from arranging a pleasant evening for a dear friend, which would be other-serving. The Maples, we are told, have just moved to West Thirteenth Street in Greenwich Village. They have Rebecca Cune over because "now they were so close" to her current apartment. Of course to be close also means to share affection, but the evening depicted offers very little of that. The story closes with Richard leaving Rebecca's apartment after walking her home, thinking "Oh but they were close"—close to committing adultery. Proximity, friendship, love, adultery—these are the issues in that the word "close" evokes in this story, and that Updike casts into punning dialectic.

The Hamiltons propose that the story is nothing short of a struggle between good and evil, and Richard, strangely enough, represents the good. They invite us to view Rebecca Cune as the "strange woman of Proverbs," a death-dealing figure who tempts men who refuse instruction in righteousness. The Hamiltons suggest that Rebecca's love of "odd things" is sufficient evidence to direct us to this of all unusual, seductive women in the Bible. They view Rebecca Cune as a "female-destroyer-temptress," and focus on Richard's moral-ethical strength when she attempts to seduce him.[5] He returns to Joan chaste, after all.

However, this theology is inconsistent with Updike's stated commitments. To quote Updike from my epigraph: your neighbor's "trespasses resemble yours in kind." There are no innocents or destroyers, not among non-sociopaths, just well-meaning people seeking consolation for their existential fears. Consistent with the Lutheran-

---

[4] Later stories make clear that the Maples, like the Updikes, spent a year in England. When he composed this story, Updike may have had no future Maples stories in mind, nor any commitment to using his own history, such as his year in England, as a control on continuity of detail in autobiographical stories.

[5] Alice and Kenneth Hamilton, *The Elements of John Updike*, 57. See Proverbs 5:3-23.

Kierkegaardian theology they illustrate, the Maples share in responsibility to love not only each other, but their neighbors as well—including the odd and perhaps cunning Rebecca Cune. "Snowing in Greenwich Village" is emphatically a story about various neighbors, from Rebecca herself, to Richard and Joan, to Jacques and Georgene, the Swedish "bomber," the butchers-in-training, and the congregation of the "poor church" down the street. If we view Rebecca Cune as neighbor—and forget for a time that her name suggests to the Hamiltons and to Donald Greiner the slang term "cunt"—then perhaps the moral playing field in the story is leveled, moral melodrama is diminished, and we begin to view Richard and Joan as sharing responsibilities for the evening's betrayals and near-betrayals.[6]

Richard and Joan obviously have differing ideas about how to love their neighbor Rebecca. Indeed, as Rebecca arrives at the Maples' apartment, theirs for only a single day, Richard's thoughts tend toward negating her as a genuine person, perhaps in order to minimize the guilt he anticipates for the manipulations he is about to enact. He notes that her smile and manner are "absent" and her coat, which he places on his and Joan's bed, is "weightless." Richard's half-conscious wish to engage with her sexually is suggested by his thought of placing her "clothes," not just her coat, on the bed.[7] In the conversation to follow we learn that Rebecca has experience as the other woman to a pair of lovers. Though that roommate relationship seems chaste enough, a matter of sharing rent and food only, Rebecca does tell the Maples that her brother, home from military service, chastised her for no longer being a "nice girl."[8] These remarks amplify Richard's interest.

Thus Updike sets up the seeming central conflict of the story, which is Richard's struggle to preserve his faithfulness to Joan when the sexual opportunity in Rebecca's apartment, perhaps imagined, presents itself. Yet the fun in the story involves Updike's careful establishing and then undercutting of Rebecca as temptress. We must be careful not to adopt Richard's view of her, which is decidedly aesthetic in both the

---

[6] Ibid., 56, and Donald J. Greiner, *The Other John Updike: Poems/Short Stories/Prose/Play* Athens OH: Ohio University Press, 1981) 74. The Hamiltons work very hard not to use the offensive word: "'Cune' is a four-letter word. It fits Rebecca 'to a T'—a letter which Updike characteristically omits, substituting instead a silent 'e'."

[7] Updike, *Too Far to Go*, 13-14.

[8] Ibid., 15.

Kierkegaardian and ordinary senses of the word. He notes that Rebecca's face suggests a da Vinci, while Joan's face is mottled and "Modiglianesque." Both thoughts suggest that for Richard the women are objects to be acquired or possessed or enjoyed. He is a freedom-loving capitalist, a buyer in a suddenly rich market. He has made purchases in a nearby corner store where "in the coming years he would purchase so much." Meanwhile, Updike is careful to present Rebecca as one who has trafficked with Communists, specifically with a friend of her roommates, and has given communal support to roommates Jacques and Georgene in their indigent ways—until, that is, she puts her foot down, ends the exploitation, and moves to another apartment.[9]

Here a theme emerges that we will revisit again in "Giving Blood" and elsewhere—whether enduring human relationships should be involved primarily in a quasi-capitalist economy of possession and enjoyment, or in a genuinely communal attitude of sharing, giving and accepting non-preferentially. The former is characteristic of the aesthetic and even ethical stages, while a just and non-preferential mutuality proceeds from the religious. As "Snowing in Greenwich Village" develops these new characters in its first act, we see that it is Rebecca Cune, not Richard or perhaps even Joan, who understands how to give, who observes ordinary proprieties in her relations with others, who notes disinterestedly the flirtations of others. She seems irritated about her Swedish "bombardier" neighbor, for instance, a girl in the apartment above who once flirted with Rebecca's one-time roommate Jacques by "bombing" his balcony with her mop. But Rebecca does not seem especially flirtatious herself. She does tell lengthy, wandering, and sometimes implausible stories about her odd and interesting past, as though she is desperate for a bit of attention. But as the story's first act ends, after nothing more titillating than Rebecca sharing a few funny stories about her roommates, brother, and vegetarian uncle, we see literally nothing that might earn her the title "temptress," let alone "destroyer."

Truly, there is no real reason to accuse Rebecca Cune of licentiousness, concupiscence or even moral relativity. She hardly seems the Hamiltons' "female destroyer-temptress," nor Greiner's tempting

---

[9] Ibid., 15-17. I use the term "act" because Updike subdivides each Maples story, using white spaces as dividers. There are usually three or four acts in a Maples story, though some have only two and others more than four.

"uniter of sex and death."[10] As Richard himself acknowledges, there is only one moment in the story that was "hard to explain" as perfectly ordinary—that is, in the third and final act, when Rebecca joins Richard at her door as he is about to leave, and she stands "unnecessarily close" to him. The Hamiltons suggest that Rebecca has offered her face to be kissed. Yet we have seen that her social conduct is slightly odd, so that her invading of a person's personal space need not be read as either intentional or provocative. After all, earlier in the evening she also stands too close to both Richard and Joan at the window overlooking the mounted police going by, and then it is she who suggests that her presence might be unnecessary. Notably, after letting Richard into her apartment Rebecca does not even remove her coat. She does not offer Richard a drink or a seat, nor engage him in the kind of conversation or banter that might keep him there longer. She merely shows him things in the apartment that she has noted as odd or interesting in earlier conversations—the stove atop the refrigerator and the huge window opening onto the neighbor's apartment across the street. Richard notices her bed, but she does not mention it herself. Rebecca's standing close to Richard for one moment as he leaves, and shifting her weight to make his height "dominating" may be a temptation offered—but it would seem to be a very chaste move for a temptress-destroyer, a uniter of sex and death.[11] As Robert Luscher suggests, Richard's sense of having been tempted by Rebecca may be simply delusional.[12]

We need to reread the story with a Kierkegaardian theology in mind. Perhaps Rebecca is a friendly neighbor who is apparently just lonely enough to lie or exaggerate to prolong a social evening because she is anxious to enjoy the hospitality of two former friends from college. In the course of conversation she describes rooming with both men and women, dramatizes a boyfriend's imitation of the devil, and later notes that her apartment is "hot as hell."[13] But since Rebecca reports no fornication of her own, and her friend's antics as a devil connect in no way to any execrable behavior on her part (indeed, she tells us these antics irritated her), these are merely thematic remarks. Even drawing conclusions about the themes we have to be careful. Updike has no

---

[10] Hamilton, *Elements of John Updike*, 57; Greiner, *The Other John Updike*, 74.

[11] Updike, *Too Far to Go*, 24-28.

[12] Robert M. Luscher, *John Updike: A Study of the Short Fiction*. (New York: Twayne, 1993) 14.

[13] Updike, *Too Far to Go*, 21 and 25.

interest in a moral economy in which some people are especially devilish, satanic, or evil simply for having sexual appetites. Furthermore, Rebecca Cune's appetite is only a matter of conjecture. Rebecca enjoys a pleasant evening with her friends, and then half-willingly accepts Richard's half-hearted offer to escort her home. She seems uneasy about the nature of her friendship with Richard—she was Joan's college friend after all—so her farewell to him at the door of her apartment is awkward. Any suggestion of other possibilities is Richard's conclusion, or more likely, projection. It is probably best to reject a dualistic reading in which good Richard is under some kind of temptation by a female agent of iniquity. In future stories, it will be difficult to find and defend a Richard who is an innocent drawn into temptation by strange and devious women. He is almost always the devious one.

The critics agree that from the beginning of this story Richard engages in sexual fantasy. He imagines undressing and bedding Rebecca (indirectly, through reference to her "clothes"), and works throughout the evening to appear interesting and attractive in her eyes. Late in the first act he "parade[s] his concern" for his young wife's health before their guest—Joan recognizes the insincerity and it annoys her—and repeatedly contrives to make himself the center of attention.[14] Throughout the story, he displays the typical traits of one living in Kierkegaard's aesthetic sphere. Though the deeper imperatives of hospitality involve a full sense of the value of the guest, Richard contrives to treat himself to pleasures—purchasing the cashews, opening the sherry with the women's attention, walking Rebecca home in the new snow. He plainly admits to us these self-serving motives, recounting how he purchases the cashews for the pleasure of making a first purchase at a corner store where he will shop for some years to come, or making a satisfying show of opening an expensive bottle of sherry in the living room instead of the kitchen. These are obvious aesthetic rotations, but there are others. On the walk home, he works to impress Rebecca with his theological insights, which neither impress Rebecca nor cause her to feign interest in order to pursue erotic goals.

Meaningfully, both of the Maples are immature, and act as rather poor hosts—both in terms of the manners of their time, and in terms of enduring hospitality rites. Neither tries very hard or very consistently to make Rebecca feel welcome and esteemed, and both take turns displaying their aesthetic self-centeredness. We recognize the truth of the

---

[14] Updike, *Too Far to Go*, 17-18.

narrator's information, that Richard and Joan are very young newlyweds, unpracticed at hosting, and unsure in their roles. One or the other of the Maples tends to act as guest rather than host.[15] It is not surprising, then, that Joan has to instruct Richard to offer and make the drinks, or that he insistently presses food upon a guest who has just politely declined it. It also seems odd that Joan allows Rebecca to sit on the floor while she occupies a beloved and expensive antique chair. Joan seems, as Richard suggests, more concerned with shaping a particular kind of evening for their "first real night" in the apartment than with making Rebecca feel welcome. This story is a parable of venial self-centeredness.

The most emphatic example of discourtesy toward Rebecca is the scene in the second act involving the mounted policemen in the street below. As Richard notes, Joan is "forgetting herself" when she sees them, and makes a quite private moment of it, hugging Richard. This is certainly a social misdemeanor at worst, but Rebecca is uncomfortable enough to say, "I think I'd best go."[16] Later Joan undercuts the kindness of her offer to have Richard walk Rebecca home, adding in the other girl's presence that Richard should pick up some cigarettes on his way back home.[17] Whether this request is about her pleasure in a bedtime smoke or her signal to her husband that he should return promptly, the remark is self- rather than other-serving. Updike's first portrait of the Maples is a rather unflattering one.

Of course Joan is ill with a cold, a factor that may partially excuse her less than kind behavior. The illness is also a very important theological emblem for Updike. This is the first installment of a theme Updike notes in his introduction to *Too Far to Go*: "One of them [Richard and Joan] is usually feeling slightly unwell, and the seesaw of their erotic interests rarely balances."[18] Here Updike links the theme of illness to an imbalance of the spouse's states of mind, as well as their libidos, pointing to difficulties of mutuality. Illness would also seem to point to fragility, perhaps a hint of mortality. Since this story is an illustration of Kierkegaard, then mortality would indeed be a central theme. Our task is to connect a consciousness of mortality in a meaningful way to the

---

[15] Ibid., 14.
[16] Ibid., 20.
[17] Ibid., 23.
[18] Updike, Introduction to *Too Far to Go*, 10.

Maples' social misdemeanors and to Richard's erotic fantasies on the evening of Rebecca Cune's neighborly visit.

As we have seen, for Kierkegaard a person's conscious or unconscious sense of mortality leads to despair. The despair is the motive energy behind any stage-shift, including the leap of faith. In this sense despair is, as George B. and George E. Arbaugh put it, both "the dreadful sickness which befalls spirit through its wrong use of freedom" and an opportunity, "a doorway to spiritual recovery and faith."[19] Though Joan's cold is hardly life-threatening in "Snowing in Greenwich Village," nor Richard's in "Marching Through Boston" or "Your Lover Just Called," the problem of mortality and the despair that accompanies it is definitely in play, as Updike subtly points to both human fragility and Kierkegaard's sickness unto death.

Throughout the Maples' marriage we see this despair in Richard's and Joan's fearful denial of mortality. Their unconscious fears tend to erupt in unkind, thoughtless, or neurotic acts. Richard and Joan may often be ill with a cold, but truly both are sick with despair. For this reason, they fail to be neighbors to others. In "Snowing in Greenwich Village" Richard makes a wrong use of his freedom in snowing Rebecca and Joan, mildly wrong in this story, manipulating them with insincere words rather than honoring them with unselfish acts of kindness and respect. Since Kierkegaard endorses creative loving rather than dutiful ethics, none of these acts need to be witless or obviously pious. Joan and Rebecca are obliged, of course, to do the same for him.

So who is snowing whom on this snowy evening in Greenwich Village? As Kierkegaard's theology predicts, each character takes his or her turn. Richard believes that Rebecca snows him and Joan. Her deadpan delivery about very odd incidents hints at a basic insincerity. Richard realizes in the second act that "Rebecca's gift...was not that of having odd things happen to her but that of representing, through the implicit contrast with her own sane calm, all things touching her as odd."[20] Richard snows both women into thinking that his attentions to them and concerns about their comfort are sincere. For reasons of social obligation, and perhaps to create the kind of evening she had been imagining, Joan snows Rebecca into believing that she, Joan, is interested

---

[19] George B. Arbaugh and George E. Arbaugh, *Kierkegaard's Authorship: A Guide to the Writings of Kierkegaard* (Rock Island IL: Augustana College Library, 1967) 297 and 295.

[20] Updike, *Too Far to Go*, 21.

in her guest's stories for Rebecca's sake rather than for their comedic value. This is an evening of wholesale insincerity, as evenings often are when shared by people who are not "close." Surely Updike has no deep moral problem with such social encounters, except as reflections of and prelude to deeper disconnections and betrayals. But in this case Updike takes care to connect social insincerity with existential awareness.

He also sets up one moment of lovely contrast, when the two Maples and Rebecca look out the window on the mounted policemen in the falling snow. This snow is essentially the same as Joyce's snow in his great story, "The Dead"—the kind that falls like God's grace and love upon both the living and the dead. Or rather, the situation is Kierkegaard's but the snow is Joyce's. Luscher also finds Joycean overtones in this story, suggesting that Richard's walk home in the dark is similar to the young boy's in "Araby."[21] This is good, but I find the themes animating "The Dead" to be the more emphatic and meaningful allusion in this story. In "The Dead" hospitality rites are also abused by insincere speech—especially but not only Gabriel's lying speech to his hostesses and aunts. The insincerity is connected with much deeper values and attitudes, and the purity of snow in both stories hints at both the coldness of death and the fundamental clean truthfulness that consciousness of mortality sometimes inspires. In this story, Updike adds the mounted police, who represent the goodness of restraints and, since they are shown moving two-by-two, a celebration of the love of two contrasted in this story with the intrigues of three. This is merely ethical goodness, but we have seen that Updike believes that social laws and codes may be an expression of Christian love. The sight of the snow and the police does inspire love in Joan, a love that flows out of her spontaneously and forgetfully as she hugs Richard and thinks for a moment of their life together: "On our first night here!"[22] The plural "our" is meaningful, and so is this momentary sincerity in an evening of inauthentic speech.

As for Rebecca's peculiar dating patterns and living arrangements, perhaps we should view them as not peculiar at all. Perhaps she merely experiments for a time with a revolutionary social movement we know was building pressure beneath the American crust of 1950s Cold War conformism, the counterculture. Rebecca, we learn, associates with American communists, which is to say, with young intellectuals

---

[21] Luscher, *John Updike*, 14.
[22] Updike, *Too Far to Go*, 19.

dissatisfied with forms of justice and personal choice and economic destiny within the current politic. However, Rebecca's friends are more bohemian than Marxist. For them, sexual freedom seems to trump revolutionary change in the mode of production. Jacques enjoys indolent flirting with the Swedish "bombardier," Georgene abandons Jacques for another man, and their rich communist friend is mostly notable for not washing.[23] There is no indication that these young communists are spying, forming cells, gathering weapons, or planning insurrections. Mostly, they seize the opportunity to exploit Rebecca's labors and engage in sexual connections not available to more dutiful, conformist young people. Call them narcissists, or to be kinder, beatniks. As for Rebecca's boyfriend, the one who likes to imitate restaurant hosts, pianists, and the devil—he is evidently a kid who fights conformism by acting out comedic defiance to accepted manners, another beatnik. Notably, each of these friends may be a figment of Rebecca's imagination, as Joan suggests with her question, "Is this *really* true?"[24]

Act three of this story involves the walk to Rebecca's apartment and brief encounter inside. As we have seen, this encounter is consistent with our understanding of Rebecca Cune as a friendly but somewhat needy neighbor. Yet the story's social facticity becomes quickly thicker in this act, and we need to account for some implied meanings. Richard seems to hope to establish a deeper connection with Rebecca by musing about the "poor church" amid taller apartment buildings. Rebecca offers only silence, which Richard feels as rebuking.[25] He tries a different tack, noting that his new apartment is remembered by some as the home of a kept woman. Rebecca deflects this remark too, changing the subject to the large windows on this street, which allow neighbors to see people they know nothing about.[26] Thus she deliberately rejects talk about mistresses in favor of talk about neighbors who watch out for each other—especially for her. Later, looking around Rebecca's architecturally odd apartment, Richard notices her copy of Auntie Mame. Readers of the late 1950s would recognize that the novel's motto—"Life is a banquet—and most poor suckers are starving to death"—is the battle cry of the

---

[23] Ibid., 14-17.
[24] Ibid., 22.
[25] Ibid., 24.
[26] Ibid., 24-5.

aesthete, and that the story is a parody of rigid pietism and abnegation.[27] Suddenly we feel a choice: people with existential hungers can indulge their senses, or seek connection with those alienated neighbors nearby. The latter is the right choice, the only non-absurd one according to Kierkegaard. But the entire evening demonstrates how little even warm acquaintances really do connect. Human connection is not natural, and people tend not to love their neighbors, not before the leap occurs.

The story concludes with one more important speech-act. As Richard takes his leave of Rebecca, believing that she has offered herself to him, he blurts a joke about the butchers who take vocational training nearby. "Don't, don't let the b-butchers get you," he says. Updike explains that "[t]he stammer of course ruined the joke."[28] Recalling that Updike theorizes that his own stuttering emerges from bad faith, a "guilty blockage" of the flow of speech, we realize that Richard's guilty conscience is at work.[29] Referring to butchering in his joke implies overtones of death, violence, flesh and blood. Richard attempts to render death a negligible joke—but the "certain guilt" he feels earlier on the steps to Rebecca's room is here expressed in an allusive form Freud would understand, as speech emerging unbidden from an anxious core self. Richard himself is nearly the butcher, the dangerous one who wants to "get" Rebecca. But on this evening, his faltering repressions win out. He goes home to his young wife.

Late in his life, Updike lent important context to Richard's anxiety in this story, writing of himself, "How repressed were we, back in those benighted Forties and Fifties? I do not recall feeling more repressed than was good for me. Even without reading Freud, one knew that civilization demanded some control of the libido."[30] Of course, civilization does not require people to be loving neighbors to each other, but sometimes, such as this evening at the young Maples' apartment, honoring a repression that emerges from conscience can lead to just that result.

Updike's attitude toward Richard's language in "Wife-wooing" is more ambivalent. The language of wooing is also the language of

---

[27] Michael Tanner, Afterword to *Auntie Mame, An Irreverent Escapade*, by Patrick Dennis. (New York: Broadway Books, 2001) 298.

[28] Updike, *Too Far to Go*, 27.

[29] Updike, *Self-Consciousness*, 111.

[30] Updike, *Due Considerations*, 465.

affection and love, yet in the end Updike again suggests that Richard speaks as a despairing man, out of touch with his deeper self and confused in his essential duties, his vocation as loving husband and father especially. These themes are amplified in "Wife-wooing," as Richard's fantasy life, which at first seems creative and funny in this intentional self-satire, develops into a portrait of his commitment to the selfishly aesthetic. However, the story ends with the very theological insight Richard most needs—that Joan's love is a gift, not an asset. Unfortunately, for years to come he will resist that insight through self-centered denial.

The form of this story is different from any other in the Maples cycle. "Wife-wooing" is a consciousness-narration in the first person, modeled closely after the Molly Bloom or "Penelope" chapter of *Ulysses* in its sexual earthiness and meditation on the nature of love. Updike acknowledges his debt by cleverly opening the story with Molly Bloom's famous interpolated, ecstatic "Yes": "Oh my love. Yes. Here we sit..."[31] The story also makes reference to the "Sirens" chapter of *Ulysses*, in which the adulterer Blazes Boylan thinks of Molly's inner thigh as "smackwarm" where a garter belt snaps it.[32] In "Plumbing," Richard muses in the first person, but those musings eventually lose the sense of a wandering human consciousness. In his musings in that later story, Richard begins to recount memories of family events in the historical present, the tense of the Rabbit novels. All other Maples stories are narrated in the third person by a limited omniscient narrator closely tied to Richard's consciousness. This story, only two acts long, is entirely comprised of Richard's consciousness narrating the events of two evenings spent at home—one evening Richard hopes will end in sex, and another that does, in spite of Richard's distracted relinquishment of his sexual hopes.

Richard's sexual excitement becomes the occasion for a meditation on time, language, God's role in creation, and the repetition or continually renewing quality of marital love. The final line of the story alludes both to the nature of marital eroticism and to the nature of grace: "An expected gift is not worth giving."[33] The story is modestly upbeat. Richard and Joan share a common task of parenting, discuss ideas together pleasantly, and even encounter theological ideas that might

---

[31] Updike, *Too Far to Go*, 29.

[32] Ibid., 30.

[33] Ibid., 36.

help them to develop into more existentially aware and thoughtful people. The pastoral marriage of Luther's day could hardly look much different.

For some reason, Richard is especially attentive to language and its uses during the winter evening of the first half of the story. Gazing at his wife's inner thigh, lit warmly by a glowing fire, he thinks of reading the word "smackwarm" in James Joyce's *Ulysses*. Richard thinks of Joyce as "splendid," and then adds that it is also splendid "to feel the curious and potent, inexplicable and irrefutably magical life language leads within itself."[34] This is not the most likely remark from a man who works with the "technicalities" of "machines" that manipulate "phrases and numbers,"[35] and the remark is not especially coherent. In a metaphysical sense, language does seem to come alive beyond the meanings achieved by its grammars and semantic potentialities, but it is difficult to understand how language leads a life "within itself." Probably the remark is reflexive, Richard actually revealing that he believes in the surplus that makes language signs mean, the mind seem independent of brain, and God exist.

Richard also takes note of the children's language use on this evening, noting the ways we struggle primitively to control and master the medium, put it to our uses. Five-year old Judith at one point doesn't understand her mother's phrase, and asks about it "enunciating angrily, determined not to let language slip on her tongue and tumble her so that we laugh." Here language is clearly a projection of ego, as it often is for Judith's father. Two-year old Dickie cries "I hate dat," about his mustard-smeared hamburger bun. Richard thinks, "Language is to him thick vague handles swirling by; he grabs what he can." Richard can identify with the boy, as he has just told himself to begin wooing Joan for a bedtime tryst, and has met with an uninterested grunt, "Vnn," and body language bespeaking retraction. Joan will not, in fact, make love to Richard on this evening. She will spend her last waking moments in bed reading about another unscrupulous and manipulative Richard, Richard Nixon, until she falls asleep. Apart from being a cleverly reflexive moment about the uses of literature, and the identification of another foil Richard to contrast with Richard Maple, it's one of the funniest moments in the entire Maples cycle: "I lie against your filmy convex back. You read sideways, a sleepy trick. I see the page through the fringe of your

---

[34] Ibid., 30.
[35] Ibid., 36.

hair, sharp and white as a wedge of crystal. Suddenly it slips. The book has slipped from your hand. You are asleep. Oh cunning trick, cunning."[36]

In this story, Richard Maple, Richard Nixon, and the Maples' own children all employ language in self-serving ways. We expect this language use of small children. The liberal ethicist Joan hates Richard Nixon, for he had manipulated and abused language in smear campaigns to defeat Jerry Voorhis for California congressman in 1946, and Helen Gahagan Douglas for senate in 1950, accusing Voorhis and other Democrats of being "soft on communism," and Douglas of being a "fellow traveler" with world communists. Though Nixon accused Douglas of voting pro-communist and being "pink down to her underwear," his own voting record was little different from hers. These nasty smear campaigns worked, and Joan cannot forgive Nixon for his "fiendish trick[s]" and "low adaptation[s]." Richard, on a determined self-serving language campaign of his own now that he and Joan are in bed together, feels sympathy with Nixon and defends him as ordinarily imperfect.

Then Richard's own campaign begins to fail: if his goal is turning Joan on, he goes about it in an increasingly strange way. He argues mildly with Joan's growing sense that Nixon's attacks on accused communist spy Alger Hiss were unjust: "Honey. Hiss was guilty. We're all guilty. Conceived in concupiscence, we die unrepentant." Once his "ornate words" wooed Joan, he thinks, but of course this evening's words are less ornate than piously, condescendingly blundering.[37] Richard also fails to distinguish ordinary faultiness from nasty, self-serving character assassination. We face challenges with the Kierkegaardian theology in this story: we are left to ponder when ordinary faultiness becomes crime or trespass.

Are Richard's wooing words Nixonian—manipulative, self-serving, adaptive, iniquitous? Hardly iniquitous. Perhaps cunning is a better word, as it is a word Richard uses to describe Joan. It is interesting

---

[36] Ibid., 32-5.

[37] Ibid., 34. Even with the help of internet search engines and dedicated librarians, I cannot find the source for Richard's theological quotation—surely it's not his original remark?—in these "ornate words." The theology sounds Augustinian, and Augustine of Hippo certainly discusses problems of concupiscence, but does not predict that "we," or all, die unrepentant. Richard may believe he is quoting a theologian, but projects his own view.

diction given Rebecca Cune's last name, and given Richard's mixed intentions in wooing his wife on the first of our two evenings. Richard views his wife as cunning, as she slips off to sleep without responding to Richard's wish to make love. However, it is his own cunning that collapses the next morning, as he takes both "a relief and a revenge" upon Joan by noting that she is no longer attractive to him. He addresses her in imagination with the unkind, "you are ugly."[38] Clearly, Richard's reality is largely a projection of his own urges for the aesthetic moment, whether that moment is realized through language or sex. In this, Updike implies through the story's opening paragraph, Richard is less like a well-adjusted post-leap husband and father than like his one-year old son: "the center, sharing nothing, making simple reflections within himself like a jewel." This is Richard's self in some form of identity crisis, greedy for life's milk bottle, sucking "with frowning mastery" and "selfish, contemplative eyes."[39]

As we attend to these quasi-satirical passages, the story begins to feel less playful and more morally or theologically charged. We also note another dimension of the story that Updike's subtle, highly wrought prose makes possible, a subtext of scientific, theological, sociological, and literary references that, taken together, construct a kind of history of marital love. This history begins in a fictive stone age, where hunter husbands wrestle meat from the hands of threatening others in "a ferocious place,"—actually a mid-century drive-in—"slick with savagery, wild with chrome." Richard's musings take him back further to the moment of creation, where quantum weirdness first appears, "as if God wills the universe anew every instant"—which is precisely what so-called "many worlds" interpretations of quantum weirdness theorizes, the creation of new worlds with every human interaction with atomic processes. Richard seems to take the probabilistic weirdness of the quantum and disruption of a uniform and predictable cosmos as signs of God's creative participation in the world. Soon Richard takes us to a medieval world in which rose windows appear above, men "joust" on their way to work, and women are "tall, fair, obscure, remote, and courteous" virgins. His use of the word "courteous" is particularly clever, as it refers to the manners of the same "courts" that gave us the courtly love tradition, with its celebration of both intense marital love

---

[38] Ibid., 35.
[39] Ibid., 29.

and idealization of adultery.[40] Richard's tale of historical development is retrograde however. By the end of the story he is the lone hunter in savage Boston. "Stone is his province."[41]

Updike's point with this textual play is both to establish Richard's learned cleverness and creativity, and to hint that the story of marital and social cooperation and discord is long and vexed. Marriage and courtship practices have involved issues of self-interest, survival, advantage, pursuit of wealth, alliances between and among kin and diplomats—and a great deal else that we would call now extra-marital specimens of naked power, or at least moral and ethical relativity. Amidst all of this vexed history, Updike wants to suggest just one Archimedean point that is relevant to contemporary Christendom— love's emergence from grace.

Joan concludes the story with an act of love, we feel, rather than the libido Richard had displayed the evening before. Greiner is correct that the concluding turn of this story is Joan's wooing of her husband, something he does not expect, and neither do readers. This is a distinctly modern moment, as a wife controls sexual congress not only by assenting to or rejecting sex proffered by her husband, but by handling the transaction completely. Richard tells the tale: "[A]t the meaningful hour of ten you come with a kiss of toothpaste to me moist and girlish and quick...." They are about to make love. We take his moral for the story seriously, but not uncritically: "An expected gift is not worth giving." Richard's language remains alienated. It is still about spending and gaining—what a gift is "worth"—but we also see that he has experienced, in a neo-Joycean story, an epiphany. His wife comes to him at bedtime of the second evening not as a figure of his fantasy or erotic projections, but as a loving partner responding to his desire, hoping, in fact, to match desires. She loves both him and their children, even in their natural selfishness, and she suspends, out of love, the contempt she feels for the other Richard (Nixon), about whom she has just been reading. She expresses a sense of generous relation with this Richard (Maple).[42]

Updike presents Joan's generous relating with Richard as an act of grace, a theological concept of ultimate "gift." Notably, Richard has offered a contrary theological principle earlier in the story, in his

---

[40] Coontz, *Marriage, a History*, 134.

[41] Updike, *Too Far to Go*, 35.

[42] Ibid., 36.

knowing speech that "We're all guilty. Conceived in concupiscence, we die unrepentant." It is unclear whether Richard here refers to medieval Catholic doctrine, or to Luther's theology, or to some other Protestant doctrine, and it makes a difference. Catholic doctrine considers concupiscence to be a tendency toward what Joan calls, speaking of Nixon, "low adaptations." Concupiscence thus understood is an arational appetite or urge that is prelude to sin. Lutheran and related Protestant doctrine holds concupiscence to be sin itself, inherited from Adam. Both traditions consider concupiscence to be both related to sin and an element of unpleasant daily life through which God punishes sin. As a Lutheran, Richard is probably speaking about his own sin. He may or may not believe firmly in the principle of concupiscent origins and the dangers of an entire life unrelieved from sin. If he does believe in this principle, he forgets it as he seeks his aesthetic fun.

What is interesting about Richard's Augustinian remark is how it sets up Joan's gracious gift, establishing the condition of concupiscence which, according to Kierkegaard, grace alone can set aside. The remark also sets up an otherwise nonsensical remark on Richard's part as he thinks back on his wedding night, a remark that takes on meaning through doctrines of concupiscence: "Who would have thought, blood once spilled, that no barrier would be broken, that you would be each time healed into a virgin again?"[43] Here a wife's virginity is posed not as a condition to a pure or proper marriage but as a mystical repetition, like the repetition of grace required for the redeeming of incorrigibly sinful human beings. In other words, Richard's wonder is not simply that wooing Joan in their seventh year of marriage reminds him of a time when Joan was a virgin to conquer and possess sexually. He is capable of such a dominating aesthetic trope, but that is not his point with this remark. He plumbs a deeper mystery, suggesting an instinct of Kierkegaard's idea of repetition, in which, through faith, nothing is ever lost. If Richard loves Joan properly, which is to say without personal grandiosity, there will never be a time when her attractions are exhausted, in which she is used goods under his eyes. Love for the nearest neighbor and presumably all others may spring forth new, every time, or so Kierkegaard argues in the poetic aphorisms of *Repetition*.[44]

---

[43] Ibid., 33.

[44] See *Fear and Trembling* and *Repetition*, eds. and trans. Howard V. Hong and Edna H. Hong (Princeton, NJ: Princeton University Press, 1983) 133: "If God

&

In these two stories we have not yet learned that Joan is the daughter of a minister, but do know that she comes from a home that can afford to give her an expensive antique Hitchcock chair, and a home in which siblings like Joan are sent to college with Christian high achievers like Bitsy Flaner, the first "girl" to enroll in the Bentham Divinity School. Joan is clearly intelligent, talented, informed, secure in her opinions—a young wife and mother who possesses a college degree, plays the piano at her church, reads biographies of active political figures not in her preferred party, speaks easily about ethics and religion. Yet she is also a woman who displays touching sentimentality about falling snow and making a home, and who chooses, presumably in open discussions with her husband, to raise four children in full time motherly caretaking. Her husband takes up the simpler task of making the money that will keep the Maples comfortable if not happy. The Maples embody these traits of the "Golden Era" Cold War marriage.

The Maples' marriage is also a Christian marriage. Updike implies this by noting Joan's volunteering at the children's Sunday School, and by having Richard speak about the social importance of churches in "Snowing in Greenwich Village" and principles of concupiscence and repentance in "Wife-wooing." But Richard is never quite serious about his theology, just as he is never quite serious about his breadwinning, parenting, or loving his wife. He *is* serious about his pleasures, though he has only begun to seize them. As Kierkegaard helps us to see, this desire for forgetful pleasure-seeking is also deeply Christian in the existential sense. Aesthetic pleasure leads to anxiety, which leads to despair, which is the most productive existential emotion. Richard will continue to follow this aesthetic path more deeply into a condition of crisis, which is where he seems not quite to have arrived as "Wife-Wooing" closes in 1960.

---

himself had not willed repetition, the world would not have come into existence."

6

Fathoms Deep in the Wrong

"Giving Blood," "Twin Beds in Rome," and "Marching Through Boston"

> There is little opiate delusion in Jesus's grim warning to his comrades that if they were true to his Gospel of love and justice, they would meet the same sticky end as him. The measure of your love in his view is whether they kill you or not.
> —Terry Eagleton, Introduction, *The Gospels: Jesus Christ* [1]

In the ninth year of their marriage, in 1963, the Maples begin living in Lyndon Johnson's America, with its dream of a Great Society, a political attempt to make love of the neighbor a national priority and matter of public policy. But Johnson was also bewitched by South Vietnam, whose defense he may have considered another national act of love on behalf of a people seeking certain existential and other freedoms. Not coincidentally, the Maples now begin to talk about civil rights and Vietnam, to take on their own ethical tasks, and to confront the possibility of ethical goodness in their own and others' lives. Like Kierkegaard, they test the power of the ethical life, and discover limitations.

It is the ethically-minded Joan's idea that the two of them donate blood for a cousin in "Giving Blood" (1963), and that they march in support of Boston's dispossessed African American community in "Marching Through Boston" (1966). During both attempts at ethical goodness, Richard objects with childish ill will, eventually falling victim to illnesses with both somatic and psychosomatic dimensions. The trip to Rome in "Twin Beds in Rome" (1964) is more his style, since it feeds his pleasure principle to tour a city of great museums, shops and restaurants. He hopes to heighten the pleasure by securing Joan's

---

[1] Eagleton, Introduction to *The Gospels: Jesus Christ*, xviii.

agreement to end the marriage, a change he believes will also secure for him *la dolce vita*. Yet during the Maples' Roman holiday Richard falls ill again, experiencing intense pain in his feet and stomach. He simply cannot diagnose or explain this pain.

Compassion becomes the focus in this story, as Joan cares for Richard in his painful distress. He hardly seems to deserve Joan's care. His speech in all three stories turns from ironic to neurotic, and springs from such a deep well of anxiety and unrestrained ego—fathoms deep—that we question how Richard might ever attain the ideal marital speech of I Corinthians 13, speech rising out of a love which is kind, rarely envious or boastful or arrogant or irritable or resentful. In this sense, Richard's speech is not just cruel and crude but truly profane—outside the temple. Richard's state of mind raises the question of whether the New Testament is at all reasonable in its demands for unselfing, for loving speech and acts in marriage. Is it possible for people like Richard ever to attain goodness? For the Maples' marriage to endure as loving partnership? For Johnson's America to attain greatness through new notions of the public welfare? Or for Dr. Martin Luther King and his followers to harness the loving impulses of nonviolent direct action for a widening of civic justice?

Beginning with "Giving Blood," Updike offers in each Maples story a kind of allusive corollary tale. In "Giving Blood," Richard and Joan are Hansel and Gretel, threatened children in a maze-like land. In "Twin Beds in Rome" Richard is another shocked young Martin Luther facing up to the mercenary foundation of his church and his beliefs. In "Marching Through Boston" Richard, Joan and the young student Carol are figures in a Salem-style bewitching. The question Updike invites us to ponder in all three allusive corollaries is what it means to be possessed or bewitched, to lack control over one's actions, to lose hope for the future, and to find one's very identity threatened by an overwhelming malign agency symbolized by Satan or witch or corrupt spiritual leader. Updike needs to bring home to an audience of ethically-committed Americans the counterintuitive existential notion that ethical choices are always conditioned by our largely uncontrolled feral inner selves. "Our Guilt inheres in sheer Existing," Updike writes in *Midpoint*, and in *Self-Consciousness* he notes that "bloody hands...go with having hands at all."[2] In these stories, this untamed and guilty self has a pathological character. Something beyond merely human mediation—better

---

[2] Updike, *Midpoint*, 42 and *Self-Consciousness*, 136.

communication or therapy or wise counsel—will be needed to heal the Maples.

Richard and Joan are now trying to decide whether to remain married. In the realm where ordinary daily choices and Christian existential consequence are married, choosing quickly becomes absurd—not only because for Updike human righteousness is an impotent imposter of God's righteousness, but also because the human consciousness is normally possessed or bewitched by its own desires, fantasies, neuroses, and often enough, pathologies. Since this is so, choices in Updike's world have a quasi-mechanical character. They are driven by the machinery of ideology, libido, psychosis, sin. The person like Richard, who employs the energies of the aesthetic sphere in the project of denying his mortality, simply avoids making choices. He pretends that he makes them, but really flows aimlessly from diversion to diversion. He forces others—usually Joan—to choose his future. The ethically-minded like Joan and President Johnson, on the other hand, have chosen a different focus for their energies: the God-given universal worth of the neighbor. But Joan's ethical efforts, which Kierkegaard reminds us are really an avoidance strategy, also become unworkable, even absurd, because her hopes for justice are destroyed by exceptional ethical situations and her own and others' moral impotence. Johnson struggled with the same problems through his perceived duty to the South Vietnamese. As badly as he and his associates wanted to create a peaceable, stable, and democratic nation both in North America and Southeast Asia, they could not realize this vision.

These next three stories sharpen our sense of Richard as neurotically selfish and aggressive, and Joan as more kind-hearted, verbally restrained, and ethically committed. It is not too much to say, in fact, that these three stories offer a distinctly feminist portrait of marriage. It is at least a portrait deeply sympathetic with a harassed wife trapped in an overly straitened role and bound to a childish husband. In this sense, Updike updates Kierkegaard, making his views on Christian marriage more relevant to contemporary practices in America than to 19th century Danish ones. Updike also comes very close in these stories to violating his stated artistic ethic of withholding judgment of his characters. He invites us to judge Richard harshly for indulging in shockingly selfish and hurtful tirades against his wife and caustic comments about his children. He calls his wife stupid, sexless, smug, the cause of his misery, his crucifier. He calls his children blasphemous brats. Slightly more moderately and accurately, Joan calls Richard self-contradicting, hateful, and sick. There can be little doubt that this is a marriage in trouble, with Richard bearing far greater responsibility for the strife than Joan.

Yet Updike's task is far more complex than placing blame upon Richard for the troubles in this marriage, or blaming unenlightened breadwinning men generally for most failing marriages of the early 1960s. Rather, his focus is on the nature of love and the human capacity to feel it, cope with it, honor it. In these stories Updike attends closely to Richard's and Joan's complex states of mind as they contemplate love, specifically Richard's tendency to minimize, deny and negate Joan's love for him in order to justify his quest for a sexual rotation. Joan's own tendency is also toward a form of denial, though a less obvious form. By focusing on ethical behavior rather than on her own root anxiety, and the anxiety her husband displays, she unwittingly aids him in misbehaving his way out of the marriage.

Updike's most important motif in these stories, however, involves Richard's psychologically strange tendency to minimize, deny, and negate *his own* love for Joan. This is the baffling, bewitched human phenomenon of the middle period of the Maples marriage. Richard epitomizes the human tendency to dishonor deep and true feelings, to reject healthy and enduring feelings of love in favor of temporary release from boredom. Lending a particular context for this exploration of human inwardness are the particular settings of these stories, the hospital of "Giving Blood," Catholic pilgrimage city of Rome in "Twin Beds," and streets of Boston on a day of nonviolent social protests in "Marching." These settings and situations help Updike to pose the question of whether and how human love might animate right action, reduce human suffering, and produce justice. Though Updike is not one to celebrate heroes, he gives us hope for the power of love in the unseen hero of "Marching Through Boston." If, as Terry Eagleton suggests in my epigraph, the measure of one's love is that they kill you, then Updike's hero in these tests of neighbor-love is a Christ-like Dr. Martin Luther King.

&

As with most of Updike's Maples stories, we stand a chance of reading "Giving Blood" existentially if we recognize the multiple meanings implied by the title. The literal meaning is evident: Richard and Joan spend the morning making a donation of blood that Joan's cousin needs for upcoming surgery. Viewed in a Kierkegaardian light the phrase "giving blood" refers to Christ's grace-filled sacrifice—his blood which, once shed, is endowed with the capacity to "give," to confer grace upon undeserving people. This quiet reference to Christian grace leads us back again to Richard's and Joan's donating of blood and to the question of what kind of giving is either occurring or possible here. Surely the two Maples give more or less reluctantly to Joan's cousin in her medical distress, and speak to each other with irritation and contempt. Their compassion is less than ideal, yet Richard and Joan do give the blood and doing so grow calmer and more aware of their love for each other. Through this carefully contrived situation the story raises deeper and more perplexing questions about what it means for married persons to give their bodies, their flesh and blood, to each other—a meaning Richard confirms as relevant by noting that he doesn't understand "this business of giving something away and still somehow having it."[3] He is speaking about a blood donation, but the remark is also theological, a principle of neighbor-love that begins at home and ripples outward.

Richard is in a foul mood on the Saturday morning of the story's action. At first, he simply seems frustrated about his role as male breadwinner, as he complains about having to make the same trip on a weekend that he makes five workdays. But then the raving speech begins: "It's like a nightmare. I'm exhausted. I'm emotionally, mentally, physically exhausted." He poses this as a problem of his sacrifices for his family, but the truth is that he has been up late attending a party with Joan, tending to two perverse projects. One involves beginning an affair with Marlene Brossman, while the other involves arranging an affair for Joan in order to reduce his guilt and increase his realm of free action. His bad conscience in these matters emerges in his speech. Richard damns God four times in this brief conversation, and calls his children "blasphemous." While Updike seems to have no special problem with the casual epithet "goddamn" or any other cursing, in this story Richard is being set up as peculiarly profane and theologically misbegotten. Then he makes the most profane remark of the story: "Well hell," he says to Joan, "every goddam body in New England is some sort of cousin of yours; must I spend the rest of my life trying to save them *all*?"[4]

---

[3] John Updike, *Too Far to Go*. (New York: Fawcett, 1979) 56.
[4] Ibid., 37.

As Kierkegaard insists in *Works of Love*, the answer to this question is yes, he must. Kierkegaard opens his study of neighbor-love with a series of meditations on Matthew 22:39: "the second commandment is like it: You shall love your neighbor as yourself."[5] The force of these meditations is best summarized by this précis which opens a chapter titled "You Shall Love *the Neighbor*":

> It is in fact Christian love that discovers and knows that the neighbor exists and, what is the same thing, that everyone is the neighbor. If it were not a duty to love, the concept "neighbor" would not exist either; but only when one loves the neighbor, only then is the selfishness in preferential love rooted out and the equality of the eternal preserved.[6]

The alert reader who is familiar with these scriptures understands that "Giving Blood" is a theological story about neighbor-love, a test really of Richard's rather nominal Christian faith (he sends his brats to Sunday School) and his capacity to give of himself. Though Richard is caught in a preferential love for Marlene Brossman, and is attempting to commit one of the sexual sins, specifically adultery, the story's focus is not on the previous evening's party and its sexual realignments but on a more ordinary failure of charity, his childishly selfish wish to avoid meeting human need with little cost, a few ounces of his blood and hours of his time. It is true that, according to Lutheran theology, performing good works brings people no nearer the righteousness of the Wholly Other God. It is also no doubt true that plenty of good works are performed by Christians burning with resentment. Nevertheless, both ordinary ethics and principles of Christian neighbor-love urge Richard to give of himself more generously and graciously.

This first of four acts in the story concerns the Maples' mutual acrimony, with each succeeding act reflecting a shift in the Maples' emotions. In the first act, Richard gripes about his fatigue and accuses Joan of unfaithful behavior at the previous evening's party. Joan recognizes Richard's stratagem: "You're not so subtle. You think you can match me up with another man so you can swirl off with Marlene with a free conscience." Richard's conscience is stung by the accuracy of Joan's insight: "Her reading his strategy so correctly made his face burn." His attempt to turn this profane matchmaking ploy into a joke fails, so Richard goes on the attack. He charges Joan with "*smugness*,"

---

[5] Kierkegaard, *Works of Love*, 17.
[6] Ibid., 44, emphasis Kierkegaard's.

"stupidity," and "sexlessness," all inappropriate, in his view, to the "Age of Anxiety." Joan is startled. She tells Richard that these are hurtful remarks and she will remember them always. Again, Richard's conscience is pricked. He realizes that he is "[p]lunged fathoms deep into the wrong." Richard cannot resist throwing "one more pinch of syllables" into a conversation that is going against him. With a remark of fatherly concern for his younger daughter's fever he activates Joan's conscience. Though she has made a strategic vow not to speak, "guilt proved stronger than spite" and she replies fittingly. Richard responds with more frankness, but no less selfishness: "Sweetie...will [the people drawing blood] hurt me?"[7]

The second act of the story concerns the Maples' arrival at a hospital, the typing of their blood, and their donation on adjoining beds. Richard and Joan reconcile during this act, demonstrating for each other a relatively unselfish love. But we should not exaggerate the Maples' unity in this section. Much of the language and imagery of reconciliation is ironic, a counterpoint to Richard's and Joan's states of mind. This imagery offers wonderfully clever allusions to questions of fidelity, faith, and the care of children: to kings and queens (which raise the question of fidelity versus fealty), the Catholic heroine-mystic Joan of Arc, the Hansel and Gretel tale (which will reappear in "Here Come the Maples"), mismatched beds, even an explicit reference to a "leap," though perhaps not a leap of faith. These images help pose the Kierkegaardian problem of anxiety and despair emerging from half-conscious fear of death. This is precisely what Richard feels as act two opens and he and Joan arrive at the hospital reception desk. Richard has already confessed a childish fear of giving blood, a "trivial" test of courage he hasn't faced before. But Richard is wrong to think his fear is trivial. Since he does not understand his dread, it only feels minor to him. His real fear is a fear of death, which closes off the possibility of ultimate choosing and thus matters more than any other fear.

Death is definitely on Richard's mind. As he and Joan pass along the devious hallways of this hospital, he glimpses "horrors!—a pair of dismembered female legs stripped of their shoes and laid parallel on a bed." This emblem of death, horror, and of a body being stripped and laid out suggest both his own death and Christ stripped and laid in a tomb. Richard then considers, as he fills out a medical history form, what death will mean to him. His wretched life will be judged: "He fought

---

[7] Updike, *Too Far to Go*, 38-40.

down that urge to giggle and clown and lie that threatened him whenever he was asked—like a lawyer appointed by the court to plead *a hopeless case*—to present as it were, his statistics *to eternity.*"[8] Significantly, Richard realizes that his indefensible wretchedness is mitigated only by sharing some part of his life—he cites "present address, date of marriage"—with "the hurt soul" Joan.[9] He understands dimly that married love partakes at least minimally of God's love, and that he has caused some part of Joan's hurt. His God will hold him accountable for these things, and perhaps, he hopes, find reason for mercy in the minimal goodness Richard has shown in marriage.

Admitted to the clinic, Richard and Joan lie down on beds set at a 90 degree angle to each other. The image implies relation but unfortunate disparity, as had their honeymoon Lake Winnipesaukee camp beds of different heights. The Maples begin to give up their blood, an image of the marital "one flesh."[10] Joan jokes meaningfully that Richard's blood doesn't seem to move much "until after midnight"—which is to say, as boozy parties wind down—and usually for other women. Joan here suggests a profane image of blood. But in a moment, as Richard and Joan settle into a more thoughtful and less combatively verbal mood, and the thoughts are of death, their blood is sanctified in Richard's mind:

> Here, conscious of a pointed painless pulse in the inner hinge of his arm but incurious as to what it looked like, he floated and imagined how his soul would float free when all his blood was underneath the bed. His blood and Joan's merged on the floor, and together their spirits glided from crack to crack, from star to star on the ceiling.[11]

The reference to "spirits" here also refers to I Corinthians 6. In the very next verse after the "one flesh" reference, St. Paul continues, "But he that is joined to the Lord becomes one spirit." Paul then warns that sexual immorality is a sin against one's own body. But what Richard imagines here is our main concern: neither extinction, nor becoming "joined to the Lord," but some kind of spiritual afterlife amid the stars.

Updike has written disparagingly of being enlisted against his will into Alice and Kenneth Hamilton's "Sunday School," so we want to be

---

[8] Ibid., 42, emphasis mine.

[9] Ibid., 43.

[10] See I Corinthians 6:16 (New Revised Standard Version): "Do you not know that whoever is united to a prostitute becomes one body with her? For it is said, "The two shall be one flesh."

[11] Updike, *Too Far to Go*, 48.

careful to honor the mature ambiguities of such imagery.[12] Updike seems to imply that in an ideal sense the Maples' marriage is sanctified, and that in conjoined acts of neighbor-love (giving blood for a neighbor in need) they realize their relational potential. With this essential realization, Richard's imagination is freed to honor this sacred quality of his union with Joan. Admittedly, this imagery is the product of Richard's childish, erratic imagination, which in a few more lines creates a pagan drama in which he and Joan are bedded together as sacrifices to "proliferant deities [who] are said to exist as ripples upon the featureless ground of Godhead." These "inconstant images," the narrator tells us, overlay Richard's more constant, evidently Christian sense that he and Joan are "[l]inked to a common loss" (loss meaning their knowledge of the crucified Jesus as well as a pint each of their blood) and therefore "chastely conjoined."[13] Richard seems transformed, either by his having given a gift of blood, or by realizing that he might behave lovingly toward Joan and others. He whispers, in a phrasing that suggests that the reader withhold full approval, "Hey, I love you. Love love *love* you."[14]

If we feel irony here, there is a reason. From the moment the Maples enter the hospital, Richard has undergone an episode of regression. Just before arriving in Boston, Richard has transformed his wife into a mother with the line, "Sweetie...will they hurt me?"[15] She praises him as she would a child for his type O positive blood, as though it were a personal achievement: "Why that's very good, Dick!"[16] The young intern who takes their blood addresses Joan throughout the scene, and not only because he has written Richard off as "a clown," as Richard concludes. The intern treats him as one who cannot make his own decisions. He asks Joan whether Richard will need coffee, both before the blood-giving and after. Early in act three Richard performs a quick soft-shoe to show his fitness after giving blood, but that act too connects him to his seven-year old self in Morgantown, the kid whose mother took him into town for dancing lessons. Joan seems to join in the regressive impulses of a medical treatment, calling the bags of donated blood "doll pillows."[17] We

---

[12] See the Introduction to this study, 5n.
[13] Ibid., 49.
[14] Ibid., 54.
[15] Ibid., 41.
[16] Ibid., 45.
[17] Ibid., 52.

need to be careful to distinguish the calming influence of regressive impulses under medical treatment, a common-enough experience for many of us, from the calm of genuine reconciliation and unity between Richard and Joan. Such a reconciliation seems doubtful because Richard has not apologized, or to put this in theological terms, repented his cruelly selfish ways earlier that morning and late the evening before. To put this in Kierkegaard's terms, he has not repented his separation from God and lack of God-inspired conscience.

The Maples' regressive behavior is really only an emphatic continuation of their childish relationship generally. Juxtaposed with their childish behavior are images that point to another way, toward responsibility and charity grounded in faith. These images reside in the story's repeated references to kings and queens, references that are kicked off in earnest by Richard's off-hand musing whether they would see the King of Arabia during his apparently widely-known stay. References to this Middle Eastern king join with other royal and saintly references. Earlier Richard accuses Joan of trying at the previous evening's party to appear "like some pale Queen of the Dew surrounded by a ring of mushrooms"—the mushrooms being, apparently, her short, stout suitors.[18] The intern reminds Richard of his younger self when he assumed adult responsibility at a newsroom and felt like "king of his own corner."[19] Later, when Joan volunteers to be stuck first, Richard ridicules the gesture: "Her full name is Joan of Arc."[20]

Taken together these references to kings and queens and national saints raise, in a playful way, a number of serious notions about responsibility, fidelity, faith, and charity (or largesse). The word "fidelity," in fact, once described the loyalty of subject to king rather than spouse to spouse. Fidelity involved the personal sense of loyalty, while fealty carried the sense of allegiance to the state or a given principle represented by royalty. When Joan notes that the King of Arabia is in residence with four wives, Richard satirizes a Christian, monogamous notion of fidelity. "Only four?" he jokes, "What an ascetic."[21] Yet this king's presence cuts another way too, raising the notion that kings and queens are said to possess royal "blood"; that mingled blood creates family and kin; that blood shared in this way

---

[18] Ibid., 39.
[19] Ibid., 45
[20] Ibid., 46.
[21] Ibid., 42.

implies rights, privileges *and* obligations; that royal authority in the Christian West has always rested upon God's endorsement of royal faith; that royal expectations of the people's fidelity is answered by royal largesse. These specimens of cultural knowledge underpin and comment upon this story's action, suggesting that Richard and Joan might, after a fundamental change of consciousness, begin to live out a calling of much more thoroughgoing and just responsibility as idealized in these royal traditions.

Despite Richard and Joan sharing names with famous kings and heroines, their marriage violates most of these sacred royal codes and expectations, specifically in honoring erotic love instead of divine love in their relationship. This confusion about love has done spiritual damage to their realm or demesne. The narrator offers us one vivid example when Richard asks about his younger daughter's health. We learn that the night before he and Joan, in order to attend a party, had left the girl home with a 102 degree fever.[22] Their quarrel in the car is another fine example of questionable priorities and spiritual disorder. By way of contrast, Richard senses that he was most kingly when first assuming adult responsibilities at work. Fair enough, but should we understand Joan as Joan of Arc in any positive sense, or is the reference ironic for us as well as for Richard? Mostly ironic: while Joan demonstrates a firmer moral sense than her husband by telling him she is "really ashamed" of his profane tirade in the car, she is hardly the spirit-informed heroine of medieval Catholic France. Her steady ethical stance is a far cry from Jean d'Arc's ecstatic religious visions, courage at war, fidelity to her king and country, and willingness to die for her faith. Still, Joan holds up better as Jean d'Arc than Richard's likeliest royal double, Shakespeare's Richard III. Shakespeare's and Updike's Richards have much in common: they are both verbally gifted but morally warped, manipulative and selfish, creators of a poisonous household. Yet the imagery of royal character and calling primarily poses a critique of Richard's and Joan's vocations as spouses and parents, and their balked acceptance of faith.

In the middle two acts of "Giving Blood," Richard pays some homage to the ethical sphere of existence, his wife's position in the Kierkegaardian scheme. Recalling those "kingly" feelings while first meeting adult responsibilities at work, he seems to come close to embracing not only the duty of an ethical calling, but its transformation of feeling, its inward benefit—a peace that passes understanding. Giving

---

[22] Ibid., 41.

the blood, he and Joan both seem calmed and moved by their small sacrifice. Richard even asks whether they might visit Joan's ill cousin. He is not really changed for the better, we realize, because the narrator tells us he asks the question "for Joan's benefit." He is performing again, and he has made a careful calculation: "He was confident of the refusal."[23]

The fourth and final act of "Giving Blood" recounts Richard's backsliding into his former raving aesthetic self. This is the incorrigibility move which often closes off a Maples story, a demonstration of Updike's claim that people are, as he notes in his introduction to *Too Far to Go*, "incorrigibly themselves."[24] The section opens with a definition of romance, one that Greiner mistakes for Updike's own definition of "ideal love": "Romance is, simply, the strange, the untried."[25] Updike's definition is in earnest, but the word is "romance," not "love." If love is a religious category of experience, romance is an aesthetic one—especially when defined as the novel, the "untried." The word "romance" could be replaced with "rotation," Kierkegaard's word for the aesthete's strategy for overcoming boredom through refreshingly novel experience. Richard does begin to experience just such a rotation as he and Joan exit the hospital. "Let me take you to lunch. Just like a secretary."[26] Joan accepts Richard's offer of the lover-secretary role in this adultery fantasy.

Their conversation then takes an oddly learned tack into the medieval humors. The Hamiltons explicate this passage nicely, connecting the imagery to the glaucomous Arab king through Islamic Galenic medicine. They note that Richard and Joan fail to balance the choleric (yellow bile), melancholic (black bile), phlegmatic (phlegm), and sanguine (blood). That is to say, the excessively choleric Richard fails to recognize that Joan's phlegmatic quality, which he calls smugness throughout this story, balances well with his own nature. The Hamiltons say that he neglects to keep his marriage "in good heart through his affection."[27] Yet it should be noted that this reading seems to partake of an ethical rather than religious emphasis. Surely it also neglects the importance of Christian meanings of blood, where its shedding redeems the human race through Christ's sacrifice. Updike hints that theories of humors in balance—the idea of balance at all—need to be, and have

---

[23] Ibid., 52.
[24] Updike, Introduction to *Too Far to Go*, 10.
[25] Updike, *Too Far to Go*, 54; Greiner, *The Other John Updike*, 139.
[26] Updike, *Too Far to Go*, 55.
[27] Hamilton, *Elements of John Updike*, 66.

been, overthrown in a practical sense by modern medicine and in an existential sense by the primacy of Christ's blood.

Notions of ethical balance are also parodied in the less-learned conversation to follow. Richard apologizes for his hurtful remarks on the way to the hospital—or at least says that he didn't mean those things—and promises no longer to pursue Marlene Brossman. Joan responds phlegmatically that she doesn't care about his flirtations. This irritates him: "That smugness; why didn't she *fight*?"[28] Richard had been gaining satisfaction through a brief time of ethical goodness, but now has to retreat again to his rotational fantasy of a mid-day date with his secretary. The two stop for pancakes at a restaurant Richard knows. He perks up under the fantasy that this is a breakfast after illicit lovemaking, picking up the check and saying "handsomely" that he will pay. But his discovery that there is only one dollar in his wallet angers him. His fantastic plot in which he plays the prosperous, generous lover is ruined, and he returns to his earlier profane self: "Goddammit...I work like a bastard all week for you and those insatiable brats and at the end of it what do I have? One goddam crummy wrinkled dollar." Spending the morning giving has not transformed him. He still wants to gain, earn, accrue, possess, and control. And punish.

Joan's reply that they will "both pay" suggests Updike's insight that both she and her husband suffer for his fantasies, or rather for his profane frustration at the inevitable failures of those fantasies to heal his existential brokenness.[29] This is existential illness with a particular psychological origin, one that Erik Erikson found in another troubled young balked believer:

> I would like to suggest that this side of Luther was a kind of personalized profanity, which in some ways is the opposite of praying, for it uses the holiest of names "in vain." Its tonal nature is explosive, its affect repudiative, and its general attitude a regressed, defiant obstinacy. It is the quickest way for many to find release from feeling victimized by the impudence of others, by the gremlins of circumstance, or by their own inanity. The degree of the release experienced, however, is in inverse relation to the frequency with which this means is employed: a chronic swearer is a bore, and obviously an unrelieved obsessive.[30]

---

[28] Updike, *Too Far to Go*, 57.

[29] Ibid., 58.

[30] Erikson, *Young Man Luther*, 246.

It seems that neither Richard's aesthetically-motivated inner life nor Joan's patient ethical goodness can address Richard's essential profanity, or their mutual marital problems. What has gone wrong is that Richard Maple has grown up mired in an identity confusion that expresses itself in hurtful ways. To put this theologically, he participates fully in original sin. For Updike and Kierkegaard, only "giving blood" has the power to lift him out of that personal inheritance. Richard is a troubled bore, but Joan needs help too. Though she willingly gives blood for her cousin, she never even suggests that they visit her. Something about Joan's love of neighbor is too cool, abstract, and finally inauthentic.

&

This is the part of Updike's career that seems most emphatically Lutheran, shaped by Kierkegaard's recasting of Luther's celebration of faith and love over-against discipline and law, or "works righteousness." These are the days of "Sunday Teasing" (1956), in which the autobiographical husband reads the Basque Catholic Unamuno and Danish Lutheran Kierkegaard, or of "Pigeon Feathers" (1960), in which the Lutheran boy David Kern comes to believe that a God who lavished extraordinary craft on a pigeon could certainly never allow him to die. Or the days of "The Dogwood Tree: A Boyhood" (1962), in which Updike speaks of being "branded by the Cross" in a specifically Lutheran fashion—"an obdurate insistence that at the core of the core there is a right-angle clash to which, of all verbal combinations we can invent, the Apostles' Creed offers the most adequate correspondence and response."[31] These stories of the late 1950s and early 1960s offer fictional corollaries to these theological confessions of the same period. While in "Giving Blood" the focus is on the nature of love and its divine form, grace, "Twin Beds in Rome" deconstructs the grandiose human will as it thinks of spreading faith. Faith, for Luther, emerges from the uni-directional grace of God, and so will and decision are problematic categories of experience requiring complex, essentially dialectical understanding. "Twin Beds" is meant to dramatize and advance such an understanding, while also illustrating most touchingly what is right and wrong with the Maples marriage.

---

[31] John Updike, "The Dogwood Tree: A Boyhood," in *Assorted Prose*. (New York: Knopf, 1965) 181.

In "Twin Beds in Rome" Richard carries his conflicted personality and his dread to the heart of Western Christendom. Richard's experience, his inner bad faith confronting a half-holy, half-corrupt city, mirrors that of another confused, tortured young man visiting Rome almost five centuries earlier, young man Luther. Richard will find himself fathoms deep in the wrong in this story too, but in a far less culpable way. It will not be his volitional self troubling him—his speech and his behavior. It will be his tortured unconscious, which in this story is very Lutheran indeed, modeled after the bad faith and tortured consciousness of Luther himself. Like Luther, Richard will leave Rome disappointed, disturbed, and searching for a thoroughly revised cosmic ideology.

Young Martin Luther arrived in Rome in 1510, serving as representative of the Erfurt chapter of the Augustinian order in a dispute to be settled by the pope. As Reformation scholar Roland Bainton recounts the visit, Luther showed little enthusiasm for either classical or Renaissance art and architecture. He saw his visit to the holy city as a time of privileged access to the saints. Through their relics he had an opportunity to "save his soul." The trip was really a pilgrimage, in other words, though its stated purpose was more practically juridical. Luther spent his weeks in Rome in "strenuous" celebrations of masses at sacred sites, in visits to "the catacombs and the basilicas, to venerate the bones, the shrines, and every holy relic." His rest was fitful, as he slept near open windows in the fetid humidity, his head pounding. Famously, Luther was shocked at the profanity and disbelief of Italian priests, whom he heard speaking flippantly in celebrations of the Eucharist: "Bread art thou and bread thou wilt remain, and wine art thou and wine thou wilt remain."[32] As Richard Marius aptly puts it, this utterance had the effect of "mocking the doctrine of transubstantiation and by extension the tradition of the church and the notion of the unseen world."[33] Yet Luther remained confident for a time in the Catholic notion of superfluous merit, and the possibility of that merit being granted to him and his family.

Finally that confidence too was shaken when Luther visited Pilate's stairs in the Basilica of St. John Lateran, by tradition stairs that the

---

[32] Roland H. Bainton, *The Church of Our Fathers* (New York: Scribners, 1941) 49-50.

[33] Richard Marius, *Martin Luther: the Christian Between God and Death* (Cambridge, MA: Belknap Harvard University Press, 1999) 82.

suffering Christ scaled just before his crucifixion. According to official church doctrine, the believer who scaled these *Scala Santa* on his knees, saying a *Pater Noster* on each step and then kissing it, released a soul from purgatory—and received a certificate of plenary indulgence to prove it. Luther completed this work on behalf of his grandfather, actually regretting before mounting the stairs that his parents were still alive and thus ineligible for this spiritual benefit. His personal crisis occurred when he stood at the top of the stairs, contemplating his just-completed assistance to his dead grandfather, and found himself saying, "Who knows whether it is so?"[34] Luther's personal pilgrimage had failed, partly because he had witnessed so much ecclesiastical corruption, but mostly because of the urgings of his conscience. He had lost his confidence in superfluous merit, and certain core rituals of his faith had become ridiculous and empty for him. Luther returned briefly to Erfurt, then to Wittenberg, the city of his professorial work, later to become his world stage. There he would nail his 95 theses to the church door seven years later, beginning the Reformation.

Rome's disillusionments for Luther, Bainton claims, were various and not completely relevant to his theological misgivings. They were however, "concomitants in his total distress."[35] For Bainton, this distress is non-pathological, simply Luther's moral and intellectual disgust with Roman impiety and extra-biblical doctrine. Half-conscious vocational doubts were also distressing to him, according to Bainton, but not enervating. For psychoanalyst Erik Erikson, however, Luther's distress is a matter of identity and development, problems appearing first in his teenage years and persisting life-long. In *Young Man Luther* Erikson argues that Luther's symptoms included youthful depression, obsessive-compulsive behavior in his early monastic years, raging abuse of opponents and enemies, stomach ailments in middle life, and the raving, vituperative speech against Papal loyalists and Satan, and later, the Jews of his day. Erikson speaks of Luther's recognition of "the psychosomatic language of the body," and his efforts to fight what he considered the machinations of the devil. Erikson considers these machinations to be merely neurotic symptoms. So, for example, Luther would eat and drink copiously when constipated or nauseated—he called it fasting because he took no satisfaction in the consuming—in order to deny the devil these forms of control or torture. For Erikson, these intestinal discomforts

---

[34] Bainton, *Faith of Our Fathers*, 51.
[35] Ibid., 49.

and "paranoid repudiations" reveal the unresolved character of Luther's failed identity achievement—his identity diffusement.[36]

In "Twin Beds in Rome," Updike recreates Luther's sufferings during his month in Rome, giving those sufferings to Richard for quasi-comic effect. He also grants Richard the same unresolved senses of identity and theological commitment. The story is colored by Updike's own trip to Rome a year earlier, a trip that gave rise, as I discuss in my first chapter, to his first public essay on Kierkegaard's ideas about faith. Like Luther, Richard Maple brings his unresolved identity to a site of ancient Christendom, along with a fearful need to save his mortal soul. There his psychosomatic symptoms both reveal and exacerbate his inner conflict over questions of love and faith. These symptoms include stomach pains and sleeping problems similar to Luther's, and also pains in his tortured feet that are all his own. As all these pains mount during a day in the Roman Forum, Richard is incapacitated by his anxiety, in terrible, knifing pain that gave no "hope of escape."[37]

Episodes of existential terror accompanied by bodily distress and pain are very real to Updike. He experienced them. In a 1999 *New Yorker* piece titled "The Future of Faith," Updike recounts two such episodes. The first occurred when Updike was in his early- to mid-30s, around the time when he composed "Twin Beds in Rome." Having given a reading and judged a poetry contest at a women's college, he suddenly felt "poised above the chasm" alongside the nubile, innocent, and obliging students. He spent that night in a dorm room, gripped in terror. "I had suffered such episodes before," he writes. "[I]t is as if one were suddenly flayed of the skin of habit and herd feeling that customarily enwraps and muffles our deep predicament." The next morning, daylight relieved Updike of the terror. Another episode was much more recent, occurring just weeks before Updike composed this essay. Coincidentally, this night-terror occurred in Italy, in a hotel room overlooking Florence's Duomo. Both times Updike experienced partial relief. At the women's college he was helped by reading a passage in a self-help book he neither names nor describes. In Florence praying helped, especially after the prayer seemed to receive an answer when a furious thunderstorm arrived, signaling to Updike the existence of a living God. "God was at

---

[36] Erikson, *Young Man Luther*, 245-46.
[37] Updike, *Too Far to Go*, 70.

work—at ease, even, in this nocturnal Florentine commotion, this heavenly wrath and architectural defiance, this Jacobean wrestle."[38]

Richard's experience in Rome is similarly frantic. The opening of "Twin Beds in Rome" suggests that Richard's psychosomatic ailments originate in the ambivalence he feels about Joan, his marriage to her, and the purpose of this trip. They want to bring their marriage to a point of "kill or cure."[39] Is it also a second honeymoon? A reward two consumerists give themselves for a marriage that may end up brief but was valiantly fought? A moratorium by which the two can come to understand the compelling reasons for their marriage's demise? Or possibly an essentially unconscious pilgrimage to the heart of Catholicism, of religion deeply invested in ethical discipline, so that they might find the practices and the will to preserve their marriage? Joan and Richard do not know, and we take Richard at his word: after long talk and thought about separating, in conversations "increasingly ambivalent and ruthless as accusation, retraction, blow, and caress alternated and canceled," the Maples obey a "marital habit."[40] They give themselves a trip, and each other a little rest. The reference to "habit" is in keeping with Updike's terrors. Such habits normally keep terrors at bay.

Soon we realize that we can no longer take Richard at his word. It becomes increasingly evident that Richard's powers of denial and reversal are working overtime. Unlike previous stories in which Richard raves at Joan, revealing his inner turmoil, in this story he speaks calmly, exerting a more persistent pressure regarding his rotation project. His cruelest remark is that Joan is "such a nice woman" that he can't understand why he is "so miserable" with her. This is a jabbing reminder that the pleasures of this trip together will not deter him from his pre-rotation separation. However, his spoken and inner speech does yield information about Richard's essential bad faith in this story and in his marriage, information we receive through clever ironies about the nature of love and marriage. These ironies are set up by an early remark about the marriage as "[b]leeding, mangled, reverently laid in its tomb"—marriage as the body of Christ. Here is the "one flesh" imagery again, conveyed through imagery of blood, but this time connected deliberately with the incarnate man-God.[41] The notion is that the love of marriage has

---

[38] Updike, *Due Considerations*, 41-42.
[39] Updike, *Too Far to Go*, 63.
[40] Ibid., 60.
[41] Ibid., 60.

a sacramental quality, that the Christian married couple is one flesh with Christ as well as with each other. But this is a story about being torn, emotionally divided, conflicted. Images of divided pairs abound in the story—from the twin beds; to the image of "mad kings" as rulers of the couple's minds; to the Italian civil war; to Hemingway's famous novel of lovers separated through death, *A Farewell to Arms*; to Joan's insight that she is "classical" while Richard is "baroque." These images express a human tendency toward conflict and division, but are paired in this story with countervailing images—Joan's joining Richard in one bed for tender caressing; the Vittorio Immanuel Monument to Italian national unity; the mad kings' armies gratefully mingling when absurd hostilities cease.

Richard's and Joan's hostilities seem increasingly absurd. Repeatedly, Richard feels or recalls his deep connection to Joan. On the bus ride from airport to city through the dark Italian countryside he recalls his wife's intimate confession years before that a gas station attendant's washing of their car window, which caused the car to rock rhythmically, gave her a "sexual stir."[42] Richard still feels the unreasonable but immediate jealousy he first felt that day. Richard also feels pleased to know that this trip is making Joan happy. Yet his thoughts about this feeling are absolutely perverse: "This was his weakness. He wished her to be happy, and the certainty that, away from her, he could not know if she were happy or not formed the final, unexpected door barring his way when all others had been opened."[43]

Richard is unable to see that he has defined something other than his "weakness"—it is his love. A few moments later, Richard sees that he has caused Joan to cry with his spoken sense that he and Joan had "only a little way more to go" to their separation. Again, his reaction is natural and his thinking about it perverse: "He fought down the impulse to comfort her, inwardly shouted it down as cowardly and cruel, but his hand, as if robbed of restraint by a force as powerful as lust, crept onto her arm." What is this force as powerful as lust? It is his love. Notably, he and Joan are mistaken for honeymooners as Richard caresses his wife's arm. But Richard insists to himself that he does not love Joan. In order to honor his program in aesthetic rotation he must deny, minimize, and negate the most sacred feeling in him.

---

[42] Ibid., 60.
[43] Ibid., 61.

Richard's emotional duplicity also finds expression in his speech. He recognizes that lines such as "You're such a nice woman...I can't understand why I'm so miserable with you" are "simultaneous doses of honey and gall." He realizes that Joan is entirely right to ignore such remarks. She realizes that this is Richard's flippant or comic speech, something to be passed over as non-serious. Richard's pondering about the trip also illustrates a lack of serious clarity. The twin beds, for example, represent for Richard a violation of the "certain technical purity" he wishes to bring to the "kill or cure" method of dealing with this faltering marriage, yet he has violated this purity himself because he has "doomed [the cure] to fail." Joan makes an apt comment the morning after Richard's agitated first night of sleep in Rome, during which he shouts in his sleep, "Leave me alone!" She tells Richard, "It was refreshing not to have you contradict yourself."[44]

Living in this contradiction and duplicity, this bad faith, is causing psychic pressures that find release in Richard's somatic life. The appearance of these half-comic symptoms in the end of act one lend the story its liveliness, and of course illustrate Richard's psychological distress. If it were true that the Maples marriage simply needed to expire, that Richard simply recognized before Joan that this was so, then Richard should feel at most regret and sympathy for her, or perhaps guilty responsibility for his share of the relationship's faltering. But this story presents anxiety of a different order. When Joan suggests a walk late in the evening of their arrival, Richard's feet begin to hurt. Since the Maples have done so little walking, Richard is not merely footsore; he jokes about an allergy to marble, but the origin of this pain is clearly psychological. They end up at an American-style bar, where Richard responds to his growing anxiety by attempting to restore some of the skin of habit and herd feeling that Updike has told us helps keep his own terrors at bay. But this bar isn't familiar enough, American enough. The hamburger is "more tomato sauce than meat," and a drunken male American voice drones on in a "distinctly female circuit of complaints"— an audible reminder of something Richard does not bring into full consciousness here, which is that his own complaints are endless, droning, self-indulgent. Identifying these complaints as "distinctly female" is perhaps to hint that Richard's inner conflict has something to do with his sense of masculine identity and calling, his failures of his own notions of male strength, his role as husband and father. Whatever

---

[44] Ibid., 61-65.

the precise nature of Richard's inner conflict, he seems also to be having an existential terror of the type Updike has experienced, a "growing dizzy emptiness within him." [45]

Throughout the story Updike connects this dizziness, and also Richard's pains in his feet and stomach, with two main sources. The first is the "exploded civic dream" of Rome itself, which seems to overfill Richard with a sense of human mortality and the vanity of human plans. The second is a certain Roman corruption regarding payment and tipping. This fiscal theme we should view in theological terms. Richard is no fiscal stickler. Buying chestnuts on the street, for instance, he "welcomed being cheated" because it gave him "a place in the Roman economy." [46] As his anxiety mounts, having such a place is what he sorely needs. He has tried and failed to find a familiar and comforting America on a Roman commercial street, so now he tries to find a home in Rome. Home and habit feeling distant to him, he is exposed to his own fear of death and to the vanity of his own aesthetic commitments. They have their own vain fiscal quality: he wants to trade up from one woman to another, in the hope of decreasing his boredom and seeking diverting pleasures in new fields of play. Significantly for this product of a Lutheran author, Richard's tips and payments are made to secure the peace of his inner life, his very soul. In other words, in his heart they are indulgences, payments meant to secure his sound and rightful place in an indifferent universe. In the medieval mind, indulgences were scrip drawn upon the Roman treasury of human merit, a treasure deposited in blood and suffering by the many saints who found their way to the Holy City in patristic days. For those who feared eternal damnation, saintly merit was available for purchase. Technically, an indulgence was freely given, and the penitent recipient then freely gave alms to the church. But because of ordinary and unsurprising human corruption the power of indulgences was often exaggerated and gifts became lucrative sales. Richard's psyche, like Luther's, recoils against such problematic expressions of human faith and merit—even though Richard thinks in this story of his subconscious as "cavernous accounting rooms." [47]

The Rome we encounter in this story is an anagogical city, filled with corollaries to the desperate human situation. As Richard and Joan ride a bus into the city, their first notable sights are the Pyramid of

---

[45] Ibid., 64.

[46] Ibid.

[47] Ibid., 64.

Cestius and the Colosseum. Updike expects us to know that the Pyramid of Cestius is a tomb. Clad in marble, the pyramid also establishes that type of stone as the material of tombs, and connects Richard's foot pain with death. Updike also expects us to know that the pyramid is the landmark for Rome's Protestant Cemetery, famous for many graves but especially that of John Keats, who rests directly beside the pyramid. Death is not the pyramid's only signified however. It refers also to a reformed understanding of faith. Incorporated into the Roman gate named after the Apostle Paul, the gate leads to the Basilica of St. Paul Outside the Walls, the burial site of the executed apostle. This is a death reference, of course, but Lutherans like Updike know that it is St. Paul's letter to the Romans that led Luther to his formulation of justification by faith alone, and revelation of God through Christ. The Colosseum slides into view, appearing to them "like a shattered wedding cake." Here we have an obvious combination of meanings: the death of saints and martyrs combined with the demise of a marriage. Of course the Colosseum also conveys the sense of the "exploded civic dream"[48] of Rome, the city's associations with classical Western cultural and Republican values, neither of which endured in the city. The word "exploded" is interesting here. Surely, "decayed" or "dead" is more accurate, but Updike seems to want to emphasize the violence that people enact upon their plans and dreams.

He also emphasizes Rome's commercial streets, such as the unnamed one where their hotel is found. The commercial character of Rome is a motif in the story. Richard quickly finds an American bar when he wants to feel at home, a shoe store when his feet begin to hurt, and (less happily) the Banca d'Italia in his painful extremity on a long walk to the hotel they can't find. All three end up useless to Richard in his pain, which is the point. The commercial/consumerist world partakes of the aesthetic, and though Richard won't admit it, the aesthetic only has value for people who feel well, who are not *in extremis*. During their first full day in Rome, Richard will be *in extremis*, and as a result will become lost in both the geographic and emotional senses.

Before this pained walking trial through the confusing streets of Rome, the focus of the story's second act, Richard and Joan enjoy a series of sites with anagogical meaning. They visit the Victor Emmanuel Monument, which Richard cannot see as a sign of unification—in this case national rather than marital—but as "stairs leading to nowhere," an

---

[48] Ibid., 67.

apt image of his own cosmic ideology. Victor Emmanuel is in fact the "funny little king" of *A Farewell to Arms*, as the Maples discuss, a clever reference to Hemingway's most compelling tale of marital love and inevitable death. Death and vanity are the points of imagining Mussolini in his Palazzo Venezia, and then climbing more stairs to the equestrian statue of Marcus Aurelius in the Piazza del Campidoglio. Curiously, Updike tells us that Richard and Joan "circled the square," perhaps another hint at the couple's perversity in a geometrical image.[49]

The churches of Rome come to represent the apostate quality of a city no longer holy, a city where death still holds sway. The Maples walk upon the tombs of "sleeping people" in the church of Santa Maria in Aracoeli: Are they only "sleeping" because this church is an "altar to heaven?" In any case, other tourists peer at a convincingly dead "child-sized greenish remains of a pope." Along the forum, the Maples visit "the abandoned church" of Santa Maria Antiqua, a sanctuary that feels to Richard "innocent of worship." The Via Sacra feels to him pagan rather than sacred. By this time, Richard has begun to feel not only inexplicable foot pain, but also a stomach pain that he can only call a "gripe"—a word that means, appropriately, both pain in the bowels and complaint. Richard's pain is clearly associated with a day spent contemplating death and decay in classical and Christian Rome. By the time he arrives at the Basilica of Constantine, built to honor the emperor who established Christianity as the religion of Rome and thus secured its predominance in the West, Richard is in such pain that he refuses to enter.[50] Rome's apostasy mirrors Richard's.

Apostasy carries the sense of revolt or rejection of faith, yet Richard's revolt is unconscious and his wish to purchase or bargain for relief from his pain indicates that there is a searching quality in him, a wish to find the God whose omnipresence Kierkegaard argues he only need acknowledge. This possibility is conveyed by a lightly emblematic narrative of the medieval Roman indulgence drama of the sixteenth century. Throughout his time in Rome, Richard is asked to pay and overpay, tip and over-tip for his pleasures and his relief. These moments begin to parody his commitment to the aesthetic, with its own pecuniary foundation. Paying for the cab ride from Termini to the hotel, Richard pays with lira coins that feel to him "the smoothest, roundest, most tactfully weighted coins he had ever given away." Richard's aesthetic

---

[49] Ibid., 64-66.
[50] Ibid., 67-68.

pleasure in the coins is significant for our Kierkegaardian understanding, but so is his reference to giving the money away rather than paying it for services rendered. This phrase "given away" recalls Richard's theological confession in "Giving Blood," his limited understanding of "giving" as an act of love generally and an act that in a Christian understanding involves no loss. A few moments later, Richard interprets the satisfied appearance of the hotel clerk as a sign that he has over-tipped the man. Richard feels no resentment until it dawns on him— there seems to be a kind of denial at work here too—that the clerk has given the Maples a room with twin beds. Richard reads this as an insult, and of course as a violation of the smooth transactions of the aesthetic realm: payments should yield expected goods and services. Of course, we suspect that Richard is also troubled about the twin beds because in a deep inner sense he still wishes to be close to his wife.

Later that same evening, he overpays for a cone of hot chestnuts. Yet this time he feels no insult. His needs have changed; he enjoys the sense of being integrated into a local economy. The next day the Maples pay admission to the forum, where Roman citizens once came and went freely, and Richard begins to pay a series of tips for visits to churches. As Richard slips a "tactful coin" into the hand of a uniformed man who had let them into the church of Santa Maria Antiqua, he begins to feel an ache in his stomach. It quickly intensifies. He feels too ill to visit the Basilica of Constantine, and a dour guard "seeing a source of tips escaping" points to an exit. The Roman economy no longer welcomes Richard. Taxis are full and will not stop, street markets simply impede the walk home, the bank and shops are irrelevant and in fact come to represent a dryness with spiritual dimensions: "The shops were unshuttered, the distant fountain was dry."[51] Lost for a time in a holy city turned profane and indifferent if not hostile to Richard's needs, the Maples finally find their hotel.

Just before arriving there, Richard expresses his distress in the most emphatic terms of the story, terms that raise the issue of his choices and of choice or decision in general:

> He felt as if he were leaning backward, and his mind seemed a kind of twig, a twig that had deviated from the trunk and chosen to be this branch instead of that one, and chosen again and again, becoming finer

---

[51] Ibid., 67-70.

with each choice, until finally there was nothing left for it but to vanish into air.[52]

This passage is crucial to our understanding of Richard's drama in this story. He sees himself as part of an existential dilemma in which choosing and continuing to choose is an absurd process of self-attenuation. According to this image, choice does not enlarge or develop individuals but rather diminishes them. The apparent reason is that choice itself is so utterly relativistic, lacking a terrain of necessity and an Archimedean point, so that to choose is to dissolve oneself into an absurd material world, absurd because it is ruled by the mad king of death. Famously, Kierkegaard writes in *Either/Or*, "When a person has truly chosen despair, he has truly chosen what despair chooses: himself in his eternal validity." The remark is Judge William's yet endorsed by Kierkegaard as powerfully true.

Updike endorses this Kierkegaardian viewpoint too. The logic of his admirably crisp version of the Judge's dialectical discourse runs something like this: to have existential or theological doubts is one thing, but to despair is to recognize the stakes of one's doubts about relating to the world. These stakes are mortal. To choose one's despair is to realize finally that death is inevitable. No conduct confined to the temporal and material offers any real consolation for this fact. To choose despair is therefore to choose oneself, over-against any inevitably absurd course of action that might divert one's attention from oneself and one's despair. Yet both the necessity of death and of the self are "posited" (Kierkegaard's word) by the absolute, so to choose oneself is also to choose this absolute. As Kierkegaard puts it, "I choose the absolute that chooses me; I posit the absolute that posits me."[53]

Updike is aware of the fact that this locution seems to posit a God on the grounds of human need alone, as though God's existence were not independent of human need. But one's own createdness, and the manifest existence of the greater delightful world itself, are for Updike apparently evidence enough for the existence of an independent Creator God that reveals Godself through Christ and works through the Holy Spirit. So he claims in the "On Being a Self Forever" chapter of *Self-Consciousness*, where he offers the mature version of his own youthful syllogism:

---

[52] Ibid., 70.
[53] Kierkegaard, *Either/Or*, 2:213.

1. If God does not exist, the world is a horror-show.
2. The world is not a horror-show.
3. Therefore God exists.[54]

Richard observes neither this hopeful logic, nor an "airtight case for atheism" of the kind that Updike confesses he felt before crafting his theistic syllogism.[55] Richard feels deeply the absurdity of his choices and his consequent attenuation. He connects attenuated feeling with his psychosomatic symptoms and his terror. For Kierkegaard, such a state of body and mind is reason for hope because the despair is clearly existential rather than what we would now call clinical, and such existential despair is a necessary prelude to choosing oneself in one's eternal validity.

The third act of "Twin Beds in Rome" concludes with no such moment of existential choosing. Instead, Updike provides the typical incorrigibility move. Finally back in his hotel room, Richard has fallen asleep in deep terror and pain, but as with Updike's own episodes of existential terror, he recovers with the aid of nothing more than sleep. He rests in the twin bed representing separation, yet Joan has also moved onto that bed and is beside him. He wakes to no pain, and sees his wife "as if freshly," as the girl in the Widener Library who had since "come to share his room." Like the comforting touch he gives Joan on the bus, this realization is love. Since the image is of the dorm room where the Maples first lay with each other, time has been defeated too. This love partakes of the unselfing that we have identified as a quality of agape. Both Joan and Richard make remarks that show they are alive to each other, refreshingly outside themselves:

> [Joan:] "Darley, it's Rome. You're supposed to be happy."
> [Richard:] "I am now. Come on. You must be starving."[56]

This heartening, unselfish moment is brief however. It is not clear whether the narrator speaks of Richard's consciousness or some independent truth with the remark that the Maples "had at last been parted. Both knew it. They became with each other, as in the days of

---

[54] Updike, *Self-Consciousness*, 230.
[55] Ibid., 229.
[56] Updike, *Too Far to Go*, 71.

courtship, courteous, gay, and quiet."[57] Strange way to be parted: though Joan here remarks that she is classical while Richard is baroque, her remark suggests what *"was* wrong" between the two of them. Richard notices her happiness and, jealous of it, "again grew reluctant to leave her."[58] While there is remarkable mutuality in this scene, perhaps Updike's point is that the love is incipient rather than existential. Despair has waned, and so Richard and Joan are able to return to their respective aesthetic and ethical ways.

This ambivalent reconciliation between Richard and Joan is not the wholehearted reconciliation that comedies train readers to desire. But the reconciliation is less important to the meaning of this story than to the nature of Richard's psychosomatic distress in the particular city of Rome. Richard is a foil to Updike's theological mentor, Martin Luther, and as such he represents the religious consciousness, tortured by commitments that seem ever more convincingly to be in bad faith. Richard's particular bad faith and existential angst are reflected in his duplicitous thinking about his marriage. He believes that he and Joan have a decision to make: either/or, kill/cure, find the grounds to remain married or effect the needed separation. But Luther's theology offers a crucial counterpoint to such thinking. Richard and Joan need not choose at all. They simply need to open themselves up to the love that Updike carefully shows they feel for each other, a love that erupts in both strange duplicitous language and lovely acts of kindness. Doing so, they might prepare themselves for another kind of opening up, the kind leading to grace. They need to open up to their own feelings of despair, which is to say a repenting consciousness of standing wholly guilty before God. Then, Luther's and Kierkegaard's theology suggests, they will know what love is, and what it can do. Then they will have the ability to choose themselves in their eternity, and perhaps their marriage need not become a ruin or their family an exploded civic dream.

"Marching Through Boston" is also about what love can do, works of love in both the domestic and larger social realms. The story puts on vivid display the sharp differences between Richard's aesthetic identity and Joan's commitment to the ethical. Richard again behaves outrageously, by almost any adult standard, while Joan earns our approval for her patience with her husband and courageous work on

---

[57] Ibid., 72.
[58] Ibid., 72, emphasis mine.

behalf of others' civil rights. She has Updike's approval too: as I have noted, he is on record claiming that Martin Luther King's civil rights movement, centering on nonviolent direct action and involving volunteers like Joan, represented a deeply religious mission, the only widespread religious impulse of the sixties to occur outside churches.[59] The question the story ponders is the same question the marchers sing throughout: "Which side are you on?" Set against the either/or dichotomies of the sixties culture wars—black/white, civil rights/states rights, man/woman, liberal/reactionary—is a much more ambivalent attitude toward the idea of "taking sides" in the social or ethical realm. Updike also gives a compelling hint that only love has the power to heal these divides and dichotomies, a hint conveyed in the comfort Richard offers to a quasi-daughter and the fear he creates in his real one.

In order to open up these questions, Updike has to establish the Kierkegaardian terms of his debate, which he does through a series of quiet ironies in the first act of the story. The brilliant first sentence, for instance, delivers such an irony through its evident focus on the massive ethical campaign of the civil rights movement seen through Richard's aesthetic perspective: "The civil rights movement had a salubrious effect on Joan Maple." Her cheeks grow rosy and her eyes shine when she arrives home and speaks of her nonviolence "indoctrination." She sips Benedictine, Updike's clever hint that she has actually relinquished her will, as a monk might accept the Rule of St. Benedict.

Usually, Joan speaks in the language of therapeutic adjustment to socially affirmed notions of psychological health and identity. Functionality is the goal. Engaged in the practices of nonviolent direct action, she says, "you have no identity. It's elegant. It's beautiful." Richard's commitment to the aesthetic entails few virtues, but seeing the absurdity of that remark is one of them. He knows that the self is primary, essential, existential, and that there is great danger in dissolving the self into a delusion of communal efficacy. He "distrusted this raw burst of beauty."[60]

The greatest irony at work in this conversation involves Joan's incoherent discussion of Christian love. She tells of a New York fashion designer who had traveled to Selma for the marches. Because this woman flirted with the state troopers, who of course worked to put down the protests, she was sent home. Richard asks, sensibly enough,

---

[59] Updike, *Due Considerations*, 30.
[60] Updike, *Too Far to Go*, 74.

whether banishing such a woman is coherent since (this is implied) King's nonviolent direct action was founded upon notions of Christian love for the neighbor and for the enemy. "I thought you were supposed to love the troopers," Richard asks. "Only abstractly," Joan replies. "Not on your own."[61] But this is bad theology, if not bad common sense. Love is never abstract. For Kierkegaard it is a pathos-filled energy, genuine recognition of the person, an urge to action.[62] Later in the story, on the streets of Boston, Richard will begin to feel Joan's ethical commitment combined with just a frisson of the erotic. It is not the march that calls his ethical self into action, but his vestigial identity as loving father: he gives comfort and friendship to a chilly teenager named Carol.

Updike ups the psychological ante in this story, hinting that after the march Richard experiences what Joan calls a "psychotic break." Joan mentions the concept of psychotic break when she recalls finding the speeches of the Reverends Abernathy and King in Alabama very moving, how "teen-aged Negro girls" had fainted at the event. Three student psychiatrists whom Joan has met at the gathering make the diagnosis.[63] Whether these teenagers actually had psychotic episodes, or rather simple responses to fatigue and excitement, the story raises the question of Richard's mental state, which comes into sharp focus in the final pages of the story. There, Richard, chilled, wet, and feverish, rides home from the Boston march with Joan, complaining of the corny speeches of the civil rights leaders they had just heard. He begins to imitate the speech of Southern Christian Leadership Conference leader Ralph David Abernathy: "Onteel de Frenchman go back t' France...." Before long (but not before making some other outrageous claims that we will consider below) he is chanting a deeply sarcastic version of this speech: "Onteel de East German goes on back t' East Germany . . ."[64] Richard says that if Abernathy is John the Baptist to King's Jesus, then he, Richard, is Herod the Great. Soon he realizes that he cannot stop his raving speech, though he is embarrassing and frightening his children. He begins to imagine himself as black character stereotypes from white

---

[61] Ibid., 74.

[62] Mary Updike came home from Selma with a similar attitude, Updike tells us in his memoir. Less attracted to her exalted mood than Richard is to Joan's, he writes "I may have...felt a generalized love for mankind, like a too-intense love for dogs and birds, rather delocalizes Eros." See Updike, *Self-Consciousness*, 135.

[63] Updike, *Too Far to Go*, 76.

[64] Ibid., 88-89.

literature, a servant at Tara in *Gone with the Wind*, Uncle Tom in *Uncle Tom's Cabin*.

This psychotic event, or perhaps merely neurotic, mock-psychotic event, is part of the usual emblematic illness theme that crops up in the Maples stories. In this story, Richard suffers with a fever as well as mental acting-out. Again, we understand this as a Kierkegaardian illness, emblematic of the sickness unto death, or sin as separation from God. Certainly Richard's condition on this day is posed as a distinctly theological illness. "He had taken something foreign into himself and his body was making resistance."[65] This description is shaped by Karl Barth's theology as well as Kierkegaard's. For Barth, human beings are creations of God and therefore bound up with the Yes of all that God creates. The No in our midst is part of what God did *not* create. (In this way, God is not responsible for the evil, the unholy No, that we experience.) Here, Richard taking sin into himself (possibly also a virus) is consistent with this Barthian theology. Richard, we understand, is not created sinful but has had sin enter into him, like a disease, possession, or bewitching. Richard's illness suggests again his mortality, fragility, and constitutional wretchedness. The notion of psychotic break amplifies this illness, and again mingles state of mind with what people once called state of the soul. Most important to this imagery is that Richard has done nothing to invite or cause these illnesses. Though Kierkegaard insists that we choose sin, Updike recognizes the more modern theological problem of neuroses and psychoses, which cause and exacerbate alienation from God but are not, of course, fully under our control.

In order to dramatize this theological problem further, Updike offers us a series of allusions to the Salem witch trials. Richard is possessed or bewitched in this story, and he is not the only one who is. The most explicit reference to the witch trials involves the Maples' choice of banner to march under, Danvers or Unitarians. "In the end it did not matter," Richard tells us, but the theological choice matters deeply. The choice is between Danvers, Massachusetts, a town remembered for the Witch Hysteria of 1692, a hysteria caused by an intense Calvinist belief in an invisible world populated by angels and demons; and the Unitarian theological tradition, a later theology that attempts to expunge the implausibly spiritual from American religion and promote rational ethical duty. This is parallel to a choice cleverly posed by the Harvard

---

[65] Ibid., 77.

course whose "section man" Richard spies among the marchers—*Plato to Dante*, the Good and God, Hellenic rationalism and medieval Christian faith. Though Updike would presumably not blame the 1692 fits of Betty Parris and Abigail Williams in Danvers (then Salem Village) on spells cast by their neighbors, he does take seriously the notion of being possessed or unwillingly controlled by a malevolent agency, whether psychological or satanic. In this story we are introduced to a kind of continuum of such possessions. On one end of this continuum there is the "spell" that leaves young Carol "unable [...] to button" her light sweater on a chilly day—the sort of bewitching that all teenagers seem to suffer—and the "psychotic breaks" that other teenage girls suffered while listening to the address of Dr. Martin Luther King. While Joan is in Alabama, Richard lives under another, more transforming spell in which his identity is changed: "I'm very tired from being a mother," he says.[66] Not only is he exhausted from tending to the children as Joan usually does, with "more than paternal tenderness," but he feels in his affection for young Carol "as if destined to give birth."[67] Later, Richard is possessed by the spirit and voice of Uncle Tom, the sentimental caretaker of innocent Missy Eva. Most alarmingly, at least in an emblematic sense, Richard, through his sarcastic remark about Abernathy as John the Baptist—"God, if he's John the Baptist, I'm Herod the Great"—morphs himself into a killer of innocent children.[68]

Psychoses, neuroses, developmental and libidinous urges, a lust for power, role-shifting caused by others' choices, sin itself—these are the forces that limit our freedom and impinge upon our identities. Like magical spells, Updike suggests, these forces work on us without our consent and often change us into people that we don't wish to be. One exceptional mysterious force is love—the one force that casts a powerful spell yet whose magic is enlarging, whose power creates a more rather than less authentic personhood. It is love for his children that turns Richard into a mother, though incompletely we suspect. Updike doesn't neglect this magical force in the story either. The fragile and touching Carol has become his charge for the afternoon, perhaps because Richard is pleased to have recognized that she, like him, is freezing. Perhaps they bond because her friend Trudy ridicules her for misunderstanding the civil rights march as a kind of labor demonstration. In the most

---

[66] Ibid., 76.
[67] Ibid., 75 and 86.
[68] Ibid., 88-89.

important line of act three, Richard thinks that "a small love was established between them." Happily, this small love has little of the erotic about it, though Richard has just fantasized about seducing Trudy's mother—until he hears her irritating speech. Greiner believes that Richard's "roving eye" has selected Carol for a possible love affair, but the story suggests otherwise.[69] Carol herself recognizes the quality of Richard's love, telling him, "You don't have to be paternal"[70]

Richard replies that he wants to be. It is as if he finally feels a passion-filled urge with the rightful quality of a calling or vocation. At this moment he feels about to give birth, which signals the purity of his caritas and surely temporary defeat of his masculine libido. Richard suppresses the "urge to tell her he loved her," instead selflessly shielding her body from physically threatening, muttering, Irish onlookers. A magic is working on Richard; he is being changed. Passing under the statues of other social crusaders in the Public Garden, he feels his heart crack open, "like a book being opened." At the same moment, the march comes to its conclusion in the Common, and participants begin to "link arms, to fumble for love."[71] Here too, Richard is under a spell; his wretched personhood is overcome by a passion larger than himself, one he cannot suppress or control. It is a passion that derives from a general altruism like his wife's, but made real in his heart by the concreteness, the unique personhood of chilly, plain little Carol, who needs and deserves his care. True to Kierkegaard's more affirmative ideas, Richard loves his neighbor non-preferentially. Perhaps he ought to feel more love for the dispossessed African Americans with and for whom he marches, but it is right and true that he feels love for the vulnerable girl Carol.

But Richard isn't changed for long. The fourth act skips forward a few hours to the drive home from the Common to the witch-trial town of Ipswich.[72] During this drive, Richard's psychotic break begins. As in "Giving Blood" his speech is profane, raving, accusatory, childish. Finally it becomes ugly, as Richard indulges in a racially-charged parody

---

[69] Greiner, *The Other John Updike*, 189.

[70] Updike, *Too Far to Go*, 81-86.

[71] Ibid., 87.

[72] To be precise, the Maples live in a bedroom community modeled after Ipswich; this story implies that they might live in Danvers, since they consider marching under that banner. For the purposes of my claims here, it doesn't matter. Both towns were witch-trial towns in the seventeenth century, lie north of Boston, and both are 30 or so miles from the city, the commuting distance that Richard mentions in "Giving Blood."

of oppressed people. He completely loses his ability to stop; if Satan were real, and were to bewitch or possess a suburban breadwinner, it might look and sound like this. "'Now, effen,' he said, 'bah some un*foh*-choonut chayance, mah spirrut should pass owen, bureh me bah de levee, so mebbe Ah kin heeah de singin' an' de banjos an' de cotton bolls a-bustin'...'" Yet this is an existential, Kierkegaardian possession. Richard's mental distress, his psychotic break, concerns his death ("mah spirrut should pass owen") and whether he will outlive it. His satire on an afterlife—listening to singing and banjos on the levee—is a cry of a more rather than less authentic personhood. Richard is in despair because he cannot grant or realize eternity without parodying the idea. A "weird tenderness" creeps over him as he rests in bed, "as if he had indeed given birth, birth to his voice..."[73] As wretched as Richard seems in this scene, he also seems to have grown nearer the leap and his authentic self, which will be very different from this raving one.

There seems to be an either/or character to these possessions of Richard and others. It is as if they must defeat deeply self-oriented possessions in order to embrace the selfless, caritative ones. Of course Richard ought to embrace the abolitionist spirit epitomized by Stowe's Uncle Tom rather than the murderous powermongering evil of Herod. Yet his behavior tends to deconstruct the privileged item in each dichotomy—such as Uncle Tom/Herod in which Uncle Tom is the preferable or privileged term—until a theological goal is accomplished. Updike names two famous women of the day, for example, the courageous Mrs. Liuzzo, who dies for her work on behalf of disenfranchised African Americans on the very day that Joan arrives home from Alabama, and Mrs. Hicks, about whom the marchers chant "RETIRE MRS. HICKS."[74] The contrast between the two is not simple. Mrs. Liuzzo was a Roman Catholic convert who, inspired by television coverage of violence on the Edmund Pettis Bridge, took her family car to Alabama. She spent two weeks there, shuttling African-American and white civil rights workers to and from the Selma airport. On March 25, 1965 she was shot in the head while driving her car from the airport. Less heroic and much more ambivalent is Mrs. Hicks of Boston. She was chairperson of the Boston School Committee and an ardent opponent of Boston-area school desegregation. Her obituary in the *Boston Globe* makes note of her unsubtle racial coding—"Neighborhood schools for

---

[73] Updike, "Marching Through Boston." *Too Far to Go,* 89-90.
[74] Ibid., 75 and 84.

neighborhood children"—but also notes that she accused suburban activists like the Maples of calling for change in others' neighborhoods rather than their own, neglecting for example to build subsidized housing in their own neighborhoods.[75] Whose side was she on? Whose side is Joan Maple on?

The story's most touching implication about neighbor love involves a similar contrast between Richard's quasi-daughter Carol and real daughter Bean. Though Richard is suffering a fever, chills, frustration, and dubiety about this march, when he meets Carol he briefly answers her need for affection, warmth and protection with the little he has to offer: a peanut, Popsicles, friendship, shielding with his body. The sense of rightness that he derives from this "small love" is so potent that he feels about to give birth. It is as though the spell of Richard's aesthetic ploys were lifted, as though he is about to learn something larger about the imperatives of neighbor-love. Yet he fails to honor the invitation to faith, or perhaps only to the ethical, that comes from feeling and acting upon genuine love, agape. He returns home to his selfishness, his tendency to abuse, and most importantly, his neglectful and deadened consciousness with regard to his own children. Little Bean, aged about six in this 1966 story, is alarmed at Richard's fit. She asks whether her father will die, then bursts into tears. Richard doesn't even slow down his minstrel rant.

How is it that he can bestow acts of love on a girl he has never before met, merely on the grounds that he feels chilled as she does, yet treat his own daughter so brutally? This is a question Updike wants us to confront. The answer goes to Richard's incorrigibility, the sickness that Joan observes in him and that is destroying their marriage. Her work for the expansion and fulfillment of American civil rights is genuine enough, and admirable as an expression of genuine religious life in this country. But as the final line of the story indicates—"But Joan was downstairs, talking firmly on the telephone"[76]—the work is a way of ignoring her husband in his foolish need, and seizing the consolations of social usefulness. Richard's kindness to Carol is in its own way more powerful, because it is more immediate and unselfish—at least momentarily.

---

[75] Mark Feeney, "Louise Day Hicks, Icon of Tumult, Dies" *Boston* (MA) *Globe,* 22 October, 2003. http://www.boston.com/news/local/massachusetts/articles/2003/10/22/louise_day_hicks_icon_of_tumult_dies/

[76] Updike, *Too Far to Go,* 90.

Richard's utterly uncontrolled voice in the final scene is, according to the narrator, "a voice crying for attention from the depths of oppression." We have to take this information for its correct inflection. We may justifiably believe that Richard deserves no one's attention for his wretched dramatics, that he needs in fact to have this behavior extinguished through the withholding of attention, as a child's undesirable behavior is extinguished. We may also believe that it is profane to label a prospering suburban white male as oppressed simply because his wife wished to stay longer at a rainy-day event than he wished to stay. But that is not the source of Richard's oppression, or rather of the oppression that at this moment he has come to feel. This is existential oppression, the terrified sense that he is indeed someday going to die, perhaps without the loving care and attention of anyone near him. Richard is entirely wrong and profane to accuse Joan in the language he chooses: "*How* could you crucify me that way?"[77] As Kierkegaard predicts, his inner self grasps and clutches unsuccessfully after the solution, Christ's sacrificial act of justification between sinning people and a chastening God. He cannot help but speak of crucifixion.

It is important also to note that Updike in no way shares Richard's dubiety concerning civil rights actions. Indeed, he implies Christ's presence in Roxbury on this day. Updike hints at this as the marchers gather on the South Side playground. "Martin Luther King," the narrator tells us, "was a dim religious rumor on the playground plain—now here, now there, now dead, now alive."[78] Richard reminds us that people thought of Abernathy as King's John the Baptist, so Updike's reference here comes into clear focus: Dr. Martin Luther King struck him as a kind of Christ—one who used his imagination and efforts to be Christ to his neighbor. The reference is not mocking. As Terry Eagleton notes in my epigraph for this chapter, a measure of King's love is that opposing powers had to kill him. Writing before King's death, Updike seems to see in him a trans-ethical passion for justice, and a deeply informed respect for love. Nonviolent direct action is based, after all, in doctrines of neighbor-love and awareness that (as King writes in his 1963 "Letter from Birmingham Jail") "sin is separation. Is not segregation an existential expression of man's tragic separation, his awful estrangement,

---

[77] Ibid., 88-90.

[78] Ibid., 83. This story appeared in *The New Yorker* only 26 months before King's assassination in April 1968.

his terrible sinfulness?"[79] King cites Paul Tillich for this definition of sin. Tillich is no favorite of Updike's but here the expression is fully in keeping with Updike's confessed views. Indeed, sin as separation is the preoccupation of the story "Separating," as we will see. For Updike, separation is sin, and can be healed only with God's grace. In this sense, there is in the end only one side for the Christian to be on.

"Giving Blood," "Twin Beds in Rome," and "Marching Through Boston" establish in the Maples marriage what Richard calls a "rhythm of apathy and renewal."[80] This is a predictably aesthetic notion about marriage, a sense of how it is felt. Yet Richard is right in a deeper sense too. In the hands and hearts of incorrigibly human souls, love will meet with apathy, result in separation, and require renewal. This renewal Kierkegaard calls repetition, a concept he develops at length in the book *Repetition* and in *Either/Or*. Even the knight of faith finds it necessary to repeatedly renew connection with God. Joan and Richard find it possible to live out love only intermittently, yet it is clear that this love has power. According to Kierkegaard, it might very well heal what is broken between the two of them, their children, and their neighbors.

---

[79] King, Martin Luther, "Letter from Birmingham Jail," in Ayers, Edward L. and Bradley Mittendorf, eds. *The Oxford Book of the American South: Testimony, Memory, and Fiction* (New York: Oxford University Press, 1997) 452.

[80] Updike, *Too Far to Go*, 74.

7

An Etiquette of Adultery
"The Taste of Metal," "Your Lover Just Called,"
"Waiting Up," and "Eros Rampant"

[A]dultery was being institutionalized as a party game...
—David Lodge, *Souls and Bodies*[1]

Like the larger American nation, the Maples in 1967 and 1968 find their hopes for progress toward a peaceable life replaced by shock and swelling misery. During 1967 the Johnson Administration and American soldiers on the ground in Vietnam seemed to be putting a long conflict to rest. Hopes for victory and subsequent peace were high. But then, during the Vietnamese Tet holiday in January and February of 1968, Americans watched television coverage of widespread, coordinated assaults by North Vietnamese Army troops and Viet Cong irregulars throughout South Vietnam, even in the center of its capital, Saigon. Within weeks, Americans became sharply divided about whether there was any real purpose in continuing to fight with and for the South Vietnamese. In these stories Updike leads the Maples on a parallel journey, from complacent hope in progressive goals to shock, disappointment, and finally despair. The Maples are at first glad to have achieved suburban prosperity and a route to even greater satisfactions through greater sexual freedoms. But somehow those freedoms do not make them feel healthier. Eventually Richard and Joan fight with and insult each other and wonder why they should continue their marital alliance.

Luckily for the Maples, unlike the nation, growing misery is propitious, especially given that they are nominal Christians. Kierkegaard calls this misery despair. As their guilt and shame mount, as they grow more depressingly aware that their efforts are existentially unavailing, that happiness is not around the corner, Richard and Joan have a chance to make that leap into a different and better life. The

---

[1] David Lodge, *Souls and Bodies* (New York: Penguin, 1990) 115.

growing intensity of this propitious misery is the focus of these four stories, "The Taste of Metal" (1967), "Your Lover Just Called" (1967), "Waiting Up" (1978), and "Eros Rampant" (1968), which are set against the growing misery and absurdity of the worsening Vietnam conflict.

The marriage grows absurd too, as Richard and Joan commit themselves to projects that seem simply perverse. Specifically, these four stories teach readers an etiquette of adultery: ways to begin affairs, ways to conceal them, ways to keep in touch with lovers, even ways for the wronged husbands and wives of adulterers to negotiate a properly sophisticated response to an affair they have discovered.[2] This etiquette of adultery existed, and Updike was not complacent about its harmful side. He has declared in one interview that couples involved in frank adultery and sexual play "could be encountered anywhere in the East" throughout the 1960s.[3] Elsewhere he remarks, "The righteous hunt for healthful satisfaction was on, and pity the child, parent, or marriage vow that got in its way."[4] Updike insists that we critique the perversity of this etiquette, but not by applying our own ethical judgments. He exposes logical contradictions in the etiquette which make the entire system collapse.

In these four Maples stories, Updike surely does indict adulterous Christians, even while he chronicles their fun. Part of his method is purposely unsubtle. He simply contrasts adults under the spell of libido with frightened children witnessing their parents' behavior. Presenting readers with various forms of this fear in both children and adults alike, and with the contrast between the aesthetically-driven gestures of erotic love and the deep ethical need for authentic parental love, Updike makes an appeal to readers' consciences. In these ways he nudges readers in Kierkegaard's aesthetic stage toward the ethical. He handles another task, pointing to the religious stage, much more subtly, providing within each of the Maples stories an allusive subtext in which waiting for the call or return of the lover serves as a parodic imitation of a more sacred task, waiting faithfully for the call or return of Christ. Through these

---

[2] The phrase "an etiquette of adultery" appears in "Gesturing" (Updike, *Too Far to Go*, 229), and refers to a "code of separation" that both Joan and Ruth require so that each is protected from details about Richard's sexual life with the other. In this chapter I try to enlarge its meaning to capture an aspect of Richard's aesthetic gaming.

[3] Plath, ed., *Conversations with John Updike*, 25.

[4] Updike, *Due Considerations*, 461.

methods, Updike manages more than an indictment of an adulterous generation. He points to a realistic route to healing for troubled marriages, through increased dedication to the children based in a shift in inwardness that might banish the ethics of a relativistic society, an etiquette of adultery and betrayal, and lead toward existential freedom to love unselfishly and creatively. This inward change has a chance to change more than Christian families. As we have seen, Updike believed that creative, non-preferential loving had a chance to change the violent national and international situation as well.[5]

The Maples marriage breaks down just as America's commitment to the South Vietnamese does, between 1967 and 1973. Updike exploits this parallel. Beginning around 1968 the Vietnam war becomes a hot topic of conversation at the parties the Maples attend. Both the war and many marriages in the Maples' neighborhood feel wrenching and defeating, mutual betrayals stemming from involvements that perhaps should not have begun in the first place. Ironically, when Joan sits down for peace talks with Richard's latest mistress and her husband (in "Waiting Up"), she discovers that the husband does not believe in war. Joan realizes that this is lucky for Richard—otherwise this wronged man might apply to Richard a doctrine of armed containment, the kind that he feels America is right to pursue in Vietnam.[6] Meanwhile, Richard feels that his aggressions should go unpunished while Ho Chi Minh's must be stopped. Perhaps Joan's insight into her husband's contradictory thinking about violent resistance to wrongs is why Richard calls her, in one sarcastic rant, "Joan Maple, lady geopolitician."[7]

Richard, "perhaps, alone in the nation," loves another great geopolitician: President Lyndon Baines Johnson.[8] Updike tells us he felt much the same during these same years. When he looks back to these days in his 1989 memoir, he smells "the poisonous vapors of a polluted and fractious time."[9] Though an anti-war stance was universally fashionable in Ipswich and ideologically necessary at *The New Yorker*— Updike lost his occasional "Talk of the Town" editorials because of a

---

[5] Updike, *Assorted Prose*, 285. Recall that in this review of Denis De Rougemont's *Love Declared* (1963), Updike notes De Rougemont's confidence that genuine Christian love could lead to "international peace."

[6] Updike, *Too Far to Go*, 121.

[7] Ibid., 103.

[8] Ibid., 127.

[9] Ibid., 115.

note he wrote supporting Johnson's refusal to run for re-election in 1968—Updike supported the war with theological arguments and reservations. "Faith alone," he writes, summarizing this argument,

> faith without any false support of works, justified the Lutheran believer and distinguished him from the Catholic and Calvinist believer. In all varieties of Christian faith resides a certain contempt for the world and for attempts to locate salvation and perfection here. The world is fallen, and in a fallen world animals, men, and nations make space for themselves through a willingness to fight.[10]

So, as long as American presidents pursued reasonable means and ends in Vietnam, Updike would support them. He felt that Lyndon Johnson's decisions regarding containment of the North Vietnamese were defensible.[11] Richard too loves and defends Johnson, and takes heat for his views on Vietnam. But, his arguments are narcissistic; as we will see in these stories, he is really only talking about himself. Ever the cool and distant one, he finds it easier to love the moon, newly immediate in the "photographs beamed back from its uncongenial surface."[12] Richard is more inclined to enjoy American pride in the Apollo program than share in American shame and responsibility regarding Vietnam. This inclination mirrors his existential dispositions, his continual pursuit of rewarding adventure, and his utter resistance to the idea that his etiquette might be corrupt, that he might be wrong, deluded, or in desperate need of authenticity.

વ

"The Taste of Metal" is among the shortest of the completed Maples stories. Updike presents it in only two acts—before a car accident and after it—rather than the typical three or four. The story begins and ends with a discussion of Richard's new dental bridgework, which at first seems to provide him with an intriguing aesthetic experience, a strange, metallic taste in his mouth. By the end of the story this taste of metal merely confirms, depressingly, his physical decay, impending death, and even hints at his iniquity. Between these sensations, Updike plots two

---

[10] Updike, *Self-Consciousness*, 130.

[11] Ibid., 148. In the same passage Updike confesses he understood but had trouble defending some of Richard Nixon's wartime decisions, such as brutal bombings of the North.

[12] Updike, *Too Far to Go*, 127.

acts of ethically shameful behavior. In the first act the Maples attend a party. Richard drinks too much and acts silly. Joan allows Richard to drive drunk, Eleanor Dennis distracts Richard with her self-serving stories about her dissolving marriage, and when Richard loses control of the car all three experience a crash into a telephone pole. In the second act the three realize the severity of the accident, which has badly hurt Eleanor's legs. Because he wants to be alone with Eleanor, Richard selfishly sends Joan off with a stranger to phone for help, sacrificing her, he thinks, as Agamemnon sacrifices Iphigenia. Richard and Eleanor exploit their privacy, kissing and groping each other in the darkened car, parting only when the flashing lights of a police car illuminate their embrace.

The story hardly makes adultery look attractive or healthful, but its concerns soon transcend sexual ethics. "A Taste of Metal" is also the most Barthian of the Maples stories. It seems to be a story about a drunken automobile accident following a boozy cocktail party, but is really a theological meditation on the No and Yes of God's character and creation. It is a story about a suburban sexual and moral permissiveness that many readers deplore, yes, but a story filled with images and utterances of rebuke for failed conscience. These images include the taste of metal, the telephone pole on which Richard's car is broken (along with his lover's leg), a remembered ocean wave that didn't care whether Richard lived or died, and the police who arrive to arrest Richard for his drunken driving and find him in the embrace of his latest lover. Taken together, these images create an agenda of negation, rebuke, decay, pain, and punishment—the essence of the Barthian No.

This agenda has theological roots in the dialectical crisis theology of Karl Barth, in the Yes and No of God's essential character as Barth finds it revealed in scripture. In his *Doctrine of God*, Barth argues that the Yes of Eastertide—the affirmation of God's saving love for humankind—presupposes the No of Good Friday. Jesus' sacrifice on the cross and return as redeeming Christ would not be necessary if humankind were not so finally, incorrigibly rebellious and alienated from God. This rebellion and alienation is sin. Sinners—that is to say, believers—need to confront the No of God's righteousness, and the pathetically unavailing character of their own efforts and dispositions.[13] Barth and Kierkegaard agree that believers need to realize and cultivate a sense of their infinite

---

[13] Karl Barth, *Church Dogmatics*, vol. 1, *The Doctrine of God*, eds. G. W. Bromiley and T. F. Torrance (New York: T. & T. Clark, 2009) 397.

guilt before a wrathful, punishing, condemning and just God. We recall one of Kierkegaard's chapter titles from *Either/Or*: "The Upbuilding That Lies In The Thought That In Relation to God We Are Always In the Wrong."[14]

The first time Updike publically endorses this theology is in 1963, in the same essay in which he first mentions his admiration for Kierkegaard. As we have seen, he writes a review of Barth's *Anselm: Fides Quaerens Intellectum* (1931, in English 1961) in which he admires Barth's theology for its "rigorous negativity," its clearheaded realization that nothing in the natural world leads us to God, that our cry for God rises out of "nothingness." Updike spends most of the essay considering Anselm's proof for God—the argument that an ideal God must exist above and beyond any conception of God people might imagine. But he rejects this taming and possessing of God, siding with Barth in the argument that liberal humanist churches (such as Joan's former Unitarian one) view God merely as (this is Barth) "the Patron Saint of our human righteousness, morality, state, civilization, or religion...This god is really an unrighteous god, and it is high time for us to declare ourselves thoroughgoing doubters, skeptics, scoffers, and atheists in regard to him."[15] Closing this essay, Updike quotes from "The Task of Ministry," in which Barth makes a series of claims that seem to give shape to "The Taste of Metal":

> We cannot speak of God. The mystics, and we all in so far as we are mystics, have been wont to assert that what annihilates and enters into man, the Abyss into which he falls, the Darkness to which he surrenders himself, the No before which he stands is God; but this we are incapable of proving. The only part of our assertion of which we are certain, the only part we can prove, is that man is negatived, negated.[16]

That is to say, we can prove that we die, but cannot prove that death itself emerges from God and can therefore be addressed or redeemed by God. The important point here is that God is present to us, properly, as a rebuking, chastening, punishing, finally annihilating No. Recognizing and admitting this God is prelude to accepting the Yes of Easter. This theology is informed by and consistent with Kierkegaard's, whose God is also Wholly Other, impossibly distant. And the leap of faith is an

---

[14] Kierkegaard, *Either/Or*, 2:335.
[15] Updike, *Assorted Prose*, 237.
[16] Ibid., 282.

acceptance of the Yes, an absurd act of trust in Christ's mediation between believer and God.

Clearly, this theology casts Richard's drunken, concupiscent, heedless behavior on the night of his car accident into a very negative light—a negative light that goes beyond our own ordinary social ethics of marital fidelity, safe drinking and driving, and other social and legal responsibilities. In the light of Updike's admiration for Barth's chastening theology, it is hard to imagine a reader finding anything other than rebuke for adultery when the whirling blue police lights shine on Richard's embrace with Eleanor Dennis. These lights will halt his groping embrace and begin a process in which Richard will be held to account for his drunken driving. If Joan has returned to the scene of the accident with the police, she will also in her way hold Richard to account for his philandering. But these will be penultimate rebukes. Richard knows he will regret this evening "in another incarnation."[17] He means literally when he is sober, but the diction implies also a moment when he encounters an utterly chastening God face to face. Barth's theology helps us to see that this existential rebuke that Richard dimly anticipates transcends the ethical-legal rebuke he is about to experience and will soon enough forget. What transcends this penultimate penalty is his unredeemed death, his total annihilation, a result of his separation from God. This is not a matter of a paltry record of Richard's deeds and misdeeds but of his inner rebellion.

Notably, this story occurs on a Friday night, and partakes of the Good Friday No. After a dental appointment earlier in the day Richard perceives the effect of the metal in his mouth as a "No spoken to other tastes."[18] Taste and savor are Biblical images of life-affirming sensations, but in Richard's case the negation of flavors probably means that he is about to exhaust the benefits he receives from the aesthetic. Sure enough, that evening he can't taste the "variety of liquids" (he avoids the more honest word "liquors") he is offered. Yet he drinks them anyway, for their anaesthetizing effect. Richard tastes metal, both literally and figuratively, throughout the evening of the cocktail party. In a figurative sense he tastes Eleanor's "brassy" manner—her highly vocal way of denying the responsibility she shares with her husband for their separation. He ponders two other annihilating metals: the Dennises' carving knife and the crumpled front end of his new Corvair car. Both

---

[17] Updike, *Too Far to Go*, 96.
[18] Ibid., 91.

present him with psychic threats—the family knife that Mack Dennis might understandably want to use against him by the end of the evening, the family car that like its owner is "unsafe at any speed," as Ralph Nader famously described the Corvair in a 1965 book. Literally, Richard tastes his new bridgework, which seems to him to amplify his shifting and troubled sense of identity. His original teeth "had been a kind of mirror wherein his tongue had known itself." But under the alcohol and the unfamiliar dental work, Richard feels first "slightly less than himself" and later "slightly more." The latter feeling he imagines is similar to a "religious conversion," but a Kierkegaardian like Updike excludes slight rebukes or changes. Later in the evening, Richard tastes the metal of his hostess's bangle earring. True to the imagery, she implies a rebuke of Richard's drunkenness by suggesting that Joan should drive.[19]

Updike's choice of title also recalls a powerful biblical connection. In Exodus the taste of metal is connected with a more serious rebuke. When Moses comes down from the mountain with ten commandments from God he discovers that his people have been rebellious; they have fashioned a golden calf to worship instead of remaining faithful to the law-giving God who has been present to Moses. To punish these people, Moses has the golden calf ground into dust, strewn into the people's drinking water, and consumed. Then God sends a plague on the people. Thus, the taste of metal also means deadly rebuke for picturing God wrongly—as small, local, manipulable, or negligible. [20]

Both the taste of metal and the car's impact with the telephone pole communicate a No to Richard, a warning that the natural world inevitably halts human hopes and deeds. Richard confirms this reading of the nature of No with a memory, triggered after the accident by the taste of metal in his mouth, which he calls "[t]hat utterly flat No...." He recalls once being caught in ocean surf while swimming, utterly losing control to the stupendous force of the wave. "[H]is struggling became nothing, he was nothing within the wave. There had been no hatred. The wave simply hadn't cared."[21] This is an experience of negation—"he was nothing within the wave"—and near-annihilation. In the last line of the story, Updike connects this image of the annihilating wave with the

---

[19] Ibid., 93.
[20] See Exodus 32.
[21] Ibid., 99.

implicit judging of the police who arrive at the accident site, as "the whirling blue light of the police car *broke upon them.*"[22]

The car accident at the center of the story is very carefully contrived to give dimension to this theology of rebuke and death. Updike uses the accident to indict Richard for layers of ethical irresponsibility—for drinking and driving; for failing to heed Joan's warnings that the road is slippery, and that he is driving too fast for the conditions; for focusing on Eleanor's exaggerated tales about her estranged husband Mack's misdemeanors instead of on the road; for buying a sporty but unsafe car. But Updike depicts Joan as irresponsible as well. She allows Richard to drive drunk, even though she sees that his judgment is impaired as well as his driving skill. After the accident, Joan—"who had a social conscience," Richard reminds us—wonders why the social world is not responding to her need. "Why doesn't anyone come out and help us?"[23] We realize, perhaps, that even during her freedom marcher days, Joan's argument about conscience is that others need to be instructed how to consult theirs. Her conscience is clear, even when it should not be.

The telephone pole Richard strikes with his Corvair is a clever image. The immediately prior story, "Marching Through Boston," concludes with Joan on the phone conferring with other activists. "Your Lover Just Called," the story after "The Taste of Metal," opens with Richard answering the phone, believing that the nonresponsive person on the other end of the line is Joan's lover. There is an important opposition here. The social realm, represented by the telephone and its wired connections, is a central existential problem for the Maples because in their current aesthetic and ethical states it distracts them from the transcendently supernatural, in the Barthian sense. The telephone as system of connection and mere talk epitomizes the ethical busy-ness that Updike disdains, or rather, regards as wholly unavailing in the existential sense. On the other hand, the telephone pole also serves as an emblem in this story of the uncompromising No of nature's rebuke for human lack of care, of mortality's rebuke for lack of eternity, of God's rebuke for lack of connection with God. Richard finds the actual crash into the pole "surprisingly unambiguous." He feels "the sudden refusal of motion, the *No*..."[24] Like the metal in his mouth that says No to life's

---

[22] Ibid., 100, emphasis mine.
[23] Ibid., 97.
[24] Ibid., 96.

flavors, this crash then is about mortal weakness, about pain, about shame, about the daily possibility and final certainty of death.

Interestingly, the telephone pole stops Richard's aesthetic fun only temporarily. Compounding his misdeeds, just after the crash he sends Joan off with a boy who happens to drive up in an old Mercury. She is to find a phone and some help. This reference to the Roman god Mercury poses this boy as a divine messenger while his offer of help poses him as a Good Samaritan. The boy demonstrates his integrity by insisting that when Joan finds a phone she will call the police rather than a sympathetic friend. But he represents an important Kierkegaardian connection too. As Joan gets into the boy's car Richard thinks how he is sacrificing her, putting her at serious risk: "As Iphigenia redeemed the becalmed fleet at Aulis, so Joan got into the stranger's car, a rusty red Mercury."[25] In *Fear and Trembling*, Kierkegaard employs the Agamemnon/Iphigenia story as a useful counterpoint to the book's central Abraham/Isaac story. Abraham, when he hears the command to kill his son Isaac, makes two "movements." The first is "infinite resignation," a total relinquishment of hope for his son's life and acceptance of the horrible act he must perform. The second is the "movement of faith," an absurd personal confidence that God will relieve Abraham of this awful task—or give him a new son. The phrase "a new son" is absurd, but that absurdity is precisely what makes faith otherworldly and an offense to the reasonable.

By way of contrast with the Abraham story, Agamemnon lives entirely within the ethical. He too comes to realize that on information from a god he needs to sacrifice his beloved child. His daughter Iphigenia must be sacrificed in order that the gods might lift the calm that keeps his ships immobilized. He does so, but Kierkegaard through his persona Johannes de Silentio notes that Agamemnon is able to make an entirely ethical calculation. He simply has to make a terrible choice between his fatherly duty to his daughter and martial duty to his men and nation. Whichever he chooses, he can weep and seek comfort afterward for being forced to make an incredibly tough choice. Abraham cannot. If he had actually been required to kill Isaac, there is no ethical calculation in the world that can excuse him.[26] He would receive no

---

[25] Ibid., 98. As an anonymous editor at MUP suggests, Mercury is also the god who leads souls to the underworld, so this boy in a truck may, like the allusion to Iphegenia, communicate the nearness of death.

[26] Kierkegaard, *Fear and Trembling*, 115.

comfort, not even his own consoling thoughts. So when Richard views Joan as another Iphigenia, he takes the role of this utterly ethical Agamemnon, living in a civic-minded but essentially Godless moral economy. He knows that eventually he will be excused whatever happens this night, even if Joan is assaulted or killed by this young man in the rusty car. He shows how determined he is to avoid any thoughts of ultimate responsibility for the night's (and his life's) errors by beginning a new affair as he waits for the police, an affair with a woman he has already hurt badly. This is simply what he does: pushing away his fears and loving responsibilities through sexual and quasi-sexual adventures.

As usual, the state of the Maples' marriage is at question as well as these existential questions, and in this as in some other Maples stories Updike's attitude toward the marriage is implied by his play with concepts of physics. The opening remarks about Richard's dental work, for example, imply strongly the idea of decay. This would be nothing but a reference to particular dental and general mortal decay if it weren't for other steady references in this story to time, stars, planets, orbits, and entropy. The Maples' marriage has begun to show the signs of its own characteristic entropy, a psychological fatigue on the part of both Richard and Joan and a related susceptibility to the temptations and machinations of others. (The Dennises will tempt and torment both Maples for the next few years.) We are not allowed to forget either that the Maples are mortal. Before the party breaks up, Richard's failed headstand leads to his feeling that "[h]e was all mortality" and that this realization is a guiding "polar cluster at the zenith of this slow whirling."[27] In other words, Richard's sense of mortality should guide him, should become the fixed star by which to set his compass. But he is giddy.

These references to physics continue. Joan represents the dimension of time. As she approaches Richard to tell him it is time to go home, her face is "neat and unscarred as the face of a clock"[28] Eleanor Dennis, who views her nine married years as "a phase" in her life, apparently believes that she has as little choice in these matters as the moon does in its phases. She and we realize a different notion of time and heavenly objects when Richard's Corvair strikes the telephone pole, and her head

---

[27] Updike, *Too Far to Go*, 93.
[28] Ibid., 93.

striking the windshield creates "a web of light, an exploded star."[29] The heated interior cools, and Richard restarts the broken car in order to fight the entropy, which physicists call disorder. Light dies, warm things cool, stars explode or burn out, women expire of head injuries—or might. Death is programmed into our universe, from the atomic level, to the planetary, to the level of the stars.

Joan's ethical energy is also in entropic decline. Since her own love for Richard has always partaken of her commitment to duty, and since fulfilling that duty is giving her so little reward or compensation, she is undergoing a kind of moral entropy. She reluctantly takes a back seat to her drunken husband and flirtatious neighbor in this story, and characteristically utters mild and undemanding rebukes about Richard's driving. She phrases them as rhetorical questions: "Darley, you know you're coming to that terrible curve?" Of course gentle reminders are never going to prevent the accident. To accomplish that important ethical task, Joan needs to act, to take the direct action she has been trained for in Mississippi, to insist on taking the wheel. But she does not. While her own "No" should come from her conscience, and she ought to speak it before they all enter the car, she accedes to a situation in which a starker rebuke from the natural world of physical forces and consequences becomes more likely, a frightening collision with an implacable reality for which she is no more prepared than Richard.

Updike satirizes the ethical through Joan, but more humorously through the angry and self-centered Eleanor Dennis, whose version of her trials with an adulterous husband is a self-justifying melodrama. She sees herself as a betrayed ethical paragon. "Looking back at myself, I was so *good*, so wrapped up in the children and the house, always on the phone...." It is understandable that she would regret an unaware goodness that has been abused by a philandering husband, but troubling that she cannot view goodness and the vocation of loving parenting as their own reward. She now views herself as experienced, wiser. But both her self-proclaimed righteousness and judgment seem ridiculous by the end of the story, as it is she who reaches out to embrace another woman's husband—and a faulty, giddy clown of a husband at that. When the police show up, it is a reprise of the scene in "Snowing in

---

[29] Ibid., 96.

Greenwich Village," the police evoking civic rightness, the snow evoking cosmic truths.[30]

If "Marching Through Boston" hints that the casually chanted motto, "Which side are you on, boy?" should be taken seriously in an existential sense, then in "The Taste of Metal" that casually spoken remark is Eleanor's "you have no idea what men are capable of."[31] What are men capable of? The Barthian/Kierkegaardian answer seems to be, *Not much good.* Mack Dennis's profane antics, if they are to be believed, demonstrate how corrupt love can be when the energy of libido combines with a giddy consciousness and seeks new objects. Mack's infidelities, which mock his work with "bonds" or solemn promises, have a cruel, taunting character. He has the "crust" to tell his wife that when he beds his mistresses he sometimes imagines that he is having sex with Eleanor.[32] He and a mistress once ordered cake for dessert in honor of Eleanor's birthday. Yet in his philandering he observes the dubious etiquette of adultery: he doesn't have the guts to ask for a candle on the cake. Richard seems little better than his friend Mack. Not only is he an irresponsible citizen, a drunken driver on dangerous winter roads, but he too has a "crust" that conceals and protects a churning interior.

What is going to penetrate that crust? Only a force that can defeat the forces of physics, of time and space and entropic processes. This divine power is represented in the story by the music of Georg Frideric Handel. In the first seconds after the accident, just as Richard and his passengers begin to recover from the shock of their "surprisingly unambiguous" whack into the telephone pole, they realize that they are no longer hearing the engine and road noise and Eleanor. Now they hear a music that must have been there all along, "mellow, meditating music" that arrives in their little world "from a realm behind time." Richard recognizes this music as a Handel oboe sonata playing on the radio. In another play on the forces of physics, he wishes the tune could be played backward, that then time itself could be reversed and they would "leap" backward from the telephone pole.[33] The most important verb in Kierkegaard's work—to leap—indicates that here we are considering a

---

[30] As in "Snowing in Greenwich Village," this snow is Joyce's. Richard leaves a party drunk, just as Freddy Malins, Brown, and perhaps Gabriel leave their Twelfth Night party drunk.

[31] Ibid., 94.

[32] Ibid., 92 and 94

[33] Ibid., 96-97.

movement toward faith, away from the unambiguous, annihilating No. This music is somehow involved. We will know how as Updike's hints grow broader.

As Richard and Eleanor wait for Joan's return, Richard begins to sober. He feels an "infinite drabness" about his life. "Never again, never ever, would his car be new, would he chew on his own enamel, would she kick so high with her vivid long legs." He turns the radio on, and the music he hears is "still Handel."[34] Which piece is playing now? Even more than his oboe sonatas, of course, we associate Handel with a masterpiece called *Messiah*. When we realize this, we think about how Joan has been "sacrificed" to get her husband and friend out of this fix, as Iphigenia had been sacrificed to "redeem the becalmed fleet at Aulis." Sitting in his cold car Richard is thus literally waiting for his redeemer, Joan or Iphigenia or Christ. Updike hints that Richard could realize this thought in a greater sense, recognize which redeemer he really needs, and receive the Barthian Yes of Easter. But instead he chooses an aesthetic rotation, embracing Eleanor. He and his new lover thus choose her thankless Thanksgiving of tuna fish sandwiches and resentment, and his unblessed mock-Dickensian Christmas, "God bless us, every one" in slurred and sarcastic speech.[35]

☙

"Your Lover Just Called" opens with the line, "the telephone rang." When the caller hangs up without speaking, Richard teases Joan that her lover has just called. She replies that the caller was his lover, and a mean-spirited story commences. We discover that Richard is ill again, on a Friday: again, he suffers both a cold and the emblematic sickness unto death. In this story, we see a brief return of the raving speech we saw in "Giving Blood," "Twin Beds in Rome," and "Marching Through Boston." As in "The Taste of Metal," however, Richard seems to have found outlets other than speech for his neurotic energy. He clearly pours his energy into adulterous relationships and, because it is just as satisfying to him, verbal manipulation of others in support of his rotation projects. It is clear that he does take calls at home from illicit lovers, while Joan testifies credibly to her sexual if not emotional fidelity. (This credibility is undercut by later stories, which establish that she has been

---

[34] Ibid., 100.
[35] Ibid., 93-95.

conducting affairs for some indefinite time.) When Richard sees Joan kissing Mack Dennis in the Maples kitchen later that evening, he speaks with accusatory energy, however, and with taunting irony—as though he had nothing at all to feel guilty about, and as though Joan were conducting affairs that offended him morally. This is another perverse story.

Once again, however, Updike disposes quickly of any suspicion that he is somehow tolerant or morally quiescent about such casual adultery. The mocking verbal play in this story exacts a severe cost: the Maples' children now live in fear. They watch their father's antics, and their mother's exhausted, ineffectual responses to those antics. As they watch, the children sense dimly the emotional risks of a home dominated by the desperate, despairing existential needs of their parents. The children's fear also has the character of dread.

Adults involved in profane sexual gaming contrasted with children's relative blamelessness and fragility—this dynamic drives the story, in three acts as usual. The first act involves empty, ironic, and manipulative speech, as Richard teases Joan about a caller who hangs up before speaking, suggesting that the caller is actually a lover of Joan's who didn't know that Richard was home with a cold. He accuses Joan—falsely, he is convinced—of conducting affairs. The story's second act begins with Richard's shock at discovering that Joan does indeed engage in intimate play with other men. Gazing through his kitchen window from the back yard, he sees her kissing mutual friend Mack Dennis, and there is little doubt that this kiss and embrace are not merely friendly and consoling, as Joan later claims. Richard notices that she and Mack move their faces to kiss as closely and lingeringly as possible, and that Mack fondles Joan's "bottom" while she laughs and talks with pleasure.[36] Meanwhile, in an upstairs window a few feet away, daughter Judith plays with her dolls.

Though it gives Richard pause to see his vulnerable young daughter perilously near this extramarital intrigue involving her mother, he does nothing to assure the child's emotional well-being. Rather, he too begins to play with dolls—Joan and Mack, whom he now sees as "two...dolls, homunculi, in his playful grasp."[37] He enjoys a few drinks and then exploits what he has just learned about Joan for his own hopes of further sexual gaming, perversely promoting an affair between Joan and Mack.

---

[36] Ibid., 107-8.
[37] Ibid., 109.

Interestingly, the third act of the story does not make the incorrigibility move that we have seen in many earlier Maples stories. Richard and Joan quarrel, and doing so frighten their son Richard, Jr. But ending their quarrel and then spending a morning in more wholesome exercise and, in Richard's case, play with the children, they come together for a calmer talk. Joan correctly diagnoses Richard as bored—a characteristic mental state for those in the aesthetic sphere, we recall. She realizes that Richard is trying to make her more interesting to him for his own purposes. Richard, meanwhile, realizes that his wife is already quite interesting, especially so when she asserts her independence from him as she has done this Saturday morning. And then the phone rings, pealing four times, pausing, then pealing twelve more times. With no particular reason, Richard imagines a lover on the other end of the line—but neither he nor Joan answers. We will see that this lover is, to use Updike's own distinction, not other, but Other.

These three acts suggest a story that is closer kin to the Kierkegaardian "Snowing in Greenwich Village" than the Barthian "The Taste of Metal." The focus is on neighbor-love rather than the severities of the Good Friday No or blessings of the Eastertide Yes. It is a story about the mismatch between flippant speech and needy people. Updike clearly has no wish to outlaw irony or teasing between marital partners. We hardly expect married people to speak to each other with constant witless sincerity. But Richard's own existential need will not be answered by flippancy, and his own teasing is hardly designed merely to entertain Joan and Mack or to engage their attention. He means to hurt, to alienate, and to control. This he accomplishes, at a cost.

The idea of Joan's lover calling is a wish fulfillment narrative of Richard's, a way of his imagining within the etiquette of adultery a greater realm of sexual freedom. He will feel less guilty with his lover if Joan has a lover too. Joan's responses in the first act hint at Updike's own attitude toward the talk. While Richard keeps pressing for the name of her lover, suggesting particular candidates, Joan replies that she has been too busy as wife and mother to conduct an affair. Richard meets this suggestion with self-justifying sarcasm, mocking the idea that he encouraged Joan to relinquish professional dreams to become a wife and mother. "You could have been the first woman to design a titanium nose cone. Or to crack the wheat-futures cycle. Joan Maple, girl agronomist." But Updike sides with Joan, who tells Richard that he is raving in a way he hasn't for years. We recognize that indeed his neurotic speech is returning.

Joan's claim to motherly busy-ness is perhaps undercut by her Saturday tennis morning and Friday cocktail-and-dinner party—neither of which involves the children. But we are probably to accept the patterns of the male breadwinner marriage, in which the husband relieves the wife of childcare duties on weekends. However, as we will see by the end of the story, these references to children are less sociological than theological. Joan tells us that the caller who wouldn't speak was not her lover but "some child."[38] Here Updike sets up a very careful contrast—child/lover, the relative innocence of children juxtaposed with the experiences of weary, needy, self-indulgent adults. Updike sets up another clever motif in this first act as well. In "Snowing in Greenwich Village," as Richard leaves his apartment to walk Rebecca Cune to hers, Joan asks him to buy cigarettes on his way home. Twice in this story Joan asks Richard to buy cigarettes. The first occurs in act one, a teasing request. If Richard goes out for cigarettes, Joan will call back the lover who has just hung up to explain why Richard is unexpectedly home. In act two, Richard does in fact go out for cigarettes. Returning home, he finds his wife involved in an apparent affair that in act one he is complacently confident cannot exist. He believes in Joan's fidelity.

Act two opens with an introduction to Mack Dennis, soon to be ex-husband of Eleanor. Updike knows that his regular readers are wondering whether Richard's and Eleanor's first embrace in the smashed Corvair has led to a further dalliance, but we learn only that Eleanor is in Wyoming (of all places) suing for a divorce. Soon after Mack arrives, Richard leaves the house for the cigarettes, so that unlike the Greenwich Village evening it is Joan who is left in the company of a sad neighbor. Mack is a bit like Rebecca Cune—easily judged as an amoral tempter, a destroyer of marital goodness, but in fact a tormented, lonely neighbor who tends to engage in self-protective speech. Updike's extended description of the kiss between Mack and Joan certainly raises questions about the nature of their relationship. Joan, for example, moves toward Mack rather than he toward her. This runs counter to her later claim to be granting a merely consoling kiss to a lonely, drunken guy-friend. Seeing this scene, Richard seems to feel a powerful response that he can only project onto other objects, as he sees a row of cereal and cracker boxes as "paralyzed." Joan's next gesture strikes Richard as

---

[38] Ibid., 103.

expressing "rebuke or regret," but it is difficult to tell whether this is an accurate reading or another projection his psyche requires.[39]

Later, when Richard begins to confront Mack and Joan about this kiss, he describes what he has witnessed as his first "primal scene." The phrase, like the phrase "psychotic break" in "Marching Through Boston," is a psychiatric term then in popular or lay usage. A true "primal scene" involves a child's witnessing or fantasizing of coitus, usually that of the parents. The child interprets the coital coupling as violence, and undergoes a psychic trauma in some cases leading to adult neuroses. Some contemporary psychiatrists suggest that a primal scene is especially damaging within brutal or troubled family situations, and that such uncanny viewings can lead to fears of aloneness and vulnerability.[40] But Richard is neither traumatized nor any longer paralyzed. He has overcome that shock and become giddy with aesthetic pleasure: "A profound happiness was stretching him from within; the reach of his tongue and wit felt immense, and the other two seemed dolls, homunculi, in his playful grasp."[41] As Joan seeks to explain or excuse her behavior, Richard compares himself to Rasputin. He jokes that Mack and Joan might plan to murder him, as Rasputin was murdered by Czar Alexander's courtiers, but the identification coils back on Richard, implying that in this setting he is the falsely spiritual, sexually voracious monster. As he has admitted to us, he wishes to control others, Rasputin-like, as though they were dolls or manikins. Joan's accusation that he has been "shockingly sneaky" in watching her and Mack rings false. She employs the etiquette of adultery, in which seeking out and criticizing adultery is a worse misdeed than committing it. But Richard is anything but innocent, anything but the wronged husband. And no one in the Maples' home grapples with the idea that there could be a very real primal scene there, if the Maples' children were to turn the wrong corner at the wrong time.

When Joan denies an affair with Mack during the next morning's quarrel, a quarrel that initiates act three, we recognize her speech as authentic and emphatic: "Go to [your lover] like a man and stop trying to maneuver me into something I don't understand! I have no lover! I let

---

[39] Ibid., 107.

[40] See for example M. F. Hoyt, "On the Psychology and Psychopathology of Primal Scene Experience." *Journal of the American Academy of Psychoanalysis*, 8/3 (July 1980) 311-35.

[41] Updike, *Too Far to Go*, 109.

Mack kiss me because he's lonely and drunk!"[42] Some might debate whether Joan's tender charity is appropriate, but her awareness of Mack's pain is important and right. Mack actually pleas for this kind of filial affection from Richard as well as Joan. He tells Richard, "Joan loves you. And if I love any man, it's you."[43] Richard, who wants to sustain his wish-fulfillment fantasy, fends off this genuine emotional appeal with a joke about Mack's Irish sentimentality. We know of Mack's adulterous antics through Eleanor's melodramatic speech in "The Taste of Metal." No paragon of virtue, Mack entertains his own mistress by ordering a birthday cake for his absent wife. Still, Mack is a neighbor in need, a man who misses his children and even his unfaithful wife. He seems to hope that his dear friends will give him some love, attention, and support as he undergoes the fear and trauma of losing a life with his wife and children. Mack and Eleanor Dennis here provide a glimpse of the Maples in a very near but not inevitable future.

In "The Taste of Metal," Richard has actively assaulted the Dennis marriage, kissing Eleanor in a libidinous, groping embrace quite different from Joan's relatively chaste and perhaps mostly consoling kiss of Mack. The scenes are deliberately parallel. In each, a woman moves toward a man to initiate an embrace, doing so for her own private purposes. The two scenes raise questions about the intention motivating such embraces—not so much the intimate behavior that we and Richard gaze upon, but the inwardness by which we understand our own and others' mixed motives and emotional needs. Kierkegaard suggests that Richard might seize a more coherent identity by making the inward move that transforms Mack from rival or manipulable homunculus in his mind to neighbor, hurt soul, friend in need. Martin Buber's famous model for this inward move is perhaps most apt: Richard might stop conceiving of Mack primarily as idea or object to be manipulated (I/It); he might encounter Mack's genuine existential personhood, his worth as another well-meaning human being, and his need (I/Thou). As I note in my introduction, Kierkegaard specifically warns in *Works of Love* that people must not confuse the feeling of love, or of being in love, with the experience of being a neighbor—which is to feel responsible for another neighbor's welfare.[44] If this is so, Richard's pose as wronged husband in the middle part of this story is completely hypocritical, given that his

---

[42] Ibid., 111.
[43] Ibid., 109.
[44] Kierkegaard, *Works of Love*, 17ff.

embrace of the leggy Eleanor Dennis in his smashed Corvair was far less chaste or innocent or based in hurt than Mack's and Joan's embrace in the Maples kitchen.

Mack is not the neediest neighbor in the story. Richard, Jr. also emerges as troubled, and Judith as vulnerable too. Both are rightful subjects of their parents' concern. But they are strangely neglected. Updike is especially direct about Richard, Jr.'s need. When Richard exacerbates a Saturday morning quarrel with Joan by clowning, carrying her tennis racket to her in his mouth and laying it at her feet, Richard, Jr. witnesses the act. It is, for him, a kind of primal scene. The narrator tells us that the nine-year old boy "laughed to hide his fright." We can imagine what sort of fright he feels—fear that his quarreling parents feel no love for each other or perhaps for him; fear that they are too involved in their games to care properly for him; fear that the mutual contempt he witnesses will lead to his parents' separation; fear of a great chaotic psychological *terra incognita* that he only dimly perceives. The boy's psychologically false position is revealed when his father offers to take him to the five-and-ten to buy him a Batmobile, a consolation prize as it were. Richard, Jr. is not consoled by aesthetic prizes: "'Yippee,' the small boy said limply, glancing wide-eyed from one of his parents to the other, as if the space between them had gone treacherous."[45]

Judith has also been unknowingly near her own potential primal scene. When Richard sees the eleven-year old Judith through her bedroom window she is barely safe from inappropriate witnessing. All she would have had to do to experience her own primal scene—her mother embracing a man who is not her father—is to walk into the kitchen. When Richard realizes this his heart feels "crowded" because his daughter is so "perilously close to the hidden machinations of things."[46] Yet Richard cares so little about this peril that he goes indoors to his wife and friend, shares a few drinks, and (as his wife eventually realizes) tries to fan this incipient affair into full flame in order to justify his own affairs and win a greater realm of freedom. He seems to forget his own insight that Mack, now separated from his wife Eleanor, seems to miss his own kids very deeply.[47] Richard does not seem to realize or to care that his own life's trajectory is moving toward a similarly alienated separation from his family.

---

[45] Ibid., 112.
[46] Ibid., 107.
[47] Ibid., 105.

Updike goes to great lengths in this story to convey a rebuking, ironical attitude toward Richard and Joan, or at least to expose the costs of their modes of living. The satire is less pointed than in "The Taste of Metal," but there is no mistaking Updike's sympathy for the vulnerable children in a home that steals their peace. This is not to say that Richard and Joan fail to love their children. Like most of us who try to do our best as parents, they fail to love the children fully or abundantly.

This is a story about the Maples' real lovers and children, but also a story about an unseen lover and figurative children. Ever the hopeful Christian, Updike poses an anagogical level to this story in which all the people of all ages in the story are named as children, and in which a lover's calls go unheeded. We have seen that Updike has a special interest in Jesus' command to 'let the little children come to me.'[48] Though Kierkegaard argues for forgetting such a merciful biblical moment, so that Christians will not indolently rely on Christ's mercy as a hedonic life nears its end, Updike argues that the "softer side" to the gospels is an anodyne to dread. In this story he returns to this theological matter in an anagogical motif in the story's first part. Joan explains why a caller has hung up without speaking (her lover, Richard says) by saying, plausibly, "It was some child."[49] (103). Later, as Richard comes into his kitchen to confront Mack and Joan for what he has just witnessed, he sees them "smaller than children."[50] If adults are calm, sanguine, in control of both practical and existential matters, then there are no adults in this story.

"Your Lover Just Called" closes with neither Richard nor Joan answering an insistently ringing phone. Either they are both too content with their rare quiet, companionable moment together to answer, or too afraid of whose lover may actually be calling. First the phone makes four peals—"icy spears hurled from afar"—then a pause, then twelve more peals. Then, the narrator tells us, "the lover hung up."[51] The numerology here is so particular, and given such emphatic attention, that it seems important to theorize what four and twelve might mean. At the simplest, most literal level, of course, they mean that at first the caller is tentative and un-insistent about gaining a response, and then unusually determined to get one. Surely most people would consider four rings too

---

[48] Matthew 19:14.
[49] Updike, *Too Far to Go*, 103.
[50] Ibid., 108.
[51] Ibid., 114.

few to call people to a residential phone, so four rings seems, so to speak, an odd number. On the other hand, the series of twelve rings seems unduly insistent. Christian numerology suggests that four means creation (four directions, four seasons) and twelve means governmental perfection (12 tribes of Israel, 12 apostles)—but perhaps this is too intricate for Updike to consider suggestive.[52] I prefer more immediate meanings for the numerology: Four is the number of Maples children, while twelve most clearly recalls the twelve apostles, representatives of discipleship. This neatly describes Richard's and Joan's behavior in this story, their neglect in honoring either the call to the parenting vocation or to Christian discipleship generally. What might it look like were they to leap into such discipleship? In their rare quiet moment, the Maples could spend some time talking not about their sex lives but about how they are going to help Mack Dennis in his distress. The lover calling to the Maples is, for Updike, the living Christ.

&

The etiquette of adultery governs "Waiting Up," but so does a thoroughly Judeo-Christian notion of waiting. For the believer, waiting is an existential category. Various teachers, prophets, and theologians have posited a particular view on how to prepare for and when to expect the Second Coming. Fifteen hundred years after the Ascension, Luther himself tended toward an apocalyptic eschatology, expecting the kingdom of God within his lifetime, and writing in his middle career "as if," one historian tells us, "the world were in its last days and the Beast were about to appear in all its horror."[53] Luther's rhetorical railing and intense preoccupation with the power of Satan seem to stem from this apocalyptic awareness. Updike's own eschatology is less apocalyptic, but rests in an intense confidence in, and argument concerning our existential need for, an afterlife. In *Self-Consciousness*, Updike tells us that Miguel de Unamuno's *The Tragic Sense of Life* informs his sense that "[t]he yearning for an afterlife is the opposite of selfish: it is love and praise for the world that we are privileged, in this complex interval of light, to witness and experience."[54] The title of this story implies that the

---

[52] I sought help with the numerology from Vincent F. Hopper, *Medieval Number Symbolism* (New York: Cooper Square, 1969).

[53] Marius, *Martin Luther*, 285.

[54] Updike, *Self-Consciousness*, 217.

Christian's existential state is to wait—which is to say, to live—in "this interval of light"—for the return of the Redeemer, and for eternity to replace absurd time.

As "Waiting Up" opens, Richard is in a state of high Oedipal and existential anxiety—an eschatological moment in its own right. He has no confidence in an afterlife or any other stay against the suspicion that his life is absurd. His immediate problem, which emerges from the existential one, is complex and goes something like this: his exciting and consoling affair with Mrs. Mason—who has apparently supplied a powerful rotation—has been discovered. The Masons have invited Joan over for a discussion. She calls the experience a "love-in" or "teach-in," but there are also shades of the Paris peace talks in this Vietnam-era story. Joan is not sure precisely what to call the session because the Masons' contemporary ethos, ethical nihilism combined with an extreme optimism about the possibility of human mutuality, is not her ethos. The Masons epitomize one cosmic ideology on such matters, which is to be "full of goodness and love," civilized and calm and determined to keep all friendships intact even when secretive liaisons among them feel like betrayals. Mrs. Mason urges Joan to be angry about her affair with Richard, for honest emotions are healthy emotions, but she clearly does not mean it. She would seem to prefer that Joan view the extramarital sex she has enjoyed with Richard as a "gift of love" that Joan might give to her—just as she would willingly give her own husband to Joan as such a gift.[55] She insists to Joan that "indignation is silly. Childish."[56] The Masons reveal that their real ethic is simple and startling: all is permitted.

The Maples, without completely understanding their own attitudes or commitments on these questions, feel differently, and here we find the story's philosophical problem. In a story that opens with evidently Oedipal feelings and memories on Richard's part—his fear of his daughter becoming a woman, his memories of a "dazzling" beloved mother from whom he seems to have made incomplete psychic separation—the central concern is with adjustment, commitments, the moral life, and anxiety. How should one live? What acts, if any, are well-adjusted people not permitted? What is the relationship between moral restraint and psychic peace? Are notions of faithfulness and indignation any longer possible, sensible, or coherent? Richard's quasi-sexual

---

[55] Updike, *Too Far to Go*, 115-20.
[56] Ibid., 121.

thoughts about his daughter and mother indicate that he is still searching for a fully developed identity and, as an expected result according to psychiatric theories, a firm sense of moral restraint. For Freud, the moral life emerges from one's Oedipal rejection of incestuous impulses.

From Richard we receive a remarkably explicit statement of what he and Joan believe in and live by: He believes in a beneficent world that requires little personal moral responsibility: ". . . there was nobody to be angry at, only tired people anxious to please, good hearts asleep and awake, wrapped in the limits of a universe that itself, from the beauty of its details and its contagious air of freedom, seemed to have been well-intentioned."[57] Richard's sense of radical human freedom combined with his instinct that the natural order is intended suggests that he is a thoroughly antinomian incipient theist—a stance which leads to no particular moral practices or restraints whatever, because the leap has not been made, and therefore no God-informed conscience is at work. The Maples' community offers little ethical or moral help, because it includes people like the Masons.

As we have seen, Updike himself has written of his antinomianism in ways that sound like Richard. His leap into faith, for example, he made in spite of the "priests and executors" who, "to keep order and to force the world into a convenient mould, will always want to make Him the God of the dead, the God who chastises life and forbids and says No."[58] Yet Richard's particular formulation leaves existential questions unanswered: has he made good use of the contagious air of freedom? Has he not, in fact, done much to cause or merit anger? Could he be the one to be "angry at"? If people are universally so "anxious to please," what has he done to please others? Has he not in fact caused others fear and pain? Even if there is theological coherency in Richard's remark, his philosophy accords with his narcissism. (Mother always waited up for him.) And finally, Richard's needs are contradictory. Far from granting others the freedom he demands, he requires explanations or apologies for minor offenses to his peace of mind, such as Joan's appearing home 35 minutes later than she promised to be home. More importantly, as this story unfolds we recognize that he requires forgiveness for his affairs.

Joan's existential commitments are less clearly stated. We have come to expect her to observe ethical commitments, and she does appeal to a "do unto others" sense of justice in her conversation with Richard's

---

[57] Ibid., 117.

[58] Updike, *Self-Consciousness*, 230.

lover: "I asked her how she'd feel..." But, arguably, an appeal to feelings cannot lead to any conclusion about the ethical rightness or wrongness of adultery, as Richard's apparent feelings would indicate. Joan is quite sure that Richard is an "awful person" (the remark is meant only partly ironically), which implies that after all she feels adultery to be essentially wrong, especially when it causes hurt to others. Yet she is unable to complete this thought, to encourage Richard to change or reform or to join her in making their marriage a creative project, or even hope that he will. Neither her ethical nor moral code is well enough worked-out to yield such conclusions or hopes. When Richard asks Joan what she believes, in "war, or a greater good," Joan responds, "I don't know" War implies a world of responsibilities and penalties in which Richard would be held to account for his adultery. The greater good implies the Masons' belief that eros is as good as agape—perhaps better—in shaping the healthy modern consciousness. Joan's parodic remark is that she "could believe in a little more bourbon."[59] This remark is funny, but also an expression of her confusion, weariness, and resignation.

This story is about a pervasive and enervating moral relativity—not only the moral confusion of the Maples themselves, but also the specific nihilism of the Masons—a condition in which all is permitted in the moral and ethical realms. Maples and Masons: the similar names indicated that the two couples struggle with similar philosophical problems. The enervating quality of their moral relativity becomes clear in the final paragraph of the story, when Richard confesses to hating Joan's absence from the house, hating it more than he would have supposed possible. If we hope that this feeling, rising out of a deeper and more sacred feeling than he feels when gazing upon the naked, sunlit body of his lover, will lead Richard to a faithful life with Joan, we are disappointed. He immediately experiences another feeling, the "abysmal loss of, with her soothing steady voice, the other."[60] Richard's consciousness, like his desire, is bifurcated. His agitation on this evening indicates that this is no way to live. His effort to feel authentic emotions (he "trie[s] to become angry" just as Joan "tr[ies] to cry") indicates a psychic confusion.[61] A moral confusion is implied by his ridiculous belief that he has taken up his mother's "old role" in waiting up for Joan.[62]

---

[59] Updike, *Too Far to Go*, 119-21.
[60] Ibid., 122.
[61] Ibid., 117 and 120.
[62] Ibid., 116.

Presumably this elder Mrs. Maple did not wait up for a husband who has been attending a meeting that seeks to understand her adultery. Again in this story the figure of the child is central to Updike's parody, but because the child is Richard himself we sense more deeply his psychic bifurcation, his status as both man and child.

Will this story offer us an antidote to its enervating moral relativity and personal anxiety? There is reason to think so. In a 2001 review of Peter J. Conradi's *Iris Murdoch*, Updike writes about a novel of Murdoch's that was a particular favorite of his, *A Severed Head* (1961). Notably, this novel takes up the same philosophical problems as "Waiting Up," through a similar fictive situation. Updike recalls that *A Severed Head*, when it appeared in Ipswich, had been "passed around among young suburban couples in the early Sixties as a species of news. This news—that love is everywhere, violent, protean, consuming, comical, cruel—never grew stale for [Murdoch]." Apart from this theme of eros running rampant, our concern with this novel is that it poses in neo-Platonic terms a question that Updike takes on through Kierkegaard's theology in "Waiting Up" and other stories: "can the Good survive the death of God?"[63] Murdoch and Updike reach different answers to this question.

The novel, like Updike's story, concerns privileged people in early middle age who believe that they have overcome conventional post-Christian morality, that they are radically free agents. In the novel the celebrant of this existential freedom is the psychiatrist Palmer Anderson, whose philosophies are often voiced by his mistress, Antonia Lynch-Gibbon, wife of the novel's narrator, Martin Lynch-Gibbon. Martin is driven to anxious distraction by Palmer's philosophy, "All is permitted," because he can neither fully accept it—for to do so would be to relinquish any claim to his wife—nor deny it—for to do so would be to relinquish both his sophisticated superiority and his pretty young mistress. In "Waiting Up," Mr. Mason's speeches about "how we must all help each other" or "about some greater good coming out of this" might be spoken by Palmer Anderson or Antonia Lynch-Gibbon. The language is therapeutic, self-satisfied, and relativistic.

This is not to say that Updike's story is somehow derivative of Murdoch's novel. This story is more of an homage. Both Updike and Murdoch, fine existentialist anti-nihilists, examine the problems encountered by those who wish to overcome conventional morality.

---

[63] Updike, *Due Considerations*, 563.

Joan's charitable kiss of Mack Dennis in "Your Lover Just Called" raises questions about whether every physical or emotional indiscretion by a married person amounts to infidelity or adultery. Surely there is a realm of ambiguity in marital ethics. But this story is less ambiguous. Richard has clearly been sleeping with Mrs. Mason, whom he does not love as he loves his wife, and he is unrepentant about his adultery. Updike engages our imaginations and consciences on this question: is the Richard we meet in this story made healthier by his sexual adventures, as he trusts, or more wretched?

More wretched: this is the answer both *A Severed Head* and "Waiting Up" suggest. In the novel Murdoch cleverly smokes out Palmer Anderson and other sophisticated moral relativists through a scene—a primal scene—involving brother-sister incest. Martin catches Palmer Anderson *en flagrante* with his half-sister. Once his incest is exposed, Anderson admits the hollowness of his entire philosophy of complete permission. Moments after being caught in bed with this sister he argues, or ruefully admits, a profound truth he has learned through his psychiatric training: no one can be morally relative about immediate experience of incest. The very body abhors this anarchic sexual conduct. Murdoch builds a case for moral restraint on this logical foundation: Since *not* all is permitted, restraints and repressions are necessary. The question is which restraints and repressions to honor. For Murdoch, enlightened persons beginning with this insight might begin to devote themselves to the Good, practicing the unselfing method of "just attention" (attending carefully to worthy persons and great art) and in doing so defeating, or at least controlling, the quasi-mechanical, deeply irrational power of libido.[64]

Updike's method for addressing the problems of moral relativity and therapeutic self-indulgence is less melodramatic and avoids any commitment to neo-Platonic disciplines which his theology cannot endorse. He does not believe in moral goodness through merely human effort, and he does not require a primal incest scene to indicate the need for certain restraints and repressions. The figure of the vulnerable child is enough, he suggests, to engage our sense of moral imperatives and to begin a search for a moral Archimedean point.

This is a one-act story, but it falls into two halves. In the first, the focus is on Richard's anxiety as he waits for Joan to return from her summit meeting with the Masons. He alternates between his authentic

---

[64] Iris Murdoch, *A Severed Head* (New York: Viking, 1961).

role as husband-parent, and a contrasting fantasy of being a child. As husband and parent he drinks bourbon, checks on the sleeping children, and considers calling the familiar number of the Masons' phone in order to check on Joan.[65] His concern for her state of mind and personal safety seems real enough, though of course he is also anxious about the newly negotiated status of his relationship with Mrs. Mason—which may entail the end of the affair. It is an affair he seems especially to enjoy, as the Mason home is like his own but "different enough in every detail to be exciting." This difference has helped to create for Richard a rotation, as have novelties such as Mrs. Mason's naked greetings when he arrives at her house.[66] But Richard's needs are pointedly regressive too, as his intense memories of his mother waiting up for him indicate.

Indeed, Updike carefully establishes a linguistic and psycho-analytical connection between Richard's mother and mistress. He thinks of both waiting for him—his mother alone with her radio in the "stationary, preferable world" of his childhood home, and Mrs. Mason "naked at the head of her stairs" in the glaring morning light. Updike employs forms of the verb "waiting" in both memories, but his more pointed linguistic connection is the more particular word "dazzling." Richard recalls his mother as the "dazzling center" of his childhood world, while Mrs. Mason provides Richard with a "dazzling welcome" when silhouetted against the morning sun at the head of her stairs.[67] That Richard feels "dazzled" by his mother hints at a balked Oedipal separation from her. It may be more normal for a man to be "dazzled" by a beautiful naked woman offering herself sexually, but Richard's use of that very verb indicates that his need for Mrs. Mason's body is connected somehow with his intense feelings for his mother.

We have seen that both Christopher Lasch and Erik Erikson explain, through their differing psychoanalytic theories, the importance of religious and existential meaning in achieving psychological health. Even if they were not sources for Updike's particular psychoanalytical and sociological diagnoses, Lasch and Erikson describe the psycho-mechanics of his situations nicely. Notably, both join Updike in viewing separation anxieties, symptoms that emerge from balked separation from the mother in the Oedipal stage, as a cause for compulsive, self-indulgent behaviors. "After the painful renunciation of the mother,"

---

[65] Updike, *Too Far to Go*, 115-18.
[66] Ibid., 117.
[67] Ibid., 116-17.

Lasch writes in *The Culture of Narcissism*, "sensuality seeks only those objects that evoke no reminder of her, while the mother herself, together with other 'pure' (socially respectable) women, is idealized beyond reach of the sensual."[68] Precisely because Mrs. Mason does call his mother to his mind, Richard has apparently not completed this "renunciation." He epitomizes something nearer Erikson's description of separation anxiety leading to identity crisis. Erikson, in fact, hopes for every man to complete painful renunciations of the mother and father both:

> We would not wish to see any boy—much less an imaginative and forceful one—face the struggles of his youth and manhood without having experienced as a child the love and the hate which are encompassed in this complex: love for the maternal person who awakens his senses and his sensuality with her ministrations, and deep and angry rivalry with the male possessor of this maternal person. We would also wish him with their help to succeed, in his boyhood, in turning resolutely away from the protection of women to assume the fearless initiative of men.[69]

Erikson is speaking of Martin Luther here, but he might be speaking of Richard—or indeed, if we get past the unnecessary sexism, of Joan in Electra rather than Oedipal terms. She too is half-adult and half-child in this story—and also one who lacks "fearless initiative" in her life. She represents the Maples at the "teach in," but only after she and Richard agree that "she might be out till eleven."[70] Speaking with the Masons she becomes as agitated as "in church"—which we know is the realm of her domineering Universalist father.[71] Both Maples feel anxieties and confused connections that stem from early childhood identity processes.

In the second half of the story, Richard and Joan talk about her frustration in dealing with two such thoroughgoing nihilists as the Masons. Mr. Mason emerges as this story's Palmer Anderson, demonic controller, knowing lecturer on psychoanalysis, and avatar of extreme existential freedom. Joan finds him irritating, and worse: "He is crazy.... He kept using words like understanding and compassion and how we must all *help* each other." Alternately kissing both Joan when she tries to cry and Mrs. Mason for more general reasons, Mr. Mason has, says Joan,

---

[68] Lasch, *Culture of Narcissism*, 204.

[69] Erikson, *Young Man Luther*, 73.

[70] Updike, *Too Far to Go*, 116.

[71] For some reason, in the omnibus Everyman *Maples Stories* he becomes a theology professor.

"stolen my identity."[72] This is an important remark on Joan's part. She seems to have some sense that her identity is tied up with her moral judgment, the foundation of which Mr. Mason tries to disassemble as he dissolves moral differences in this conversation. For example, he views the newly exposed affair as a beneficial revelation, the cause of unexpectedly good sex with his wife. Soon he calls Richard "good old Richard," a genial epithet that is undercut as he then calls Richard a "son of a bitch," and finally an "old seducer"—as though each is meant with equal, amiable warmth. Clearly, the latter two epithets express barely concealed aggression.

Inevitably, an American story of the late 1960s has to turn to talk of the Vietnam War. This one does when Joan notes that the Masons "don't believe in war. They think indignation is silly. Childish.... He kept talking about some greater good coming out of this." This is when Joan confesses that she does not know whether to believe in either war or a greater good, nor in her parents' commitment to punishment for wrongdoing, nor in a more recent moral economy in which non-censorious acceptance of human desire might lead to social comity. She believes, for the moment, in anesthesia: a little more bourbon. She cannot conclude that the Masons are, as Richard suggests, "awful people." "*You're* the awful person," she tells Richard. This too seems a remark based in moral confusion, and we do not have to make a loosely ethical, personal conclusion to say so. After all, if Richard is awful for having this affair, then Mrs. Mason is equally awful, and so is Mr. Mason for promoting the logic that leads Richard and the Mrs. into the affair: better sex means better health. It is notable that the story closes with both of the Maples independently reaching the conclusion that they have no stomach for "love-ins, or teach-ins" or keeping in touch with the Masons as a couple. Richard says it for both of them: "But it's you...I seem to want most." Joan will hew to this view all the way up to and beyond the moment of their divorce decree. Not Richard. In the typical incorrigibility move, "Waiting Up" ends with the return of his compulsive wish for the "other," presumably Mrs. Mason, who will feed his Tristanism, overestimating his worth in a libidinous overflow of feeling.[73]

It may be natural for us to want to see Richard and Joan behaving with moral integrity, to assuage their children's fears and meet each

---

[72] Updike, *Too Far to Go*, 120.
[73] Ibid., 121-22.

other's needs with faithful, patient attention. But for Updike that is a secondary matter. Such duties still partake of the ethical and therefore still lead to dread. In a sense then, moral relativity is beside the point for Kierkegaard and Updike, even when it leads to execrable behavior. To be more precise, moral relativity and the behavior it yields are far less important to Kierkegaard and Updike than the psycho-theological drama or process in which they take part—the drama of tormented consciousnesses, homesick for God but invested in potent systems of denial of that homesickness. When this denial is in full sway, neurotic symptoms result, such as Richard's bifurcated personality in this story. He desires both his exciting lover and his comforting, consoling, and reasonable wife. But even his psyche will not allow him to have both. Weird, tormented, dreadful feelings result, such as the kind revealed in the terrifying dream he experiences late in the next story, "Eros Rampant."

Still, in the conclusion of "Waiting Up" Updike provides us with a more hopeful way of reading Richard's abysmal sense of loss. After he confesses to Joan that he wants her most, he immediately longs for "the soothing steady voice" of "the other." In that 1963 review of de Rougemont's *Love Declared*, in which Updike first uses the litany of Kierkegaardian code words, he also uses the same word "other" to refer to the lover, equally coyly: "This exalted arena, then, is above all others the one where men and women will insist upon their freedom to choose—to choose that other being in whose existence their own existence is confirmed and amplified."[74] Notably "that other being" is singular. To accommodate Richard's current world-view, it would need to be plural, since Richard believes in his new freedom to choose gratifying partners serially. But Updike is actually implying in both the de Rougemont essay and this story that there is really only one Other who overestimates him existentially, permanently, in eternity. In "The Taste of Metal" he called that being Messiah, the one believers in deep trouble are waiting for.

Clearly, in Oedipal, ethical, and more deeply Christian terms, Richard Maple is in trouble. The only hope we have for his responding to his dread occurs briefly, as he realizes that his wife is so dear to him that he hates having her away. The rest of the story is humiliating for Richard, and to a lesser degree for Joan. The two have not in any way worked out a way to live, to pursue "health" through reduced

---

[74] Updike, *Assorted Prose*, 299.

repression. They are confused, tormented, torn between goals. They numb their pain with liquid anesthetics. It may be worth noting that Updike first published this story fully ten years after the stories that come before and after it in sequence, "Your Lover Just Called" (*Harpers*, January 1967) and "Eros Rampant" (*Harpers*, June 1968). It is also the only story published in the distant and, compared with *The New Yorker*, *Harpers*, *Atlantic Monthly*, and *Playboy*, distinctly minor *Canadian Weekend Magazine*. Did Updike compose "Waiting Up" in sequence, delaying its publication and publishing outside the United States in order to spare feelings? Or did the story have to emerge from Updike's own systems of denial in order to find its place in the Maples cycle? No matter the circumstances of its origin, "Waiting Up" is a dark, psychologically tangled story with humiliating confessions at its center.

&

"Eros Rampant" (1968) completes this four-story cycle concerning the etiquette of adultery. The story that comes after it, "Plumbing" (1971), is distant in terms of both time and theme, as three years pass before it appears in the Maples cycle, and since the core problem it addresses is death rather than adultery. Perhaps it is inaccurate to suggest that "Eros Rampant" addresses only adultery. The story seems in fact to address the causes of adultery in the "rampant" or unchecked quality of eros, or the instinct for self-preservation expressed in physical love. The narrative presents Richard's experiences with his lovers, a terrible, hurtful discussion with Joan about the affairs both have been pursuing, and an examination of the affairs' putative causes. The familiar three-part structure gives way in this story to a four-part arrangement. In this case, act one involves a playful meditation on the nature of love, its Oedipal, consumerist, obsessive, feral, despairing, and even unselfish valences. Act two shows us that Richard actively pursues affairs (this time with his secretary Penelope Vogel) and treasures his memories of affairs which have lapsed. Act three involves a hurtful discussion with Joan, whose retaliatory affairs come into deliberate focus. The fourth and final act is far from the typical incorrigibility move of a Maples story. Instead, Richard's knowledge of Joan's affairs, and dream about her in which she has adopted his aesthetic mode of living, casts him into emotional vertigo. It is a very dark story, but it seems to deliver Richard into a state of dread, that nearly breaks through his fundamental flippancy.

The word "rampant" offers associations of its own, which give shape to the first act of this story. In medieval usage, the word refers to one of the prototypical poses used in heraldry, or the part of heraldry involving the design and display of family coats of arms. The rampant pose, typically of a real or mythical animal, suggests aggression or fierce assertion, vitality, an unrestrained energy. The *Oxford English Dictionary* notes that in the rampant pose the left (sinister) foot is the only one touching the ground, while the right (dexter) is raised, along with both arms. The face is in profile. Conventional meanings are not entirely clear, but the contrast of the sinister with the dexterous seems to be in play, both for medieval families and Updike's Maple family. "Eros rampant" suggests that in the Maple family, the sinister and the rightful are in tension. The energy of physical love, self-preservation, and self-assertion rage fiercely and unchecked.

Indeed it does. Feral animals in the household mirror their human owners in displaying uncontrolled, instinctive sexual energy. The Maple children display lively Oedipal excitements; Richard's affairs have become routine and apparently take up significant amounts of his vocational time; Joan has entered into retaliatory and consoling affairs of her own with friends and counselors. Meanwhile, the dog Hecuba lives in constant adoration for her owners, and the cats Esau and Esther (more to come on the mythical and biblical associations of these names) enter into and then are surgically released from a rhythm of incestuous coupling and conceiving. Esther's spaying in this context seems the only positive image, positive because a release from the erotic drive seems merciful and welcome.

As Richard's secretary Penelope Vogel says in the next act, it's a bad scene. Her first name, along with that of the cat Esther and dog Hecuba, raises the issue of classical feminine faithfulness in contrast to male greed and fierce, warring energy. The more famous Penelope waits faithfully for her husband Odysseus for twenty years, fending off the greedy suitors who would couple with her in order to gain Odysseus's property, should he not return from war. Esther, a Jewish woman of the Old Testament, wins the hand of the Persian king Xerxes and courageously and faithfully turns her husband's heart toward the plight of the Jews rather than the greedy machinations of his counselors. Hecuba, wife of the Trojan king Priam, loves her children so much that their deaths during the Trojan War causes her, in her grief, either (depending on the version of the story) to bark like a dog or to be turned into a dog by the sympathetic gods. Whether we view the Maples' naming of pets as learnedly clever or outrageously pretentious, all three mythical/biblical figures represent courageous, steadfast faithfulness—an expression of love quite different from the erotic. If any of the three lived in a Christian world we might speak of agape or caritas, since all demonstrate a self-forgetting love for their children. Though the first act of this story catalogs a wide variety of love's manifestations in the Maples household, this faithful, self-forgetting type is conspicuously missing, except in these allusions.

The reference to Esau runs counter to this spirit of self-forgetting. The biblical Esau of course sold his birthright—with all the ethnic, communal, and spiritual responsibilities it implies—for a mess of pottage, antidote to an immediate animal hunger. If this reminds us of Richard in his aesthetic appetites, we are justified. In this story, the cats Esau and Esther become characters in a kind of parable concerning the torments of Richard's feral, which is to say aesthetic, love. For a time the tom Esau was forced by lack of other female cats to mate with his sister Esther, though he did so happily enough, and productively: thirty kittens in two litters per year. Once Esther was fixed and no longer went into heat, Esau was forced to "venture from the house in quest of the bliss that had once been purely domestic."[75] Perhaps this parable explains Richard's own extra-domestic questing after bliss, since he is, like all the rest of us, subject to animal drives and urges. But of course Joan is sexually healthy and apparently willing. And why would Updike contrive to place Esau and Esther in an incestuous relationship, when he could as easily have brought two cats into the Maple house from different litters and different parents? The imagery seems to suit Richard's consciousness rather than Updike's: Richard feels his marriage to be a union with a kind of chaste sister, his sexual urges for his wife (which we will encounter in this story) in his mind best escaped. We will have to explore the Oedipal roots of his love for Joan.

Perhaps the feline incest expresses the complexity of love in marriage, since the exigencies of parenting and mutuality require a different sort of love than the erotic. Husbands and wives do establish a filial closeness that often exists in tension with erotic adventuring—agape versus eros, *Kjerlighed* versus *Elskov*. This parable, however, seems

---

[75] Updike, *Too Far to Go*, 125.

more emphatically to express Richard's state of mind, the obsessive and forbidden quality of his urges for Joan and other women. We note, for example, his image of Esther's womb as "vaster than a cave" and Joan's own hidden pubis as an "absurd persuasion" to which he feels "captive."[76] There is a certain logic to these thoughts. Richard's aesthetic consolations require that he *feel* freedom rather than authentically *own* it. Joan represents a certain kind of psychic, ethical, and legal captivity, a No to his misdeeds that faintly echoes God's No.

So this first act playfully initiates a contrast between myths of divine-endorsed faithfulness and empirical realities of feral desire. As act two opens, Richard's dinnertime seduction of his secretary Penelope Vogel complicates his own position of feral freedom. We sense a compulsively serial quality to Penelope's liaisons, and her brittle loneliness parodies the satisfactions of sexual rotations. Richard struggles to control his own racist attitudes in reacting to Penelope's affairs, wondering against his will whether her black lovers render greater animal satisfactions. He nearly offends her with his rapt questions about the races of these lovers. This Penelope may not be able to remain faithful to any of her suitors, but she does assert a sincere faithfulness to an ideal of faithful love. She declines Richard's offer to come up to her apartment, with a frank "No" that resonates for us since encountering it in "The Taste of Metal." We believe her when she says that she has "developed a good ear for sincerity in these things," and then suggests that he might be too wrapped up back home. Richard thinks that her earlier remark about finding it hard to "back up" when you find "something that works" is a remark about preferring black lovers. But her "level gaze" at Richard hints that she senses he is the one who has "something that works" at home.[77]

Just as Penelope is about to reject Richard's implied request to sleep with her, Eleanor Dennis arrives at the restaurant where they have met. Eleanor's presence reminds us of his love history, which shows the same compulsive serial quality as Penelope's. When he mentions Eleanor, Marlene Brossman, and "the little girl who used to steal his hunter's cap"[78] in one equalizing sentence, we realize how strange is Richard's conscience. Surely there are moral differences between women one has

---

[76] Ibid., 126.
[77] Ibid., 128-32.
[78] Ibid., 132

seduced under the gaze of one's wife and a girl one remembers as a childhood crush.

The third act of this story opens with Joan's announcement to Richard in a private bedroom conversation that she knows about his dinner with some "little office mouse." Mack Dennis has relayed this intelligence from Eleanor to Joan, who sensibly believes that Richard has slept with the office mouse, Penelope. Richard's denial, "I never have" confirms that he has been seeing the girl. This conversation is about to get out of Richard's control, for a time at least. It represents a reversal of mood, not because Richard regrets his affairs once they are exposed to Joan's ethical viewpoint, but because in retaliation she soon makes clear that she is seeing, perhaps sleeping with, Mack Dennis. And not only him.

When Richard asks Joan when she converses with Mack, she has not prepared a plausible lie. She says "Oh—" and searches for a scenario. Meanwhile Richard's "heart falls through her silence."[79] This remark hints at more than the familiar double standard that allows men to have affairs while denying their wives the same right. Richard is too sophisticated to allow himself such a traditional double standard. He is obliged to grant Joan any freedom or privilege that he seizes for himself; indeed, he has encouraged her to have affairs. Yet he realizes that some force in him, which we will name later, fills him with alarm and requires him to seek Joan's denial of the affair with Mack.

He doesn't receive a denial. Joan admits that she and Mack "understand each other."[80] In his hurt, Richard admits that he has tried to sleep with Penelope, and flinches as Joan steps toward him aggressively. His fear of Joan's striking him reveals his recognition that he merits punishment. He has been awful again. This is not an ordinary quarrel about fidelity between the Maples. When Joan asks whether he wants to know who she was sleeping with Wednesday, Richard feels that "a continent has lapsed between them." Joan continues in her retaliatory attack, naming an assistant director at her museum as another lover. Richard, we are told, is "stunned."[81] He works to put Joan on the defensive, questioning her about her affairs, but only succeeds in confirming—to his great discomfort—that she has had numerous affairs

---

[79] Ibid., 133.
[80] Ibid., 134.
[81] Ibid., 135.

over many years. He learns that mutual friends of theirs know about these affairs.

Now, in a story that began with love for and among children and pets, we begin to contemplate love with a new seriousness, and a new psychological depth. The passage describing Richard's shocked reaction is complex:

> Love, a cloudy heavy ink, inundates him from within, suffuses his palms with tingling pressure as he steps close to her, her murky face held tense against the expectation of a blow. "You whore," he breathes, enraptured. "My virgin bride." He kisses her hands; they are corrupt and cold.[82]

Could it really be love that Richard is feeling? If so, it is definitely eros rampant, not the patient, forgiving, un-insistent, generous love of I Corinthians 13, nor the neo-Platonic corollary Murdoch calls "just attention." This love is violent, contradictory—Joan is both whore and virgin—anxious, and related in Richard's consciousness with the bodily corruptions of death.

Admittedly, Christian culture has grappled with an unjust and dichotomous view of women's character for centuries, as Kierkegaard himself has observed, according to the Arbaughs: "For S.K., as for Catholic mysticism, there were two understandings of women, the temptress who leads man into sin and the mother who leads her child to God."[83] Richard seems particularly prone to a crude dualism regarding women, perhaps because of his obvious separation anxiety disorder, in which only his mother can be wholly comforting and pure while all other women are objects of sexual attachment alone, whores or nearly so. Richard's psychic confusion is mirrored in this moral and ethical contradictoriness: dining with Penelope, Richard has taken deep and exciting pleasure from a recitation of her past lovers. Listening to a similar recitation from Joan, he is filled with terror. He might make a similar, probably longer, recitation of his own affairs, and yet he has not thought about the terror his philandering must be causing Joan. Some psychic blockage keeps him from making this simple deduction or seeking logical consistency in these matters.

At this point in this third act, the children come into their parents' bedroom and interrupt the conversation. Judith has been bullying Richard, Jr. by blocking his view of the television, so he is very upset.

---

[82] Ibid., 136.

[83] Arbaugh, *Kierkegaard's Authorship*, 183.

Characteristically, their father holds no one responsible, explaining Judith's behavior in terms of a developmental process no one can control. "'She can't help she's growing'"—as though Judith has simply grown into Dickie's line of vision, and as though her intentional taunting of her little brother were not obvious. Apparently no one is responsible for the Vietnam war either, for Richard at least. Just as he pities his growing daughter he "pities Johnson for his Presidency."[84] He neglects to notice that each has been an aggressor in the conflict under discussion. Eros being rampant again—or is it Thanatos now?—Dickie charges out of the room prompted by Judith's victorious sneer, the baby girl Bean runs into the room frightened, and down the hall Dickie passes along his torment, puncturing John's quiet "communion with his dinosaurs." Joan has begun to cry. To paraphrase the line of Updike's which I quote in the beginning of this chapter, pity the family that gets in the way of the pursuit of healthful sexual satisfaction.

Before moving to the story's fourth act and denouement, we should note Updike's conscious and clever play with geopolitical and psychosexual horizons for these domestic themes of eros and conflict. Through these themes Updike carries forward his deconstruction of specifically Christian and generally human responsibility, which he feels underpin an unrealistic view of the human capacity for goodness. Richard's reference to President Johnson is just one of a number of utterances dedicated to this task. As in the first two Maples stories, the Cold War functions here as an anagogical corollary to the Maples marriage, and troubled Christian marriages in general. In a general sense, this corollary seems to suggest that male and female consciousness is, like democratic capitalism and sino-soviet totalitarianism, so contra distinct that conflict is inevitable—and this conflict must inevitably shape the world we live in. In this story Updike carries the corollary further. Just after learning of Joan's affairs, which Richard is shocked to discover are much more complex and involved than he had ever imagined, he finds himself at a party making an uncharacteristically dove-ish argument (Joan speaks earlier of Richard's "horrible pro-Vietnam stand") about Vietnam: "He allows that Asia is infinitely complex, devious, ungrateful, feminine: but must we abandon her therefore?"[85] This remark says more about Richard's troubled new insights into his wife's private life than about America's involvement in

---

[84] Ibid., 138.
[85] Ibid., 134, 139.

Southeast Asia, and indeed it is the conflation of the two that matters. Updike suggests that to know persons and nations is basically hopeless. Stratagems and arguments that seem at first sensible and coherent later confront a tangled, hidden, sundry reality and then dissolve. Is Johnson to be pitied for resolutely managing such a reality or hated for arrogantly believing in unrealistic stratagems in the first place?

Updike is after a complexity here—a "reality-embrace" he calls this complexity in his memoirs—that he reports finding in short supply in the late 1960s, when he was unjustly labeled an unequivocal supporter of America's military involvement in Vietnam, and, as we have seen, a moral quietist who would not condemn adultery. In the Vietnam-era chapter of his memoir *Self-Consciousness* Updike reports how a brief reply in 1966 to an English newspaper reporter led to a *New York Times* article listing him as an author who had taken sides with other authors arguing for an American war in Vietnam. He wrote a long letter to the *Times* laying out a nuanced view of American responsibility for and in Vietnam, condemning the bombing of the North and all manner of "terror and coercion on all sides." Updike's explicitly political position is that a war that Americans entered step by step, as rationally as it could in a liberal impulse to protect human rights, must be exited step by step with a certain kind of realism. The North Vietnamese would not negotiate meaningfully with a suddenly pacific opponent, he argues. Yet Updike's argument—which he lays out with great care—is not finally geopolitical in nature but theological. It rests upon the Augustinian principle that Original Sin cannot be disowned. No one, Updike argues, least of all a privileged and "enlightened few" who conducted protests on or near America's college campuses, could disown their share of responsibility for their own bloody hands. Some hands were bloody in those days because they had flipped the voting machine's lever toward the war-makers, Truman, Eisenhower, Kennedy, and Johnson. But all American hands are bloodied with the wars and revolutions that have secured freedoms and responsibilities. "The world is fallen," he writes, "and in a fallen world animals, men and nations make space for themselves through a willingness to fight." Christ, Updike asks us to recall, beat up money-changers and said that he brought not peace but a sword to His world.[86]

If men are at war with women in this story, and the democratic West with the communist East, then so is Eros at war with Thanatos, the

---

[86] Updike, *Self-Consciousness*, 130.

pleasure principle with the chastening death drive. We associate Eros with the pleasure principle, and the pleasure principle with the aesthetic. To say that Eros is rampant in this story is to say that Richard runs rampant in a world where notions of love are cheapened by—to repeat part of this story's catalog—Beatles and Monkees songs, crooners singing of amore, and casual philanderers meeting in restaurants and museums and counseling offices. According to Freud, Eros is a unifying force, an instinct which, given a free rein it is never in fact granted, has the power "to combine single human individuals, and after that families, then races, peoples and nations, into one great unity, the unity of mankind."[87] But Freud insists that personal, familial, racial and international wrongdoing must be explained, and it is the death drive that provides the explanation. The death drive is a force countering the unifying pleasure principle, a force that first leads innocently enough to religious and political institutions which seek to restrain natural human erotic instincts, but eventually defeats the unifying work of Eros in civilization, leading people into aggression, conflict, war. For Freud, then, human beings are battlefields of Eros and Thanatos, the former leading to civilizing unity and the latter to widespread domestic and international aggression.

Eros in this story is compulsive, mechanical, duplicitous, and frightening. The Maples live in service of their pleasure-seeking egos, and as long as this continues they will fail to create the innocent ideals of houses, cars, cats, and flowers that in this story their children stick onto the refrigerator door. Updike punctuates the story with martial language to this effect. Like the America in which they live, Richard exploits territory Joan "has surrendered,"[88] Joan acts like President Johnson amid the Tonkin Bay controversy in seizing false excuses for a fight,[89] continents come between the two Maples.[90] The marriage is total war.

The fourth and final act of this story fulfills its Freudian trajectory by presenting us with a dream filled with fear and repressed impulses. Richard has fully exploited his new powers over Joan by pumping her for exciting information (exciting for him) about her lovers, details of

---

[87] Sigmund Freud, *Civilization and Its Discontents*, ed. and trans. James Strachey. (New York: Norton, 2005) 118.

[88] Updike, *Too Far to Go*, 140.

[89] Ibid., 136.

[90] Ibid., 135.

their liaisons, and her "precisely mixed emotions" about the affairs.[91] After the exacting conversation and unloving lovemaking, Richard's silent forgiveness of his wife is "wasted" because she is sleeping. For the aesthetically-minded Richard, forgiveness is not an inward shift in consciousness and movement toward reconciliation, but a performance—and here the performance is unattended. Richard sleeps while dreaming that he is awake. In this dream he walks to his kitchen, where he finds Joan on the floor of the brightly lit room, practicing yoga. She casually admits a number of previously undisclosed affairs, and twists her body provocatively. Richard asks a question he might ask himself, "Why?"[92] We do not know what specific question Richard means to ask, but these seem likely: why is his own love not enough for her? Why do they behave this way? Why is life so short and filled with dread? Richard wakes in terror when the dream-Joan admits to having sex with men who come to the door to sell septic tanks—utterly casual sex and bodily waste in profane combination. Richard wakes to one of his full-blown anxiety attacks, the first we have seen since his and Joan's trip to Rome years before: "Richard's terror persists, generating mass as the reality of his dream sensations is confirmed."[93]

This anxiety attack arises, as have Richard's others, out of bad faith. Where Richard might have decided to love his wife in forgiveness, and in forgiving her for betrayals, recognize that he needs to repent his own, he instead dwells upon the pleasure he receives from experiencing shocks and from understanding his wife as "complex, devious, ungrateful, feminine." Only a perverse person—Kierkegaard would say an aesthete—would find deviousness pleasant to encounter. He walks to his kitchen, where now objects are "faithfully themselves," and finds the contentedly mated cats, released now from the rampant erotic. He has some inkling that there has been an intruder in the house, so he looks for "signs of criminal entry." All he finds are "clues" of another kind of crime: "tacked-up drawings done by children's fingers ardently bunched around a crayon, of houses, cars, cats, and flowers."[94]

This too is a complex thought. Updike seems to alter the definition of "crime" here, to include the widespread crime of parenting poorly or inattentively. Perhaps the Maples' children express some anxiety

---

[91] Ibid., 140.
[92] Ibid., 142.
[93] Ibid., 143.
[94] Ibid., 140-43.

through their drawings of ideal home and their father has aided and abetted their dread. But this passage communicates no specific anxiety of this kind, no definite sign of their father's guilt. More likely Updike here expresses the Kierkegaardian idea, paraphrased in Updike's comments on the Vietnam War, that people are born guilty, live guilty, and die guilty. This is as true of those who make the leap of faith as those who do not. The Wholly Other God decides who is redeemed. Richard notes that he lives in a nation that has photographed the moon and lived on its surface. Others may find a triumphant America in a nation that can accomplish such things. Like a later fictional character of his (Alf in *Memories of the Ford Administration*), Updike finds that the sky doesn't really care.

જ

By the time of Richard's latest night-terror in the final pages of "Eros Rampant," we are sure that he is psychologically and spiritually *in extremis*. He is a bright, attractive and charming man when he wants to be, but filled with neurotic sexual tension, with concupiscence as understood by Augustine—as a mortal sickness, a sickness in origin (*morbus originis*). To connect him further with Updike's theological heroes, he is as existentially desperate as young Luther was before he joined his mentor Staupitz in Wittenberg, as Erik Erikson argues:

> The fact is that this potentially so passionate man [Luther] found he could not feel at all, which is the final predicament of the compulsive character. That is, he could not have the feelings which he so desperately wanted to feel, while on occasion...feelings had him in the form of phobic terrors and ugly rage.

Erikson's turns of phrase capture young Martin Luther and young Richard perfectly in their existential angst. Twenty-five year old Martin Luther proceeded from this phobic and ugly stage of life to an equally chilling theological conviction, a "final totalism" of God in "the role of the dreaded and untrustworthy father."[95] This God could only terrorize

---

[95] Erikson, *Young Man Luther*, 164. I am convinced that Updike had read *Young Man Luther* by 1958, and read it carefully, but this is not the place to make that argument. For differing reasons, both Updike and Erikson are interested in the collision of faith and psychological illness—and fascinated by Martin Luther as one in whom this collision occurred. As for my mention of Augustine,

him, and Luther knew that he could not live or worship in such terror. So through intellectual rigor and frantic personal need Luther came to understand this God as revealed through Jesus Christ—revealed as incarnate, near, loving, and willing at the greatest cost to redeem fallen people. In their terror, Richard and Luther both come to a point of near-total desperation, to the propitious desperation of dread. Luther emerged from this dread to seize a caritative or infused identity, according to Erikson, a capacity for real loving-kindness. Richard, on the other hand, remains in crisis so far, and has difficulty performing the simplest works of love.

We know this: for Richard the etiquette of adultery has failed, and failed utterly. He has tried to turn adultery into a consoling game, a source of aesthetic pleasure, food for his narcissistic ego, a way to enlarge his spirit after dull Saturdays with his suffocating children, a field in which to display his considerable wit and managerial skill. But he has forgotten that love springs from the deepest personal well, and makes its own demands. Libido is giddy, and thrives upon contradictions, double standards and hypocrisy. But love will not survive contradiction. As Richard realizes, excruciating jealousy has taught him that his love for his wife is alive and vital, and so his casual liaisons are under threat. His own affairs may remind him of his wife's affairs, which raise feelings of terror and the great existential question for him: why? Why can't she be faithful to him? Why can't he be faithful to her? Why can't they love each other more fully? Why does happiness elude them? Why are they so easily bored? Why do they both feel unwell? Also under threat is his entire commitment to the aesthetic sphere. Richard has proven a resilient adulterer, and we will see further affairs in his life. But the character of his dread has changed; his games have turned deadly serious.

---

concupiscence and original sin are so pervasive in the writings that citing any single instance would be silly.

8

Frightened People Discussing

"Plumbing," "The Red-Herring Theory," "Sublimating," and "Nakedness"

> Without the empty self and its characteristic interior emptiness and yearning, the economic and cultural shape of the postwar era, including its youthful bravado, escalating inflation, and unquenchable consumer desire, would have been unthinkable.
> —Philip Cushman, *Constructing the Self, Constructing America*[1]

As they approach middle age and the end of their marriage, Richard and Joan Maple achieve a new material prosperity. They move up to a large old house and rent a vacation home on what appears to be Martha's Vineyard. They still debate with friends about the Vietnam War, but these debates seem to be a projection of inner anxieties rather than genuine worries about America's international policies. Existentially, the Maples seem to be emptier than ever, epitomizing the selfhood that Philip Cushman and other psychiatrists view as essential for the processes of consumerism.

In the next four stories—"Plumbing" (1971), "The Red-Herring Theory" (1975), "Sublimating (1971), and "Nakedness" (1974)—Richard and Joan, like their nation during the same period, turn relentlessly inward and alarmingly violent. Their inwardness, expressed primarily through their careful tending of their sexual lives, leads them first to neglect a larger world that includes their own children. Eventually this relentless inwardness leads to verbal and physical violence between them, and the Maples' children are terrified. During these same years, President Nixon ruthlessly bombs North Vietnam at Christmastime, as he attempts to extricate American troops from Vietnam, partly to redirect

---

[1] Philip Cushman, *Constructing the Self, Constructing America A Cultural History of Psychotherapy* (Boston MA: Addiston-Wesley, 1995) 214-15.

war funds to the domestic economy. Thus Updike suggests that the empty consumerist self and society both tend to be violent and engender fear in others.

When we last met Richard and Joan Maple they were both filled with fear, an emotion that grows more intense in these stories. Joan's fear is immediate and practical. She is frightened to realize how angry she is with Richard, so furious that she is willing to hurt him with a recitation of her affairs. This recitation is a clear violation of the etiquette of adultery, yet Joan cannot resist. Apparently she is also frightened to realize that he will use these confessions ruthlessly against her. Richard's fear is more frantic and deeply felt. He has had a telling and frightening dream in which Joan is so involved in the love of other men that she no longer cares about his feelings, a possibility so real that it gives him another of his night terrors. These next four stories also express the Maples' fear, which is found in denial as well as in frank confession. Through these fears Updike develops tensions that he feels are often lacking in the American civic and religious debate—tensions about what it really means to die, to stand before a Wholly Other God, to explain to this judging God both the things one has done and those one has left undone. Speaking in Kierkegaardian terms, to live in denial of this terrifying fate, to fail to choose oneself as mortal yet redeemable and possibly authentic is to live in dread. Because Richard and Joan now live with such acute dread, we begin to feel a new possibility in these stories. Richard and Joan seem on the verge of some momentous change. But what kind of change?

Whatever kind, it is represented in "Plumbing" by a changing of houses. In *The Sickness Unto Death*, Kierkegaard tells a brief parable about a man who finds his "dwelling-place distasteful." The chimney smokes, or some other problem bothers him. So he leaves his dwelling, but he does not take another one: "he continues to regard the old one as his habitation; he reckons that the offense will pass away." "So it is," Kierkegaard explains, "with despair." The one who despairs makes vain changes that are not changes at all. Defiantly refusing to become themselves, these people make their way into adulthood, live an entire life among objects, reflect just a bit, and sadly, "never really manage in their whole life to be more than they were in their childhood and youth."[2] So it is with the Maples, even as they gain new possessions and purchasing power in these years approaching middle age.

---

[2] Kierkegaard, *The Sickness Unto Death*, 191.

"Plumbing" establishes the new mood of the Maples stories. Since Richard is now middle-aged, his sexual adventures are often recalled now rather than acted out. This is a story of memories, a plumbing of the past for the meanings of home, parenthood, work, death, faith. Indeed, the story is modeled after Charles Dickens's *A Christmas Carol*, though rather than Christmases Past it is Easters Past that move Richard to a Scrooge-like epiphany: the recognition that he is guilty, in need of repentance. Throughout, Richard (who is never named; this is one of the two Maples stories Updike says belong by virtue of "internal evidence") shows evidence of being sober, meditative, even guilty, as he freely admits. Because this story occurs wholly in memory, Richard has no social poses to cut; he is able to be frankly self-critical and finally self-indicting. In one stunning memory, Richard and Joan quarrel so violently that Joan throws a book at Richard, wishing it were a heavier ashtray. Richard, who views himself as a prisoner in his own home, argues back and eventually, provoked by a blow from Joan, strikes her in the side—and finds the sensation pleasant. The terrified Maples children watch from the stairs, causing Richard to ask an acute question: "What are they saying, what are these violent, frightened people discussing?" They are afraid of "change, natural process, the passage of time, death."[3]

The story's first act opens with an emergent theme in these later Maples stories, a paradoxical treatment of time. Richard and his "old plumber" have entered the grave-like cellar of the Maples' "new house" to peer at an "antique joint."[4] The fact that the "new house" is older by far than the "old plumber," and both are older than the "antique joint," suggests that time, here, is in a kind of philosophical flux, a frame of indeterminacy. The plumber calculates the age of a lead joint as first thirty years, then forty, then fifty. Both his talk and Richard's suggest that for Updike time has the character of Bergson's *durée* rather than *l'étendu*—the fluid, subjective, existential character rather than the conveniently scientized, spatialized clock time by which we manage our existences. Similarly, the plumber's accounts can track minutely the parts he installs,

---

[3] Updike, *Too Far to Go*, 150.
[4] Ibid., 144.

1 1 ¼ x 1" galv bushing	58¢
1 3/8" brass pet cock	90¢
3 ½ " blk nipple	23¢

but can only express time spent in labor—that is, in human acts—in large, underdetermined slices:

Labor	$550

Richard and his plumber here contemplate (as they will confirm in act three) a time in which "we are outlasted," in which our very existence comes to seem absurd because our time is so pointlessly brief, and because after our untimely deaths the world we love goes on without us. Another paradox of time: throughout this tale Richard will think of himself and his family as "feeble ghosts," as though they are already dead.[5] Since they are unredeemed and living in dread, in a sense they are enacting a kind of living death rather than purposeful life. A future that might appear to them perfectly open and free in fact appears wholly closed, a prison they built, or, like Jacob Marley, a chain they forged link by link.

The Maples' plumber, on the other hand, lives comfortably in this absurd time and labors with a meaningful sense of vocation because he acknowledges and is able to work with "the eternal presences of corrosion and flow." Significantly, he also dwells upon the ways things are joined—lovingly so that they last, or vainly so that they do not. He serves, then, as a model for Richard of the well-adjusted soul, a wise priest. Updike conveys this idea anagogically. The plumber shows Richard the ancient plumbing he and Joan have just purchased and become responsible for. A lead joint demonstrates that workers, including the plumber himself as a boy, once had a different conception of time when it came to their work. They patiently melted and poured lead, performing "sixteen distinct motions" to complete a joint that would last and last. Richard and the plumber ponder a pipe so corroded that it is at the point of failing. It also illustrates this preoccupation with things joined. The plumber says, "See, they cast this old soil pipe in two halves."[6] But the seam between the halves is supposed to be on the sides,

---

[5] Ibid., 150.
[6] Ibid., 145.

rather than the bottom where liquid rests, and so this pipe is about to fail.

If we are reminded of the Maples' marriage, we have followed Updike's signals. He first has Richard realize, in a digestive metaphor, that "we think we are what we think and see when in truth we are upright bags of tripe."[7] This corroded soil pipe also carries waste, so that what is implied here is the non-ideal, impure character of humanity, of the failing, fractured self, implicated as a cause in the imminent failure of the Maples' marriage, also improperly joined. Of course no Plumber is responsible for its joining; they are.

The second act of "Plumbing" orchestrates Richard's memories, mostly profane, of two Easters, two houses, and many deaths. These are Dickensian memories of Easters Past, yet Richard himself is the ghost who guides the memories. Unlike the first-defiant Scrooge, Richard from the beginning encounters his memories in a self-indicting mood. The first is a memory of the house the Maples have just sold and left after twelve years in residence. Richard projects his emotions onto the family move, concluding that the former home's familiar rooms and stairways "do not seem to mourn, as I had thought they would."[8] Defying time, the house "is young again" without its burdensome tenants; defying rationality, it "greets Richard with a virginal impudence" even after its non-virginal experience of the Maples. Richard says, "I feel guilty that we occupied [that house] so thinly."[9] Twelve years before, the Maples had hired a witch, a friend of Joan's, to exorcise the house. Perhaps the reason the witch-friend did not find any ghosts haunting the house is because they were themselves the ghosts. Since Richard and Joan had not moved in, the haunting had not yet begun.

Mimicking the cadences of Dickens's ghosts, Richard recollects a vivid memory: "I see a man in a tuxedo and a woman in a long white dress...."[10] This is an early Easter morning, which the man and woman, Richard and Joan of course, honor by staying late at a party and becoming drunk. They hide Easter eggs, tiptoeing in the muddy yard. Later that morning, their children celebrate Easter with chocolate treats but Richard recalls "from the perspective of a sober conscience" the "apparition" (the language of haunting continues) of the early morning

---

[7] Ibid., 145.
[8] Ibid., 146.
[9] Ibid., 147.
[10] Ibid., 148.

with Joan. He sees the two of them as "Easter bunnies." Drunkenness on Easter combines with this language to convey a childish, flippant denial of Christ in this scene, but also conveys the Maples' affection for their children and faithfulness to Christian ritual, vestigial though it is. So far, the imagery is dialectical.

Vestigial Christianity is the focus of Richard's next memory as well. The scene has shifted to Bean's bedroom. He teaches the Lord's Prayer to his younger daughter. The two have attended different Sunday Schools and so "they have trouble with 'trespasses' versus 'debts.'" This "trouble" is not only a problem of language, Updike implies, but a problem of vapid permissiveness by which the entire Maple family lives: they have too little consciousness of trespasses. Richard moves on to his older daughter, who feels that reciting a prayer with her father is embarrassing. "Daddy, no, don't!" He recognizes that he too is embarrassed—"too easily embarrassed," because in relenting to his daughter's wish he denies her spiritual protection she needs and deserves. As Richard notes with more than one meaning, as he walks out of Judith's room he "leaves her to the darkness."[11]

Updike's point is that the whole family lives in darkness, the darkness of a life committed to the logic of imminent and inevitable death. His next scene, the story's most shockingly dark one, amplifies this sense. Richard and Joan fight both verbally and physically in front of the children. "She hits him; he knocks her arm away and punches her side, startled by how pleasant, how spongy, the sensation is." Updike does not spare the condemning images: "Children sneak quietly up and down the stairs, pale, guilty, blaming themselves, in the vaults of their innocent hearts, for this disruption." The dog hunches as if being whipped. Richard's sense of his wife's body as he strikes it is of a "sack of guts"—the word "guts" recalling reference to dead bodies, such as Hamlet's epithet for the body of Polonius: "I'll lug the guts into the neighbor room."[12] After noting that he and Joan have been "discussing" death (the polite verb suggests denial), he calls himself and his family "[f]eeble ghosts."[13]

Needing images of a less profane family life and Easter memory, Richard recalls the Easters of his childhood. The Easter eggs were more

---

[11] Ibid., 149.

[12] William Shakespeare, *Hamlet*, eds. Barbara A. Mowat and Paul Werstine. Folger Shakespeare Library (New York: Simon and Schuster, 2003) 3.4.212.

[13] Updike, *Too Far to Go*, 150.

than sickly-sweet candy; they were "ingots" suggesting value, "theaters" suggesting meaning-filled human play; "worlds" suggesting the world-conferring power of grace. Employing an Easter diction, Richard recalls that these eggs "arose" out of excelsior the purple hues of royalty, arising "from the same impossible-to-plumb well of mystery where the stars swarm, and old photographs predating my birth were snapped, and God listened." This remark says more, of course, about Richard's youthful Christian consciousness than about any change in God or God's response to people. His memories suggest that he was aided as a child by a culture that lived in consciousness of "corrosion and flow." Richard felt that his home was "haunted" by "menaces," but that, unlike the home he has made for his own children, the adults around him knew the place of both funeral homes and "Jesus signs"; parents and grandparents read obituaries and war news with knowing equanimity. In a remark with theological significance, Richard reports feeling that the newspapers in which these stories appeared were not about the past but about the future. Death was not an end, but a ground for a further movement, for a life with a God who listened even while death took its toll.[14]

Richard closes act two by asking whether his children sensed "the frivolity of our Easter priesthoods," his and Joan's trivializing of the Passion good news. He has his answer in nine-year old Bean's talk about death and her wish to have no more birthdays: "I don't want to have a birthday. I don't want to be nine."[15] Though Richard tempts his daughter with images of future freedoms (biking on Central Street) and the consoling fun of sexual attractiveness and activity (she can wear a bra), Bean does not want to grow older because she realizes that aging is a process that leads to death: "Because then I will get to be an old, old lady and die." Richard is mute at this remark. He imagines that "all the men ever with her will be on this point dumb."[16]

If there were no gospels perhaps this would be true, but Updike points to them immediately, a hint that there may be men in Bean's future who, like him, read and know and embrace this good news. The reference is circuitous: Richard thinks with sadness that with this move, all his family will leave behind them will be "scuff marks and a half-scraped Snoopy decal on the window frame." He thinks about the season, springtime, when he typically performs a feeble act of protection,

---

[14] Ibid., 150-51.
[15] Ibid., 152.
[16] Ibid., 153.

"putting screens in the windows." But Bean's window does offer an image of a more robust spiritual protection. Everyone reading *Peanuts* in the 1960s knew that Charles Schulz's precocious children and wise dog Snoopy enacted stories and principles from Christian scriptures.[17] The half-scraped decal on the window implies the half-owned faith of the home's tenants, a faith that—feeble as it is—confers some protection against the absurdity that has led to Bean's existential listlessness, if not against her future suffering and death.

As act three begins, readers must wonder whether Richard, like Scrooge, has learned anything elemental about himself through his memories. Seemingly not. Though his plumber-priest (a priest or theologian is one who plumbs mysteries) speaks again of "corrosion and flow," and recommends an anagogical Passion story ("dig it up and replace it with [new pipe]"), Richard protests. Thoroughly aesthetic in his understanding and feeling, he does not want to see damage done to the things he tends, "my lawn torn up, the great golden backhoe trampling my daffodils." But the plumber urges him to reconsider because new pipe and pump are important enough to outweigh temporary aesthetic disruptions. They will "outlast your time," he tells Richard.[18]

This phrase is more pregnant theologically than it seems. To outlast our time means to transcend time itself. Richard enacts an emblematic resurrection in the final lines of the story, stepping upward out of the cellar bulkhead, an emblematic grave. But he steps into a merely natural world in which even the "temporary, timeless clouds" outlast him. This story suggests that we live in Bergson's *l'étendu* and encounter only the certainty of our deaths. We fear his *durée* because we cannot realize it, situate ourselves in it, put it to use. This story hints at another way—to view time as our home. Updike suggests this meaning through Richard's remark that in seeking to buy their latest home the Maples had become "usurpers" of the future of the children living there. Richard has said that buying a home is buying "a history, an archaeology of pipes and cut-ins and traps and valves."[19] This is his authentic personal view, one he realized for himself. His remark about the children's future is less

---

[17] Robert Short's *The Gospel According to Peanuts* (Louisville KY: Westminster John Knox Press, 1965) was a bestseller in 1965 and remains in print.

[18] Updike, *Too Far to Go*, 154.

[19] Ibid., 145.

conscious, more off-hand. Yet it correlates with his sense of his own children, that their parents' fears are stealing their future too—a future filled with blessedness and gratitude. Updike believes that these children need—they deserve—to view the future as a home. Surely they need and deserve what the plumber-priest has already: a basic sense of safety, the opportunity to learn a common purpose with parents and other believers, a calling that provides work in service of neighbors' needs, a wise perspective on human corrosions and flow, and a confidence in the ability to outlast time.

&

If "Plumbing" represents a break from the problems of the Maples' adultery, those problems return in "The Red-Herring Theory," another conversation between the Maples that begins with flippant taunting but turns malicious. Richard and Joan have hosted a party, which in this neighborhood is an occasion for erotic realignments: "Their friends had come, shuffled themselves, been reshuffled, worn thin with the evening and then, papery post-midnight presences, conjured themselves out the door."[20] "The Red-Herring Theory" consists of the cleaning-up conversation in only one act. The story's focus is on rotations, sexual gaming, cunning stratagems, language used to deceive and to hurt. The two Maples discuss the partygoers, labeling them as "fish" or active lovers, and "red herrings" or false leads convenient for concealing affairs. They also discuss both the etiquette and strategy of adultery. Both Maples drink brandy during the conversation, she more than he, so that eventually Joan loses her composure and attacks Richard directly, rather than through teasing observations. Instead of an erotic conclusion to the evening Richard hoped the sexy talk might lead to, the two of them work together to clean up the mess. Yet this story ends with the incorrigibility move, as Richard decides upon a way to enter into and hide yet another affair.

Updike has written often of his childhood love of Agatha Christie's mysteries, and of course the red herring is a plot device for which Christie is known. She knew that dog trainers would drag a red (or smoked) herring along a trail to train the dog to track smells. Then, when it was time to train the dog to trail game, a red herring would be

---

[20] Ibid., 155.

dragged across the game trail at a sharp angle. In this way trainers tested the dog's tenacity in tracking the game scent.[21]

This is a story that discusses red herrings but also employs one. It only seems to be a domestic story, but is actually about the entire American polity—and beyond. First, Joan attempts to discover the true nature of Richard's relationships with some of the evening's guests. Entering into the game willingly, Richard takes his turn at this sleuthing. Both Richard and Joan make discoveries and each follows false leads, as we will see. However, Updike cares little about what the Maples learn through sleuthing about each other's affairs, or even determining guilt for marital tensions. Instead he suggests a Kierkegaardian response to devious and selfish behavior that many people in the 1960s and 1970s called "Machiavellian," contrasted with more responsible and responsive behavior arising from a theology of the "king's two bodies."

In this story Richard is the Machiavellian person, though he uses the term himself, pejoratively. Responding to Joan's "red-herring theory"—that adulterous spouses need a red herring to deflect attention from the real lover—he says, "That's too Machiavellian to be real. That's decadent, sweetie."[22] If there was resurgence in interest in Machiavelli in 1970s America it was related less to an interest in Early Modern political realism than in a popular psychological personality test that appeared to much acclaim in 1968. Developed by psychologists Richard Christie and Florence L. Geis and later discussed in their *Studies in Machiavellianism*, the test sorted people into "high Mach" and "low Mach" categories. Richard and Joan correspond nicely to these categories. Richard is "high Mach," willing to conceal, cheat, and manipulate for his own purposes. Taking the personality test, he would tend to rate highly a statement

---

[21] It is possible that Updike also plays with a more ancient meaning of red herring. According to the Oxford English Dictionary, during the sixteenth to eighteenth centuries, speakers of English might use the phrase "neither fish nor flesh nor good red herring" to denote any object or person with a mixed or confused character. The "good red herring" had become a common high tea and breakfast food—the kipper—and lodged in the English mind therefore as a quite definite, familiar substance. Any object of confused character—say, a friend who according to the evidence may be either loyal, disloyal or even malevolent— could be said to be neither fish nor flesh nor good red herring. This meaning applies nicely to this story, in which Richard and Joan lack the authenticity of "good red herring," an authenticity Kierkegaard says they may achieve by releasing grandiosity. *Oxford English Dictionary*, 2nd ed., s.v. "red herring."

[22] Updike, *Too Far to Go*, 157.

such as *It is safest to assume that all people have a vicious streak that will come out when it is given a chance.*[23] Joan's personality is "low Mach." She is ethically more sound, simply less inclined to use such methods. She would tend to rate highly a statement such as *There is no excuse for lying to someone.*[24] Readers of Christie's and Geis's work learn that high Mach personalities reap gains. One of their studies asked groups of three persons to divide ten dollars. High Mach personalities left the study an average of $5.57 richer, while low Mach personalities left with an average of only $1.29.[25] We recall that in "Giving Blood" Richard has difficulty understanding "giving something away and still somehow having it."[26]

Juxtaposed with Richard as Machiavel is Joan as a medieval sovereign queen.

> Joan rose, regal in her high-waisted, floor-length, powder-blue party dress, and seized the brandy bottle on the piano; its long neck became a scepter in her hand. She took up a dirty snifter, tossed its residue into the fireplace, listened to the sizzle, and poured herself a tawny, chortling slug. "Poor Ruth," she [said] carefully, seating herself again in the director's chair.[27]

All of the regal imagery—her dress, snifter-orb, and scepter, even her command early in the conversation—establish Joan as pre-modern and pre-Machiavellian, or potentially so. Through these assignments, which are wholly in character for both Maples, Updike offers a theological alternative to modern advantage-seeking. Richard may be ruthlessly interested in power and frankly coercive in getting it, but Joan is only temporarily so, not constitutionally. She has the potential to enact a theology of the "king's two bodies," a decidedly low-Mach form of sovereignty in which the king or queen, inspired by the example of Christ as incarnation of spiritual love, seeks to take loving responsibility for subjects, for whom she is so responsible that they are her second

---

[23] Richard Christie and Florence L. Geis. *Studies in Machiavellianism* (New York: Academic Press, 1970) 364.

[24] Ibid., 13.

[25] Ibid., 165. Not surprisingly, recent studies employing the Christie and Geis personality taxonomies tend to involve the disciplines of management and marketing.

[26] Updike, *Too Far to Go*, 56.

[27] Ibid., 158. This passage also marks the first appearance of Ruth, Richard's eventual second wife.

body. In all this, Updike may be informed by Ernst Kantorowicz's famous 1957 *The King's Two Bodies*, which notably includes a theological reading of *The Tragedy of King Richard II*.[28] Or he may be informed by Luther's theology of "two kingdoms" and a more general knowledge of royal responsibility in medieval times. Both theologies assert a similar general theory, which is that a spiritual world exists with and in the physical world, and the wisely responsible person honors both through loving conscience. Throughout his work Kierkegaard also develops a similar theory, which is that the human person is a synthesis of body and spirit, responsive to relative bodily needs and absolute spiritual ones.

Throughout the Maples stories Updike plays with references to kings and queens, but he is no royalist. He has no interest in hierarchies of anointed Christian leaders or regimes of Christian law. Instead he believes, with Luther, that such hierarchies should be replaced by networks of spiritually active and informed citizens. He implies the possibility of a just, clement society under the rule of no one sovereign but of citizens acting with love. To cite one previous example, the marchers following Martin Luther King through the streets of Boston must not depend upon a "king" to secure their freedoms or that of their neighbors, but must instead enact neighbor-love in their own lives.

In "The Red-Herring Theory" Richard and Joan vie for control of the conversation, but Joan initiates it, and indeed she is unusually culpable in it. Updike's imagery suggests that Joan, newly aggressive, is not so much trying to gain information about Richard's affairs as to gain control in the household. From a certain ethical perspective, Joan's project is sensible enough. She is merely trying to protect a realm of action in Richard's game. However, we must remember that Updike promotes marital love over power, unselfing over violence. First playing for power, Joan enjoys some brandy with her teasing conversation about the etiquette of adultery. But drinks that are at first part of her swagger cause her to become drunker and less strategically sharp. Late in the discussion, Richard routs her through a verbal cruelty to which she cannot rise, an accusation that because she maintains "so many" red herrings among her own relationships she had been a painfully obvious flirt on a recent sailing trip. Her silence in response recasts her in Richard's mind as his moody, secretive mother. She claims that she had merely wanted "to talk" in a way she feels deprived of: "It doesn't

---

[28] Ernest H. Kantorowicz, *The King's Two Bodies: A Study in Mediaeval Political Theology* (Princeton, NJ: Princeton University Press, 1957).

happen that often."[29] But this is a shot fired in retreat, an effort to recast herself as oppressed wife, victim in the situation. She certainly is Richard's victim often enough, but this night's conflict is mostly her responsibility and emerges from a bid on her part to exert a power she has learned from what she calls the "women's lib" movement.

To the extent that this feminine power pursues justice and seeks equality between husband and wife, we surely approve of Joan's self-assertion. We also approve of her elevated self-esteem, her queenly poise, in this scene. Yet the orb and scepter she holds are duplicitous images, and Joan is making a largely improper use of her emerging power. Literally grasping symbols of power, she proposes an interesting theory that gains Richard's attention and gets him talking about his secrets. This seems to be her object in the discussion. But in seizing a brandy bottle and snifter, emblems of alcohol use and a habit that has become so regular that Richard has noticed it, she has grasped after a dubious power. She will quickly become drunk (or drunker), and will, as Richard puts it, use the alcohol to anesthetize herself and thus lose her "edge."[30] This is the aggression or edge he employs to carry his flirtations into sexual liaisons, to exert his will in general, to seize what he wants in the aesthetic realm. Losing her edge, Joan abdicates both her Machiavellian power, and the more caritative powers that emerge from her incarnational, spiritual identity.

Midway through the post-party conversation, the metaphor of the red herring gives way to the metaphor of fresher fish and fishing. "Jim is your fish," Richard guesses, "and you teased him with your red herring." Through this biblical imagery, crime mystery gives way to divine mystery—for the reader if not for the Maples. This is a gentle reminder of the Ichthus to fishers of men less profane than those attending the evening's party, to loaves and fishes as holy food, to casting a net on the other side of the boat. A series of non-profane reminders of this sort begins to appear. Sitting down, Joan's long dress ceases to look queenly and makes her appear pregnant, an image we should take as a reminder of the children sleeping in innocence upstairs.[31] Joan dismisses the idea of Mack and Eleanor remarrying, which ought to please the Maples if they loved their friends, by joking about wasted lawyers' fees.

---

[29] Updike, *Too Far to Go*, 162-3.
[30] Ibid., 161.
[31] Ibid., 160 and 155.

A more emotional turn in the story occurs when Richard, fully engaged in the game of sleuthing, mentions Mack speaking at length to Linda Donnelson. "Joan's face froze," he notices, "the way a gust of wind will suddenly flatten choppy water."[32] She is hurt. Richard supposes, incoherently, that Mack cannot interest Joan since their affair cooled after the Dennis divorce. But if protecting an affair with Sam Donnelson were Joan's object, why should Joan be so stunned and hurt by Mack speaking to Linda Donnelson? She may worry that Mack is informing Linda of an affair between Joan and Sam, but would not be so thoroughly chilled or stunned by the news. Joan clearly has deep feelings for Mack, though Richard's denial in this scene, his poor sleuthing and gamesmanship, reveals that he is ignorant of them. These genuine feelings thrust Joan out of the game. She goes on the attack with hurt sincerity and energy— and some drunken license. She tells Richard that she doesn't like him very much. His response, teasing her about Sam's fine body, is unanswered. Joan is silent, and now Richard becomes frightened too. "Her silence frightened him," Richard confesses, "he became again a little boy begging his mother to speak to him, to rescue him from drowning in the blood-deep currents of her moods, of her secrets."[33]

Richard's Machiavellianism has coiled back on him. Like all sin, his devious and manipulative selfishness is self-destructive as well as other-destructive. (Joan participates in this sin as well, of course.) Richard might gain some help with his separation anxiety disorders if he encountered Joan sincerely, and with love. But he has alienated her once again, and activated that part of her ethical self that participates in God's judging, punishing No. Finally speaking, she tells him that he is cruel. Desperate for affirmation from this wife turned opponent turned spurning mother, Richard begs to know why she likes him: "Tell me," he begs, "why we shouldn't get a divorce." He isn't pleased with Joan's answer: "I've never been lonely with you. I've never for an instant felt alone when you were in the room."[34]

Joan's remark about never being lonely with Richard is a gift—it confers a genuine personhood upon him, little as she intends the remark as a gift and little as he deserves it. She is simply speaking from the heart, seemingly trying to understand the nature of this love herself. The remark is a hint at the struggling love that exists between them in spite

---

[32] Ibid., 161.
[33] Ibid., 162.
[34] Ibid., 163.

of their sufferings with each other, and a hint at the personhood that might be his if he would honor Joan's love enough to allow her to speak this frankly and honestly with him always, or at least much more often.

The Richard we meet in these stories—still compulsive, cruel, selfish, unfaithful—is not going to cure himself. Nor is he going to adopt Joan's ethical stance, meet her implied wish for a faithful relationship and join her in justice-seeking social crusading. As if to demonstrate his incorrigibility, he attacks Joan once more this evening, responding to her retreating shot about seldom getting to talk and knowing that Richard doesn't want her to feel alive. He tells her she is alive only to others. Again apparently speaking honestly rather than in calculated attack, Joan tells Richard that his self pity makes him sound just like Ruth—who will eventually become the next Mrs. Richard Maple. In the brief coda to follow, Richard sits on the sofa "trying to see through the tangle to the light. Joan was on to Ruth; that space was gone. There remained one area of opportunity, one way to beat the system; its simplicity made him smile. Sleep with your red herring."[35] With this perverse line, the story ends.

Fathoms deep in the aesthetic, Richard sees the light and his escape in yet another arbitrary sexual liaison, another shuffle of the cards, sleeping with his red herring. Readers alerted to Updike's theology know that in losing the scent of the religious in a pursuit of the aesthetic red herring, Richard ignores the light of the world—the, Ichthus the fish. The tangle he struggles through is the net in which he is now caught.

Theodor Adorno, in a challenging 1939 critique of Kierkegaard's notion of Christian love, picked up some of the same threads of Biblical imagery as Updike does in "The Red-Herring Theory." He also echoes Updike's implied questions about power, ascendancy, and justice:

> The neighbor of the gospels implies fishermen and peasants, herdsmen and publicans, people whom one knows and who have their established locus of life of simple production which can be realized by immediate experience. One cannot imagine the Gospels taking the step from this concrete, unproblematic neighbor to the abstract, universal idea of neighborhood.

Adorno claims that Kierkegaard had his own Danish neighbors in his day, but in his writing substitutes for them an abstract Christian neighbor "who belongs to a different society." Adorno implies that the

---

[35] Ibid., 164.

only way to meet a neighbor's need is through revolutionary transformation of the mode of production. Kierkegaard strikes Adorno as being guilty of the very reification that mystifies neighbors, distracts them from their real neighbors living in economic oppression, and keeps them from joining in the historical processes that the economic classes must complete. "Hence," he continues, "he deprives both of their sense."[36]

Updike, whose Christianity also foresees a radical justice for all persons, and who posits the establishment of this justice as the daily task of believers, understands Kierkegaard more penetratingly. For Kierkegaard, the wife is as concrete and immediate as a neighbor can be, and the home the simplest locus of production. Perhaps Adorno has not read *Works of Love*, because in that book Kierkegaard is quite specific about how to find the neighbor. One could venture out into the world and travel its breadth in a vain search for this neighbor. "But Christianity," Kierkegaard writes, "is never responsible for having a person go even a single step in vain, because when you open the door that you shut in order to pray to God and go out[,] the very first person you meet is the neighbor, whom you *shall* love."[37] For Updike and his Danish mentor, love is an act in service of a real, nearby person, not a feeling.[38] In gratitude to God and with God's help, the personal act (or work) of love will penetrate the social sphere and transform power and precedence into love and justice. Learning to use power, Machiavellian or not, is at best a way to remediate proximate evils, but there is nothing about genuine Christian inwardness that will support a behavior based in manipulation. The mystery of "The Red-Herring Theory" is how the *vita passiva* can become the ground for assertive action and social transformation.

&

"Sublimating" shares the mock-comic spirit of "Your Lover Just Called" and "The Red-Herring Theory," stories whose initial comedic effect turns chilling. For a plot model Updike this time takes the television sit-com, and also employs the one-liners and other gags of the form, as

---

[36] Theodor Adorno, "On Kierkegaard's Doctrine of Love," in *Søren Kierkegaard*, ed. Harold Bloom (New York: Chelsea House, 1989) 26.

[37] Kierkegaard, *Works of Love*, 51.

[38] Ibid., 96.

when Richard offers to cut Dickie's hair with hedge clippers and the boy backs away toward his brother in wide-eyed fright. (Cue laugh track.) The tension in this story is laughable and sham also, like the marital tensions of *The Honeymooners* or *Bewitched*, programs the Maples kids might be watching. But Updike's situation involves narcissism and its effects, and the comedy is bitter.

The psychiatric theory on which "Sublimating" is based is threadbare and unconvincing—which is not to say that sublimating itself is a sham. Updike repeatedly affirms the sublimating of sexual energy as an essential human function. It is one of his familiar intellectual formulae.

Freud notified us of our servitude to sex, our freedom in the face of the erotic life, and the motive sexual energy that we inevitably tap for many purposes, including culture-making and novel-writing. Perhaps Updike's most explicit reference to sublimating and most convincing evidence of his belief in it occurs in a late 1990s essay, "Lust," first published in the *New York Times Book Review*. Freud, Updike tells us, caused an intellectual revolution in the West. A traditional view of lust as sin, a tenet of Catholic theology handed down to Protestants, has been replaced by an ethic of health based in sexual satisfaction. Freud introduced the notion of libido, and in doing so deconstructed lust. Now, in Freud's wake the sins of which we are truly ashamed are impotence, frigidity, and unattractiveness. Thus, Updike argues, "the Gospel of Freud has triumphed." We all now recognize the "polymorphous-perverse torrents" (Updike apparently means libido) at work in us and in our neighborhoods, at a cost to our "as yet unreplaced institutions, marriage and the male-headed family." Pornography and advertising have changed social expectations, and unleashed sexual urgency has brought us increased "divorce, out-of-wedlock pregnancies, and a rise in literally mortal venereal disease."[39] Updike's disgust with this situation is so palpable that we wonder whether he means it when he suggests that, as Freud has convinced us, the human animal "must lust [...], one might say, *or else sublimate*." Not an entirely ironic remark: Updike goes on to suggest that lust joins us with "the beasts of the field," a sexual appetite that "calls into activity our most elegant faculties, of self-display, social intercourse, and idealization."[40]

---

[39] Updike, *More Matter*, 43-44.
[40] Ibid., 45, emphasis mine.

We recognize that this treatment of lust is characteristically dialectical. Updike has always made clear that human sexuality is a source of both degradation and innocent joy. Still, whether or not Updike with his divided mind believes Freud's theories to be powerful and true, he does not let the father of psychiatry off the moral hook. Freud's emphasis on sexual satisfaction met with widespread acceptance in 1970s America; so did the idea of our helplessness before sexuality. And so, writes Updike, "[t]he righteous hunt for healthful satisfaction was on, and pity the child, parent, or marriage vow that got in its way."[41]

"Sublimating" directly confronts this righteous hunt for sexual satisfaction. Updike not only exposes wrongheaded uses of Freudian theories in the project of 1970s sexual license, but suggests that the Freudian drama, essentially a war between the life-affirming libido and the death drive, proposes no solution to the terrorizing, imminent reality of death. Mikhail Bakhtin once observed that he remained a Christian in the adamantly secular soviet state because socialism showed no care for the dead.[42] Updike suggests that his own calculus regarding Freudianism is similar. Freud's greatest intellectual error was in positing mere quasi-mechanical drives in place of the desperate personal terror that is ground for the leap into faith. Failing to be Kierkegaard, Freud thus fails to offer an adequate portrait of the existential human situation.

Updike concedes and indeed celebrates Freud's insight that sexual energy drives human behavior. This story employs the entire Maples family as a catalog of developmental stages and illustrations of the sexual energies they present. The four acts of the story all prepare for the ironic final line, in which Richard responds to Joan's hopeful but doubtful suggestion that sexual abstinence is "cleansing" and productive of the kind of energy "that went into the Crusades." Richard replies, "'Yes, I think...we may be onto something.'"[43]

This is heavy irony for this story's conclusion. All five of the Maples in this story are sexual beings, seeking (sometimes frantically) outlets for their sexual energy. As for Joan's suggestion that she and Richard are storing sublimated energy, few thoughtful contemporary Christians, least of all the Maples, would wish to use available energy to embrace or repeat the Crusades, violently chauvinist and racist as those military

---

[41] Updike, *Due Considerations*, 461.

[42] Tzvetan Todorov, *Mikhail Bakhtin: The Dialogical Principle*, trans. Wlad Godzich (Minneapolis, MN: University of Minnesota Press, 1994) 4.

[43] Updike, *Too Far to Go*, 179.

maneuvers were. Furthermore, both Maples have been having dreams and visions in which they see themselves dead. Joan's visions are more frightening to her because none of those who know her—not even her children—are much affected, in her imagination, by losing her. Richard simply does not grapple with his own dreams of his death. He renders them aesthetic dramas in which funeral attendees grieve his loss bitterly while he watches—Richard as Tom Sawyer in the church balcony, enjoying the show. The Maples are emphatically not onto something with their sexual moratorium.

Joan's reminding us of the Crusades is important for more than one reason. The remark reminds us of iniquitous, violent Christian energy (which will receive ironic comment in this story), but suggests also sexual abstinence in the Catholic tradition generally, which of course leads us to Martin Luther's struggles with monasticism. Luther also supposed for a time that chastity was clarifying, but during his nineteen years in a monk's cowl he nearly killed himself (and, he thought, probably did destroy his digestion) with acts of penitence, self-punishment, extreme denial of physical comfort and need, and other offenses against his carnal and psychological self. Eventually he came to see the beauty in such simple things as good food and drink, warm blankets on the bed, pleasant physical exercise—and of course, joyful sexual intercourse with a beloved wife. Oddly, the Maples' sexual moratorium is also a sin against the religion of the sexual revolution, which according to Updike obeys the Freudian insight: "happiness is sexual happiness."[44]

Act one of this story involves the image of Richard's cabbage. Sex being a "sore point" in the marriage, they have decided to give up sexual intercourse, even though their eighteen-year marriage has made them feel one flesh: "even their birth pangs, with a pang, seemed to merge."[45] The Maples do not seem to realize that all they have given up is physical pursuit of the orgasm. They can never give up their sex, their deep identity emerging from procreative instinct. Richard's cabbage epitomizes this larger sexual identity, the stages of human sexual function. At first the cabbage is a stereotype of birthing imagery, evoking the myth that babies are found in cabbage patches. (That this myth is used by parents to conceal actual sexual processes from children seems

---

[44] Updike, *Due Considerations*, 461.

[45] Updike, *Too Far to Go*, 165. Joan has recently called their sex together "lousy," 163.

important in this tale of unnatural denial.) Next, the cabbage becomes an emblem of the psychologically complex self, especially the "leaves and leaves of female psychology, packed so snugly the wrinkles dovetailed." Next, Bean's teasing about the cabbage spurs Richard to adopt it in fun as a substitute child. Eventually, Richard compares his cabbage, loyally eaten beyond its freshness and the pleasure it first gave, as one of his mistresses, one of the kind Richard leaves as soon as Joan discovers and mocks them.

These are parables of carnal life. They are matched in this story by Richard's meditations on ideality, the implication being that our incarnation is a window onto the spiritual and sacred. He is charmed by the "pure sphericity" of the cabbage, a "secret sphere...he had drilled back into reality."[46] Where does this ideality lead him? Back to his wife, with whom, he imagines, he is so closely and spiritually wed that his own eyes and Joan's merged into one shared eye. Significantly, this third eye seems to take Joan's ethical viewpoint rather than Richard's aesthetic one as its dominant trait, since it is Joan's "dry female-to-female clarity" that "always ousts his erotic mists."[47] Again, this imagery poses the Maples as one flesh, and the cabbage represents this wedded flesh. Like a typical marriage, Richard's cabbage might become monotonous to devour over time; its heart might be bitter enough to burn the mouth; but it is a hole drilled into reality.

The story's second act contemplates the less-than-ideal nature of human sexual identity, to some comic and some chilling effect. Richard's thoughts about his own affairs in act one give way now to thoughts of Joan's contrasting ones. Hers have been less easy for Richard to discover, and so he learns of them after the fact, after Joan's healing over her hurts and wounds has concluded. These affairs occur against the backdrop of her quotidian housewifely duties, the "[s]ame old grind" of driving the kids to their chosen activities. Updike connects Joan's affairs with the children's athletic activities, suggesting that they emerge from the same energy—an energy properly sublimated in the children's parts, but perhaps not in hers. He suggests further through John's latest project, building a guillotine out of a sharpened snow shovel because his sixth grade class is studying revolution, that sublimated sexual energy has had catastrophic as well as beneficent effects in human history. Here Updike presents an irony and a history lesson that he has more recently

---

[46] Ibid., 165-168.
[47] Ibid., 168.

confessed as a preoccupation about the days of the sexual revolution and Vietnam conflict: "Make love, not war became a chant—as if people hadn't, for millennia, been finding time for both."[48] The guillotine reminds us that in Vietnam American forces took over a warring project from the defeated French. John's simple school project becomes a sign of Updike's concern for the particular form that sublimating may take in the political realm in a nation like mid-century America.

The sit-com trope Updike echoes and ironizes in this story is the idea that people deprived of regular sex become intensely irritated. Updike also plays around with half-serious references to castration anxiety. Both are stock situations for television comedies, and neither holds up well to psychological analysis. We get an example of this castration anxiety when Richard worries about John building a guillotine: "Jesus, he better not lose a finger."[49] Richard's excess energy and fixation upon castration is evident in his pruning of bushes on the Maples property, and again receives comic treatment when he offers his son Dickie his haircut and, as I have noted, the boy backs away toward his younger brother, displaying exaggerated fright. It is as though both sons are castrated already: "They looked like two chunky girls . . ."[50] Even Joan's speech becomes comically allusive. "Daddy's upset *about something else*, not about your hair," she tells the boys. Her own response to the sexual moratorium is also comic and silly, as she gushes over the sensation of driving through an automatic car wash, and the "little hose" you can hold if you put money in it.[51]

Richard's frantic pruning around his house may exaggerate sublimated sexual energy, but it does serve an emblematic purpose for Updike. Dickie chides his father for pruning too aggressively: "You didn't leave any green," he says. "There can't be any photosynthesis." This worry refers to a genuinely serious problem: whether Richard isn't committing violence upon a living thing—not his yews but his marriage. We laugh when Richard responds by inviting his sons to stick their heads into the guillotine, but we are told that he "mutilates" a flowering trumpet vine, and his vision of a world from which "the organic" has been "scoured" is both alarming and intriguing—alarming because

---

[48] Updike, *Due Considerations*, 459.
[49] Updike, *Too Far to Go*, 169. Is he thinking of threats to his own "finger" when he ponders Joan's "even white teeth?"
[50] Ibid., 171.
[51] Ibid., 172, emphasis mine, and 170.

Richard's denial of his incarnate life is heretical, and intriguing because we sense in his wish, perhaps, a contempt for his merely physical self, unredeemed at present by a genuine awareness of spirit or relation to God. Late in the story he illustrates the hollowness of his materialist commitments when he fails miserably to console Joan for her death-visions: "It's part of being one with Nature."[52]

The second half of act two riffs on the two older Maples children's Oedipal dramatics, realistic-enough evidence that though children they are fundamentally sexual beings. Judith, sixteen, has awakened to her newly sexual body and adult-tending mind. She puts both on obvious display, squirming and stretching in her "hip-hugging Levi's" and exposed "silken underpants," and making speeches about the immaturity of her male siblings. Dickie can only defend himself by noting the truth about Judith, that she is a "young sociologist"—like her mother, a preacher of liberal justice—who "flaunts her charms"—mostly her "pearly belly." If Judith reproduces her mother's ethical commitments (or are they pretensions?), she has also learned, like her father, to exploit raging and unkind speech: "You," she tells Dickie, "are a very *spoiled* and *selfish* and *lim*ited person." This attack might just as well be directed at her father, truly enough, and indeed in a moment Judith labels him a "narcissist"—a cut so close to the bone that Richard speaks as sharply to her in rebuke as he ever has during her life.[53] With Judith's precocious diagnosis, act two ends.

Updike's third act compares the Maples' sublimations or substitutions for sex. Joan has made another visit to the erotic car wash. With all three of her children in the car, plus two others and the dog, it was, she says, "a real orgy." Richard, meanwhile, has viewed a pornographic film in Manhattan, where he has taken a business trip. He uses the tale to turn his conversation with Joan toward himself, and much of his chatter is irrelevant. But two remarks seem important. First, Richard refers to this porn theater as a circle of Hell, filled with suffering people separated from one another spatially and emotionally. Then he notes that porn films turn the joy of sex into labor: "God, how they work."[54] This is not the first time Updike has referred to the sex act as work—in *Rabbit, Run*, Harry's lover Ruth commands him in the midst of

---

[52] Ibid., 171 and 179.
[53] Ibid., 173-4.
[54] Ibid., 177.

their first lovemaking to "Work!"[55] In that novel, Updike is after an ironic comment on Harry Angstrom's hollow sense of calling; the same is true in this story. As Updike has noted in his nonfiction, the sexual revolution, by the time it was expressed in the "Playboy philosophy" of sexual pleasure as psychological palliative, had turned good sex into a "new work ethic."[56]

Here we have arrived at a central suggestion of this story: every human joy, divorced from the motive energy of love (*agape*, not *eros*), may become "work" understood in a pejorative sense—toil, the sweat of our brow.[57] The Maples have turned marriage into work, parenting into work (Joan: "All I've heard all week are children's complaints"), sexuality into work, and, in the next moment of this story, time with the neighbor into work: "We have to go to dinner tonight with the new Dennises." Joan's instincts help her to suggest some needed weekend leisure in bed with Richard, but perversely he quashes the idea—and his wife's gesture at mutuality—by insisting on an afternoon of golf. "See," Joan says in the final line of the act, "you're sublimating."[58] And they remain separated.

The sit-com spirit of the story ends abruptly with the opening of its final act. Sublimating no longer results in an irritable, frantic energy or comically unrealistic threats to the phallus; now we enter into the genuinely subliminal realm in which death is an active terror rather than a deep inner death wish. I have discussed how this scene prepares for the story's final line. More is going on, however. Notably, Richard's materialist suggestion that through death he and Joan will become "One with nature" is prompted by Joan's stereotyping of sublimating a moment before: "It's as if my senses are jammed permanently open. I feel all one with Nature."[59] The remark is both silly and unknowingly prescient. The best way for the Maples to be "one with nature" is to reject the pieties of pervasive eroticism, which devalues carnal expressions and turns them into toil, and to enter into the deeply satisfying repetitions of loving sexuality. This would be to express their human nature in an authentic way, as Freud himself recognized. As Updike notes, Freud

---

[55] Updike, *Rabbit, Run*, 84.
[56] Updike, *Due Considerations*, 461.
[57] Genesis 3:19.
[58] Updike, *Too Far to Go*, 176-77.
[59] Ibid., 178.

warned against a cheapening of sexuality through profligate spending of sexual energy:

> Some obstacle is necessary to swell the tide of libido to its height.... In times during which no obstacles to sexual satisfaction existed, such as, may be, during the decline of the civilizations of antiquity, love became worthless, life became empty, and strong reaction-formations were necessary before the indispensable emotional value of love could be recovered.

When Updike quotes this passage in a 2000 essay, he goes on to review unwelcome chastening responses to the profligacy of the sexual revolution: evangelical pieties, and revelations of the violent underside to the porn and sex-salon worlds. He concludes the essay with less profane memories of life with his parents, who had experienced both the Flapper days of the 1920s and urgent seizing of erotic moments during the forced separations of the Second World War. His point is that even the seemingly repressed generation of his parents knew plenty about sexual freedoms, and yet still valued the inhibitions of self-preservation so that sex never became "paltry."[60]

References to death give a theological character to the observation. Again, we remember, these are frightened people discussing their anxiety-producing fates. Luther and Kierkegaard would never suggest that love or sex, either one, can or should be measured, apportioned, regulated, or controlled—all functions of legalism. Both love and sexual expressions of love are to be given freely, but in full knowledge of eternity, so that no one is degraded or cheapened, no one distracted from God's revelation by the merely profane.

&

With "Nakedness," a relatively light-hearted and affirming story, Updike closes out the days when the Maples share a home together, discussing their fears with each other. Kristiaan Versluys chooses to seize the story from Updike, to render it a paean to the goodness of semiotic delay, the "vacillation and interaction between interpretive schemes and epistemological paradigms," and the "representation of life experience as a constant repositioning of the self within a discursive field of ever-shifting meanings." It is true that the cultural meanings of nakedness are

---

[60] Updike, *Due Considerations*, 463-65.

the focus of this story, and the young nude bathers walking down the beach its fictive occasion. Versluys implies that he finds Updike intentionally at work on this project of semiotic relativity—but it seems an uncharacteristic project for a man so God-haunted and concerned with psychological and existential meaning. For Versluys, the story's epiphanic moment involves Richard's realization of "gnostic wisdom" while bathing nude, alone in a tidal pond. This is a wisdom that somehow causes a moment of peace and mutuality between him and Joan—though they will, we are told, quarrel again soon. Versluys admits that one ever-shifting meaning Richard tries to pin down in this tale is "what nakedness is, what adultery is." But he makes no attempt to discern Updike's definitions. Versluys then suggests that Richard, during a solitary swim, realizes that "everything makes sense." This is what matters.[61] Precisely what now "makes sense" to Richard in this sweeping way—about nakedness, adultery, signification, or life—Versluys's reading does not explain. And what about the ticks that then crawl up Richard's naked legs?

Updike provides us with a broad hint as to *his* notion of the focus of the story, which seems quite different from Versluys's semiotic reading, when Joan realizes that an incident she witnesses, nudists being kicked off the local beach, was like Masaccio's *Expulsion from the Garden*. Richard teases her for her pride in demonstrating to herself, though apparently not to him, the "relevance of a humanistic education to modern experience."[62] The relevance of forms of knowledge will become the story's theme.

Joan's education *is* valuable and important, and Richard's too. Knowledge surely shapes behavior, and liberal learning poses opportunities for meaning-making, for reform of the consciousness, for consolation in existential anxiety. We recall that Luther was an essayist and educator in the humanist tradition of his day. As Erik Erikson suggests, "He most carefully studied the classical textbooks (*Glossa, Ordinaria, and Lyra*), and kept abreast of the humanist scholars of his time and of the correctives provided by Erasmus's study of the Greek texts

---

[61] Kristiaan Versluys, "'Nakedness' or realism in Updike's early short stories," in *The Cambridge Companion to John Updike,* ed. Stacey Olster. (New York: Cambridge University Press, 2006) 39-42.

[62] Updike, *Too Far to Go,* 185.

and Reuchlin's study of the Hebrew texts."[63] In referring to the Masaccio painting, the erudite Updike reminds us that Richard is not the first to be bewitched by the aesthetic pleasure of gazing at women's bodies, not the first to grapple with the meaning of narratives of innocence and experience, not the first to differ sharply with his spouse's view of the world yet experience the renewal with that spouse of a deep and enduring bond. He and Joan had privileged educations at Harvard and Radcliffe, and this story tests whether their knowledge can be brought to bear on these mysteries of mind and body that others have encountered before them.

Of course, the story also addresses social and ideological disputes and differences that concerned Updike in the later 1960s and early 1970s. In his memoirs he confesses his irritation with unsubtly ideological liberals and student radicals, neither group apparently able to engage in any dialectical thinking at all, any weighing of priorities, seeking of warrants, contemplating of tensions, or forming of commitments that admit to doubt. Joan in this story represents these liberals. Her reflexive sympathy for the young nudists walking down the beach and distaste for the young "pig" policeman who stops them come too quickly and with too little reflection. Notably, the young people themselves reject her sympathy. The nudists stand in for student radicals generally, though it must be admitted that they are granted little speech in this story, making no real argument on behalf of any ideological position. Richard, who may be growing up, represents Updike's interest in dialectical thinking here. He wishes not to label the young cop a "pig," searching for a paradox that would contain the young man's union with the nudists he pursues and also his disunion in role and perhaps perspective. He watches the dressing kids "like a sorrowing angel." Richard even senses a sadness in the situation that could only be expressed wordlessly, some meaning transcending linguistic framing. [64]

One sadness both Joan and Richard confront is their age, which is to say their bodily decay and sense of mortality. Daughter Judith is now old enough to live with a man. The Maples' gazing upon taut young bodies makes them realize that their own middle-aged bodies are far less fit and attractive. Joan is "plump," and Richard feels an impulse to cover

---

[63] Erikson, *Young Man Luther*, 198. Versluys may be pleased to know that Luther "could be as quibbling a linguist as any scholasticist and as fanciful as any humanist."

[64] Updike, *Too Far to Go*, 180-85.

his own flesh when he sees the male nudist's "godlike thorax." Dialectical thinking leads Richard to another observation, that with their greater age even the maddening Maples grow in mutuality, as when Richard "unthinkingly match[es]" his wife's gait on the sand. This instinctive bodily mutuality is both significant itself, and emblematic of an inward mutuality that becomes evident in the story's third and final act. In this first act, Richard finds that his wife's "lustrous volume" is "real enough...for now."[65] Apparently his deep, instinctive bond with Joan is still subject to the temporizing effects of his rotation projects. The day may come when she is not interesting enough to him.

The passage of time is evoked in the Maples' aging bodies, as we have seen, but contrasting this decay is their renewed sense that they were courting now, as they had in Harvard's Widener Library years before. Updike suggests here that through love we do in fact reverse time, may indeed recover innocence. Ironically, this is exactly the intended program of the young people on the beach, a program of regained innocence that Updike means to address and test. Of course the hippies' project of recovering innocence is in direct reaction to doctrines of Original Sin, a doctrine whose mythic originating moment is commemorated in paintings such as Masaccio's *Expulsion from the Garden*. Updike stages a contemporary retelling of that myth in the first act of this story, casting the young pig in the role of the "sorrowing angel"—like the one in Masaccio's painting who is also armed to the teeth and reluctantly intent on driving the nonviolent and unarmed sinners out of Eden. This casting of the nudists is only seeming, however. The better players for the roles of Adam and Eve are Richard and Joan.

Act two of this story is quite literally a meditation. While Richard mows and trims the grass around his rented cottage, he muses upon three moments of his own nakedness, and nakedness depicted in Bible, Apocrypha, and Western painting.[66] Richard returns in these mediations to what he knows of origins—his own origin in God's creation, non-Christian myths of creation, the origin of his separation anxiety disorder. In this fictive time, Richard experiences his disorder without any active feelings of terror—or rather only one remembered moment of alarm as he and a lover, in mid-intercourse, hear a step in the room below them.

---

[65] Ibid., 182-83.

[66] Of course grass is a traditional image of common or universal death. In "The Dogwood Tree" Updike refers to God as "the Author of the grass." Updike, *Assorted Prose*, 182.

(More on that scene below.) As Richard ponders, his thoughts of origin and creation seem to shift to thoughts of castration and annihilation, and he uses these thoughts as a springboard for a contemplation of what, finally, strikes him as genuinely profane and genuinely innocent. A *Time Magazine* review of a film in which Bridget Bardot appears briefly naked raises this question. The review makes the comic remark that nakedness is no big deal: there is a naked woman in most American homes around eleven o'clock each night.

Updike continues his dialectical approach. In this middle section of the story, his preoccupation is with the opposite of innocence, which we will have to call sin. The most vivid sin in this story is Richard's own, as he admits, the moment when his lover and he believe, to their shock, that they are about to be discovered in coital embrace. The scene is presented in terms we have come to think of as Lacanian, and Freud is definitely involved. Richard and his lover gaze into a mirror beside their bed. Ironically and characteristically, the narcissist Richard admires his own body rather than his lover's. This seems to participate in the Lacanian confession of the Freudian faith: Richard seems to reenact in the mirror an earlier time, the *infans* stage of his own development when he first encountered a mirror and, making gestures that the mirror allowed him to witness, realized his primordial self, prior to its dissolution into an awareness of others and prior to his fuller immersion in language that would teach him he is not only an "I" but also a subject. This narrative would fit with our understanding of Richard's self-obsession, and the mirror here does accomplish a shift of attention to Richard's aesthetic pleasure, his tendency to make pictures, or rather portraits, in which he is the sole subject. His lover lying beneath him tries to get into the picture, but Richard finds her image negligible. Still, he notes that his own head is "startled, sheepish." A process of self-critique is thus already begun when he hears an alarming step downstairs.[67]

Dubiously, and no doubt because of his deconstructive method, Versluys does not even address the phrase, "the mirror had become a screaming witness to the fact that he was where he should not be ("Dirt is matter in the wrong place," his mother used to say)...."[68] An emphatic line in an emphatic scene—here Updike does some screaming witnessing of his own. Richard believes that he is too sophisticated morally and ethically to honor simple obligations such as faithfulness to one's spouse.

---

[67] Updike, *Too Far to Go*, 186-87.
[68] Ibid., 187.

Worse yet, from Updike's confessed point of view, Richard ignores not only duty but also Joan's obvious hurt. This is a failure of neighbor-love. Instead of feeling such neighbor-love, Richard feels fully justified in seeking sexual pleasure with whichever woman attracts him. Yet we note that he does not secure any agreements first with these women's husbands, their families, or members of their community—the very people before whom a wedding promise is made. He speaks to Joan about his liaisons only when she catches him at them. Richard's duplicity becomes clear in this epiphanic scene when we find that he is filled with bodily shame at his adultery, moved for the second time in the story by an impulse to cover himself. (The first occurs on the beach, when he sees a nude body more fit than his own.) Then his unconscious delivers another chastening blow. Significantly, the voice of theological nay-saying, "Dirt is matter in the wrong place," is Richard's own normally permissive mother. It is her voice Richard hears naming him as dirt, dust, mortal, unredeemed, out of place. This is fitting in an existential sense. Richard's neuroses originate in his love for this mother, a love never apparently transformed and given ethical-moral character by his accomplishing a healthy separation from her. Richard's obsessive coupling with women and dependent possession of his wife both stem from this separation anxiety, which has become a disorder.

Is Updike's intention comic or clinical when in the very next scene Richard contemplates, with a pair of sharp clippers in his hand, the meaning of the phallus in Japanese pictures he has seen? The dialectical answer is, comically, both. Clinically speaking, castration anxiety is linked to fears of loss consistent with separation anxiety disorder. The greatest loss to be feared is loss of the love object, that is, the mother. Here Richard's shame at being caught *in flagrante* in adultery is connected to his mother. In fact, the scene is—to connect it with themes we saw first in "Waiting Up"—a so-called primal scene in which, thanks to the mirror, Richard sees himself caught in the forbidden act that, in spite of taboos, he connects to his mother. The act becomes shameful to him, and he has the chance to renounce it, to repent, and begin to build a system of restraint. Freud's theories of course posit such a system of restraint as the origin of morality in the individual and collective mind. To speak of the comical content of this scene, Richard fears the violent response of a man less morally sophisticated than himself, more primitively protective of his wife's virtue, willing to act upon the jealousy that we have seen (in "Eros Rampant" especially) Richard feels sharply about Joan as he learns about her affairs.

Perhaps Updike is after something simpler yet. In a story governed by the Adam and Eve myth, he feels unmanned by his own sin. Hearing the step downstairs, and watching his lover stride downstairs unafraid and shameless, he cowers on the sun porch clutching his clothing to his chest. While mowing the grass (another image of severing, and an enduring image of common—rather than individual—mortality), he contemplates his lover's shamelessness, and its corollaries in the nudes of Titian, Manet, and Goya—three female nudes in the odalisque pose that strike Richard as expressing this "shamelessness." But in his own nakedness Richard has been ashamed and shameful indeed, and it is significant that the next nude that occurs to him, Edna Pontellier of Kate Chopin's *The Awakening*, becomes naked to meet her death—perhaps in Richard's unconscious self the known cost of shamelessness, the death that sin merits.[69]

It is difficult to track the logic that brings Richard to his next memory. This one comes to him while he pushes his lawnmower down a set of cellar stairs, another emblematic grave. Richard recalls arriving at this rental cottage ahead of his family, to confirm that it would be suitable. Joan, we are told, assented to this plan because "there was something in her, these days, that also wanted to be alone." Whether this something is weariness with Richard, or perhaps another affair to conduct, we don't know—but the line suggests strained mutuality. Richard lives alone in the cottage in "a profound chastity and silence." Richard's chaste isolation is emphasized further when he walks to a local pond where wild swans live, swans that "seemed gods to him." The reference is to another myth of origins, this time Leda and the Swan, made famous, as Richard's humanistic education made known to him, by Yeats's poem of that title. (Also incidentally, the subject of many paintings, including female nudes). Leda's rape by Zeus, disguised as a swan, begat the dangerous beauty Helen, whose face launched a thousand warring ships and led to "Agamemnon dead." Neither Yeats nor Updike needs to tell us this story, but Yeats does ask the question that this story also asks: did Leda put on any of the god's knowledge when his loins shuddered into her, or only his power? To frame the question in a Kierkegaardian way appropriate to the Maples stories, were human beings created with a capacity to learn and change, or only

---

[69] Ibid., 188.

to exercise their wills in selfish and destructive acts? An answer arrives through the quasi-Biblical imagery of the rest of the scene.

Richard strips at the edge of this pool and, in one of his typically profane reversals, feels that it would be "sacrilegious" to waste such an opportunity. He wants to do something "transcendent, something obscene." Clearly, this is an aesthetic rotation that he wishes to enact. Refreshing novel experience is the key, whether that experience is profane, obscene or transcendent. He mimics Rodin's Thinker, grows bored, sees himself as "a Baptist" or prophet, and then experiences an epiphany in which sex falls away from him and "he seemed indeed the divinely shaped center of a bowl-shaped Creation."[70]

This morphing includes a "Baptist." As the prophet John stood at the margins of waters he preached a Baptism of death and self-denial. Unlike Richard's vestigial and self-confirming Christianity, John preached a Baptism of "repentance for the forgiveness of sins."[71] The first person John baptized was Jesus himself, about to begin His ministry. Jesus later asks his disciples, "Can you drink the cup that I must drink, or be baptized with the baptism with which I must be baptized?"[72] This baptism is not a washing but a dying, a drowning of the corrupt self, a self-denying *matanoia*. Not so Richard's private ritual. Significantly he does not touch the water. He views the pool in a reductive image, as a "bowl-shaped Creation," more like the womb than a world in which to act out a mission. Significantly, just before becoming the Baptist he gives up the pose of "thinking." This is an exercise in wish-fulfillment, Richard retreating from careful thinking and other adult responsibilities, from the possibility of loss, from the compulsions of his own tormented sexuality, to the womb. Updike makes his sly hint at a Christian notion of the incarnation, though, in the dozens of fleas which deflate Richard's fantasy. They give him back his body, seek to taste his blood, and place him back into a world that makes its own painful and irritating demands. Back to dread for Richard.

This is a story about incarnation—the body as felt, seen, represented, mythologized, owned and disowned, lost to death. Updike takes the incarnation seriously, as he illustrates frankly in his poem "Seven Stanzas at Easter." The poem begins,

---

[70] Ibid., 186-89.
[71] Mark 1:4.
[72] Mark 10:38.

Make no mistake: if He rose at all
it was as His body;
if the cells' dissolution did not reverse, the molecules
 reknit, the amino acids rekindle,
the Church will fall.

Five additional stanzas embroider upon the physical reality of Biblical story, and caution against a too-easy dissolution of Christian mystery into metaphor and myth. The poem ends,

Let us not seek to make it less monstrous,
for our own convenience, our own sense of beauty,
lest, awakened in one unthinkable hour, we are
 embarrassed by the miracle,
and crushed by remonstrance.[73]

The lyrical voice supplies what Updike's memoirs do—straightforward confession of core beliefs. In this case the core belief is one that he has repeated often, as in this meditation, published sometime in the 1990s, on The Song of Solomon: "Judaism recognized that the body is the person, a recognition extended in the strenuous Christian doctrine of the bodily resurrection."[74] While the critic has deconstructive freedom to ignore such confessions, we do so at the cost of reading opaque, unrewarding and frankly monotonous Maples stories. What keeps readers from tiring of Richard's continual vacillating between love of his wife and compulsive need for alternative attachments is the core Christian drama the stories enact: can Richard save himself, or will he be saved? Can the quasi-mechanical energy of libido be mastered or are we lost to compulsive lust? Shall we adopt a modernist, materialist economy, such as Spinoza's sense of blessedness, derived from a sanguine acceptance of our deaths; or accept Christ's grace and leap into an absurd faith in the afterlife?

Acts one and two of this story strip Richard and Joan of their characteristic pretensions and self-delusions—strip them naked. First, Joan confronts the distressing reality that she is unfit, ideologically and bodily, to traffic with the revolutionary youth attempting (futilely and a bit arrogantly) to recover Eden through her own favorite practices: free

---

[73] John Updike, "Seven Stanzas at Easter," *Telephone Poles and Other Poems* (New York: Alfred A. Knopf, 1962) 72-73.

[74] Updike, More Matter, 49.

love, meditation, the diminishing of authoritarian power, the enlarging of human freedoms, the fulfilling of justice. This chilling realization makes her feel (and the outdated diction is important) like "a nincompoop."[75] Then Richard, who has sought for some less evident paradox, "some wordless sadness," is stripped by his own unconscious of the illusion that he is bodily attractive and guiltlessly justified in his life of self-gratification. He has indeed confronted a "wordless sadness," one brought home to him in a series of inner realizations that he will not dwell upon. His daughter sees him and Joan more "clearly than they see themselves"—and doesn't want to be with them. Richard sees himself as shameful and ridiculous in the mirror of his lover's bedroom and in his memory. In a moment of mythic and ritual self-aggrandizing at the margins of a pond, feeling briefly godlike, he finds himself defeated by mere insects. These first two acts of the story illustrate the reality of bodily and psychic decay, the loss of beauty and defeat of consoling illusion.

Act three suggests a Kierkegaardian response to such a dread-filled reality. The setting is what we call the master bedroom, site of marital union. This island cottage is decorated in white and white alone, so that the imagery is of purity and spirit, "white and breezy." Joan undresses and Richard watches. Her poses remind him of nudes with uplifted arms, Ingres' urn-bearer and Munch's Madonna. Richard seems to speak of more than the immediate moment when he answers Joan's question, "Don't you have something better to do? Than watch me?" He answers, truthfully, "No." He undresses too, and stands with Joan. Notably, he is not, as he so often is, sexually urgent, and he is pleased with Joan's pleasure in the calmly mutual moment. This is a moment of some unselfing for Richard. Joan's "No" to his unasked question is intentionally ambiguous. She may be saying no to sex she assumes, rationally enough, that Richard is requesting. She may be expressing pleased surprise that Richard still finds her attractive and compelling, in all her middle-aged plumpness, that he has answered her question with a no. Updike tells us that "This nakedness is new to them," and to the extent that the Maples are experiencing middle-age decay more sharply than ever before, and experiencing it together in a common sympathy, it is new to them.[76]

As Edward Mooney argues in "Repetition: Getting the World Back," the novella *Repetition* dwells on the theme of "sudden loss and

---

[75] Updike, *Too Far to Go*, 184.
[76] Ibid., 190-91.

wondrous restoration." Constantin Constantius examines three tales of sudden, excruciating loss: Abraham about to lose his son to an absurd commandment from God; Job actually losing all his material blessings; and a young man very much like Kierkegaard himself, who has rejected a young woman and now wishes for her back. The young man's tale is the most ironic in Kierkegaard's eyes, and not coincidentally, the most like Kierkegaard's own experience with Regine. This young man writes letters to Constantius, begging for his counsel and comparing himself, in his suffering, to Job. Like Job he has lost what he loved, and knows that none other than God can grant him relief and consolation. He notes that Job, stripped of all he cared for, related to God in opposition, deeply angry resentment. We come to realize that faith can contain this paradox, that to accuse God of wrongdoing is a kind of righteousness—not because one is correct in the accusation itself, but because of the pathos-filled personal acknowledgement of, and assumed relation to God.

Mooney notes a coolness about the young man's letters, a complacency about whether he really regains the love of his young woman. His interest in repetition has an academic and aesthetic quality—perhaps it reminds us of Richard's pondering of the aesthetics of European nudes—that hints at a limited personal involvement, a limited suffering. Abraham and Job, on the other hand, reached out to God in desperate, overwhelming *need*. In a real way, they asked God to give back to them not just a son (in Abraham's case) or property and family (in Job's) but a world that makes sense. Their repetitions were authentic, rising not out of their manipulations but their need. All they had to offer God was an openness to God's existence; God then engaged in an act of world-conferring grace. Mooney observes the metaphysical importance of such a moment:

> Kierkegaard holds that our initial, premoral and prereligious connection with the world and others is insufficient, a first or aesthetic immediacy, bound to end in "boredom and nihilism." With the world-conferral of repetition, we are granted a "second immediacy," a vital connection through which things and persons matter, a connection more adequate to our human and spiritual needs.[77]

---

[77] Edward F. Mooney, "Repetition: Getting the World Back," in *The Cambridge Companion to Kierkegaard*, eds. Alastair Hannay and Gordon D. Marino (New York: Cambridge University Press, 1998) 293.

More than simply a primitive confidence in the afterlife (which Updike considers essential to human wholeness), repetition involves a person's opening up to a world of possibility, not with dread but with faith.

In what way can a story about an aging married couple, troubled by infidelity, confronting utopian nudist kids, be a story about such a mysterious concept as repetition? As Mooney suggests, "repetition is linked with Christian doctrine in which saving value is first wondrously embodied, then lost or stripped away, and finally faithfully expected to return: not on the strength of a rational prediction, and not on the basis of a metaphysical axiom known to be true, but on the strength of faith that baffles reason."[78] The aging Maples have about lost their chance to gain attractive lovers, and this loss may open them up to such an unreasonable thought, such new knowledge.

---

[78] Ibid., 299.

9

Consecrated Unhappiness

"Separating," "Gesturing," and
"Divorcing: A Fragment"

> But at the end of 1969, Al Worden, assigned to Apollo 15, showed that an astronaut could end his marriage and remain on a space crew.
>
> —Andrew Chaikin, *A Man on the Moon:*
> *The Voyages of the Apollo Astronauts* [1]

In the final few Maples stories Updike charts a time of stunning, accelerating change. In the late 1960s and early 1970s, just as the American nation found it possible to send men and vehicles to the moon for scientific exploration, it also decided that divorcing was an elective decision meriting little social stigma. Like astronaut Al Worden, who was surprised when he was assigned to pilot the Command Module on Apollo 15 even though he was a divorced man, Richard cannot shake his own feelings of surprise and guilt when he journeys to the Cambridge City Hall to retrieve records he needs for his divorce. Clerks there treat him as though his task were normal and sanctioned. Seeking his "anti-license" feels neither normal nor sanctioned to him. It certainly does not feel consecrated.

If the controlling dynamic of the middle years of the Maples' marriage was fear and debilitating dread in the face of possibility, then the controlling dynamic in these, the bleakest three stories in the cycle—"Separating" (1975), "Gesturing" (1979), and "Divorcing: A Fragment" (1979)—is annulment, negation, abandonment, and resulting misery. Richard attempts to perform an authentic separation from Joan—his desire since sometime before their 1963 or 1964 trip to Rome. But he is

---

[1] Andrew Chaikin, *A Man on the Moon: The Voyages of the Apollo Astronauts* (New York: Penguin, 2007) 349-50.

merely gesturing; he is unable to perform the acts he desires and wills. A power resides in the marriage that is greater than any residing in his person, so all Richard's assaults on his marriage to Joan amount to empty motions. This is not to say that he does no harm to Joan or to their children. On the day when he announces his separation from his family, Richard knows that in confessing his guilt about the separation he is dumping an emotional mountain on his son Dickie. As that separation nears its conclusion in formal divorce, Joan is suicidal over her loss of Richard's companionship and partnership. In these later stories, psychological pressures and processes are no longer funny.

Perhaps surprisingly, Richard's relationship with Joan remains his central preoccupation even as he commences another committed relationship. His second wife-to-be, Ruth, hardly receives mention in his thoughts. Updike does not suggest with this neglect of Ruth that divorce is always wrong, or that the Maples' particular divorce was a mistake. His focus is on the complicated rightness of marriage even when spouses are vexed by the animal urges we saw in such stories as "Eros Rampant," "The Red-Herring Theory," and "Sublimating." Updike's dialectical thinking raises increasingly more compelling and distressing questions, including the unanswerable one Dickie asks Richard in "Separating"— "Why?"[2] Why can a loving father find that he can unload intolerable guilt onto his son? Why are so many like the Maples, unable to comfort each other faithfully and love their children attentively? More generally and philosophically, why would a loving God insist on marital faithfulness from creatures whose nature, as created, seems driven by psychological needs and urges that apparently demand multiple sexual and emotional attachments? Richard comes to wonder, and we do with him, whether the Christian marriage must inevitably be a state of "consecrated unhappiness."[3]

"Separating" is arguably Updike's masterpiece. Yet this tale, a guilt-ridden husband's announcement of his plan to leave his family home, deprives us of information we expect in these fictional circumstances. Neither "Separating" nor any story set around its time describes how Richard falls in love with Ruth, determines with her that the two of them should marry and make a new family together, brings Joan to understand the situation, and reaches an agreement with Joan (an only

---

[2] Updike, *Too Far to Go*, 211.
[3] Ibid., 234.

half-willing one, we know) to try a separation in order eventually to agree to a divorce. Because we are deprived of this information, because Updike neglects full and sufficient reasons for the Maples to separate, he must have another focus. Richard's and Joan's explanations to the children, and also their consoling remarks, certainly ring hollow in this story. What seems to matter is the way the children are told the half-expected but nevertheless evidently shocking news, that their family would be further separating. I offer the qualification "further" because this story, like the others in the Maples cycle, is not fundamentally or exclusively about marital troubles, or union and dissolution. Rather, "Separating" is about processes of separation that affect all families, such as the child's progression through Oedipal or Electra dynamics toward emotional and vocational maturity, or through schools and family changes that bring them to their own independent homes. Some of these forms of separation are welcome, such as an educational trip to another country, and some are not, such as leaving home for a day at a hated job or school. But for Updike separating from loved ones is as inevitable as the processes leading to death.

So, for example, Judith returns from a separation from her family—an academic adventure in England—that will soon be repeated and we presume lengthened as she establishes a career, perhaps meets a partner ("Grandparenting" reveals that she does), and makes her own adult home. Updike asks us to consider, through his usual quiet implications, whether Richard's moving on to another home is morally and existentially really so different. Is his leaving the Maples home simply another painful-hopeful stage in the life of a developing adult personality? By what requirement, law, or tradition do we judge Richard ineligible for the satisfactions that his daughter pursues?

Separating from loved ones is a task that Richard has already failed at, conspicuously. Throughout the stories, Updike poses separation anxiety disorder and resulting narcissism as a cause of Richard's identity crisis, as a source of his incorrigible selfishness and neediness, his desperate fear of loneliness, his terrors when away from home or outside his usual habitual routines. Even a cursory reading of recent psychiatric research into panic and separation anxiety disorders will convince us that we have no business making clinical judgments about such complex subjectivity deficiencies.[4] But we are making literary judgments here,

---

[4] See, for example, Katherine Shear, et. al., "Prevalence and Correlates of Estimated DSM-IV Child and Adult Separation Anxiety Disorder in the National

and Updike has surely suggested through his narrative patterns that Richard has separation issues: obsessive feelings about his mother's body (he can't bear to look at her while they sunbathe; he recalls feeling as though he were "drowning in the blood-deep currents of her moods, her secrets"); compulsive demands for the attention of his wife and other women he associates with his mother; episodes of panic regarding intense feelings of doom (he dreams terrorizing dreams of death in Rome at age 32, and fantasizes compulsively about his funeral at age 39); and a pervasive, continuous feeling of anxiety that might be predicted both by psychologists and by psycho-theologians such as Søren Kierkegaard.[5] The important thing, as I have argued, is to understand Richard's psychological and psychosomatic symptoms as related to his incorrigibility, as posing an impediment to the Kierkegaardian phase-shifting that might occur in his spiritual life. Updike learned from Freud, but was changed by Kierkegaard. Richard is unwilling to change, not wholly unable. Updike cleverly combines these psychiatric and theological horizons in the first paragraph of "Separating": the Maples feel "internal misery" in a summertime world so beautiful that their "sad, murmuring selves [are] the only stain in Nature."[6]

To separate: what other connotations are at play in this story? Clearly, to separate is to leave one's spouse for a trial period, a non-marital moratorium. The Maples have arrived at a strategy "for their dissolution" that amounts to a humane process for telling the children, giving Richard time to pack, and ending in what Joan calls his "wonderful departure." To part company: The Maple children have already shown that they suffer no obvious anxiety regarding their own separations; Judith has just spent a fulfilling year in England, and all four have already eagerly scheduled "jobs and camps and visits" for this summer that will "scatter" them.[7] Perhaps the most importantly, to sin: as we have seen, the sickness unto death is alienation both from God and from one's authentic self, a "disrelationship" to use Kierkegaard's own translated language from *The Sickness Unto Death*, "in a relation which

---

Comorbidity Survey Replication," *American Journal of Psychiatry* 163 (June 2006): 1074-1083. Reading this sort of professional clinical literature is a bit like reading Kierkegaard's works: you have brief moments of clarity but mostly feel chastened about what you do not know.

[5] Updike, *Too Far to Go*, 186 and 162.

[6] Ibid., 192.

[7] Ibid., 194-95.

relates itself to itself." This is to say, he continues, that despair as symptom of our sin does not simply befall us but results from our failure to recognize in our existence the hand of God "who made Man a relationship."[8] For Updike, this is what he has to say as a writer, "the hymning of this great roughly rectangular country severed from Christ by the breadth of the sea."[9]

Leaving his wife is not the deepest form of separating that Richard hopes to carry to completion. It is, to use Kierkegaard's phrase again, "becoming another." Also in *The Sickness Unto Death*, Kierkegaard describes two men who despair at not willing to be themselves. The first is the man who accepts the routines of Christendom, goes to church every Sunday, understands the parson's preaching, and dies. The parson then "introduces him into eternity for the price of $10—but a self he was not, and a self he did not become." The other man who wills not to become himself, indeed a "lower" sort of man in terms of existential seeking, is the one who lives in un-thoughtful "immediacy." He is a comical man, humorously innocent in his envy of others. He sees other men no better off than himself, living in immediacy themselves, and he desires the "most crazy of all transformations," to become them, to be another as easily as changing coats.[10] But this is beyond foolish. To become another, even if it were possible, is a further separation from the God-created self. Richard, however, is caught between the richly layered past with his family, memories of these times the focus of such stories as "Plumbing" and "Sublimating," and a future in which he inhabits the home on the town green where Ruth lives with her young sons. Between them is the moment Kierkegaard thinks we hardly ever inhabit, an existential moment therefore, the "unthinkable now"—a present in which Richard is going to have to take responsibility for his petty existential hopes, is going to have to exact a cost on his children. In "Separating," this moment arrives. In the story's denouement, Dickie pays dearly for his father's dreams and, without meaning to, makes him pay too.

---

[8] Kierkegaard, *The Sickness Unto Death*, 148-49.

[9] Updike, *Self-Consciousness*, 103.

[10] Kierkegaard, *The Sickness Unto Death*, 186-7.

As an alternative to Richard's pettiness, "Separating" offers references to Jesus' parting, or separating, from his disciples and other believers. Richard takes the role of comic Christ. These references crystalize in a parodic Last Supper (wine drunk with broken lobster bodies rather than broken bread), a Passion story (Richard's tearful emotional suffering occurs on a Friday; he meant to make his announcement at Easter), and an Ascension (his "wonderful departure" in Joan's sarcastic phrasing), all these mocking ecclesiastical images appearing in the second of three acts. These images suggest the miracle by which the New Testament makes its central claim about separating, that "neither death nor life, neither angels nor demons, neither the present nor the future, nor any powers, neither height nor depth, nor anything else in all creation, will be able to separate us from the love of God that is in Christ Jesus our Lord."[11]

If this seems a hopelessly pious focus for a story about such a difficult moment in the history of a modern marriage, then we might consider the complications that arise from a claim Updike's modern Kierkegaardian hero Miguel de Unamuno makes. He offers another way of thinking about the centrality of the self in hungering for immortality and thus for faith:

> Sacrifice yourself to your children! And sacrifice yourself to them because they are yours, part and prolongation of yourself, and they in their turn will sacrifice themselves to their children, and these children to theirs, and so it will go on without end, a sterile sacrifice by which nobody profits. I came into the world to create myself, and what is to become of all our selves? Live for the True, the Good, the Beautiful! We shall see presently the supreme vanity and the supreme insincerity of this hypocritical attitude.[12]

But is Richard, in leaving his family, embracing a True, Good, and Beautiful, honoring his deep, immortality-hungering self? No, Richard has rarely sacrificed anything meaningful to his children. Furthermore, as we will see, Richard has no coherent self, and the bagatelle of gestures of which he is composed can honor little but immediate urges.

---

[11] Romans 8:38.

[12] Miguel de Unamuno, *Tragic Sense of Life*, trans. J.E. Crawford Flitch (New York: Dover, 1954) 46.

Richard should not leave his family, but this is not the point of the story. The focus is on Richard's warring conscience, which desires goodness as much as it desires immortality, but which is caught in a trap created by his continual aesthetic machinations. The way out of the trap is communicated by imagery from the Passion and Ascension stories, but Richard will seek a profane freedom that entraps him further. Unamuno would call him Christophile but not Christian: since he cannot embrace a resurrection faith, he simply admires a Syrian teacher of the first century and remains in despair. His Biblically-tutored conscience in this story will try to lead him home by another way, but it will fail.

The story opens with a dispute over the etiquette of separation. Much of the story concerns Joan's futile struggle to see her way to announce the separation adopted over-against Richard's. Thus, in the gasping final moments of their mutual homemaking they reiterate their affable antipathy—affable perhaps because what is antipathetic comes from a shared despair. Joan displays her care for the children, insisting that they be told one by one, while Richard seeks the easier route out of his house, making an announcement at the table. Yet he too wants to show his children that he cares about them. When Joan informs Richard that his children are individuals, not just "some corporate obstacle" to his freedom, she seems to be honoring Kierkegaard's own obsession with 'the individual.' Yet we wonder how truly alive she is to each child's personhood. Richard detects "an edge of false order, a hidden plea for control" in Joan's plan. They remind him of his wife's other ethically-based habits, her "chore lists," "financial accountings," and "too-copious lecture notes." Still, whether or not her love of the children is purer, she is correct in her prediction that if Richard is allowed to make a general announcement, "They'll start quarreling and playing to each other instead of focusing."[13] This is exactly what they do.

The action of this story illustrates the effectiveness of aesthetic strategies and their *telos*—Richard gets what he wants and as a result punishes and disgraces himself. Since in his family Richard loves least, he has the power, but it is only the power to separate and alienate himself from those who love him. The opening act of this story suggests such paradoxes of success and failure, love and dread. The season has accomplished a "stunt of renewal," yet Richard and Joan have not enjoyed any of it, haven't gotten their tans or played any tennis. The tennis court that once proved the Maples' marriage could "rend the earth

---

[13] Updike, *Too Far to Go*, 194-95.

for fun" now falls into entropic decay, which Richard only halfheartedly attempts to reverse or repair with "crumbling of handfuls of clay." Richard himself feels like a handful of dust, in a "mood of purposeful desolation." "In his sealed heart," Updike writes, suggesting that this heart contains a deeper truth because it is "sealed" from Richard's full consciousness, "he hoped the day would never come." Though the Easter season has just passed, Richard's separating day is a Friday—a day for crucifixion, not renewal. Richard's consciousness, we are told, has "moved through a world of insides and outsides, of barriers and partitions." This imagery connects with the tennis court, whose game is made possible by these demarcations, "in" and "out" making the difference. But because of Richard's lassitude, the net and tapes that make "in" and "out" possible are still rolled up and stored; his court makes for only an absurd, nonsensical game. The first act's final image amplifies this sense of the absurd: Richard's toiling to secure his family, "replacing screens and sash cords, hinges and latches," serves the incongruous purpose of making his Houdini-like escape more wonderful.[14]

The story's second act is governed at first by this imagery of futility and mistaken safety—Richard changing a lock on a screened porch. Since it is easy to push through a screen, we wonder why replacing this lock is so important to Richard. His facility in making the repair is also at question. Here we encounter the set-up for the Passion story sequence about to come—Richard as ineffective carpenter, Richard as profane Christ. He knows that unlike the real Christ he can do nothing to protect his family from "insects, rot, death." Each of the family members present (Dickie is in Boston) is then placed in the scene, while "Time, like the sunlight, continued relentlessly." Here Richard is less Christ in the garden than Quentin Compson at Harvard, tormented by passing time. We see that simply leaving his family, depriving them of his company and losing theirs, is not Richard's preoccupation. Death and time remain his existential problems—and the absurdity and sense of human fragility they yield. When he asks Judith whether she wants to live in England "forever," the word's meaning expands beyond what he meant by it (the duration of Judith's adult life), and comes to mean eternity. He begins to cry. [15]

---

[14] Ibid., 194-96.
[15] Ibid., 196-97.

Next, Richard presides over a Last Supper. Not simply a profane Eucharist, this meal offers paradoxes and ironies that need to be sifted through. First of all, the Christian imagery is persistent, ample, and significant. The body and blood are present, and Richard's sin is evident in his act of breaking the lobster's back, the ritual body, adding to Jesus' suffering. The salt of his tears "flavor" his champagne, a sign of Richard's desolation (the Bible connects salt with the desolation of the Dead Sea) but also of the "savor" that he might have if he were to accept the Eucharistic meal genuinely, as spiritual nourishment from a bodily risen Jesus Christ.[16] The flavor of salty tears is of course also central to the Passover meal, the historical occasion for the Last Supper with the disciples.

Explicating all this imagery we may neglect more practical matters, such as the Maples' questionable judgment in serving champagne not only to a collegiate nineteen-year old but to fifteen-year old John. His anger and chiding of his parents over their decision both to conceal their problems from him and the other children and then to spring those problems upon them as a *fait accompli* comes off as dramatic and false, compromised by his drunkenness. The chaotically practical and liturgically sacramental come together as John, drunk and shaken both, contrives a symbolic meal of his own—a halved cigarette, paper napkin, and lettuce leaves. No nourishment can come from this absurd meal, prepared for him in a way by his father. Judith tells her brother to be mature, but as she says so she is literally blowing smoke.[17] What kind of maturity helps a teenager to accept his parents' separation with equanimity?

The next scene might be taken for a renewal of Richard's parental love and resulting restoration of order, but it is not. Richard takes John outside to spit out his absurd meal and help him gather his composure. Father and son run to the Maples' field of games, tennis and family baseball. When John complains not of the separation but of his school, his lack of friends, and his history teacher, his father characteristically proposes another separation: "'We'll think about getting you transferred. Life's too short to be miserable." Here Richard feeds his son the motto of the aesthetic. If pleasure wanes, seek a rotation. Don't be dominated by questions of difficult fidelity. Returning to the table, now become a

---

[16] See Matthew 5:13.
[17] Ibid., 202.

"party," Richard's aesthetic sense is offended that his family has taken pleasure without him.[18]

As we have seen, Richard and Joan have conducted their affairs according to a sophisticated etiquette stipulating honesty as essential. An affair might be carried out in secret, but once discovered it needs to be admitted by the participant and then accepted by the other. But children are to know none of this. The aim of this etiquette seems to be to apply a veneer of rationality to the deeper irrational passions of libido. In act three of "Separating," as the farewell dinner proceeds, the veneer splits. The Maples' carefully calculated ritual is revealed as a thoroughgoing fabrication and concealment. Unlike the Eucharist, which through frankness and honest confrontation of the crucifixion turns the cosmic embarrassment of Jesus's death into a ritual of death's defeat, this fabricated ritual has offered overt pretenses about the separation's causes. There is no mention of Ruth. The ritual has also involved a great deal of denial about the real state of relation between Richard and Joan. Richard, for example, at one point explains to the children why he is leaving, and needs to finish a sentence by saying that he and Joan "do not love each other." He finds that he cannot speak the phrase—not, we realize, because he is afraid to hurt his children with such an annihilating phrase, but because it is not true. He may not feel libidinous excitement, psychic titillation, or sexual arousal when with his wife (not often enough for his wishes anyway), but he does feel the urge to cooperate with her, keep her from harm, talk with her, listen to her, support her in her chosen calling. And this, though he can neither realize nor honor it, is love. When Joan moves into the next part of her prepared speech, an assurance that she and Richard have "always, especially, loved our children," the utterance cuts two opposing ways. It seems true that the Maples have loved their children profoundly if not attentively, but in the midst of such emotional cant and spin as that the Maples' children are experiencing this evening, John for one is "not mollified."[19]

Joan is therefore being ironic (intentionally or not we cannot tell) when in the opening of act three she agrees with Richard that the children's lack of suspicion about "a third person" was touching. Richard's gratitude for Joan's concealment of his guilt creates a problem for him: "Guiltily, he realized he did not feel separated."[20] This is to say

---

[18] Ibid., 203-4.
[19] Ibid., 201.
[20] Ibid., 205.

that he loves his wife. Every act he performs for the rest of the evening will be an act of bad faith, now, as Richard denies his own feelings. We need to recall that for Kierkegaard feelings are far from uncontrolled, misleading, psychological phenomena. They are the very index to human passion, the will to live, the capacity to love. When Hegelian rationality fails us, Kierkegaard argues, feelings save us. Unamuno, explicating Kierkegaard's insights, writes,

> Feeling does not succeed in converting consolation into truth, nor does reason succeed in converting truth into consolation. But reason going beyond truth itself, beyond the concept of reality itself, succeeds in plunging itself into the depths of skepticism. And in this abyss the scepticism of the reason encounters the despair of the heart, and this encounter leads to the discovery of a basis—a terrible basis!—for consolation to build on."[21]

Richard's own feelings will initiate just such a process as this story closes.

Joan tells Richard, in wholly alienated language, that he still has "Dickie to do." From this moment on Richard will be afflicted by a "mountain" of guilt—an interesting image within the story's Christian symbolism. Matthew suggests that genuine faith can move mountains.[22] Genuine faith; bad faith—this is the governing dialectic for the rest of the story. Dickie, we learn, is "most like a conscience" to Richard. The mountain of guilt moves toward Richard and then in him; Joan sleeps beside him "as if slain." He wakes her while dressing to meet Dickie's late train and says that he would undo everything if he could. Because she understands that Richard's sins and even his weaknesses are fundamental to his identity, she asks, astutely, "Where would you begin?" Instead of pondering the question carefully, he decides—his narcissism and power of denial at work—that she is "giving him courage."[23]

If Dickie represents Richard's conscience, at first Richard has little to fear in the way of moral or spiritual critique. Dickie seems very much another apparential aesthetic self, seeking his satisfactions and complacent in his gratitude. He shows no surprise that his father has met him with a ride at this "terrible hour." After his two friends have been

---

[21] Unamuno, *Tragic Sense of Life*, 105.
[22] Matthew 21:21.
[23] Updike, *Too Far to Go*, 205-6.

dropped off, Dickie begins wheedling for relief from the mowing work he performs—an echo of John's complaint and wish for relief from his "scud" of a history teacher. Surprisingly, Richard does not immediately suggest that Dickie quit his job or get another he likes better. His suggestion that eye drops might work better this summer is perhaps irrational—the ineffective carpenter is now ineffective healer—but expresses an unstated belief in fidelity to responsibilities. Richard then acknowledges that picking up Dickie was not a kindness to him; it allowed him to make his "sad" announcement. Dickie shows a stoicism that his father has lacked this day. He is even able to swallow his father's transparently false suggestion that the separation "should have no practical effect" on Dickie's life, just an emotional effect. Richard's life proves that emotional effects have vivid and far-reaching practical results.

The two Maple men then drive past the church they "went to" (we note the past tense) and Richard's lover's lit bedroom window. The juxtaposition of imagery is deliberate, but to say that the church is sacred and the lover's window profane is too simple. Richard hopes to marry "the woman" (he cannot name her for some psychological reason)— which is to say that he hopes to cherish, protect, honor, and obey her, that his vow has meaning (at least for the time being), and that he hopes for some divine blessing upon the union. The opposition here is not between the sacred and profane but between a genuine *metanoia* and what Dietrich Bonhoeffer identifies as an antinomianism requiring no real discipleship, the complacent expectation of "cheap grace." This opposition leaves open the possibility—though ample textual evidence militates against it—that Richard is ready for commitment, discipleship, that he ought to marry Ruth, and be a good stepfather to her sons. Then he might help introduce them to a worldview that prepares them to make existential decisions. He might also offer that same worldview to his biological children during his opportunities to be with them, be a cooperative and thoughtful partner to Joan, repent his sins when he commits them, and so on. Richard, though, wants his grace as cheap as he can get it. Driving home, he makes a brief speech to Dickie about his and Joan's decision to separate. They will see how living apart feels. They do not plan to divorce. For Richard if not Joan, all of these are lies. When Richard arrives home, he asks Dickie whether he has sensed his parents' unhappiness, the boy answers, honestly, "No." He talks easily enough with his father, but Richard observes cues that Dickie is "stunned."

Then Richard utters perhaps the most moving piece of dialog in all Updike's work. He tells his son how he feels as he shares all this shocking news. "I hate this. *Hate* it. My father would have died before doing it to me." Rather than causing self-indicting feelings or a repentant consciousness in Richard, this remark causes him to feel "immensely lighter...He had dumped the mountain on the boy."[24] Richard offers to lie to the boy's boss, an obvious cheapening of vocational responsibilities parallel with his offer to transfer John out of his demanding school. Dickie, serving as his father's conscience now, refuses to play the permissive and dishonest game: "No, that's all right."[25] This exchange suggests that Richard has not only unloaded something emotional onto Dickie, but has somehow exchanged roles with him, shifted to the boy the adult responsibilities of forbearance, awareness, fidelity, and ethical choosing, while he, Richard, deceitfully blames his separation from his family on Joan. On the ride home Richard had told his son that he and Dickie's mother are separating because she doesn't make him happy—as though that was a wife's absolute responsibility, and as if any person might finally mediate the happiness of any other person.[26] Dickie must hear that since his father is unhappy, he and his siblings have also "failed" to provide adequate love or diversion.

We should not pass over this odd load-shifting without noting that it reiterates the spiritual meaning of the Passion story that Updike has coded so carefully into this story. Dickie here is forced to assume the role of suffering Christ, taking on the burden of his father's sin—a burden he in no way shares or bears responsibility for. Taking on that burden, he renders the world bearable for the sinner, his father. Richard's reference to his own father also has theological as well as psychoanalytical resonance. Both Abraham and the Creator find cause to load a mortal burden upon their sons—though, unlike Richard, both shift that mortal load in full awareness of human need, and out of wholehearted, faithful love. We should also note the Oedipal dynamics of the remark, which

---

[24] Ibid., 209.

[25] Ibid., 208-210.

[26] Kierkegaard is adamant about the impossibility of such "mediation," one of the key tenets of his attack on unduly optimistic Hegelian systematics. But it is not happiness that Kierkegaard claims cannot be taught, counseled, or urged. It is faith.

are related. What does it mean psychically for a man to admit that he is morally less strong, less worthy than his teenaged son? Lacking just cause, shame must be the result. Thus we enter into the existential dialectic—Richard as justified by grace; Richard as shameful reprobate.

"Separating" ends with a fourth act or coda. Richard's guilt is still front and center: Joan is still pictured as "slain," now sleeping in a "deep trough," an emblematic grave. She wakes and joins Richard in Dickie's bedroom for a goodnight talk and kiss. Updike again raises the issue of Richard's separation anxieties. First Joan talks with Dickie, then stands, her naked body in thin nighty silhouetted by moonlight for Richard to see. She is the sexually vivid mother standing by her son's bed—and Richard is both husband and son, relentlessly confused. Dickie, on the other hand, seems to have separated properly from Joan. He shows an ability to make his own decisions, to meet his own responsibilities faithfully—no compulsive or narcissistic complaining about his job or his shocking new situation. Then Richard makes a speech that illustrates his emotional deficits and returns us to Updike's Ascension theme: "Dickie, listen. I love you so much, I never knew how much until now. No matter how this works out, *I'll always be with you.*" Dickie responds with what can only be called unqualified love. He kisses his father passionately, we suspect pleadingly, and moans the "crucial, intelligent word: '*Why?*'" Updike concludes the story with a few lines of poetic prose:

> *Why.* It was a whistle of wind in a crack, a knife thrust, a window thrown open on emptiness. The white face was gone, the darkness was feature- less. Richard had forgotten why.[27]

The only sensible way to read Richard's forgetfulness of his lover's face—and it is a reading that accords with the story's refusal to make her a real or compelling rival to Joan and to the Maples' children—is that in a moment like this one she is too light to register on the scales of Richard's heart and mind.[28] The other two sentences simply tell us what is existentially important about Richard's latest erotic rotation. It will mean nothing, a whistle of wind, a forgotten word, emptiness.

What do we make of Ruth, who appears in this story twice as a "white face," and once as the object of a simple and quite lovely expression of affection? Updike strikes me as deliberately mysterious

---

[27] Updike, *Too Far to Go*, 211, emphasis mine.
[28] We should not confuse her with Martha Updike, with whom John remained married for more than thirty years, until his death.

about her. We are told that she is frightened these days, of what we can only imagine—probably not the censure of her neighbors. She is also soothing to Richard. We cannot deny that Richard may love her, in the manner of Kierkegaard's first love. At the very least he feels protective and solicitous, as he wishes "to shield [her] from [his] tears"—though this too is a questionable tactic, since Richard's tears might teach Ruth about what sort of marriage and family she is helping to break up, or what sort of feeling underpins that family.[29] In "Gesturing" Richard will make an interior speech in which he supplies language by which to judge Ruth—not the woman, but the woman in Richard's consciousness. Richard notes that to a married man lovers, "however we love them, are not us, are not sacred as reality is sacred."[30] Ruth is not (yet) "us" in Richard's consciousness. His plural personal pronoun includes Judith, Dickie, John and Margaret. So Updike makes it difficult for us to celebrate the end of the Maples marriage and of the intact Maples family.[31]

In "Separating," the mocking Last Supper and Ascension both remind Christians that theirs is a religion of separation, of desperately desired relation denied or at least deferred. Yet it seems that the Christian story also lives in believers' conscious and subconscious minds, shaping their behavior as much as any Oedipal drama. Richard, under the duress of having to speak hurtful and self-serving lies to his family, cannot help but speak the kinder language of the gospels, to appropriate the roles of goodness that he has encountered in the churches he has irregularly attended. It seems that love demands such language. Feeling a love for his children that he forces himself to deny, a new language rises up in him. He confesses his weakness: "My father would have died before doing [this] to me." And his love: "No matter

---

[29] Updike, *Too Far to Go*, 195-6.

[30] Ibid., 231.

[31] Could Updike ever have considered Richard's incorrigibility to be a narrative liability, an element that consigned the Maples stories to one sort of monotony, Richard's implacable apostasy always closing out a story otherwise filled with narrative creativity, wit, and variety? Why should Richard be denied always the kind of epiphany and subsequent *metanoia* that his author experienced while reading the pumpkin-colored Anchor paperback *Fear and Trembling* in the 1950s? Are Christian faithfulness and Christian vocation really so uncongenial to narrative requirements and readerly tastes? Even knowing that Kierkegaard posits difficult, protracted identity transformation utterly governed by a God that knows God's mind, Richard annoys.

how this works out, I'll always be with you. Really." It is far from the raving speech with which he has degraded himself and punished his wife over the years. It is a soothing language of loss and recovery, acknowledging iniquity and desiring forgiveness. Even as he unconsciously appropriates, cheapens, and abuses the Passion-Ascension narrative for his narcissistic purposes, Richard seems to desire its message of suffering redeemed and death defeated.

Certainly others have read the story differently. James Schiff reads "Separating" as a tale of Richard's resistance to nature's tendency toward disorder. He affirms Richard's attempts both to confront this entropic tendency with his home repairs, and to live in harmony with nature by pretending to no artificial ordering in it, such as his wife's over-orderly plans for announcing the separation to the children. Schiff is especially good on the double thrust of the story's final line, in which Richard forgets why he wanted the separation. Is he moved to forgetfulness of his mistress by the power of his son's love? or is he deceiving himself, conveniently forgetting his motives in order to shirk responsibility (for the moment at least) for the pain he is causing? Both seem at work, as Schiff sees clearly. He also sees a staged Last Supper in the Maples' celebratory dinner. But with regard to that dinner he makes a dubious remark: Richard, Schiff writes, "kills the marriage rather than have it kill him, and his anticipated resurrection lies outside of his marriage, where he will be joined with another woman."[32]

This argument presumes that the man we meet in Updike's memoirs would appropriate the power of the Christian Passion to dramatize Richard's need to begin a second marriage with a woman who, in all the Maples stories, is scarcely real. It is very difficult to see how the Maples' marriage poses a *mortal* threat to Richard. This story, among others, illustrates powerfully that life with his family is precious to Richard, that he and Joan share a deep mutuality even while they disagree on certain matters of style, sex life, worldview, and method to accomplish tasks. Richard craves a resurrection, certainly, but not the false resurrection of another marriage that, because of his incorrigibility, is very likely to reproduce the same tension, pain, and boredom as his first marriage. (We see in "Grandparenting" that this is so.) Updike's personal confessions make clear that the resurrection he foresees for Richard is the real one, the one he honors through praise for the

---

[32] James A. Schiff, *John Updike, Revisited* (New York: Twayne, 1998) 124.

Apostles' Creed in "The Dogwood Tree: A Boyhood": "the resurrection of the body; and life everlasting."[33]

&

In fact, far from presenting Richard's relationship with Ruth as life-saving, a marital resurrection, Updike's next story in *Too Far to Go*, "Gesturing," calls into question the seriousness and depth of Richard's love for her. With Ruth, he now finds his identity even more severely divided. One Richard still essentially occupies his home. Now living in a nearby beach cottage, he talks daily and intimately with Joan; he sometimes sleeps with her; he takes his meals with his family. As the Maples agree, "it was not healthy, not progressive." Richard realizes that he is the very incarnation of his wife's love, having taken her meals for so many years of cellular death and renewal: "[H]is body, every cell, was composed of her cooking."[34] The other Richard takes a Boston apartment, and finds satisfaction in his own housekeeping. He experiences sexual and other rotations with Ruth. "It was an interim," Richard realizes, "a holiday."[35] But it is not a marriage, or a model for marriage. It is *Elskov* or first love.

This story represents the moment when Richard realizes that all his aesthetic hopes, his quest for more than a decade to get out of his marriage and into a more intense love with another kind of woman, have turned out hollow, have failed him utterly. He may have fun with Ruth, but still has fun—and more than fun—with Joan. He discovers that his satisfaction cannot be secured by the pursuit and possession of novelty in his life, and freedom to pursue this novelty. Indeed, he discovers the reality of aesthetic repetition, its *telos* in boredom.

While religious repetition for Kierkegaard partakes of the eternal, restores personhood, lends meaning to life, and presents itself to the believer as a "beloved wife" of whom one never tires, aesthetic repetition lives in hope alone, hope pictured as a "charming maiden" who slips through the fingers—thus, a vain hope. The pursuit of aesthetic repetition is often shrewd, but always frantic, a seeking after novel

---

[33] Schiff also had access to the "Seven Stanzas at Easter" poem I cited in my last chapter. There, as in "Dogwood Tree," Updike states a defiant credo of belief in bodily resurrection.

[34] Updike, *Too Far to Go*, 215.

[35] Ibid., 222.

291

experience. At a deeper philosophical level, aesthetic repetition is an emblem of what it means to maintain identity through change—an impossible task, finally, in which the self comes to seem fractured, tormented by the threat of boredom, and terrified of the final result of change, annihilation.[36] Richard's relationship with Ruth, both courtship and marriage, is a literal aesthetic repetition. And she is the figurative representation of the "charming maiden," hope. Joan is of course the "beloved wife" whose existence points to the assurance—not just the hopeful possibility—of fidelity.

In the perverse world of "Gesturing," Joan seems to promote and participate in fidelity's opposite, faithlessness. She opens the story by returning from sex in the city. Meeting Richard, she insists on a genuine separation. But we trust Richard when he sees her play as a bluff. She wants Richard back, and shrewdly allows him his hollow freedom so that he can experience its failure. Joan has made a gesture. By the end of this elusive story Updike is able to show that our gestures enact both our existential futility and its opposite, both the ways that our acts are absurdly unavailing, and the ways that these gestures take on a life in those we love and with whom we live. This insight becomes the ground for Richard's realization—which his incorrigibility will keep him from honoring—that his marriage is sacred, a stay against his terror, a meaningful fabric into which he is woven, a union that is real in both body and mind—not an idea but a reality.

"Gesturing" is the only Maples story to appear first in *Playboy* (in January of 1979), a reasonable choice given the story's frank and adulterous treatment of sexuality. Indeed, in this story Richard manages to betray not only his wife but also his lover before she becomes his wife. This betrayal he accomplishes by sleeping with his legal and spiritual wife, Joan. This bizarre reversal is part of the perverse fabric of this story, which Updike intends for us to sense and confront. It is not too much to say, in fact, that "Gesturing," in spite of its appearance in a magazine based on what Updike himself calls the "Playboy philosophy," the

---

[36] Kierkegaard, *Repetition*, 131ff. I do not want to lose sight of another meaning of repetition. After the leap, believers are charged with meeting neighbors' needs in such a sweeping way that we begin to talk of justice. Thus Kierkegaard's notion of repetition, of theology-for-the-individual, is not, as Edward Said views it, so decidedly different from or inferior to his favored Marxist-materialist processes. Both Kierkegaard and Marx hope for essential fairness, material justice, enough. Cf. Edward Said, *The World, the Text, and the Critic* (New York: Harvard University Press, 1983) 120-125.

wholly free pursuit of sexual satisfaction, is the one Maples story that makes an explicit rather than implied defense of marriage, and does so on evidently Biblical grounds. No other Maples story can be properly understood without reference to Richard's realizations in "Gesturing."

"Gesturing," in turn, must be understood in the light of events that unfold in "Separating." In that story Joan has uttered the reason for separating that she and Richard think (dubiously) is best for the children to hear, that the Maples parents "did not make each other happy enough, somehow." Richard has made the more shocking argument, in his thoughts if not in speech, that he must leave Joan because "*they do not love each other.*"[37] There are at least two problems with this thought. First, Richard is about to speak for Joan, making a claim that she would probably deny. In both this story and "Divorcing: A Fragmant," Joan attempts through both calculated indirection and raw, direct emotional plea to convince Richard to come back to her. Secondly, he is able to think his denial of love for Joan, but not speak it, certainly because he believes the children would find the idea dreadful, but also because his conscience will not allow such an untruth. "Gesturing" tests Richard's assertion, and therefore the entire rationale for establishing a new life with Ruth.

The opening act of the story runs directly counter to Richard's viewpoint. Richard drives Joan's car from her house (formerly theirs) to pick her up at the town train station. As he is driving, too late to have met her train, he meets her on her walk into town. "Even from a distance," the narrator notes, implying an emotional as well as physical distance, "they smiled to see one another." As they talk in the car, Joan makes her bluff, raising the question of their current life and asking Richard to leave town. She presumes that if Richard is living in Boston he will no longer spend so much time with her or the children, that he will prepare his own meals. Her calculation is that these "freedoms" will eventually seem onerous to him, and he will return to his marriage and the family. A mail truck emphasizes the unified quality of the couple, honking in friendly acknowledgment of the Maples as known neighbors. Richard reverses his course toward the Maples' house, another emblem of Joan's desire, and Joan continues her bluff. She states a diagnosis of their marriage that recalls Richard's in Rome, when he says that they have come very far and have only a little way to go. She says, dishonestly, "Things are stagnant...stuck; we're not going anywhere."

---

[37] Updike, *Too Far to Go*, 201, emphasis Updike's.

Richard hears the bluff and responds defensively, saying that he will not give up Ruth, and Joan continues in her bluffing mode. She suggests that Richard move to Boston.

Notably, she offers aesthetic reasons she thinks Richard will like. Neither the kids nor Richard will likely be bored there. Joan offers Richard the language to counter her bluff: "'Is this too sad? Do I seem brutal to you?'" He knows that "it was a bluff, a brave gesture; she was begging for reprieve." He decides to exploit her tactic, using her pride against her to get his way—more shrewdness in service of the aesthetic. He muses about the many ways that he is still her husband and his children's father, how even his bodily self is provided by Joan's nourishing. This is a theological emblem, expressing the sense that the Maples are still one flesh, joined together through time and space. Yet he offers a weak counterargument couched in shallow therapeutic language: "She was right"—not that she meant to be—"it was not healthy, nor progressive." It was no longer "convenient to love one another."[38]

The force of the story's opening act is to clarify positions: Joan's touching wish to get her husband back, in spite of a satisfactory lover and time for him; Richard's shrewd but hollow assertion that he finds it inconvenient to love Joan. Narrative hints and silences and ironies make clear that not only Joan but both Maples still feel a powerful mutual attraction. This, not merely Richard's selfishness, is why he spends so much time at home, even after his children "plodded through homework or stared at television." This is why he still sleeps with Joan. This is why he smiles to see her after a brief parting, and why he sympathizes with her touching stratagems.

In the second act Richard finds an apartment, calls Ruth with the news, and becomes irritated with her tepid response. It seems that Richard will not always find it "convenient" to love her either. The subtext of this act involves theologically charged emblems of human brokenness—the beautiful disaster of the Hancock Tower, emotional black holes, the crowded and hungry city itself. These emblems provide ironic context for Richard's and Ruth's words and actions, suggesting that their relationship, like Richard's with Joan, rises out of this brokenness rather than a "healthy" or "progressive" sense of human well-being.

---

[38] Ibid., 212-15.

The Hancock Tower is a truly brilliant and arresting image in this story. Updike turns the actual design problems of the building—its opening was delayed for five years as designers struggled to determine why the building regularly shed huge 500 pound panes of glass—into a correlative to human nature. The building is beautiful, praiseworthy, suggestive of a loving Designer, and yet disastrously flawed, fragile, and dangerous. In his nonfiction, Updike describes men and women as "radically imperfect and radically valuable."[39] He captures this and more in his description of the Hancock Tower in "Gesturing."

Richard accepts his apartment as soon as he sees the skyscraper. We imagine psychological reasons why—because the building thrusts skyward in masculine assertion, because it serves Richard's narcissism by reflecting his image and his world back to him. But the building also suggests an impersonal reality. Like men and women, according to Kierkegaard and others, the building is "suspended in a...state of incompletion"; it is therefore a "beautiful disaster"; its beauty derived from its Designer's love: "the architect had a vision." Richard understands that its blue verticality was meant to contrast with the "horizontal huge blueness" of the sea, but beyond this aesthetic language we recognize references to God (verticality, the sky) and immersion in life (horizontality, the sea).[40] It is the divine verticality that fascinates Richard, though his love neglects to grapple with the fact that the building is literally deadly. If the building expresses God it is a Barthian God, ready to punish, rebuke, and kill unless a redeemer-builder intervenes, paying for the repairs.

Attuned to his aesthetics, Richard calls Ruth rather than Joan to announce his new address. Richard implies he might have called either woman—there is an emotional equivalence rather than new preference for Ruth—and because he knows that Joan's sadness upon hearing the news will mar his rotation. But he is not having a rotation; he is shaken. Ruth precludes any possible rotation by hearing Richard's anxiety, feeling her own, and uttering a self-protecting put-down: "Don't do it, if you don't want to." She and Richard quarrel, partly because he requires "lover-babying" for which she has little patience, and partly because Richard has been honest about the likelihood of his children's unhappiness at their father's move.[41] Part of the etiquette of adultery she

---

[39] Updike, *More Matter*, 851.
[40] Updike, *Too Far to Go*, 216.
[41] Ibid., 217.

asks others to observe, evidently, is that she should not be reminded of any pain she is helping to cause.

Richard clearly does not find unalloyed aesthetic enjoyment in this new relationship. He is quite frank about the "tedious formality both [of them] observed, the pretense that they were free, each within their marriages, to do as they pleased; guilt avoidance was the game." Ruth is willing to play this game, observe this etiquette of adultery, while Richard notes regretfully that Joan's words "always opened in, transparent with meaning." Ruth then utters an expression of affection that is patently insincere, non-transparent: "'What else can I say,' Ruth asked, 'except that I love you?'"[42] Yet she has not in a strict grammatical sense said that she loves Richard. Language theorists would say that her question had an illocutionary effect, and not only or necessarily the effect of saying to Richard, *I love you.* Here she also says, plainly, *I am tired of this conversation,* and *I believe that my emotional confession should compel you to move forward with our relationship.* If Richard and Joan have often failed to meet standards for love laid out in the New Testament, Richard and Ruth do no better. Cleverly, given the title of this story, Updike has each of them then gesture unseen. On one end of the phone line Ruth exhales cigarette smoke in exasperation. On his end Richard stays on the phone, suppressing the urge to hang up, which might signal a giving up on the relationship. It is that serious, this gesturing.

Act three presents extended metaphors involving ash trays, further views of the Hancock Tower, the apartment's tile floor, and an anecdote about Ruth taking the name Maple, for real and for pretense. All of these motifs revolve around the story's touchstone, the couplet Richard finds etched into his apartment window.

> *With this ring*
> *I thee wed* [43]

This is the governing idea of the act, so that its metaphors and anecdote comment upon marital fidelity. Richard enjoys bachelor housekeeping. Ever the aesthete, he actually enjoys contrasting Joan's frugal tidiness with Ruth's wasteful messiness. Yet the casual phrase, "When a woman left...," poses both women as somehow equivalent in his deeper mind. Worse, his unconscious also has him thinking about

---

[42] Ibid., 218.
[43] Ibid., 221, italics Updike's.

dust, corpses, death. Ruth's cigarette butts become bodies. Her leavings are "long, pale bodies prematurely extinguished." Her ash trays are a "messy morgue." Richard objects consciously to the unthrifty waste; he objects unconsciously to death, which almost always seems premature, and which he somehow associates with Ruth.[44]

Interestingly, Joan's association with death is less bodily, more psychiatric. Joan smokes her cigarettes thriftily close to the filter, so that her ashtray becomes a "nest of filters, discreet as white pebbles in a bowl of narcissi."[45] Joan's "compulsive economy" strikes Richard as part of her "discreet death wish"—a repression or defense mechanism which seems to give rise, in Richard's mind, to her scrupulous ordering and management of people and objects, and her typical erotic restraint. In a baffling counterpoint to his associating Ruth with bodies and morgues, he then calls Ruth "love" and "life." This, he believes, is why he loves her. Now Joan and Ruth come to represent the warring instincts, Thanatos and Eros. Joan is familiar, associated with restraint; Ruth is erotic, associated with the life-force. In psychoanalytical theory, especially the kind the Maples have learned, restraint can devolve into aggression, violence. The erotic is the proper business of society.

The point Updike suggests seems to be different, altered by a theological viewpoint that would chasten hopes in Freudian sexual license: Joan's death wish is not a morbid, disabling preoccupation. To be sure, she feels anxiety and dread of the sort Kierkegaard predicts for one still "becoming." She fears death half-consciously, and she is afraid to choose herself in eternity. Yet she is alive to others, lively in her daily tasks, witty and transparent in speech, kind and generous, desperately hopeful for a future lived in love. In ways that Richard does not fully bring to conscious understanding, he prefers Joan to Ruth because Joan has an inkling of her own and others' mortality. Her "discreet death wish" is a function of her incompletion as an identity, but it points to her readiness for a leap of faith. In this story, we see her attempting to choose love and fidelity with Richard over adventure and infidelity with Andy. Unlike Ruth, who thinks first of her "beautiful unblinking assumption of her own primary worth," who thinks "better other-destructive than self-destructive," Joan is able to think of the primary value of others, even her boyish husband.[46] With her ring/She did wed.

---

[44] Ibid., 219.

[45] Ibid., 219. Narcissists flower around her.

[46] Ibid., 219.

In moving from Joan's love to Ruth's, Richard may not be choosing life but repeating his own death instinct. Another line from the Book of Common Prayer governs the imagery of this scene: Dust to dust; ashes to ashes.[47]

All this from a paragraph on ashtrays. Updike derives even more complicated theological and psychological meanings from the image of the gigantic blue mirror, the Hancock Tower. Luscher considers the building to be a metaphor for the Maples' marriage, but the suggestion is grounded in little verbal evidence, and is only partly correct. If we pay close attention to the many associations Updike builds up around the skyscraper, we discover the Kierkegaardian references that we have come to expect. It is meaningful, for instance, that Richard notices how images are reversed in the mirror of the building, but motion is not. A cloud moving from left to right in the sky behind the building will move that same direction even when reflected from somewhere behind Richard, the viewer. It took Richard "an effort of spatial imagination" to work this out. So it goes theologically. Something about our motion, or our becoming, is difficult to grasp, but once grasped is understood as resistant to human manipulation or altered viewpoint. Our becoming is true in any frame of reference, or can be.

Kierkegaard's entire scheme is based upon the metaphor of motion or change, a dialectic between (say the Arbaughs) the "static being of the ancient Eleatic philosophers and the Flux of Heracleitus," or "being-within-becoming, or repeated identity through change."[48] Without engaging more deeply than is necessary or useful into this philosophical problem, we can trace out the philosophy we need. In *Repetition* especially, Kierkegaard rejects notions of temporal change that deny real, existent, thoroughgoing transformation. One reason is clear: the leap of faith is a change from life-in-death to life-in-eternity. Parmenides and his fellow Eleatics in the 5th century B.C. posited a monism in which everything that can be thought exists. Change, the argument goes, is impossible because the transformed object must already have existed in order for us to think about it. Many philosophers find this argument wholly unpersuasive, but there it is. Heracleitus's famous remark about never being able to step in the same river twice has been variously interpreted, and its specific grammatical content disputed, but at bottom it concerns identity through change. The river is and is not the same

---

[47] *Book of Common Prayer* (New York: The Church Pension Fund, 1945) 333.
[48] Arbaugh, *Kierkegaard's Authorship*, 97.

river; in some sense the change or motion of the river makes it a river. Applied to human beings, this notion of flux suggests that even though body and mind undergo constant change (Richard knows that cells fed by his mother are all gone; his cells owe their existence to Joan's cooking), the person remains a person, Richard remains the Richard both women fed.

Thinking about the Hancock, Richard notices that the "disaster sat light on the city's heart," that in "rain or fog it vanished entirely." These remarks suggest that the Hancock and Richard are "becoming" similarly. The Hancock is a giant looking glass for the narcissist. Richard confirms these suspicions: "Even unseen, it was there; so Richard himself, his soul, was always there." Here again, we have a theological affirmation of the immortal, unchanging soul. A man or woman is more than a flowing river of nutrients and wastes and gestures, but a soul, an incarnation whose very hairs may be numbered by a loving God.[49] There is a social corollary to this insight within Richard's view. First he notices that while his beloved modern building can attenuate and even disappear from view, the "brick chimney pots and ironstone steeples" (metonymic for home and church) "intensify their substance" under the same conditions. As the self recedes, the social and religious fill the void. Similarly, while glass panes replace plywood panels on the Hancock with no logic and with slow, "brainless" work, the window pane "near his nose" carries a message of "comic vow": *With this ring/I thee wed.*[50] Idiotic flux versus holy constancy: the values suggested are clear as glass. In his state of mind, Richard thinks the vow is comic in the humorous sense— laughable. Updike expects us to read the word in its literary sense as well, as related to happy, blessed union through marriage. The writer of this verse and other names and dates were "armed with diamonds," a phrase that suggests that their marriages, or rather their constant love, gave them strength, a kind of just power.

The skyscraper becomes Richard's "companion and witness." Like Richard, it represents modern narcissism dedicated to frantic change, and sinful imperfection. In a few more lines we learn that the building is "hideous" at its foundation and has "tangled mucky roots." Nevertheless, Richard loves the building, and thinks it loves him. But Richard's love, we are told, requires him to gaze at the building at a great distance. Meanwhile, inches from his nose is a graceful, simple litany of

---

[49] Matthew 10:30.

[50] Updike, *Too Far to Go*, 220-21.

fidelity. All he has to do is change his depth of focus to see it. Updike allows us to focus on one or the other, the distant wreck or the near promise. Characteristically, Richard falls in love with an emblem of "beautiful disaster," and finds the elegant wedding litany of the Book of Common Prayer an "irritation."[51] Updike makes certain that we read it "etched bright by the sun's fading fire"—imagery of both truth and death.

Richard calls the dirty black-and-white tile floor in his apartment a "Vermeer floor," referring to the Dutch Baroque painter who tended to use tile floors to establish the realist perspective that he was after.[52] The remark establishes the artifice or unreality of Richard's relationship with Ruth, who joins in a game which is literally played out upon this checker-board floor—nude Brillo-scrubbing leading quickly to sex. Because Ruth becomes "a plump little steed" on her hands and knees, the game seems to be emblematic of chess rather than checkers. While this imagery renders her a masculine warrior, a knight, she is not a very powerful piece. Notably, throughout the Maples cycle if Joan is not Jean d'Arc she is the queen. (In "Red-Herring Theory" she holds a scepter and orb, and this is far from the only such reference.) Richard is enjoying his aesthetic holiday, and so he values the strangeness of Ruth in her equestrian posture, complete with "nether mane." But the two of them clean only the white squares, which is not a sign of their cleverness. It is a sign of their indolence, of their willingness to work for the appearance of cleanliness (or purity: the metaphor is of goodness) rather than thorough cleanliness for its own sake. Just as they observe a false "tedious formality" about their moral freedom, and pursue a false work of rinsing renewal, they observe a false etiquette of adultery—or rather, Ruth tries to. She learns that Richard has made love to Joan in the apartment. Ruth reveals an expectation or instinct for fidelity that she has not thought to honor with regard to Joan, wailing into the phone, "'In *our* bed?'" Self-oriented to the core, Richard reminds her that the bed is his.[53] These two are emphatically not one flesh, not fed with the same food, not (yet) wedded for eternity.

---

[51] Ibid., 224.

[52] See for example Vermeer's *Girl with a Wine Glass* (1660). Some art historians propose that Vermeer used mechanical lenses, the *camera obscura*, to achieve his precise perspective positioning.

[53] Ibid., 223.

This third of four acts ends with an anecdote about wedding rings. In a telling image, Ruth takes off her genuine wedding ring and puts on a false one as "concession to imposture." Apparently Ruth cannot stand even for hotel staff to know that she and Richard are not married to one another. Her false ring refracts light, and, as she imagines it, signals to the skyscraper which is beautiful only at a distance. She resents taking Richard's name, and he takes delight in the shame that makes her use it to get her room key. He imagines her unkindly as a "prim, fearful, and commanding" presence to children when she was a teacher—surely a projection of his own assessment of her manner.[54] We have no way of knowing yet within this fictive moment whether Richard and Ruth can grow to love and trust each other unreservedly, but it has not happened yet, and their mutual aesthetic gaming seems aggressive and mutually aggravating. Indeed, seen clearly, moving to Boston has afforded Richard two fragile and flawed mirrors to love: the skyscraper and Ruth, who mirrors his sense of self-primacy and shrewdness in gaming for novel satisfactions.

These three metaphors and one anecdote would seem to be very difficult to turn to a positive reading of Richard's relationship with Ruth. At best, the two of them seem to be learning to be married, to establish a rewarding mutuality within a realm of rewarding self-assertion. Their pleasures seem to rest in novel sexual activities; their troubles seem to rest in establishing a coherent narrative that legitimizes their relation-ship. Even Richard recognizes that they are forced to play the game of "guilt avoidance" because, after all, something they are doing makes them feel guilty.[55]

Ironically, in the fourth and final act of this story Richard falls in love with his wife. He does so over another meal with Biblical resonance, and speaks in Biblical terms of the way that he and Joan are one flesh, that they and their children constitute a sacred reality. Still, it is hard to approve of this love, for Richard's heartfelt speech about his sacred union with Joan is only a gesture, not a deliberate act. Having made a commitment of sorts to Ruth, Richard now views Joan as an aesthetic trespass, and she cannily presents herself as a source of aesthetic "fun." Twice she uses the word "fun" to describe offers she makes to Richard, in act three to make love with him in Boston, and in act four to arrange

---

[54] Ibid., 224-25.
[55] Ibid., 218.

an "illicit" dinner in their town.[56] Though Ruth is the former teacher, Joan seems intent on teaching her husband a lesson too, a kindhearted lesson that she still has much to offer him in terms of bodily satisfaction, adventure, intellectual interest.

In this final act Updike also leads us through a complex series of allusions, parables, and theological concepts. We move from the Maple children's boredom, to John's love of the *Kung Fu* TV program, to Richard and Joan meeting an older couple who illustrate the possibility of marital fidelity (or endurance), to the Maples running out of wine, to Joan's sharing odd and funny moments she has experienced with her steady lover (and someday second husband) Andy. There is a logic beyond conversational flow binding these sub-episodes together, and much of the logic is Kierkegaard's.

The children's boredom, for instance, is an evident reference to the great fear of those in the aesthetic stage, that their hopes for novelty will be quashed by everydayness. Does Updike imply that the children have learned an aesthetic economy from their father, and that it is failing them? Or that Richard's fear of boredom is basically adolescent? Both, probably. All three of the Maple children still at home find themselves bored when their "bossy visitor" of a father is around. John emerges as a foil to his father's boredom. When Richard was young, he virtuously read science fiction, while young John now wastes his time watching the wild West martial arts fantasy, *Kung Fu*. Richard takes comfort in the idea that John is learning a system of ethics—"oriental passivity, relieved by spurts of mystical violence"—just as he had assembled an ethics from his youth's heroes: "coolness from Bogart, debonair recklessness from Errol Flynn, duality and deceit from Superman." Updike indulges in brief satire here: these are aesthetic rather than ethical qualities, and even so Richard typically displays precious little of the cool or the debonair. Furthermore, Superman's deceits were in support of the good and just, and the Man of Steel was also faithful to his girl. Richard employs his own self-serving duplicity, asking John insincerely (for the answer won't matter) if he would be less bored were his Dad still living at home. John recognizes the question as a gesture, a performance on his father's part. We know that Richard has been staging these self-affirming dramas in his Boston apartment, emptying ashtrays with a smile formerly put on

---

[56] Ibid., 223 and 225.

for his parents and schoolmates, and then children, and now for the "blue skyscraper."[57]

When Richard and Joan leave their bored children they sit down to a repetition, a dinner of wine and seafood that recalls the champagne-and-lobster Last Supper of "Separating." This experience troubles Richard because Joan's attractiveness and charm tempt him to reunite with her. As though to mock their separation, an older couple from town stops by their table, illustrating the possibility of life-long fidelity. Richard offers Joan a "veiled compliment" about how much he has expected of his marriage to Joan, knowing that she would offer so much to it. He suggests that maybe this older couple expected less. Joan replies wisely that the theory is "too easy," but this is not an actual dispute. Richard is tipping toward her, realizing again how valuable he finds her.

Emblematically, this is no Last Supper but the feast of the Wedding at Cana.[58] This is why Updike makes such a point of the Maples running out of wine. Joan is amazed that one bottle of wine isn't enough for two people any more—a comment about her heavier drinking these days. But it is also an image of the love for each other they have been discussing: Richard thinks there has also been too little love. He offers to buy another bottle but is dismayed at the "waste." He finds himself generously giving Joan all he has remaining in his glass. When Jesus attended a Cana wedding feast in which the wine ran out, he performed his first miracle and established his divinity by turning water to wine. The parable affirms marriage and connects it with a celebratory joy and the miracle of divine providence. Richard and Joan witness no miracle, but they do experience a repetition of their love. This is a dinner of uniting rather than separating—and their remaining wine becomes an emblem of their love and their joy: if they share it, there is enough.

Joan, however, seems in no mood to honor such a mystical union between herself and her husband. She has a project for the evening, one that emerges from her "do-unto-others-as-they-do-unto-you" ethic. She is determined both to be charmingly attractive and to push Richard's nose into some adulterous adventures of her own. Her hope seems to be to pique Richard's interest in her. But she is ruthless too (partly because she is slightly drunk), pressing past his pleas that she stop. Whether the project is working, or Richard feels a love for Joan that she does not have to coerce, something deeper than jealousy, he is struck by more than her

---

[57] Ibid., 219-20.
[58] John 2:1-11.

sexual possibilities. He finds himself thinking of her perfect teeth, "immaculate soul," and "mischievous demons" beneath the polished surface. Her lover Andy only admires the surface.[59] Richard loves, in other words, Joan's whole person, her flaws as well as her goodness; he loves her for herself. Again, he feels forced by his aesthetic project to be duplicitous, promoting Andy's character so that Joan will retain her lover rather than renew her calls for Richard's return. Though Andy is a "churchman" who tithes, Richard knows that Andy does not understand Joan as he does. Andy cannot. He has not been one flesh with her for over twenty years.

At this point Richard realizes an elegant and powerful defense of marriage. He seems perfectly sincere, sober, and collected as he thinks these remarks, though his libido may also have been activated by Joan's physical self, her face "pink as a peony" and her eyes "a blue pale as ice. He saw through her words to what she was saying—that these lovers, however we love them, are not us, are not sacred as reality is sacred. We are reality. We have made children. We gave each other our young bodies. We promised to grow old together."[60]

Can Richard affirm this powerful theological description of marriage, this argument in favor of an eternal and sacred union between married persons, their love made incarnate through bodily commitment ("with my body I thee worship") and the children they helped to create? It seems so. Joan makes a gesture with her hands while telling her raunchiest story of the evening, about a plumber unexpectedly entering the house just as she cries out in coital ecstasy with Andy. (This is the plumber who understands the "eternal presences of corrosion and flow.") Her drawing a *v* in the air strikes Richard as a lovely gesture: "eager, shy, diffident, trusting: he saw all its meanings and knew that she would never stop gesturing within him, never...." This "never" that Richard imagines embraces eternity, and has the character of an ideal marriage vow: "...though a decree come between them, even death, her gestures would endure, cut into glass."[61]

Cut into glass, like the wedding vow. This language is emphatic and convincing. If libido is involved, it is sublimated into a compelling poetry expressing the character of ideal human and divine love. The remark admittedly also expresses Richard's incorrigible wish to leave his

---

[59] Ibid., 229-30.
[60] Ibid., 231.
[61] Ibid.

marriage, to allow Joan's gestures to become memories, or to experience them intermittently and from much greater emotional distance. Richard's ideal marriage is one in which he possesses all women he desires. For this reason, it is difficult to view Richard as having made a leap of faith, even though he is now talking about love surviving death. From a Kierkegaardian point of view, he teeters on the edge of something important.

Embedded in this denouement is a much quieter suggestion about the Maples' status as "us," coded in two references to the phrase "had it." The first is set up when Joan makes her grand entrance on the Maples' stairway—she knows how to dramatize too—dressed for dinner in her prettiest dress. Richard must be struck by her loveliness because his thoughts immediately express doubt about his marriage to Joan really having ended: "He must be wary. They had had it. They must have had it." Here, "had it" means ended it, finished it off. Later, Joan uses the phrase differently in her raunchy tale of being heard in intercourse by her plumber. "'The backdoor bell rang, Mr. Kelly stomped right in, you know how the kitchen echoes in the bedroom, we had *had* it.'"[62] She looks to see whether Richard knows what she means by "had it." "'Just at the *very* moment.'" Her meaning is quite different—they had *had* their audible sexual climax. Updike's arrangement of these echoed phrases is intended. Though Richard's use of the phrase is unspoken, Joan ends up using the very same phrase. The Maples not only share cells nourished by the same food, and children created through their shared bodies, but they share a common language, a quick mutual understanding of each other's elusive expressions. Realizing all this, we may sympathize with the two of them for finding emotional reasons to leave one another, even though they share so much history. Or we may feel frustrated with Richard for walking away from something so profound, real, and sanctified with Joan for something so uncertain and necessarily duplicitous with Ruth.

&

Updike has nowhere (to my knowledge) explained why he did not complete the story that we presume would have been titled "Divorcing." That gerundive title would not resonate or multiply in meaning as so many others have—"Waiting Up" or "Plumbing" or "Separating." There

---

[62] Ibid., 227 and 231.

is only one ordinary force to the word "divorcing," to dissolve a marriage according to legal custom. The most interesting feature of this fragment is that its focus on "divorcing" is not fulfilled in ways that title would lead us to expect. The Maples pay no attention to the legal and domestic agreements that a divorce requires, and we know that "Here Come the Maples" depicts the actual divorce proceedings. This story fragment focuses on the inward process by which two people in intense partnership find the strength to do without that partnership. Only Joan's method is strictly honest. She will have to cope with losing a partner she loves, and she wonders whether she can literally live with the loss. Richard denies this love, but both his acts and feelings illustrate its existence. The story's subtext suggests not only that it feels like death to be trapped in another person's suicidal state, to feel responsible for a person in that state and unable to help, but that a marriage ending is itself a kind of death, one that produces tremendous grief.

Joan tells us plainly about her attitude toward the divorce: "I wake up every morning reciting reasons to myself why I shouldn't jump in the river. You don't know what it's like," she tells him. Richard is still convinced that his boredom during the marriage is somehow equivalently weighty and compelling: "Well do you know what I felt like...lying beside you all those years waiting for something to happen?" Richard's rhetorical question is ridiculous and alienated, a shocking failure of sympathy. More than any other place in the Maples cycle, here Richard becomes the demonic Kierkegaard manipulating lovely Regine, manipulating her because he knows best existentially. Joan reiterates her wish to die, and Richard listens with little patience and no expressions of understanding. Joan's choice of suicide method is interesting, given that she and Richard met at Harvard: like infamous literary Harvard-man Quentin Compson, she wants to jump in a Boston-area river.[63] Death hovers over the story. Richard wonders whether dying can be worse than watching—or is it feeling responsible for?—such emotional pain in a person he loves.

And then the story takes an entirely new tack. Richard thinks, "he wanted to die with her." This wish opens up the possibility of his guilt, of propitious self-contempt—Kierkegaard's motive energy for the leap into self-worth. More importantly, the remark suggests that Richard still feels himself to be one flesh with Joan. Certainly he has experienced a shift in his balancing of Eros and Thanatos in a way that may open him

---

[63] Ibid., 233.

up to a new moral seriousness. The *telos* of the erotic gives him no joy now, for the painful moment at least. If readers have not caught the irony that Richard's pursuit of health through sexual freedom has not worked existentially, this time Richard tells us himself: "He wished to be out of this, this life and health he had achieved since leaving her, this vain and petty effort to be happy. His happiness and health seemed negligible, compared to the consecrated unhappiness they had shared."[64] Consecrated unhappiness: this is the phrase that must be explained and justified to readers for whom happiness is the rightful achievement of the human experience.

According to Kierkegaard there is no reason that Richard needs to live in any sort of unhappiness, though at first it will seem so to him. He needs to make two great renunciations before reaching the world-granting joys of faith. In order to achieve the growth required to move into the ethical, he will have to renounce the temporal, momentary, libidinous (or sublimated) pleasures of the aesthetic. He may on the way to the ethical enter into a preparatory or intermediary stage of irony, a bitter knowledge of the hollow vanity of aesthetic/erotic pleasure. Judging by the above remark about wanting to be out of "life and health," he may be there already. Once he occupies the ethical and discovers eventually that his existential problems are still not solved—as Richard may very quickly, because he has witnessed Joan's failed participation in the ethical with some acuity—he may enter a final intermediary stage, humor. This is a bitter humor that recognizes the vanity of human efforts to achieve or act out goodness, the comical quality of human effort generally.

But it is not yet faith because he has not yet made the second great renunciation. The leap of faith requires the prior renunciation of all claim to intelligence, rationality, moral goodness, or any other efficacious power on the question of life's meaning. This renunciation is not made with joy. No happy outcome seems possible even to the incipient believer at the verge of faith. Yet, through God's grace the believer does make the leap and enjoys a religious repetition, a gaining back of all that had been renounced and seemingly lost, gained back with the blessed assurance of faith and the neighbor to love.

So when Richard speaks of "consecrated unhappiness" he is honoring an instinct in himself that tells him that his love for Joan participates in a divine love, and that his wish for her health and well-

---

[64] Ibid., 234.

being is a wish that might expand to many other neighbors, if he were to allow the arrival of grace. On this day Richard is not ready for that movement of faith. He despises his questing after happiness and health, resigning himself to "a numb marching forward, like a soldier in a discredited cause, with tired mottoes to move him." These mottoes are basically duplicitous, and include, we are told, his self-serving theory that Joan was depressed even when living with him. This motto does her little good now, and Richard does not help by glancing at his watch because he has a date, or by telling Joan about all the things she has: "You're healthy, you have the children, money, the house, friends; you have everything you had except me. Instead of me you have a freedom and dignity you didn't have before."[65] Of course this freedom and dignity are just as vain as his own petty pursuit of happiness. She simply does not value them, perhaps because they do not participate in any power great enough to heal existential wounds like hers.

God help her, she simply loves Richard. She does not want to be free of him, or to assume the dignity of being independent. Being joyously co-dependent or married is what she wants. Suddenly, Richard sees her painful, hunched crouch as "a hatching one, her immobility a nesting hen's."[66] If Richard's insight is anything other than a sexist, self-serving projection, it might indicate that Joan's calling, the place where her self's passion meets the world's need, is to be a mother—not only to her children but to any around her who need nurturing, who might benefit from her voluntary care.

"Divorcing: A Fragment" concludes (and of course we have no way of knowing whether Updike ever planned for this moment to serve as a conclusion) with a reversal of mood and a hopeful moment for Joan in her suicidal depression. Richard argues that Joan's talk of death is a sin. He probably knows too little theology to make an informed judgment about this matter, and he takes no account of Joan's limited responsibility while ill with depression. He is simply trying to talk Joan into a better frame of mind, largely for his own benefit. His next words make this clear: "Why must this go on and on? I hate it"—words that echo his complaint to Dickie just before telling the boy that his own father would never have done this to him. "I feel glued fast. I come here to see the children, not to have you make me feel guilty." If we are going to number sins, Richard's shift of attention to his feelings while his wife

---

[65] Ibid., 234-35.
[66] Ibid., 235.

is suicidal seems another. But Joan is neither shocked nor surprised by Richard's remark. She jokes with him, "You feel about as guilty as a—" She searches for the simile, arriving at "bedpost."[67] This is not an especially witty simile, but Joan and Richard both laugh—perhaps because the nearest object at hand really does communicate the wooden quality of Richard's sense of culpability and sympathy.

Actually, Joan is not quite right. Richard often *feels* guilt, but he rarely expresses that guilt or allows it to change his behavior, to turn him around in repentance. Still. there is a Kierkegaardian hint in the laughter Richard and Joan share. They may have entered into the intermediary stage of humor, where both realize how unavailing and hollow their own existential modes have been. They live now in bitter amusement at their shared folly—not folly in marrying but in imagining that they had a way of living figured out.

"Divorcing: A Fragment" does provide us with one essential concept for understanding these three bitter stories. It is the notion of "consecrated unhappiness." The phrase, understood rigorously, does not imply merely that while all marriages are sacred, some are unhappy, and that most marriages exist in consecrated happiness. A clear-sighted Augustinian theology tells us that all married persons are broken and for this reason help to create their own unhappiness. For some, the sanctified quality of the marital bond will lend patience needed to cope with this unhappiness. Richard has not received this patience—though in "Gesturing" we see him recognizing vividly the sacred reality of a Christian marriage. He even recognizes that for the believer marriage survives death, not as a legal-social institution but as a deep history of mutual love, shared memory, and mutual work on others' behalf— neighbor-love. In these two stories and one fragment, we experience a Christian marriage breaking down in the social realm, but enduring in the inward realm, in the God-haunted consciousness and consciences of two normal human beings, a man and woman who are "radically imperfect and radically valuable."[68]

---

[67] Ibid.
[68] Updike, *More Matter*, 850.

Reality is Sacred

"Here Come the Maples" and "Grandparenting"

> Now it was Buzz Aldrin who enacted a spiritual observance in a strange and distant place. In the weeks before launch, he had searched for some gesture that would be worthy of the moment, and he had decided to celebrate Communion. Deke Slayton had warned him against broadcasting any religious observance over the air; NASA was still coping with a controversy stirred by the Genesis reading on Apollo 8.
>
> Andrew Chaikin, *A Man on the Moon:*
> *The Voyages of the Apollo Astronauts* [1]

Early in the Maples marriage, in 1961, Alan Shepard visits space, the first American to do so. Then, throughout the rest of the decade he and other astronauts conduct a series of tests of their abilities, capacities, and equipment. By the end of that decade these astronauts land on the moon, where they conduct tests, think hard about their existences, and in at least two instances risk offending others by celebrating Judeo-Christian scripture and sacrament. Before the Maples' divorce in 1976, twelve of these astronauts walk on the moon. By that time, as Buzz Aldrin's lunar Eucharist illustrates, it had become deeply American to care about both scientific materialism and Christian spirituality, the two systems for meaning-making that Richard contends with in these final two Maples stories.

Throughout the Maples cycle, Richard and Joan are existential astronauts and, in a nondenominational sense, Christian scientists. In "Giving Blood," Richard imagines marks on a ceiling as "constellations" in an effort to forget that his blood is dripping away into a plastic bag. Finally relaxing a bit, he has an epiphany in which he realizes his spiritual connection with Joan. Suddenly their spirits move "from star to

---

[1] Chaikin, *A Man on the Moon*, 204.

star" on the ceiling.[2] Liftoff. "The Taste of Metal" involves the unforgiving physics of a car crashing into a pole. Both before and after the crash in that story, Updike plays with both time and with entropy, noting our inexorable advance toward heat death. Almost exactly a year before the moon landing, in "Eros Rampant," Richard feels stunned and adrift because of Joan's confessions of adultery. He dreams of "the lunar face of the electric clock" before talking with a wanton and morally relativistic dream-Joan. His terror "gains mass." He struggles with "acrophobia," feels on the edge of a "vortex."[3] "Plumbing" is essentially about scientific versus theological dimensions of time. In "Sublimating," Richard realizes that Joan knows a "truth" about his recent behavior, which is a "transparent vista of scoured space."[4] In "Separating," Richard and Joan tell their children that they need "space and time" to think about why they don't make each other happy.[5] Dickie shows his father another view of "space" with his existential question, "Why?" which shows Richard a view of "emptiness," of "darkness [that] was featureless."[6] "Here Come the Maples" brings the theme into the most emphatic and dramatic focus, as Richard turns a description of the four fundamental forces of modern physics into a self-serving parable about time, habit, boredom, and love—in doing so, turning the "great logical engine"[7] of relativity and the quantum, the immense and the infinitesimal, into a man-sized excuse for betrayal. Consistently throughout the Maples stories, Richard thinks of love as a "force" not under his control.

While Updike clearly respects good science, in the Maples stories the physics concepts of space, time, and impersonal forces such as entropy become emblems of an empty, airless, hostile, cold, and nugatory existence. It is the world in which Kierkegaard's passion-filled individual, acting with love, has no place. Though unaware, the Maples bring this world into being with their own essential nihilism, which also

---

[2] Updike, *Too Far to Go*, 48.
[3] Ibid., 143.
[4] Ibid., 172.
[5] Ibid., 200.
[6] Ibid., 211.
[7] Ibid., 246. All of Updike's quotations from the pamphlet in which he finds a description of the actual four forces of modern physics are in italics in the story, "Here Come the Maples." I eliminate the italics in order to avoid creating confusing differences of emphasis. Readers of this chapter may or may not be consulting Updike's original text, and realizing that he uses these italics.

displays as cold and hostile. The one force that works counter to this airless space is love. As we will see in "Here Come the Maples," Richard simply does not know how to think coherently about love. But in some ways he does not have to: love is a force in his world, and in his psyche. For this reason, he cannot help but be brought into Joan's orbit, though he tries mightily to generate his own escape velocity.

In these two final stories of the Maples cycle, "Here Come the Maples" (1976) and "Grandparenting," (1994) the divorce decree comes between Richard and Joan. But a force as profound and permanent as any in physics, one that transcends the merely legal and social, gets most of Updike's attention. As their marriage ends, and then as they come back together more than a decade later to meet their first grandchild, the Maples are very much one flesh, their past "cut into glass" in a lasting reality. They still have loving work to do as a couple, and though legal decisions may dissolve some part of their partnership and obligation to each other, a deeper endorsement of their marriage remains in force. These stories surely supply reasons why the Maples might have remained legally married. But more importantly they point to the aspects of marriage that make it a sacred reality rather than merely a legal construct or arrangement, a reality that even divorce does not and cannot end, a reality that can replace the nugatory, airless space of existential absurdity. Indeed, these stories link the processes of arrived faith with the erotic/agapic love moving between married lovers, or even complicatedly committed ones.

ॐ

"Here Come the Maples" is filled with images of sickness and healing. These images emerge from Joan's hospitalization for vaginal bleeding as Richard first begins to court her, and from Richard's largely-psychosomatic arthritis symptoms as he pushes this divorce forward to a legal decision. Updike implies a horizon for the story in which the keys are health, freedom from physical pain, and relinquishment of mental compulsion. In order to achieve this health on his own terms, Richard in the final days of his marriage has to navigate a moral and psychic landscape riven with internal contradictions. His state and culture now allow no-fault divorces, precisely the legal doorway that Richard believes will allow him into a realm of permanent good health and happiness, the kind he has felt in Boston. Yet his psyche directs his attention to images of marital solidarity and stability, such as the courthouse clerk's framed family portraits, or his own vivid personal memories of married life with Joan. The story comes close to implying that Richard and Joan ought to remain married. But Updike is after something less ethically-minded and practical, something more existential. He and Joan do of course secure a divorce in this story. Whether they finalize a spiritual or psychic divorce is another matter. In becoming ex-spouses, the Maples begin to be neighbors to each other, as they should have all along, and their conduct with each other implies the nature of a more genuinely healthful identity, one on Updike's terms, not Richard's. The Maples are ready for remission from the sickness unto death.

The story's central paradox is implied by its title. Even as the Maples' divorce is decreed, they keep moving along together, as though, Richard thinks, they are arriving together at a party. The odd phrasing "here come the Maples" is drawn from juridical rituals of Massachusetts' Puritan past, in which the bailiff announces the litigants arriving in court to make their pleas and give testimony. This archaic language remains in use in the joint affidavit that the Maples file in request of their divorce. Joan finds it funny, "the way it was worded. Here we come, there we go."[8] This title and the opening lines of this story set up interesting tensions between Puritan and modern expectations for marriages in Massachusetts. In three hundred years the state interest in marriage has evolved. Once there was a theocratic civic vision in which the marriage promise is so sacred that almost no divorces are allowed. Now there is one in which marriage is a great elective, and no-fault divorces are granted on demand. Here Updike chronicles a shift in American social and legal practice in which original Protestant marital and disciplinary regimes are all but abandoned in favor of a permissive ethic of temporary, serial marriages, and other emotional and practical partnerships. Updike's attitude toward this marital change is complicated. Surely he has no longings for theocracy, and certainly none for puritanical mores. This sociological shift is not his primary focus, though it provides an interesting question: What state or individual forces, if any, might counteract the primary "natural" forces that destroy marriages—love, habit, boredom, and time? Or is there any countervailing supernatural force that might sacralize marriages and thus also help keep them intact?

---

[8] Ibid., 251.

The affidavit sets up another interesting tension. The state of Massachusetts threatens perjury penalties for those who swear falsely that "an irretrievable breakdown of the marriage exists."[9] In the final lines of this story, Richard and Joan both swear falsely to this question, knowing that the state will not care to apply its own penalties for their very real perjury. This means that the Maple divorce is not strictly legal in an ideal sense. In this way Updike shows that the new complacency about marital commitments can and does lead to logical and psychological contradictions and incoherence, to lies, even to crimes. Some part of Richard finds it difficult even to look at his and Joan's signatures on their marriage license, broken pledges of their marital promises both to the state and to each other.[10] Even the wedding day and honeymoon photos that "survived" picture the marriage as a matter, at least partly, of public order and well-being. In one of these photos, the family gathered for the wedding is pictured beside a parking meter: "The meter, a slim silvery representative of the municipality, occupies the place of honor in the grouping, with his narrow head and scarlet tongue." Another pictures Richard on the honeymoon, juggling three croquet balls. They are red, yellow, and green, the color of a traffic light. In keeping with his giddy character, Richard has a firm hold on the colors that tell him to go freely or go with caution, green and yellow, but the red ball signaling stop hovers in the air, out of his hands.[11] Municipalities use these colors as signs because when people fail to stop, accidents happen.

This concern for state and municipal order soon shifts to the matter of cosmic order. The four forces that Richard feels destroy marriages appear in the long third and final act of this story. Richard has begun to read a "scholarly extract" that has come in his mail, a description for scientifically literate non-physicists of the four basic forces known to physicists by 1935: the gravitational, the weak, the electromagnetic, and the strong.[12] While running errands across the city Richard ponders these forces, recasting these natural forces as existential ones:

---

[9] Ibid., 236.

[10] Ibid., 240.

[11] Ibid., 241-2.

[12] We can deduce a less random reason why Updike would have first read this actual "scholarly extract." It is the transcript of an address by Professor Steven Weinberg, given (as the Acknowledgments page of *Too Far to Go* tells us) before the American Academy of Arts and Sciences. Updike had just been

> In life there are four forces: love, habit, time, and boredom. Love and habit at short range are immensely powerful, but time, lacking a minus charge, accumulates inexorably, and with its brother boredom levels all. He was dying; that made him cruel.[13]

It is difficult to know just how to receive this theory. Does Updike also believe that the forces of love, habit, boredom and time really work on us in these ways? Or by confusing partly-volitional forces with inexorable ones as old as the universe, is Richard attempting to excuse himself from responsibility for his pending divorce?

The answer—a dialectical, Kierkegaardian one—is that both are true. For the person dwelling in the aesthetic sphere, love is a powerful, obsessive fascination with typically short duration. This is first love, Tristanism, love as a libidinous feeling. Habit, on the other hand, has a constructive role in helping the despairing to cope. It aids in human forgetfulness of existential terror and its causes. We know this because when Richard leaves behind his daily habits—as with his trip to Rome in "Twin Beds in Rome," or to a strange, bitterly cold Northern city in "Grandparenting"—he falls prey to his existential night-terrors, his naked fears of death. As for time, it is indeed inexorable and irreversible ("no minus charge") for one who has not chosen himself in eternity. Boredom is of course the great *bête noir* of the aesthetic personality, the clearest sign that the existential strategy of pursuing pleasure is not working to keep dread at bay.

Richard's theory of existential forces, then, is a description of very real forces and their actual dynamics, but only from one point of view: his own, the aesthetic. Updike casts the whole theory into ironic doubt when Richard, looking for this scientific pamphlet, instead pulls from his pocket a prescription for painkillers, a copy of his marriage license, and the affidavit testifying to his opinion that his marriage has irretrievably broken down. These carefully chosen items imply the deeper purposes of Richard's version of the four forces. The theory kills his pain by lifting responsibility from him; it explains why he married in the first place, because he underwent the complex experience of desire and mutual need called "falling in love"; and it explains why Richard is unable to continue to honor his wedding vows, because he believes he requires a rotation with the neighbor's wife. We are reminded of the forces that we

---

inducted into that same academy and received a reprint of the talk in its January 1976 bulletin.

[13] Updike, *Too Far to Go*, 249.

have seen working on him throughout his marriage—his psychic and psychosomatic pain related to Oedipal dynamics that are certainly not under his full or even significant control, his deep appreciation for his wife's wit and kindness as well as her sexual allure, and his giddy need to pursue serial sexual associations to keep boredom at bay and his narcissism in good form.

The four acts of "Here Come the Maples" juxtapose this powerfully explanatory theory with a series of Richard's memories of his life with Joan, most of these memories carrying the freight of Updike's emblematic subtext. The first act calls the Maples "lucky," for no-fault divorces have come to Massachusetts just in time. Richard recalls his wedding day. He and Joan were just kids, he realizes, kids at deadly risk, Hansel and Gretel entering a gingerbread courthouse. The second act takes us into the present-day building. It is still in Richard's mind the home of sorcerers. Richard must secure his "anti-license." He sees family photographs on the clerks' desks, including one showing a wholesome, patriotic African American family. He recalls other wholesome photos: a group shot of those attending his wedding, another capturing innocent honeymoon games. He walks out of the courthouse ashamed. He has defeated no preying evil. Act three is set on the subway. Richard fills dead time by reading the pamphlet on physics. His mind shifts from reading to his own honeymoon memories, to courtship memories at Mass General hospital, to his current psychosomatic arthritis symptoms and his doctor's comments on them. Act four depicts the Maples' last marital task, getting each other to the courthouse for the divorce decree. They share memories, jokes, and wry, learned observations (the courtroom is a Daumier) until the judge grants the divorce. On the way and at the courthouse, they seal the new vow with a kiss. This is by far the most congenial, friendly, loving day we witness in the Maples' marriage, a day of bonding rather than separating.

Act one opens with the explanation of the phrase, "here come the Maples." The first and last lines of the act also call the Maples "lucky," for two reasons. The first reference refers to the fortunate adoption of no-fault divorces by the state. The second compares this luck with the Maples' expectation when attending parties, that something "lucky" might happen—Updike's sardonic joke about casual sex described as "getting lucky." Both forms of luck seem a bit perverse. Richard realizes suddenly that he will have to retrieve a copy of his marriage license from the Cambridge City Hall. The task causes anxiety for Richard because he still has his doubts about finalizing this divorce, doubts that are amplified by the unpleasant guilt he feels as he recalls memories of the summer of 1954. Richard recalls his wedding day as a showcase for his then "regressive impulses," and he believes or assumes that Joan's impulses were similar. Richard recalls the ride in his parents' car to Cambridge on his wedding day, trying to sleep beneath his jacket like a child "hiding from a thunderstorm."[14] When he arrives, Joan speaks with contrastingly calm humor from behind the door where she is bathing.[15] The bathing/baptism connection hints that Joan had a clearer sense of her identity and calling that day, of a purer spirit working in her.

In act two, the sojourn into the Cambridge City Hall later that day, Updike has his fun by picturing the elderly female clerk as a witch who retrieves the "sorcerer's tome.[16]" She limps on her apparently cloven hooves, her hair "lifeless as dried paper." But the contents of the giant book are ordinary enough. Joan's signature on the original marriage license seems to Richard "firmer, and bluer" than his, and he notes that her profession is listed as "Teacher" while his is "inferiorly...'Student.'"[17] Yet Updike hardly suggests that Richard's and Joan's relationship was initiated entirely by Richard's frantic psychological need, or that his agreement with Joan to enter into a marriage was on his part wholly immature or hollow. Present events illustrate a different view. Richard can barely tolerate the pain of watching his "anti-license" being written out. (Clerks are the copiers of the 1970s.) He forces himself to think about memories of 1954, captured in "a few slides." In one, Richard seems similar to a metal post and parking meter, while Joan seems like a dancer about to perform. The parents of the groom and bride seem "half-lost" and "benevolent." Richard focuses on the ambivalent qualities of those pictured, except Joan. She is very much herself, energetic, confident, ready to dance. In contrast, in another slide taken by a friend who drove the new Maples to their honeymoon cottage, Richard is shown easing his anxiety by performing a stunt, juggling the croquet balls.

---

[14] As I argue in "Young Man Angstrom: Identity Crisis and Works of Love in *Rabbit, Run*," (in *Religion and Literature*) Updike borrows his thunderstorms from the one Luther cowered under, pledging his life to God and to the Catholic priesthood if spared death by lightning strike. Thus, a thunderstorm merges with a chastening, terrifying God, as it does during the initial golf-and-theology match between Rabbit and the Reverend Eccles in *Rabbit, Run*.

[15] Updike, *Too Far to Go*, 238.

[16] Ibid., 240.

[17] Ibid., 240.

Briefly Richard returns to real time to request a notary public. He finds her to be a "young black woman" whose nearby desk is "bristling with...images of fidelity and solidarity and stability, of children and parents, of a somber brown boy in a brown military uniform, of a family laughing by a lakeside; there was even a photo of a house...."[18] These details are carefully selected. For an American black family to send young men to war is especially moving, given that African American citizens faced real civic injustices in segregated Boston throughout the years of the Maples marriage, and considering that this war is against another people of color seeking fuller citizenship, the Vietnamese. The photographs of children, a lakeside, and a house all recall images that Richard's unconscious supplies or that Richard views in regretful consciousness in this story: his own children, the lake where he and Joan work together at camp, the house Richard has continually repaired. Richard's conflicted consciousness in pursuing this divorce is clear when he has to suppress an urge to ask this woman's pardon for his request that she notarize an affidavit supporting the divorce. He then casts his mind back to the juggling photo to escape these pictures mocking his betrayals, and sees that the "red ball still hung in the air, somewhere in a box of slides he would never see again." More shame: Richard does not know the signal for stop. He thinks of another kind of travel, less local. He knows that the honeymoon cottage he shared with Joan was "a capsule of silence, outward to the stars."[19] Escaping the City Hall, Richard recalls that this is the site of his neglect. He had forgotten to kiss Joan after the wedding vows. Again, he feels ashamed.

We see in the story's third act that non-erotic or only partly erotic love was in fact the primary motivating force behind the Maples' marriage from its beginning, as the lovely and unusual courtship illustrates. As in "Nakedness," Updike associates Richard and Joan with Adam and Eve. They first speak to each other while studying photostats of Blake's illustrations to *Paradise Lost*. Their courtship has a quality of Edenic innocence, but not of Edenic human perfection. Images of illness and healing surround the budding relationship. Joan's platelet deficiency requires her to miss her first date with Richard, a beer after their literature exam. In order to get to know her he has to brave a maze-like hospital, the protective watchfulness of Joan's family, and "other suitors." The fact that he does brave these impediments suggests that his

---

[18] Ibid., 242.
[19] Ibid., 239-43.

interest in Joan is non-sexual—or rather, healthily sexual, with a deep interest in the intellectual and emotional person as well as the attractive sexual one. (Richard is not going to get lucky in a crowded hospital room.) Joan does (cannily?) inform Richard that she is a virgin, an admission she tells him she made to her incredulous doctor as he treated her for vaginal bleeding. But in those days, the man who in a few years pursues sexual adventures frantically to feed his aesthetic commitment merely holds Joan's hand "in its little cradle of healing apparatus." Richard's first visits with Joan reveal in him a sense of chaste caritas rather than rampant eros.[20]

The issue of healing is central to the entire Maples saga, since throughout their marriage their illnesses and psychosomatic maladies express their greater sickness unto death, their acceding to sin/separation. The nearest they ever are to spiritual health, Updike suggests, is here in the hospital, as their love takes shape, where Richard feels the impulse to give and serve rather than to take and be served. The fact that Richard later views this situation as regressive—as a tale expressing their deep need for reassurance and companionship rather than the satisfactions of liberated adult sexuality—is no indication that Updike shares his view. These courtship scenes, colored by Richard's chaste and selfless caring, are the touchstone of this story. They depict a love that is not a weak force, not a mere feeling, fragile and easy prey to time and boredom, but a force for healing, comforting, and deep mutuality. Joan's hand is "unresisting and noncommittal" in Richard's memory, a characteristic emotional stance we have come to recognize in her. But we also gather that young Joan recognizes in young Richard a man worthy of her love, worthy of her ethical commitment, even though he is aesthetically-minded himself. Many marriages begin in the hands of very young and inexperienced men and women who have much to learn; this is one of them.

These act three memories are spurred by Richard's visit to the same hospital for an appointment with his "arthritis man," who diagnoses his pain as psychosomatic. Naturally enough, as Richard manages his marriage's demise he is undergoing significant psychic stress. His physician tells him that the pain will stop when his brain "stops sending out punishing signals."[21] The "arthritis man" is here making an amateur psychoanalytic diagnosis, one emerging from the Marcusan thesis that

---

[20] Ibid., 246-48.
[21] Ibid., 248.

improving one's health requires the defeat of the superego, the sender of punishing signals.[22] Of course there is an obvious alternative thesis: Richard's superego may be functioning properly and rightly. His symptoms may point to a psychic war within him that might be positively resolved when he drops his plan to divorce or otherwise harm Joan. He could take her side in things, and decide to keep working on the marriage. This thesis would imply that health may be sought through marital fidelity and commitment as well as through shedding restraints—a clinical possibility that Richard's doctors do not even view as debatable or interesting.

It is in the context of these and other memories that Richard ponders the nature of the four forces. As we have seen, out of the raw materials of the four basic forces known to physicists he constructs for himself an elaborate existential machinery. Seeking natural and cosmic excuses for his giddy desires and null solidarity is only one purpose for this machinery. Deep in the dark tunnels of the Boston subway, Richard is in personal anguish and feels personally negligible. He identifies with the "weak forces" of atomic physics, and cheers inwardly for gravity, which the tract describes as negligible at the atomic level but predominant in objects a hundred kilometers across or larger. Richard envies such forces of attraction. The subway train stops at the Kendall stop on its way from Cambridge to Boston, and Richard is cast back immediately to memories of his train ride with Joan to their first summer job as a married couple. Again, we hear of his feelings of inferiority or weakness, as Joan wins "every game" of naked croquet.[23]

The laws of physics begin to resonate with both personal and theological meaning. Richard is struck by a description of the weak force's decay in an atom's nucleus, which Weinberg describes as being "like a flaw in a bell of cast metal which has no effect on the ringing of the bell until it finally causes the bell to fall into pieces." Again, Richard makes a personal connection, since his own despair and psychological makeup cause him to seem also perfectly functional, to ring like a bell, but then turn either ruthlessly selfish or desperately fearful. In quick

---

[22] This is an interesting moment in a story where lawyers and a judge also misapply the standards of their own profession, granting the Maples a divorce on grounds based on falsified testimony. Updike may be setting up a theme here, human faultiness viewed through the professions. I consider another possibility below.

[23] Ibid., 244.

succession, Richard recalls the rest of his trip to the summer camp on train and boat, blaming Joan for unpleasant occurrences over which she had no control, or no more than he had. Or rather, "He both blamed her and wished to beg her forgiveness for what neither of them could control." He returns to the pamphlet and learns of the incommensurability of relativity theory and the quantum, but reverie overtakes him as he recalls the Harvard literature class in which he first saw Joan. Then he dwells on the early courtship days in the north Boston hospital.[24]

After thinking about this hospital courtship and honeymoon days with Joan, he contemplates another scientific sentence that takes on existential resonance: "The theory that the strong force becomes stronger as the quarks are pulled apart is somewhat speculative; but its complement, the idea that the force gets weaker as the quarks are pushed closer to each other, is better established." Here Richard thinks, "Yes... that had happened," nearness to Joan had caused love to grow weaker. So he proposes his theory about love, habit, time, and boredom—proposing, as we have seen, that love and habit have no lasting power. "Love and habit at short range are immensely powerful, but time, lacking a minus charge, accumulates inexorably, and with its brother boredom levels all."[25]

But the scientific language accords with neither his theory nor with his present state of mind. A few minutes earlier, Richard has cheered inwardly for gravity, a force that seems weak at the atomic level but later becomes immensely powerful, governing the motion of planets and stars. He is hardly going to cheer inwardly for habit, time, or boredom, the forces that threaten all the pleasures he lives for. Like all of us, Richard wants love, wants it badly and cheers inwardly for its victory. So when Richard lists his four existential forces and equates love with the so-called strong force, powerful only in the short term (read: first love) but ever diminishing as quarks (read: lovers) are pushed together, he has offered a contradictory theory. He has reassigned love a different corollary physical force in order to propose his self-serving theory. He was correct the first time, cheering for gravity. Love is more like gravity than it is like the strong force: love is not actually strong only over the short term, as it seems when it is mistaken for lust. Love is like gravity, seemingly negligible at the local, human level but actually a force that

---

[24] Ibid., 245.
[25] Ibid., 249.

binds the universe, the sun and moon and stars. The creator-God, after all, is love.[26] Since for Kierkegaard sin is nothing but separation from God, Richard's sin is to believe that boredom and mortality (he calls it "time") are more powerful than love. His belief or fantasy that love is not holy and omnipotent is his sin. He simply does not acknowledge the existence of the most powerful force in the universe.

Richard's contradictions and confusions in act three make the action of act four all the more poignant. The section begins *in medias res*, with Joan obviously answering Richard's question about whether a deer couple, a stag and doe, lived on their Lake Winnipesaukee island when they were newlyweds. Joan cannot recall, and asks whether Richard wants her to feel guilty. He does not press the matter, though the acuity of his memory is immediately confirmed as Joan recalls the placement of the marriage license bureau in Cambridge City Hall just as he does. This stag and doe remind us of the great buck in Faulkner's "The Bear," a natural-celestial confirmation of the worthiness of those allowed a glimpse of the great, mysterious animal. Just as Ike McCaslin was allowed to see the buck on the Mississippi delta by virtue of his reverence for nature and creator, so Richard and Joan are allowed to see this loving union of stag and doe by virtue of their own loving union. It is hard to imagine how the image of the stag and doe can be taken for anything other than an endorsement of the Maples' marriage, even if Richard has imagined them. Whether supplied by memory or by his active unconscious, his vision of the deer indicates his deeply felt union with Joan. Notably, Richard's wife-to-be Ruth is never mentioned in this entire story, nor is Joan's husband-to-be Andy.

Richard admits the "eggshell thinness" between his determination to part from Joan and his contrary wish to remain with her. All she has to do is "raise her voice" to halt this divorce proceeding—though we note that raising her voice has not been effective in the recent past. Richard imagines her "hatching" inside this thin egg, an image that recalls her hatching posture in "Divorcing: A Fragment." But Joan overtly questions whether she really needs to move bravely toward this divorce. "I assume I must be [brave]. No?" Richard replies, "Yes."[27] She is obviously quite

---

[26] I John 4:8.

[27] Updike scatters references throughout this story to previous Maples stories and themes. This is the Barthian Yes and No we saw in "Taste of Metal," reversed or perverted. References to blood, mismatched beds, childish regression, illness, witches, African American neighbors, stars and planets, time,

ready to resume her marriage to Richard, and does not share his putative need to outgrow any regressive impulses that might have led her into this union. She implies the same as Richard arrives the morning of the proceedings to drive her to the courthouse. She thanks him, then adds "I guess," acknowledging the irony of thanking him for helping her with an act she would rather not perform.

The lightness that Richard suddenly feels expresses something other than what he proposes: "All those years he had blamed her for everything—for the traffic jam in Central Square, for the blasts of noise of the mail boat, for the difference in the levels of their beds. No longer: he had set her adrift from omnipotence. He had set her free, free from fault."[28] This theory too is confused. Richard certainly might regret his unfair blaming of Joan for experiences he has found unpleasant and out of his control, but he cannot "set her free, free from fault" in any coherent sense. He can set her free from his torments, a freedom she does not seek. But what Richard offers inwardly to Joan he actually seeks for himself only—to be utterly released from fault. Or perhaps, what Richard desires is not just a regressive state of utter irresponsibility, which would suit his current circumstances and soothe his conscience. What he really desires is the experience of grace, the sensation of a peace that passes all understanding, which Luther and Kierkegaard and Barth suggest he might have if he were to repent. Richard's feeling of lightness, then, is actually a merely aesthetic sensation of getting finally the freedom he has longed for. His freedom from Joan involves not only the opportunity to unite with Ruth but the relinquishment of responsibility for his "nearest neighbor." Since there is no true incompatibility between Richard and Joan, and since loving the neighbor is for Updike an absolute duty, this is a basic betrayal. Or it would be if he could accomplish it.

The remainder of the story expresses the kinds of ironies and perversities that earlier lead Richard to call his affidavit an "anti-license."[29] While pursuing this divorce he admits to himself repeatedly that there is no legitimate cause for it. Indeed, this is not a strictly legal divorce. Richard can point to no cause of a marital breakdown, no

---

bathing, modes of travel, lying—these are others. The Judas kiss at the end of "Here Come the Maples" is one in a long list of scriptural allusions—not the last because of "Grandparenting."

[28] Updike, *Too Far to Go*, 253.

[29] Ibid., 241.

significant physical violence, only his own sexual dissatisfaction. When his lawyer asks whether there were "personal and emotional incompatibility" that Richard would swear to, he knows that such testimony would be "profoundly untrue," something readers of previous stories have recognized already. The Maples will have to lie in order to secure this divorce. Ironically, even in an era of permissive "no fault" divorces their own plea does not meet the minimum legal requirements. Yet Richard, in the company of his older lawyer, feels like the young athlete about to go into the game to accomplish the heroic act. He hears inwardly his favorite word: "Go."[30]

The story closes with a legal proceeding as mock-wedding. Richard and Joan enter the sanctum on the arms of their lawyers, like brides on the arms of their fathers. The room is decorated in green, the color of permission to go. Unlike the depictions of God that might appear in a church, here "[d]ead judges" look down on the proceedings. The judge takes a quasi-ecclesiastical role, seeming to Richard "altogether good," and, strangely and irrationally, immortal. Richard is repelled by everything around him, with the notable exception of Joan. The two seem utterly married in these last moments of the marriage, and in the light of the four forces Updike's phrasing of the situation is pointed: "Richard inertly *gravitated* toward Joan, the only inanimate object in the room that *did not repel him*."[31] The love that exists powerfully between them is precisely like the gravity existing between large objects.[32] Yet both Richard and Joan then lie about an "irretrievable breakdown" that they know does not exist between them, using the traditional utterance of the wedding vow, "I do." Partly because he had forgotten to kiss Joan at the conclusion of their wedding ceremony, Richard now kisses Joan.[33] But it is also a Judas kiss, marking a mutual betrayal of an incarnate love.

The emotional force of this concluding story of *Too Far to Go* is to affirm the loving bond between Richard and Joan Maple. In order to make this point, the story subtly redefines love—rejecting Richard's definition of love as a powerful but short-term force and replacing that definition, through the irony of his confused and contradictory thinking,

---

[30] Ibid., 255.

[31] Ibid., 255, emphasis mine.

[32] Or around or through large objects. Updike's diction here is rather Newtonian. He is not thinking of the classic Einsteinian model of a slice of gravity, the bowling ball distending a rubber mat.

[33] Ibid., 255-56.

with a definition of love as a mutual caring, a partnership in action, an instinctive gravitation toward the loved one amid a world of repellant objects. Richard's sinful obduracy is also vivid to us, though as usual the extent of his responsibility for this obduracy is open to debate. Certainly Joan offers him opportunities to rethink his plans, cues about their option to renew their relationship together, but he seems able to construct reasons (however feeble) not to accept her offers or observe her cues.

And so there go the Maples—as a formerly legally married couple in the state of Massachusetts. Yet there is a sense in which the title "Here Come the Maples," with its emphatic present tense and composite subject ("the Maples," not "Richard and Joan" or even "Richard and Joan Maple") suggests a differing view of the marriage. Viewed theologically rather than legally, the Maples remain "the Maples" for as long as their love for each other persists, for as long as God blesses their union, and for as long as they continue in mutual acts of non-erotic love.

☙

One such mutual act is the subject of the final Maples story, "Grandparenting," in which the Maples take up the shared task of grandparenting Judith's first child. Their mutuality remains palpable, a decade and more after the divorce and after second marriages have commenced and lasted for both. "Grandparenting" presents evidence that Richard's epiphany about Joan's gesturing in him forever is indeed true. The sadness readers feel as the Maples' legal partnership dissolves is a sadness that has been prepared for us, so that the Maples saga is a correlative for human alienation and separation, which is in turn an anagogical corollary to human separation from God. Both correlative and corollary fill readers with sadness perhaps verging on, or evoking, despair. It is in this sense that *Too Far to Go* is a composite tale evoking Kierkegaardian concepts. More importantly, the stories prepare for readers a Kierkegaardian experience, a vivid experience of the contours and structure of the despairing existence possible in either the aesthetic or ethical spheres.

"Grandparenting" makes clear, as no Maples story before it has, that Richard's and Joan's commitments to the aesthetic and ethical modes of existence during their marriage evolved into a mutual search.

If we associate the word "search" (or the idea of searching) with Kierkegaard, it is because of Walker Percy's *The Moviegoer* (1960) rather than Kierkegaard's own writings. In Percy's novel, Binx Bolling sets out on a search for something other than the two bad choices he sees as available to him: the theism Binx believes 98% of Americans embrace, or the atheism and agnosticism the other 2% do. He wants to find something rare, something immune to the malaise of everydayness, and his instinct tells him that the answer is nearby, around him, part of the fabric of his life in the neighborhoods of New Orleans. He feels that the movies, which he loves, are "onto the search." But they "screw it up." The films' stories of searching always end in despair (and this is Kierkegaard's despair) because their characters, finding themselves at first in a propitiously "strange place" that might be productive of an alternative to everydayness, eventually settle down into a normal ethical existence and surrender to everydayness. [34] Binx's search, he hints, will continue to examine the strange, the rare, the odd. His search will be for God—but not the tame, knowable God of hegemonic American Christendom, the 98%. It will be a search for the Wholly Other God, faith in whom is thoroughly absurd, sweeping in its demands, and yet wholly world-conferring. [35] All of this is Percy's particular interpretation of Kierkegaard's scheme, and a distinctly Catholic one at that. Though Percy's epigraph from *The Sickness Unto Death* notes that the specific character of despair is that it does not know it is despair, the Catholic Percy suggests through Binx that some people grow aware enough of the absurdity of their existence and sense their despair with enough clarity that they actively search for something to believe in other than the tame pieties of American Christendom or the vacancy of unbelief. They choose God.

Because Updike hews closely to the logic of Luther's Augustinian theology, or Kierkegaard's interpretation of it, he will not allow his characters to find God through their own effort or initiative, as Percy seems to. However, Updike joins Percy in recognizing a searching activity among the most world-aware and self-aware people, a wish to figure out existence in some fundamental and distinctly God-haunted if

---

[34] In Binx's movies this "strange place" is simply a previously unvisited locale, but both Percy and Updike imply that it can also be in one's conscious apprehension, in the conscience, or in the unconscious. In Buzz Aldrin's case, on the moon.

[35] Walker Percy, *The Moviegoer* (New York: Knopf, 2001) 10-14.

not God-aware way. As this story takes place in 1986 or 1987, Richard sees this searching quality in Joan, his ex-wife for some ten or eleven years. For instance, late in the story she tells Richard and her second husband Andy about Judith's delivery of her first baby. Joan has realized, because of her view during her own four deliveries, that the womb is more than a "place for transients"; it is a "whole other life in there. It's a lot to give up." Richard has been admiring his ex-wife all evening, contrasting her with Ruth and Andy at the second spouses' expense. One of her most attractive features, he realizes, is her curiosity and seeking quality. She was always "groping for the big picture, searching for the hidden secret, in keeping with all those sermons she had had to sit through as a child." He is impressed—though we have to deduce this—with Joan's having come to a sophisticated theological conclusion, that life itself is less an inhospitable stopping point for alien transients than a beautiful, joyful, praiseworthy journey, hard to give up.

Richard believes that for Joan, "[l]ife is a lesson, a text with a moral."[36] We have seen, with Kierkegaard's help, that Joan's confidence lacks a sense of mystery, that it partakes of the ethical urge. Yet she is still on a search for the "hidden secret," and so is Richard. Early in the day he admires this search, and later that evening he joins in it, to his terror. This search, we realize, has always been a dynamic part of the Maples' mutual life together. Even their most selfish and profane speech and behavior has involved a searching quality, the sense that a better life lay before them. "Grandparenting" asserts that this mutual life has not ended, that in both memory and through the mutual experiences of parenting they are still really one flesh, divorced only by decree and spatial distance. And the former Maples are still searching together, plumbing the mysteries of life and death and faith, and incarnate consequences of their partnership.

In the four acts of this story, Richard reveals that the aesthetic motive has finally collapsed for him. He has accepted the ethical life, his own interpretation of it. He provides insights into his and Joan's deeply

---

[36] John Updike, "Grandparenting," in *The Afterlife and Other Stories* (New York: Knopf, 1994) 312. Again, I use *Too Far to Go* for the first seventeen stories, and *The Afterlife and Other Stories* for this final one, because the omnibus *Maples Stories* makes a few odd changes to the stories that, believe it or not, change some of my meanings and arguments. My dangerous Corvair becomes a Mustang. Vietnam becomes abortion. And using the original periodical publications would be very inconvenient to readers and me both.

compromised second marriages, and competes with Andy for Joan's primary affection. Finally, he experiences a repetition of the force that has always baffled him, the "adhesive force, a something," that we call love. Because Richard has become much kinder and much less selfish, because he can now be forgiving and hospitable even with people he doesn't like, because his libido is now finally under control, because he is faithful to Ruth in spirit and in body, because he recognizes religious hypocrisy when he sees it—he may even be a post-leap person.

The first act of "Grandparenting" revisits differences between Ruth and Joan, differences we have seen before. Joan comes off as far more attractive, though that isn't the point. Early in the story Richard recalls his wife Ruth and her thoughts about his trip to the Hartford hospital to support Judith in her birthing and to meet his new grandchild. Ruth, Richard thinks, has a "crisp way of seeing things; it was like living in a pop-up book, with no dimension of ambiguity." Joan, on the other hand, remains the liberally educated girl who accompanied Richard to a great E.E. Cummings reading at Harvard, willingly listening to stanza after stanza on "Immortality" while the other students around them grew restless. Not only is Joan more of a thoughtful, intellectual person than Ruth, but we learn, less petty. Ruth, who might give thought to Judith's challenges as a first-time mother going into delivery, offers didactic instruction on a birthing mother's need for space ("'You need *space* when you're having a baby. You need *air* to *breathe*'") in a transparently jealous and manipulative strategy to keep her husband at home.[37] She criticizes Richard and Joan for giving Judith a "terrible upbringing," but takes no responsibility for any harms she may have helped to cause. She calls all of the Maples, including Richard, "ragamuffins" and Andy a "fop." Richard calls this way of seeing things "crisp," but he is being forgiving and quite generous. She is harshly judgmental.

When Ruth renews her pressuring during a phone conversation that evening, Richard resists for mixed reasons. On the one hand he is jealous of Andy, whom he fears this child may come to accept as his real grandfather. On the other hand he dimly recalls the love he felt when holding Judith when she was his own first child. The story is filled with imagery that conveys this aura of competition and human

---

[37] Ibid., 298. Here, Ruth is linked to "space," that image of the nugatory and empty and annihilating. One of the delights of reading the Maples cycle is watching Updike resurrect themes and images he has established in earlier stories. He must have reread his own stories carefully, and often.

competitiveness generally, from the Super Bowl on television, to Andy's reading a book about nineteenth century Christian explorers' battles with malaria and African unbelief, to the *Wall Street Journal's* (implied) ethic of competitive capitalism. Richard recalls Judith's high school graduation, how in performing a dance she had seemed suddenly a grown woman. He thinks of adulthood as being "a body out in the world, competing."[38] Even Judith's marriage to Paul Wysocki seems to Richard a losing bet, a competition for an excellent mate lost. On the other hand, Richard goes to Hartford because he remembers the "adhesive force," the "something" that banished his fear as he held baby Judith for the first time thirty-one years earlier. He feels that he is "*in this together*" with her, as she had wordlessly suggested to him the moment he met her. His wish to be with her now is part of that feeling of adhesive force that banishes fear, that eternal commitment to the person—both of which are aspects of love. Kierkegaard denies that erotic love or *Elskov* could have these qualities, but not Updike. As we have seen in his writings about Denis de Rougemont, Updike feels that the erotic and agapic, *Elskov* and *Kjerlighed*, are inextricable. But Richard expects *Kjerlighed* on this trip.

So we find in the first act of the story that there will be a struggle between competition and caritas, one red in tooth and claw and the other passionate and loving. Both are involved in a perfect early sentence which begins with unselfish wonder at natural processes, "And now [Judith's] body was splitting, giving birth to another...," and ends with a petty wish to compete: "...and he'd be damned if he'd let Joan be there having their baby all to herself."

Richard hardly seems ready for the competition. Indeed, Updike helps us to see that his personality is now so contracted—a deliberate word deserving attention—that he seems more ethically-minded and less spunky than Joan ever did in the first seventeen stories. He sees himself not only as the last family member to arrive at the Hartford hospital, but also, even though Andy is no kin to Judith, "the least." Joan's welcome a few minutes later makes him feel like a guest, and an "inconsequential" one at that. He feels he needs to lie about Ruth's resistance to this trip partly, we surmise, because he doesn't want to appear the cuckold. Both his contracting libido and kinder, gentler identity seem involved when Joan sits next to him and he shifts over to avoid their "touching

---

[38] Ibid., 299.

rumps."[39] He makes room for people. Much later in the story, Joan urges him to think hard about where his car is, so that they can find it and get out of the bitter cold. Richard realizes that he doesn't do much thinking: "Ruth was so much more decisive and clear-headed than he that he rarely had time to think."[40]

Richard also seems a bit contracted as he contemplates his relationship with his son-in-law. He doesn't like Paul, finds his pony tail and troubadour hobby affected (or perhaps effete), and senses an insolent and sneering manner in him that we certainly never see. When Richard imagines Paul as "a tall dry stalk you want to pull up and throw away," and admits surprise that Judith's marriage has lasted five years, he seems nearer to Ruth's "crisp," unambiguous judging than to his own former narcissistic energy and instinctive rivalry with any man near a woman. Richard has become a sourpuss.

Or is it a Prufrock?—as act two opens, he allows himself a non-nutritive snack (dare he eat a lemon Danish?), feels no wish to be near the action in the delivery room, and suffers a number of his wife's barbs on the phone. She disapproves of his being in a hotel, his interrupting her television program, his rendering her a "grass widow" while he pays attention to this other family.[41] Richard doesn't bother to fight back, a far cry from the man who, when a younger Joan asks him to remember to buy dishwasher soap, replies "Remember it yourself."[42] Much later, when a nurse asks him whether he would like to hold his new grandson, his namesake, his reply is a directly Prufrockian "Do I dare?"[43]

To be fair, there is a heartening quality to Richard's change, one that Kierkegaard would approve. Richard in this apparent ethical stage seems to have learned to forgive and tolerate genuinely, not in the giddy, libidinous, forgetful way in which he had forgiven or passed off offenses during his adulterous days. Ruth comes off as a real shrew in this story, and does so in depicted action, not in memories that Richard might alter to make her appear badly. Yet Richard seems to understand Ruth's feelings of fear and jealousy, and to forgive the mean-spiritedness there. She has been suppressing her goodness. He recognizes it in her when she is "at last, touched" by his news that he alone among the blood relatives

---

[39] Ibid., 300-301.
[40] Ibid., 311.
[41] Ibid., 303.
[42] Updike, *Too Far to Go*, 168.
[43] Updike, *Afterlife*, 316.

was not in the delivery room. And he smiles when she treats his staying in a hotel without her as if it were "a kind of infidelity." He takes genuine joy in Ruth. He likes calling her because her voice on the phone has a "throaty, shapely quality" that reminds him of their days of aesthetic rotations, days which were "secretive, urgent, humid." Richard is able now to enjoy these days as memories rather than trying frantically to repeat them or turn them into rotations. As we see in his tolerant patience speaking with his wife, he has come to understand Ruth's meanness as rising out of fears that he has helped to shape or to cause. She fears his infidelity because he practiced infidelity with her; she fears his leaving her for his family because he has left his family for her.[44]

This story ends with the assertion, "Nobody belongs to us, except in memory."[45] We will deal with this statement and the denouement later. For now, we have to consider how memories shape Richard's behavior throughout this story. Given the dialectic between Richard's seeming personal contraction (yes, on the day that his daughter gives birth Richard undergoes contractions) and seeming gentleness, we might consider whether the past is a place in which he ought to dwell. Surely we approve, or find no reason to criticize, when Richard recalls holding his baby daughter for the first time, feels adhesive love for her, and commits himself to her welfare.[46] We may be slightly less approving when he recalls the "secretive, urgent, humid" courtship days with Ruth. But now that he is a second husband, how much time should he spend recalling Joan before he married her?

When Joan finds him returning from the hospital cafeteria and asks, "Where were you?" the correct answer is *In the past*. She tries throughout this story to drag him into the present—*be alert because Judith is about to deliver; think where you left your car so we can go to warm hotel rooms*—but Richard is drawn to oddly arbitrary memories, such as the Cummings lecture during their undergraduate days at Harvard. First, he recalls with pride how the Dadaist poet had held the two of them rapt— "[Cummings] was jointly and privately theirs, fluting Wordsworth's Immortality Ode"—while their dimmer fellow students grew restless. Later he recalls how older art-loving Cambridge ladies attended Cummings' reading even though they were the subject of one of his more satirical poems. (This is an odd memory, spurred by Richard's

---

[44] Ibid., 303.
[45] Ibid., 316.
[46] Ibid., 299.

surprise at Joan's aging since he has seen her last, so that she too now looks like a "Cambridge lady.") This memory seems at first to be cutting and condescending, but it need not be read that way. Richard seems to admire the affection that these Cambridge ladies had felt for the poet even after he had specifically criticized and wronged them by reading his poem, sarcastic at their expense. Richard now identifies with the poet he recalls as a verbally gifted "homunculus," because like Cummings that night he too would like to be forgiven and attended to.[47]

Richard is thrust into a fairly complicated present when Joan asks him, at Judith's behest, to join Andy in Judith's hospital room. Richard plays the humble homunculus in the initial meeting, though we recognize his irony coming alive: "Keep reading, Andy. I'll just cower over here in the corner." This remark initiates a competition between the two men, a duel between rivals for a lady love. The great American gladiatorial contest, the Super Bowl, provides emblematic context. Andy offers his comfortable chair to Richard, whose response would reveal much to someone more acute than Andy: "Absolutely not, Andy. Survival of the fittest. To the victor belong the spoils, or something." Richard refers less to the "spoils" of the comfortable chair than to Joan. She has become a prize to Richard. It is interesting how Richard's response rewrites his and Andy's history. Andy was never a real rival to Richard, and he certainly did not win Joan through greater manly fitness or a will to survive. Even as she began sleeping with Andy, Joan nearly begged Richard to come back to her, threatening suicide, and then much more mildly ridiculing Andy's fastidiousness to Richard.[48] In "Gesturing," when Richard suggests to Joan that she must be no more inclined to give up Andy than he is to give up Ruth, Joan replies, "'I would if you asked. Are you asking?'"[49]

At this point in "Grandparenting," midway through the second of its four acts, certain key concepts of Kierkegaard's theology appear. First, Richard tells us that Andy was an Episcopalian "the way a Chinese Mandarin was a Confucian, to keep his ancestors happy."[50] If this is so, Andy lives in the moribund Christendom which Kierkegaard rails against, and engages in what Updike calls the "sin of church worship"[51]

---

[47] Ibid., 302-4.
[48] Updike, *Too Far to Go*, 230 and 232-5.
[49] Ibid., 196.
[50] Updike, *Afterlife*, 305.
[51] Updike, *Picked-Up Pieces*, 110.

in Kierkegaard's theology. Andy practices an inherited and therefore non-desperate, non-passionate faith. Ironically, he is reading a history of Christian explorers of Africa, marveling at their faith in facing malaria. Of course Andy's own Episcopalianism makes no allowance for faith as a safeguard against disease; this is not a matter of faith at all, but of superstition. And for a modern-day Anglican to read with admiration the lives of such "explorers" suggests that Andy is less than fully alive to questions of justice and intercultural respect.

Richard at first satirizes Joan's latter-day selfhood in similar fashion, but soon changes his mind. First he recalls that Cummings had written sardonically about women like Joan who live in Cambridge. In "the Cambridge ladies who live in furnished souls," a modernist curtal sonnet published in *Broom* in 1922, Cummings writes of self-satisfied Cambridge ladies who "believe in Christ and Longfellow, both dead." Their "furnished souls" express their materialism, and make them "unbeautiful."[52] However, Richard sees Joan as a Cambridge lady only before the baby is born, before Joan makes remarks about the womb and the nature of life, remarks proving that she is still a lively seeker.[53] After hearing these remarks, Richard seems to give her the benefit of his doubt, returning in memory to an image of her wheeling her bicycle across Harvard Yard—not a Cambridge lady but the bright girl who held her own as the only female in a seminar of high-achieving Harvard literary men.[54] She is still the clergyman's daughter who ten years earlier found "the concept of God...not only dim but oppressive," but we have no idea of her inward state now, and we believe Richard when he diagnoses in her a profound interest in existential mystery.

The real Kierkegaardian question of this story is whether Richard himself is so diminished or contracted as to be far from propitious despair, far from an unconscious search for cosmic meaning. His own role in this story is also framed by a poem Cummings had read at Harvard in the middle 1950s, Wordsworth's "Intimations of Immortality from Recollections of Early Childhood," which Richard recalls as a very long poem that eventually bored the student audience as Cummings fluted stanza after stanza. Wordsworth's neo-Platonic argument is that the soul finds its origin with God and from God. The child is dimly able to recall this origin of the soul, and thus lives in union with its nature, in

---

[52] E.E. Cummings, *100 Selected Poems* (New York: Grove, 1994) 8.
[53] Updike, *Afterlife*, 312.
[54] Ibid., 304 and 311.

joy and "heaven-born freedom." But the adult lives a life that is "a sleep and a forgetting," so that the soul's vision of a better place is lost:

> At length the Man perceives it die away,
> And fade into the light of common day. (V, 18-19)

Updike's allusion to this particular poem lends a specifically Romantic theological gloss to Richard's personal diminishment. The suggestion is that at his cruelest during his adulterous years, Richard was nearer to his "heaven-born freedom" and thus to the leap than he is today. His psychosomatic symptoms, his night terrors, his compulsive serial attachments, his aggressive and excessive speech, his arthritis—all emerged from his despair and therefore signaled a dynamic process of searching for God. The Richard about to become Grandpa has traded in his sporty Corvair, which was "unsafe at any speed," for a gray Taurus, the everyman sedan, with three bridge stickers signifying his newfound sense of social compliance.[55] We may like the elder Richard's manners better, but may also regret his retreat from danger, which once seemed about to lead him, in his desperation, to God. The leap into God's presence is an emphatically present moment. It is a choosing of oneself in time with an eye toward eternity. As this story commences, we find Richard living in a dim past, avoiding images of present age and decay (his own, the hospital's, Joan's) by dwelling on the innocent courtship days at Harvard.

All this changes as Richard engages in his duel with Andy, the main subject of act two. Joan leaves the two of them in Judith's room. As she leaves, she asks whether they will be all right. Andy doesn't bother to answer, so Richard, with more politeness, does. "Happy as clams." He eventually asks whether they might turn on the TV for the Super Bowl, or rather, for the commercials introduced during the game. Andy takes the pose of one who has little interest in sports, or any other specifically American ritual like the Super Bowl. At this moment, Richard realizes that "This is fun," and he laughs. Laughter will become the telling symptom of the inward change he is about to undergo, and that Joan will undergo with him. Humor, after all, is the inter-stage emotion between the ethical and the religious.

Watching the game, Richard is struck by the drama of contrasting quarterbacks and game plans. One team plays a low-risk, systematic, ball

---

[55] Ibid., 311.

control passing game, while the team he favors is led by a scrambling quarterback who tosses high wobbling balls requiring acrobatic catches. When such a catch is made, he yells in delight, and then explains to Andy, "It was a miracle." Living more dangerously, he eats the crackers that Joan remembers he enjoys, and then a banquet of unhealthy snacks—cheese curls, Twizzlers, and candy bars. Richard shares them all with Andy, whether out of kindness or to spite his rival's dietary pieties we do not know. Andy seems to rise to the competition with Richard— but Updike hints that Richard is winning. The two discuss the ways that players fight for the ball in the scrum after a play is over. Richard tells Andy, "Watch what happens *after* the tackle." As he develops a clever argument he wonders how long Joan and Andy had been meeting for church choir practice, drinking beer together, and then making love before he, Richard, knew about it. In reply to Richard's observation that players steal the ball after the tackle, when a play is officially over, Andy smugly murmurs "Survival of the fittest."[56] But this football parable speaks to what is happening in the room between these two: Andy thinks the play for Joan was whistled dead when the Maples divorced. In fact, the play has gone on unofficially. Out of the ref's view Richard has the ball in his grasp. Joan is really his this evening, even though Ruth has nothing to worry about.

Richard wins a victory in this contest, but through no present effort of his own.[57] Joan arrives to announce the birth of the baby, whom Paul announces is to be named after Richard. The new grandfather is hardly bowled over with either joy or gratitude. His first reaction to Joan's appearance in the room is to utter "No!" and to experience terror at the thought of his own impending death. The drama of the Super Bowl and duel of "the fittest" with Andy appear idle to him, a "waste of minutes while his final minute was rapidly approaching."[58] Because of his death-terror and distaste for Paul he can barely be gracious when honored with the child's naming.

Yet in the third act we realize that Richard has indeed won a victory. Leaving the hospital together, Andy, Joan, and Richard walk in the bitter cold toward the parking garage. Finding it closed, Andy cries out a "petulant and ineffective" curse, which brings both Richard and Joan to laughter. Andy wonders why no one told them the garage closed

---

[56] Ibid., 305-8.
[57] It is a very Lutheran victory.
[58] Ibid., 308.

at night,[59] and Richard gently taunts him, "I bet they thought you could read." Andy swears again, appearing hilarious to Richard in an Astrakhan toy soldier's hat. His breath in the near-zero cold makes a "streaming white flag" which signals to Richard, and to us, Andy's surrender.[60] Richard and Joan are so united in spirit by their new status as grandparents that when Richard leads the other two down a blind alley on a search for his car, the former Maples both laugh again. They find the car. It is during the ride to the Vanderhavens' hotel that Joan reveals the mystery she has been grappling with all evening, the nature of the womb and what it tells us about life's transience. Richard recognizes the search in her, while Andy "listened to her as one does to second wives, in confidence the search is over. Or that there is no search." As Richard drops off the Vanderhavens at their hotel he is tempted to kiss Joan before she leaves the back seat—but instead jokes with himself that he wouldn't enjoy their icy faces touching, and besides, his neck doesn't turn as easily as it used to.[61]

The last time we saw Joan in the back seat of a car with Richard at the wheel, he drunkenly smashed up his new car and broke the leg of a woman he would soon make his new mistress. This time he is moved by a deeper appreciation for his ex-wife, an appreciation that seems far from lust. She is a woman who still seems one flesh with him, joined more firmly to him than to Andy certainly, and who has just joined him in the task of grandparenting. She has not joined Andy in this task, not the false and rival grandparent. Richard is the maternal grandfather of the third Richard because incarnate reality is sacred. This is Richard's victory, and it has nothing to do with his fitness, but with the history of his love.[62]

Act four combines another night terror, Richard's first in decades, with the Maples cycle's most vivid honoring of non-erotic love. Richard's night in his hotel room is emblematic of his change during the past few hours, the repetition of his youthful desperation. Like the temperature outside, he is "flirting with zero." In a room that is cold as death, he feels

---

[59] Ethical Andy Vanderhaven's question recalls his wife Joan's just after the car accident she experiences with Richard and Eleanor Dennis in "The Taste of Metal": "Why doesn't anyone come out and help us?" Updike, *Too Far to Go*, 97.

[61] Updike, *Afterlife*, 310-312. This kiss is important to mention because this is the last we see of Joan Maple Vanderhaven. Updike picks up the thread of the forgotten wedding kiss, the strange divorce court kiss, and now the Maples' reunion kiss.

[62] Another Lutheran victory.

his existence compressed "to nothing," a sharp contrast to the "heated, pumping blood" of the womb from which his grandson has just emerged. Richard's fear of death is partly fear for this child, who has also left a warm, protected life in union with his creator, to enter a bitterly cold world in which death is the expected outcome. Grandfather Richard, however, dwells mostly upon his own existence. He feels a "homunculus" again, this time a small figure at "the far end of God's indifferently held telescope." As a "newly hatched grandfather," he feels the universe wants to crush him "to make room for newcomers." Richard falls asleep "a little," but we are to recognize this as a full-blown night-terror. The literary markers are too clear. For decades, no modern American chain hotel has offered twin beds, yet in this room Updike contrives to give Richard twin beds, and calls special attention to them. Clearly, this scene is meant to recall Richard's terrors in "Twin Beds in Rome," and to return him to that kind of existential desperation. This time, though, Richard is merely anxious, filled with dread, not psychosomatically ill.[63]

The next morning, Richard seems to backslide on his promising desperation. He learns that his football team—the team that performs miracles—has lost the Super Bowl, and he soon realizes that he is perversely more jealous of Paul and the new baby than of Andy. His vow to cut back on coffee suggests a return of his diminished Prufrockian self, and indeed he feels groggy from having been "compressed in the night." However, he is soon renewed by a repetition. Visiting Judith in the hospital and listening to her describe her labor, Richard is brought near to tears by her description of the pain she endured. Suddenly, he is not grandfather but father, and a father who recognizes her existential situation with some wisdom: "He blinked and stood and kissed her lightly on the forehead, that wide pale brow that from the start, love her as much as he could, held behind it her secrets, her sensations, her identity."[64] He thinks in terms of physics—how his night terror had compressed him a few hours before, while just a few hours before that Judith had been split in two.

Now *he* is about to split in two. On his way out he meets and holds his grandson for the first time. He experiences a powerful repetition of the moment in 1950s England when he had held Judith for the first time. Richard is suddenly both father and grandfather, two callings based in

---

[63] Updike, *Afterlife*, 313-14.
[64] Ibid., 314-15.

fidelity, love, and care. This baby boy also "adhere[s] to his chest and arms," just as Judith had thirty-one years earlier. This is Richard's way of saying that there is a type of love—Kierkegaard calls it *Kjerlighed*—that makes bonding with each child both natural and powerful. Richard knows that his children are not, never were, "his own." They have existences, anxieties, and their own searches to cope with. Yet he knows that he loves these children, and that this love has the magical quality of adhering him to these souls or selves otherwise independent of him.

What do we make of Updike's final line of "Grandparenting," Richard's insight that "Nobody belongs to us, except in memory"? It is a line that justifies the fiction-making art, of course, to the extent that that art draws upon and seeks to understand memories. Coming from Richard, the line is a bit alarming. He seems ready to inhabit a world of memories alone, memories that are consoling because they are carefully selected and edited. For this very reason Kierkegaard's "Unhappiest Man" lives in memory only, memories of a past that never actually occurred, and in a future based in self-consoling fantasy.[65] One problem with such a life is its denial of the present, in which the work of repetition, both ethical and religious, must occur. Richard needs to renew continuously his relation to God and neighbor, as all Christians must do. The rhythm of sin, repentance, grace and joy must be repeated over and over again in the believer's life, and the effort to meet the neighbor's need is endless. But the believer meets these repetitions with joy rather than regret because of the inward change. This is the change that, thanks to the elderly bohemian Cummings, Richard hears in Wordsworth's "Immortality Ode":

> Our birth is but a sleep and a forgetting:
> The Soul that rises with us, our life's Star,
> Hath had elsewhere its setting,
> And cometh from afar:
> Not in entire forgetfulness,
> And not in utter nakedness,
> But trailing clouds of glory do we come
> From God, who is our home:
> Heaven lies about us in our infancy!

---

[65] Kierkegaard, *Either/Or*, 1:219-30.

Richard seems to recognize now this God-haunted nature of his mortality, this sign that his real destiny is not an icy cold room but a joyous present—and possibly another Richard.

The Richard we meet in this final Maples story is onto the search, and can recognize a searching quality in others, especially those he loves. These searchers include Joan and Judith, but not Ruth, at least not yet. Though Richard now lives often in memory, he is quick to compete over ideas and values, to laugh, and to love, to live in a dynamic present. He experiences existential terror and personal feelings of "contraction," but he is also open to moments of grace and love, such as the sensations he experiences holding his first grandchild. There is a kindness in Richard now, an alertness to others' pain that seems wholly new, and which partakes of the unselfing imperatives of the gospels. We have to ask whether in the ten years since Richard's divorce from Joan he has made the leap and become a knight of faith.

His night terror in Hartford seems to militate against a sanguine faith. Yet Richard's author John Updike encountered such night terrors throughout his adult life, long after making his own leap. Perhaps Richard's clinging to memories also militates against a life guided by loving conscience. Yet Updike closes *Self-Consciousness* with an interesting and dialectical remark about memory and conscience. He has just returned home from an Advent season church service, where he has heard the "very unlikely, much illustrated passage from Luke telling how Gabriel came to Mary and told her that the Holy Ghost would come upon her and the power of the Highest would 'overshadow' her and make her pregnant with the Son of God..."[66] Updike knows, as Unamuno teaches, that these kinds of mythic implausibilities cause believers to question their hope for life in eternity. Updike also knows, though, that doubts founded in intellect also deconstruct. He writes, "when we try in good faith to believe in materialism, in the exclusive reality of the physical, we are asking our selves to step aside; we are disavowing the very realm where we exist and where all things precious are kept— "Here the key terms cease to be Unamuno's and begin to be Kierkegaard's: "the realm of emotion and conscience, of memory and intention and sensation.[67]"

---

[66] The gospel reading in Updike's church that day was Luke, 1:35.
[67] Updike, *Self-Consciousness*, 250.

So Updike affirms a certain kind of memory. Perhaps what matters is the quality of Richard's memories in "Grandparenting." Since they are almost entirely memories of non-erotic love—of holding his first child, of sharing the intellectual joys of college with young Joan, of realizing Judith's confidence at her high school commencement ceremony, of hearing Joan's voice for the first time in a Romantic poets course—and since Richard displays neither morbid regret about leaving these times behind nor pious disowning of his younger self, the memories are consistent with authentic personhood in the Kierkegaardian sense. Possibly Richard has already accepted grace, and the experience of faith is simply incommensurable, a life to be lived rather than a topic to be discussed or pondered.

Bibliography

Adorno, Theodor. "On Kierkegaard's Doctrine of Love." In *Søren Kierkegaard*, edited by Harold Bloom. New York: Chelsea House, 1989.

Arbaugh, George E. and George B. *Kierkegaard's Authorship*. Rock Island IL: Augustana College Library, 1967.

Bainton, Roland H. *The Church of Our Fathers*. New York: Scribners, 1941.

------. *Here I Stand: A Life of Martin Luther*. Nashville TN: Abingdon, 1980.

Bakhtin, Mikhail. *The Dialogic Imagination: Four Essays by M.M. Bakhtin*. Translated by Caryl Emerson & Michael Holquist. Austin TX: University of Texas Press, 1981.

Barnes, Jane. "John Updike: A Literary Spider." In *John Updike*, edited by Harold Bloom. New York: Chelsea House, 1987.

Barth, Karl. *The Doctrine of God*. Volume 1 of *Church Dogmatics*. Edited by G. W. Bromiley and T. F. Torrance. New York: T. & T. Clark, 2009.

------. *Dogmatics in Outline*. trans. G.T. Thomson. New York: Harper, 1959.

------. *The Word of God and the Word of Man*. Translated by Douglas Horton. Boston, MA: Pilgrim, 1928.

Benjamin, Jessica. *The bonds of love: psychoanalysis, feminism, and the problem of domination*. New York: Random House, 1988.

Bloom, Harold. Introduction. In *Søren Kierkegaard*. New York: Chelsea House, 1989.

Bonhoeffer, Dietrich. *The Cost of Discipleship*. New York: Macmillan, 1959.

Book of Common Prayer, And Administration of the Sacraments and Other Rites and Ceremonies of the Church. New York: The Church Pension Fund, 1945.

Boswell, Marshall. *John Updike's Rabbit Trilogy: Mastered Irony in Motion*. Columbia MO: University of Missouri Press, 2001.

Buber, Martin. "The Question of the Single One." In *Between Man and Man*, translated by Ronald Gregor Smith. London: Collins, 1979.

Bukdahl, Jørgen. *Søren Kierkegaard and the Common Man*, edited and translated by Bruce H. Kirmmse. Grand Rapids MI: Eerdmans, 2001.

Buunk, Bram P. and Pieternel Dijkstra. "Men, Women, and Infidelity: Sex Differences in Extradyadic Sex and Jealousy." In *The State of Affairs: Explorations in Infidelity and Commitment*. Mahwah NJ: Lawrence Erlbaum, 2004.

Chaikin, Andrew. *A Man on the Moon: The Voyages of the Apollo Astronauts*. New York: Penguin, 2007.

Chesterton, G.K. *Orthodoxy*. San Francisco CA: Ignatius, 1995.

Christie, Richard and Florence L. Geis. *Studies in Machiavellianism*. New York: Academic Press, 1970.

Collins, James D. *The Mind of Kierkegaard*. Chicago: University of Chicago Press, 1953.

Connell, George. *To Be One Thing: Personal Unity in Kierkegaard's Thought*. Macon GA: Mercer University Press, 1985.

Coontz, Stephanie. *Marriage, a History: From Obedience to Intimacy or How Love Conquered Marriage*. New York: Viking, 2005.

------. *The Way We Never Were: American Families and the Nostalgia Trap*. New York: Basic Books, 1992.

Crowe, David. "Young Man Angstrom: Identity Crisis and Works of Love in *Rabbit, Run*." *Religion and Literature* 43/1 (Spring 2012): 81-99.

Croxall, Thomas H. *Kierkegaard Commentary*. New York: Harper, 1956.

Cummings, E.E. *100 Selected Poems*. New York: Grove, 1994.

Philip Cushman, *Constructing the Self, Constructing America: A Cultural History of Psychotherapy*. Boston MA: Addiston-Wesley, 1995.

De Bellis, Jack. *John Updike: The Critical Responses to the 'Rabbit' Saga*. Westport CN: Praeger, 2005.

------. *The John Updike Encyclopedia*. New York: Greenwood, 2000.

De Rougemont, Denis. *Love in the Western World*. New York: Doubleday Anchor, 1957.

Derrida, Jacques. *The Gift of Death*. Translated by David Wells. Chicago: University of Chicago Press, 1996.

Dillenberger, John. *Martin Luther: Selections from His Writings*. New York: Anchor, 1961.

Duncomb, Jean and Dennis Marsden. "'From Here to Epiphany . . .': Power and Identity in the Narrative of an Affair." In *The State of Affairs: Explorations in Infidelity and Commitment*. Mahwah NJ: Lawrence Erlbaum, 2004.

Dupré, Louis. *Kierkegaard as Theologian: The Dialectic of Christian Existence*. New York: Sheed and Ward, 1963.

Duvall, John N. "Conclusion: U(pdike) and P(postmodernism)." In *The Cambridge Companion to John Updike*, edited by Stacey Olster. New York: Cambridge University Press, 2006.

Eagleton, Terry. *The Gospels: Jesus Christ*. New York: Verso, 2007.

Eller, Vernard. *Kierkegaard and Radical Discipleship*. Princeton NJ: Princeton University Press, 1968.

Elrod, John W. *Kierkegaard and Christendom*. Princeton NJ: Princeton University Press, 1981.

Emerson, Caryl and Michael Holquist. *Mikhail Bakhtin: Creation of a Prosaics*, Stanford CA: Stanford University Press, 1990.

Engel, Stephanie. *The Initial Impact of Psychoanalysis on Feminism in America*. Cambridge MA: Harvard University Press, 1976.

Erikson, Erik H. *Young Man Luther: A Study in Psychoanalysis and History*. New York: Norton, 1993.

Faulkner, William. "The Bear." In *Go Down Moses*. New York, Vintage, 1991.

Feeney, Mark. "Louise Day Hicks, Icon of Tumult, Dies," *Boston* (MA) *Globe*, 22 October, 2003. http://
www.boston.com/news/local/massachusetts/articles/2003/10/22/louise_d
ay_hicks_icon_of_tumult_dies/

Ferriera, Jamie M. "Faith and the Kierkegaardian Leap." In *The Cambridge Companion to Kierkegaard*, edited by Alastair Hannay and Gordon D. Marino. New York: Cambridge University Press, 1998.

------. *Love's Grateful Striving: A Commentary on Kierkegaard's* Works of Love. New York: Oxford, 2001.

Forell, George Washington. *The Luther Legacy: An Introduction to Luther's Life and Thought for Today*. Minneapolis, MN: Augsburg 1983.

Freud, Sigmund. *Civilization and Its Discontents*. Edited and translated by James Strachey. New York: Norton, 2005.

------. *Five Lectures on Psycho-Analysis,* ed. and trans. James Strachey. New York: Norton, 1989.

Fromm, Erich. *The Heart of Man: Its Genius for Good and Evil*. New York: Harper&Row, 1964.

Garff, Joakim. *Søren Kierkegaard: A Biography*. Translated by Bruce H. Kimmsee. Princeton NJ: University of Princeton Press, 2007.

Gomes, Peter J. *The Scandalous Gospel of Jesus: What's So Good About the Good News?* New York: HarperCollins, 2007.

Greiner, Donald J. *The Other John Updike: Poems/Short Stories/Prose/Play*. Athens OH: Ohio University Press, 1981.

Hackstaff, Karla B. *Marriage in a Culture of Divorce*. Philadelphia PA: Temple University Press, 1999.

Hamilton, Alice and Kenneth. *The Elements of John Updike*. Grand Rapids MI: Eerdmans, 1970.

Hamilton, Kenneth. *The Promise of Kierkegaard*. Philadelphia PA: Lippincott, 1969.

Harrington, Joel F. *Reordering Marriage and Society in Reformation Germany*. New York: Cambridge University Press, 1995.

Hohlenberg, Johannes. *Søren Kierkegaard*. Copenhagen: Hagerup, 1940.

Hopper, Vincent F. *Medieval Number Symbolism*. New York: Cooper Square, 1969.

Hoyt, M.F. "On the Psychology and Psychopathology of Primal Scene Experience." *Journal of the American Academy of Psychoanalysis* 8/3 (July 1980): 311-35.

Hunt, George. *John Updike and the Three Great Secret Things: Sex, Religion, and Art*. Grand Rapids MI: Eerdmans, 1980.

Jackson, Timothy P. "Arminian Edification: Kierkegaard on Grace and Free Will." In *The Cambridge Companion to Kierkegaard*, edited by Alastair Hannay and Gordon D. Marino. New York: Cambridge University Press, 1998.

Jeffrey, David L., ed. *A Dictionary of Biblical Tradition in English Literature* . Grand Rapids MI: Eerdman's, 1992.

Jodock, Darrell. "What is Goodness? The Influence of Updike's Lutheran Roots." In *John Updike and Religion: The Sense of the Sacred and the Motions of Grace*, edited by James Yerkes. Grand Rapids MI: Eerdmans, 1999.

Johnson, Roger A. *Psychohistory and Religion: The Case of Young Man Luther.* Philadelphia PA: Fortress, 1977.

Jolivet, Regis. *Introduction to Kierkegaard.* London: Frederick Muller, 1950.

Joyce, James. *Dubliners.* New York: Oxford University Press, 2008.

------. *Ulysses.* New York: Oxford University Press, 2008.

Kantorowicz, Ernst H. *The King's Two Bodies: A Study in Mediaeval Political Theology.* Princeton NJ: Princeton University Press, 1957.

Karant-Nunn, Susan C. "Reformation society, women and the family." In *The Reformation World*, edited by Andrew Pettegree. New York: Routledge, 2000.

Kernberg, Otto. *Borderline Conditions and Pathological Narcissism.* New York: Jason Aronson, 1975.

Kierkegaard, Søren. *Concluding Unscientific Postscript to Philosophical Fragments.* Edited and translated by Howard V. Hong and Edna H. Hong. 2 volumes. Princeton NJ: Princeton University Press, 1992.

------. *Either/Or.* Edited and translated by Howard V. Hong and Edna H. Hong. 2 volumes. Princeton NJ: Princeton University Press, 1987.

------. *Fear and Trembling* and *Repetition.* Edited and translated by Howard V. Hong and Edna H. Hong. Princeton NJ: Princeton University Press, 1983.

------. *Fear and Trembling and Sickness Unto Death.* Translated by Walter Lowrie. New York: Anchor, 1954.

------. *Practice in Christianity,* Edited and translated by Howard V. Hong and Edna H. Hong. Princeton NJ: Princeton University Press, 1991.

------. *Repetition.* In *Fear and Trembling* and *Repetition.* Edited and translated by Howard V. Hong and Edna H. Hong. Princeton NJ: Princeton University Press, 1983.

------. *The Sickness Unto Death.* See *Fear and Trembling and Sickness Unto Death.*

------. *Stages on Life's Way: Studies by Various Persons.* Edited and translated by Howard V. Hong and Edna H. Hong. Princeton NJ: Princeton University Press, 1988.

------. *Works of Love: Some Christian Deliberations in the Form of Discourses.* Edited and translated by Howard V. Hong and Edna H. Hong. Princeton NJ: Princeton University Press, 1995.

King, Martin Luther. "Letter from Birmingham Jail." In *The Oxford Book of the American South: Testimony, Memory, and Fiction,* edited by Edward L. Ayers and Bradley Mittendorf. New York: Oxford University Press, 1997.

Kurlansky, Mark. *1968: The Year that Rocked the World.* New York: Random House, 2005.

Lasch, Christopher. *The Culture of Narcissism: American Life in an Age of Diminishing Expectations.* New York: Norton, 1979.

Lindberg, Carter. *The European Reformations.* Oxford UK: Blackwell, 1996.

Lodge, David. *Souls and Bodies.* New York: Penguin, 1990.

Lowrie, Walter. *A Short Life of Kierkegaard.* Princeton NJ: Princeton University Press, 1970.

Luscher, Robert M. *John Updike: A Study of the Short Fiction.* New York: Twayne, 1993.

Mackie, J.L. *Ethics: Inventing Right and Wrong.* Harmondsworth, Middlesex UK: Penguin, 1977.

Malantschuk, Gregor. *The Controversial Kierkegaard.* Translated by Howard V. and Edna H. Hong. Waterloo, Ontario: Wilfred Laurier University Press, 1976.

Marcuse, Herbert. *Eros and Civilization,* 2nd ed. London: Routledge, 1987.

Maslow, Abraham. *Toward a Psychology of Being.* 2nd ed. New York: Van Nostrand Reinhold, 1968.

Marino, Gordon D. "Anxiety in *The Concept of Anxiety.*" In *The Cambridge Companion to Kierkegaard,* edited by Alastair Hannay and Gordon D. Marino. New York: Cambridge University Press, 1998.

Marius, Richard. *Martin Luther: the Christian Between God and Death.* Cambridge, MA: Belknap Harvard University Press, 1999.

Marty, Martin. *Martin Luther.* New York: Penguin, 2004.

Mintz, Steven and Susan Kellogg. *Domestic Revolutions: A Social History of American Family Life.* New York: Macmillan, 1988.

Mooney, Edward F. "*Repetition*: Getting the World Back." In *The Cambridge Companion to Kierkegaard,* edited by Alastair Hannay and Gordon D. Marino. New York: Cambridge University Press, 1998.

Morson, Gary Saul and Caryl Emerson. Bakhtin: Creation of a Prosaics. Stanford CA: Stanford University Press, 1990.

Murdoch, Iris. *A Severed Head.* New York: Penguin, 1976.

------. *The Sovereignty of Good.* New York: Ark, 1985.

Palmer, Parker. *Let Your Life Speak: Listening for the Voice of Vocation.* San Francisco CA: Jossey-Bass, 1999.

Percy, Walker. *The Moviegoer.* New York: Knopf, 2001.

Plath, James. *Conversations with John Updike.* Jackson MS: University Press of Mississippi, 1994.

Quinn, Phillip L. "Kierkegaard's Christian Ethics." In *The Cambridge Companion to Kierkegaard,* edited by Alastair Hannay and Gordon D. Marino. New York: Cambridge University Press, 1998.

Richards, Barry. *Images of Freud: Cultural Responses to Psychoanalysis.* New York: St. Martin's, 1989.

Ricoeur, Paul. "Kierkegaard and Evil." In *Søren Kierkegaard,* edited by Harold Bloom. New York: Chelsea House, 1989.

Rieff, Philip. *Freud: The Mind of the Moralist.* Chicago: University of Chicago Press, 1979.

Rohde, Peter P. *Kierkegaard: An Introduction to his Life and Philosophy.* New York: Humanities, 1963.

Rose, Gillian. "Reply from the 'Single One': Soren [sic] Kierkegaard to Martin Buber." In *Martin Buber: A Contemporary Perspective,* ed. Paul Mendes-Flohr. Syracuse NY: Syracuse University Press, 2002.

Rudd, Anthony. *Kierkegaard and the Limits of the Ethical.* New York: Oxford University Press, 1993.

Ruddick, Sara. *Maternal Thinking: Toward a Politics of Peace.* Boston MA: Beacon, 1995.

Schiff, James A. *John Updike, Revisited.* New York: Twayne, 1998.

Said, Edward. *The World, the Text, and the Critic.* New York: Harvard University Press, 1983.

Samuels, Charles Thomas. "John Updike: The Art of Fiction No. 43." In *The Paris Review* 45 (Winter 1968). http://www.theparisreview.org/interviews/4219/the-art-of-fiction-no-43-john-updike

Seaburg, Alan. "Leslie Pennington." In *Dictionary of Unitarian and Universalist Biography, an on-line resource of the Unitarian Universalist History & Heritage Society,* 1999-2013. http://www25.uua.org/uuhs/duub/articles/lesliepennington.html

Shakespeare, William. *Hamlet.* Edited by Barbara Mowat and Paul Werstine. Folger Shakespeare Library. New York: Simon and Schuster Paperbacks, 2003.

Shklar, Judith. *Ordinary Vices.* Cambridge MA: Belknap Harvard University Press, 1984.

Short, Robert L. *The Gospel According to Peanuts.* Knoxville TN: Westminster John Knox, 1965/1999.

Steiner, G. *In Bluebeard's Castle: Some Notes towards the Redefinition of Culture.* New Haven CT: Yale University Press, 1974.

Strauss, Gerald. *Luther's House of Learning: Indoctrination of the Young in the German Reformation.* Baltimore MD: Johns Hopkins University Press, 1978.

Tanenhaus, Sam. "The Roommates: Updike and Christopher Lasch," *The New York Times,* June 20, 2010, http://www.nytimes.com/2010/06/21/books/21roommates.html?_r=0

Taylor, Mark C. *Journeys to Selfhood: Hegel & Kierkegaard.* Berkeley CA: University of California Press, 1980.

------. "Natural Selfhood and Ethical Selfhood in Kierkegaard." In *Søren Kierkegaard,* edited by Harold Bloom. New York: Chelsea House, 1989.

Todorov, Tzvetan. *Mikhail Bakhtin: The Dialogical Principle.* Translated by Wlad Godzich. Minneapolis MN: University of Minnesota Press, 1994.

Unamuno, Miguel de. *Tragic Sense of Life,* translated by J.E. Crawford Flitch. New York: Dover, 1954.

Updike, John. *Assorted Prose.* New York: Knopf, 1965.

------. *Couples.* New York: Knopf, 1968.

------. *Due Considerations: Essays and Criticism.* New York: Knopf, 2007.

------. *Endpoint and Other Poems.* New York: Knopf, 2009.

------. Foreword to*Too Far to Go: The Maples Stories.* New York: Fawcett, 1979.

------. "Grandparenting." In *The Afterlife and Other Stories.* New York: Knopf, 1994.

------. *Hugging the Shore: Essays and Criticism.* New York: Vintage, 1984.

------. *In the Beauty of the Lilies.* New York: Knopf, 1996.

------. *Memories of the Ford Administration.* New York: Knopf, 1992.

------. *Midpoint and Other Poems.* New York: Knopf, 1969.

------. *More Matter: Essays and Criticism.* New York: Fawcett, 1999.

------. *Odd Jobs: Essays and Criticism.* New York: Knopf, 1991.

------. *Picked-Up Pieces.* New York: Knopf, 1976.

------. *Rabbit, Run.* New York: Knopf, 1960.

------. *Rabbit Redux.* New York: Knopf, 1971.

------. *Rabbit is Rich.* New York: Knopf, 1981.

------. *Rabbit At Rest.* New York: Knopf, 1990.

------. "Rabbit Remembered." In *Licks of Love: Short Stories and a Sequel, "Rabbit Remembered."* New York: Knopf, 2000.

------. "Seven Stanzas for Easter." *Telephone Poles and Other Poems.* New York: Knopf, 1962.

------. "Søren Kierkegaard." In *Atlantic Brief Lives: A Biographical Companion to the Arts,* ed. Louis Kronenberger. Boston MA: Little, Brown, 1971.

------. *The Centaur.* New York: Knopf, 1962.

------. *The Early Stories, 1953-1975.* New York: Ballentine, 2003.

------. *The Maples Stories.* New York: Everyman's Pocket Classics, 2009.

------. *The Poorhouse Fair.* New York: Knopf, 1959.

------. *Too Far to Go: The Maples Stories.* New York: Fawcett, 1979.

------. *Your Lover Just Called: Stories of Joan and Richard Maple.* Harmandsworth, Middlesex, UK: Penguin, 1979.

------. *John Updike, the Early Stories: 1953-1975.* New York: Ballentine, 2003.

------. *Self-Consciousness: Memoirs.* New York: Knopf, 1989.

Versluys, Kristiaan. "'Nakedness' or realism in Updike's early short stories." In *The Cambridge Companion to John Updike,* edited by Stacey Olster. New York: Cambridge University Press, 2006.

Walsh, Sylvia. *Kierkegaard: Thinking Christianly in an Existential Mode.* New York: Oxford University Press, 2009.

Wannenwetsch, Bernd. "Luther's Moral Theology." In *The Cambridge Companion to Martin Luther.* Edited by Donald McKim. Cambridge UK: Cambridge University Press, 2003.

Weinberg, Steven. "The Forces of Nature." In *Bulletin of the American Academy of Arts and Sciences* 29/4 (January 1976): 13-29.

Weinstein, Arnold. *Northern Arts: The Breakthrough of Scandinavian Literature and Art, from Ibsen to Bergman.* Princeton NJ: Princeton University Press, 2008.

Wood, Ralph C. *The Comedy of Redemption: Christian Faith and Comic Vision in Four American Novelists.* Notre Dame IN: University of Notre Dame Press, 1988.

Wordsworth, William. "Ode: Intimations of Immortality." In *The Oxford Book of English Verse: 1250–1900,* edited by Arthur Quiller-Couch. Oxford: Clarendon, 1904.

Yerkes, James, ed. *John Updike and Religion: The Sense of the Sacred and the Motions of Grace.* Grand Rapids MI: Eerdmans, 1999.

Zaretsky, Eli. *Secrets of the Soul: A Social and Cultural History of Psychoanalysis.* New York: Vintage, 2004.

Index